1997

The Margins of the Text

The Margins of the Text

Edited by D. C. Greetham

Ann Arbor
THE UNIVERSITY OF MICHIGAN PRESS

Copyright © by the University of Michigan 1997
All rights reserved
Published in the United States of America by
The University of Michigan Press
Manufactured in the United States of America
⊗ Printed on acid-free paper

2000   1999   1998   1997   4   3   2   1

A CIP catalog record for this book is available from the British Library.

Library of Congress Cataloging-in-Publication Data

The margins of the text / edited by D. C. Greetham.
     p.   cm. — (Editorial theory and literary criticism)
   Includes bibliographical references and index.
   ISBN 0-472-10667-8 (hardcover : alk. paper)
   1. English literature—Criticism, Textual.   2. Manuscripts,
English—Editing.   3. Discourse analysis, Literary.   4. Transmission
of texts.   5. Textual criticism.   6. Marginalia.   7. Editing.
I. Greetham, D. C. (David C.), 1941–   .   II. Series.
PR21.M29   1996
820.9—dc20   96-30221
                                                        CIP

Contents

Preface

In any collection of essays the usual prefatory expressions of gratitude for collaboration and support become not just an expected scholarly formula; they underwrite the very existence of the book. For me this current collection was a particular personal challenge in the collaborative mode, for it was toward the end of a decade-long attempt to put together a multidisciplinary collection on scholarly editing for the Modern Language Assocation (MLA) that I was approached by George Bornstein about the possibility of editing this collection on textual margins for his series with the University of Michigan Press. Although the actual contributors to the *Scholarly Editing* volume were unfailingly gracious and generous, the administrative and bureaucratic wounds of MLA were still very fresh, and thus my first response to George's suggestion was: never again. But after a few tentative inquiries with scholars known for their work on the ideological or bibliographical margins, it became clear to me that there was a good deal of excitement about the subject that might be quickly, and relatively painlessly, translated into a book. Almost everyone I approached immediately agreed to contribute (and even those few whose other commitments prevented them from collaborating promised to buy the book), so it looked as if we had a winner.

If this turns out to be so, it will be primarily because of the collegiality, expertise, and expedition of the contributors themselves. Yes, our original schedule slipped a little in the last stages of submission and revision, but virtually everyone both met the deadlines and responded with courtesy and tact to my editorial suggestions. After having said never again, I'll admit that I'd happily work with this team, this series editor, and this press again. Therefore, in addition to the primary gratitude to the contributors themselves, I also offer my thanks to George Bornstein, for prompting and guiding us; to Susan Whitlock, our editor at Michigan, for her ministrations to our text; to the two anonymous readers for the press, for their advice and support; and to several City University of New York administrators (President Frances Degen Horowitz, Provost Geoffrey Marshall, and English Ph.D. Executive Officer Joseph Wittreich), for their support of matters textual; and to a number of graduate assistants (Thane Doss, Patrick Curran, and Page Delano), for their help in getting the book out.

Introduction: Out of the Text and into the Margins

D. C. Greetham

In 1992 I mounted a conference session at MLA on "Race, Class, and Gender in Scholarly Editing" on behalf of MLA's Committee on Scholarly Editions (CSE). The title (and ultimate content) of the session was a recognition that several of the most ideologically contested issues in contemporary critical debate had not been accorded a full evaluation (or even acknowledgment) among textual critics and bibliographers. There was no agreed function for class, race, gender, and so on, in the intellectual operations of scholarly editors. And this despite some disturbing raw data: the session was in part a response to the institutional history of CSE and its forerunner, the Center for Editions of American Authors (CEAA), for, of the three hundred–plus volumes awarded seals of approval by these bodies, only two were of texts by women (Woolf and Cather), and there were none by persons of color. Did these data mean anything? Was scholarly editing an activity peculiarly supportive of the sort of "definitive" editions formerly sponsored by CEAA/CSE and thus inimical to (say) feminist or cultural materialist concerns? Was there perhaps something patriarchal, elitist, even racist, about the very construction of the traditional scholarly edition, with its approved clear text of accepted "authorized" readings and its separate apparatus of "rejected" readings (and thus literally "inferior"—at the bottom of the page or the back of the book)?

These questions were obviously not to be answered, or even properly confronted, in a single MLA conference panel, but the very asking of the questions about race, class, and gender encouraged a broader interrogation of previously marginalized types of discourse, indeed, of the margins themselves (in bibliographical as well as ideological terms) as the site for new ways of looking at textual scholarship, the history of the book, and the history and current status of scholarly editing and bibliography as marginalized activities. These matters were taken up in a couple of sessions at the 1993 MLA, at which I presented a general position paper on textual margins.

In the meantime George Bornstein, series editor of the University of Michigan Press series on scholarly editing and literary theory, had suggested that the issues raised in the 1992 MLA session might be developed into a collection of essays for this series. Accordingly, I began the task of approaching leading textual theorist-practitioners in the various modes of "marginal" text and textuality, and the plan for such a book gradually took shape.

It became clear that there were two (closely related) ways in which the topic of the textual margins could be approached. The first, drawing upon the first MLA session, would be concerned with the margins of (textual) discourse and would explore the function of discourses not previously recognized as significant to scholarly editing. This resulted in essays by the three original MLA panelists (Gerald MacLean on class, William L. Andrews on race, and Brenda R. Silver on gender), supplemented by Ann Thompson on feminist editing, Jonathan Goldberg on gay textuality, and Jonathan Bate and Sonia Massai on adaptation. This latter essay links nicely with Brenda Silver's essay, which also deals with adaptation. This section would be introduced by an expanded version of my position paper on philology as a marginalized activity, written for the 1993 MLA. The second section would attend to the textual margins in the bibliographical sense (the margins of the book), with the understanding that the current interest in marginalia, commentary, and apparatus was itself a manifestation of a poststructuralist concern with the "supplement" as against the formalist preoccupation with the "text itself." Thus, the two parts of the collection would both be studying the effects of margins as a form of cultural "discourse." This second part would begin (logically enough) with the textual function of titles (in two essays—James McLaverty on titles and "entitlement" in eighteenth-century bibliography and Thomas L. Berger on Shakespeare titles) and would end (again, logically) with W. Speed Hill on commentary. Between would be essays by William W. E. Slights on the ideological function of marginal notation in John Dee; Evelyn B. Tribble on the move from marginal annotation to formal footnote in the seventeenth and eighteenth centuries; Michael Camille on medieval glossing and graffiti; and Mary Keeler and Christian Kloesel on the semiotics of the margins in Peirce.

In the arrangement and specific content of the collection seen as a whole, there are inevitably cross-references and intertextual resonances. For example, the Slights essay on Dee's marginalia provides a specific context for the implementation of many of the general concerns about commentary raised in Hill's essay. Moreover, Slight's study is implicitly a commentary on Keeler and Kloesel's problems with Peirce's marginalia, especially in the problem of the agency of voice and authority. The bibliographical and sociocultural issues surveyed in McLaverty's essay on titles are given exemplification in the different production and publication contexts covered in Berger's essay on Shakespeare titles, which provides the raw materials for a reader to arrive at the sort of theoretical conjunctions and disjunctions that McLaverty confronts. Goldberg's essay on a gendered reading of textual cruces can be used as a gloss on Thompson's account of a specifically feminist approach to editing, particularly since they both deal with the varying cultural responses to the works of the same author. The Silver essay on adaptation is a modernist gloss on, and extension of, the Bate-Massai essay on adaptations of Shakespeare, for Silver takes up the challenge (raised in Bate-Massai) of adaptation as a so-called inferior discourse (belated and nonauthorial), and shows how empowerment may pass to the secondary discourse, especially when the adaptation is in a different, and perhaps more popular, medium than the original, a condition exacerbated by "male" adaptations of "female" texts. And, as a group, the several essays on the canonical status of Shakespearean texts can be read as a gloss on Andrews' much more practical concern for getting a body of previously noncanonical literature available to a reading public: in a sense Andrews is in the bibliographical position of early editors of classical and medieval texts, where the primary aim of such collections as those of the Early English Text Society was to publish documentary editions of otherwise little-known works—in the case of EETS, as the linguistic data for the construction of the *Oxford English Dictionary* (*OED*). Andrews thus posits a "pre-hermeneutic" condition for editing, a concept that I address in my essay on philology. There are many other such webs and networks of glosses in this book on glosses, and the fixed print sequence unavoidably masks the full range of intertextual implication. Readers will doubtless construct their own glossing systems, perhaps aided by the index of topics.

As a whole, the collection spans several periods (medieval, Renaissance, eighteenth century to modern) and several disciplines (drama, literature, art history, politics, and philosophy) and offers a wide-ranging consideration of a single topic as it is manifested in various genres, formats, and media. The contributors are among the most respected textual/critical theorists in their fields (Thompson is co-general editor of the new Arden Shakespeare [Arden 3], Goldberg is a leading authority on Renaissance gay studies, Silver on contemporary feminist studies, and Hill is the general editor of the Folger edition of Hooker, and so on). Indeed, some of them have earned special recognition for their work on textual margins (Camille for *Image on the Edge,* Tribble for *Margins and Marginality*).

As a collection, it is, of course, very much of its cultural moment, for essays on such topics as gay editing and annotation would have been almost literally unthinkable a few years ago, and an entire book devoted to ideological and bibliographic margins would similarly have been regarded as obtuse, if not perverse. In 1634 Fermat could famously complain that the margin was too small to hold the proof for his last theorem (to be solved only with the aid of computers in 1994); and in *Arcadia* Tom Stoppard plays upon this sense of bibliographical constriction by having his 1809 ingenue Thomasina Coverly similarly complain that "this margin being too mean for my purpose, the reader must look elsewhere for the New Geometry of Irregular Forms" (*Arcadia* [London: Faber, 1993], 1. 4.43). The joke, of course, is that much of Stoppard's oeuvre can be considered as a form of "looking elsewhere," of constructing a supplementary, marginal gloss on a previous text (e.g., *Rosencrantz and Guildenstern Are Dead* on *Hamlet, Travesties* on *The Importance of Being Earnest*), and that, as an exemplary postmodernist author, he has proved not that the margins are too small but, rather, that, even in their very supplementarity and belatedness, they are larger and more powerful than the text itself.

In other words, these days the margins are a peculiarly privileged position, as the formalist concentration on the primacy and unity of text has retreated before a concern with supplements, frames, contexts—and belatedness. In Stephen Barney's collection, *Annotation and Its Texts* (New York: Oxford University Press, 1991), Derrida remarks that in "scholarly, academic discourse" it is in the margins of the text, its notes and supplements, that there is "the highest concentration" of the information necessary for "calculating the strategic positions" of a book or even an entire field ("This Is Not an Oral Footnote," 200); and in the same collection Ralph Hanna III argues that the margins of annotation contain a "guilty knowledge" that is so potent that it must not be admitted to but, instead, is fragmented and dissipated throughout a volume ("Annotation as Social Practice," 180–81). In some of my other writing, specifically on textual criticism and poststructuralism, I have similarly noted the paradox whereby the readings recorded in the text itself ultimately draw their authority from the "rejected" variants in the apparatus, so that "textual empowerment passes from the lower to the upper" ("[Textual] Criticism and Deconstruction," *Studies in Bibliography* 44 [1991]: 22; reprinted in *Textual Transgressions* [New York: Garland, 1996]). For a series on the interlacing of current editorial and literary theory, it would seem that the margins of textual discourse and the margins of the book are indeed an inevitable topic in these days of "post" (structuralism, colonialism, modernism, feminism, Marxism), of deferral and dispersion, of the edges and the interstitial.

Part 1
The Margins of Discourse

The Resistance to Philology

D. C. Greetham

Students of corrupt textual transmission will probably have already spotted that my title, "The Resistance to Philology," is a conflation of the titles of two essays by Paul de Man: "The Return to Philology" and "The Resistance to Theory," published as companion pieces.[1] It is a purposeful conflation, and its results embody the problem all textual scholars are confronted with: an institutional resistance to philology, just as de Man was confronted with an institutional resistance to theory in the early 1980s. In the first of these essays de Man recounts his experience in Reuben Brower's course The Interpretation of Literature, at Harvard in the 1950s, in which Brower insisted that students "were not to say anything that was not derived from the text they were considering. They were not to make any statements that they could not support by a specific use of language that actually occurred in the text."[2] This constraint on interpretation should be familiar enough to those textual critics who have tried to follow G. Thomas Tanselle's injunction always to look in "the text itself" for meaning and thus for intention.[3] But de Man regards this "mere" (i.e., "close" or "text-based") reading as "deeply subversive to those who think of the teaching of literature as a substitute for the teaching of theology, ethics, philosophy, or intellectual history" (24), and he claims that Brower's approach, obviously deriving from the practical criticism of I. A. Richards and other formalist critics, was of a piece with the "turn to theory" in the 1970s and early 1980s, which de Man sees as a "return to philology, to an examination of the structure of language prior to the meaning it produces" (24). So much for Tanselle's injunction.

I have severe reservations about this claim,[4] but my demurral is not based on de Man's thesis that the presemantic, prehermeneutic philological

9

model for theory denies what he calls an "ethical function to literature" (25)—the common charge against theory made by critics such as Walter Jackson Bate and Alvin Kernan.[5] Rather, my "resistance" to de Man's conflation of theory and philology is that such a conflation falls into the trap of circumscribing philology, and thus the bibliographical and textual research that characterizes its current operations in the scholarly world, by the foundationalist and positivist (i.e., prehermeneutic) requirements that so many literary critics seem to accord bibliography and textual study and which have led us to the current marginalized condition of textual study in the academy.

For example, while sensibly questioning whether philology can ever be "prior to literary and cultural interpretation,"[6] as de Man would have it, Jonathan Culler still regards his own promotion of what he calls "antifoundational" philology as somehow inimical to, or in sharp contrast to, the present functioning of philology as a "scientific" enterprise. He dreams of a philology that would show how "philological projects rely uncritically on literary and cultural conceptions that come from the domains of thought that are supposedly secondary"[7]—a division between primary and secondary that is another figure for the condition of estrangement or schism[8] that has brought us to this pass. And Richard Lanham, in a conference sponsored a few years ago by the Modern Language Association (MLA) and the Ford Foundation,[9] charged that textual critics ought to abandon their claims for positivist definitive print editions and instead acknowledge that text could be electronically manipulable, fragmented, versionist, and, well, "critical." Paradoxically, so great was Lanham's own faith in the definitiveness of print that he retained the charge unmodified in the published version of his paper,[10] even though the discussion after his conference presentation made it quite clear that such textual critics as Hans Walter Gabler, John Miles Foley, Michael Warren, Gary Taylor, Donald H. Reiman, and a host of Franco-German geneticists had already put into practice Lanham's prescriptions for us, practices of which Lanham was clearly ignorant.[11] De Man, Culler, and Lanham are thus laboring under an outmoded view of the philological model that textual critics as diverse as Jerome McGann, D. F. McKenzie, and Tanselle have frequently called to question, as witness Tanselle's insistence on the one hand that it is a delusion to think that textual scholarship is prehermeneutic, or that it "merely prepares the way for scholarly criticism and is not itself part of the critical process,"[12] and on the other that the old collocation of bibliography and science will not withstand scrutiny.[13]

But we have to acknowledge that this collocation is a deeply entrenched one institutionally, that bibliographical and textual research and writing are typically regarded as different in nature from other forms of text production, and that a textual or bibliographical book is indeed thought of as prehermeneutic, or "noncritical," by our colleagues, our students, and those administrators who have charge over our promotion, tenure, and salary. It is no betrayal of confidence, and was certainly no news to members of the MLA Division on Methods of Literary Research who heard the early version of this essay, that the title of the session in which it was presented ("But It's Not a *Book!*") comes from the experience of Gerald MacLean, in whose home institution a scholarly edition or a bibliography was counted as exactly one-half of a "real" book in personnel and budget commmittee decisions,[14] and that a former chair of my department would regularly go through an applicant's *curriculum vitae* checking off the publications that were "not-books." This peculiarly structuralist, semiotic bibliographical universe, in which a book is known by what it is not (a "bibli-eme" perhaps?), is part of a general cultural resistance to philology that is all too easily documented.[15]

Some years ago C. H. Sisson spoke forcefully for the marginalization of textual/bibliographical study when, in reviewing an edition of Pound for the *Times Literary Supplement,* he pronounced that "the prestige of fiddling with minute variants and bibliographical details should be low. It is, intellectually, the equivalent of what is done by clerks everywhere, labouring to pay [earn?] wages and to feed computers. Such things hold the world together."[16] Such disdain for the apparently "mechanical" and the "clerical"—a desire to see its operations as different in kind from genuine criticism or scholarship—is rarely stated as bluntly as in Sisson's review, but there is a long tradition of critical hostility to the philological edition, perceived as that which, according to Lewis Mumford and Edmund Wilson, puts editorial "barbed wire" between the author and reader,[17] preventing the reader from getting direct access to the text. Indeed, an important rhetorical aim of Wilson's case against the "fruits of the MLA" (those editions sponsored through the Center for Editions of American Authors [CEAA]) is that there is a professional, "professorial" *trahaison des clercs,* a conspiracy by the "clerisy" of the professoriate to use the mumbo jumbo of supposedly scholarly method to deny the amateur (like himself) any role in the transmission of the canonical texts of American literature.

Wilson's conspiracy theory was doubtless colored by the fact that his own proposal for a user-friendly uniform edition of that literature, based on the Pléiade editions of French literature, had been turned down by the National Endowment for the Humanities (NEH), which decided to fund CEAA directly. And there is an obvious irony in NEH's having later ceased such direct support and having been a major contributor to the Pléiade-like Library of America,[18] but his designation (throughout *The Fruits of the MLA*) of *professor* and *professorial* as the most polemical of his terms of abuse emphasizes the gentleman-amateur's dismay at the professionaliza-tion and institutionalization of editing. And it is this fear that the tech-nicalities and arcane vocabulary of scholarly editing had denied a role to the amateur and that large-scale multivolume editions of the canonical authors demanded heavy institutional investment that led John Gross to the nostalgic wish for "earlier, simpler days" in his review of the Cambridge Lawrence:

> A true collected edition at last, then, and one fitted out with all the accouterments of sound scholarship—fully annotated, with every source conscientiously cited and with the texts (as far as one can judge) scrupulously transcribed. How could anyone interested in Lawrence fail to welcome such an undertaking? And yet I must admit that, faced with the first volume, I also felt a pang of affection for earlier, simpler days. The Huxley collection, and the Harry T. Moore collection for that matter, were books, to be bought and read through; with the Cambridge edition we are in the presence of a Project: all the more incongruous in the case of the early letters, since so many of them show the young Lawrence and his friends conducting their own informal—and intense—literary education, seizing books in whatever cheap edition or reprint they could afford. By contrast, the Cambridge editors are inescapably involved in the task of bringing literature off the streets and into the library or the seminar room.[19]

This desire that the edition should somehow be compatible with, or even "look like," its subject, that a youthful, bibliographically rough-hewn author should not be constrained by the "apparatus" of Dryasdust modern scholarship, was promoted with even greater critical fervor in Paul Delany's review of the same Lawrence volume:

> The editorial commentary arouses more mixed feelings. It is sharply incongruous to see Lawrence's vital personality so cribbed and con-fined by the scholarly apparatus; he would, of course, have detested

the whole enterprise—though that need not be a final criticism of such posthumous tributes. In any case, Professor Boulton has labored devotedly to provide us with chronologies, maps of every place Lawrence went, lists of his college textbooks, glosses on Midlands slang and thousands of other facts. Too many, I suppose, for some tastes and most purses.[20]

Gross's affections for earlier belletristic modes of textual scholarship becomes here an attack on the very rationale for modern bibliographical scholarship. One of Fredson Bowers's favorite informal definitions of responsible textual critics was that they should put all their cards on the table, but Delany would apparently prefer them to keep some of their cards up their sleeves. And Gross is similarly concerned about overt display: "the actual editing is very good: the notes are informative without being fussy, the textual apparatus is decently unobtrusive."[21] The loaded vocabulary of this damning with faint praise ("without being fussy," "decently unobtrusive") suggests that an edition is the more decorous if its scholarly pudenda have been kept out of sight.

The suspicion of editorial plenitude and the desire for an epistemological or visual fit between edition and subject meet in Rosemary Dinnage's review of Morton Cohen's edition of the Lewis Carroll letters for the *New York Review of Books*:

> The standard of editing is modern and extravagantly good. The twenty years' labor was supported by money from six prestigious American endowments. Fifty-eight librarians, curators, archivists, and keepers receive acknowledgment, and there is another couple of pages of names of guides and advisers. The edition has a chronology, family tree, and bibliography (fortunately selective), and there are biographical notes, which must have involved much toil, for almost every recipient. . . . If these were the letters of a novelist, philosopher, or poet of world stature they could not be more ceremoniously and impeccably presented—indeed there *are* writers of world stature who have never been paid the compliment of an edition like this. But Carroll is, when all is said and done, the author of a couple of classic children's books.[22]

This is damning not with *faint* praise but with critical eulogy. If only Cohen had turned his obvious editorial talents to the work of a *real* writer, instead of a minor Oxford don's part-time scribbling. There is no argument here over the discipline of textual criticism itself, no quibbling over vital personalities being confined or old, friendly editions being superseded. And yet in one sense the reaction is even more dangerous to the status of textual scholarship, for it assumes that editing, commenting, and annotating are a chore, an activity nobody with any professional self-esteem would indulge in for pleasure. This notion is hinted at in the other reviews, in which, for example, Sisson's "clerks" and Delaney's "labored devotedly" imply a similar doggedness, but the "toil" that lies at the center of Dinnage's comments is more telling, since it is seen as misdirected. Delaney detects almost a perverseness in the Cambridge Lawrence's having foisted all this unnecessary material on Lawrence lovers, whereas Dinnage admires Cohen's tenacity over twenty years but finds it difficult to reconcile with the limited merits of its object. Textual scholarship becomes almost a masochistic experience, undertaken only for the greater good of deserving or undeserving authors.

One might object that this is no more or less than textual critics have been claiming for a century and more: that their labors were to allow the text "to speak for itself" and that in this claim they were aligning themselves with one of the central theses of nineteenth-century criticism in general, expressed in Arnold's famous dicta that the critic should attempt to cultivate "disinterestedness" in order to "see the object as in itself it really is" ("Function of Criticism") and to avoid the "personal fallacy" that might make our "affinities, likings, and circumstances . . . overrate the object of our interest" ("Study of Poetry").[23] The sublime assurances of this "impersonalist" criticism, when married to the technical sureties seemingly conferred on scholarship by Lachmannian stemmatics or historical and analytical bibliography, have meant that textual scholarship has to the outside observer retained its nineteenth-century positivism long after such claims had been given up, or even thought desirable, in other parts of the academic map.

But the schism is not wholly of others' making: textuists have in part contributed to it, by the use of a seemingly forbidding arcane technical vocabulary and methodology in such areas as descriptive and analytical bibliography and by continued appeals to the definitive, the positivistic, and the permanent in some forms of scholarly editing: so, for example, the "definitive" edition of the Anne Frank Diary was published (with much public acclaim) several years after the 1988 publication of the "critical" edition by the Dutch Institute of War Documentation; neither edition is, in fact, complete or definitive.[24] All too many of us have tried in the past to assert a moral, and certainly a cultural, superiority over the ephemeral, prejudice-bound interpretations of our colleagues and have wanted our text productions to be regarded as cultural monuments and thus as permanent, as positivist, as definitive, in other words, as noncritical, or nonhermeneutic. Is it any wonder that the noncritical chickens might have come home to roost and that what was once an epistemological virtue has now become an institutional liability?

There are doubtless good reasons for this determination of difference and for our having both embraced it and now being branded by it: for example, descriptive and analytical bibliography, like any other account of complex physical states, requires a similarly complex terminology, and one can understand the psychological and the financial temptations to claim definitiveness for a textual edition. Put as bluntly as may be, authority so defined as definitiveness is almost a requirement in securing foundation or federal funding, for no bureaucrat is likely to loosen the purse strings for an editorial project that admits, even celebrates, its critical bias and its likely ephemerality. And no man but a blockhead (not even for money) would spend decades working on a scholarly edition if it could be superseded at any moment. But, if scholarly editing and scholarly editions were truly definitive and timeless and not a product of their cultural assumptions and cultural practices (of what Clifford Geertz calls "local knowledge"),[25] then Erasmus would not have felt it necessary to replace Jerome's Vulgate or Johnson (and Theobald) to reedit Shakespeare after Pope or John Kidd to question Hans Walter Gabler's "definitive" Ulysses and to produce his own Dublin edition (i.e., if the legal and other problems surrounding the edition are ever resolved).[26]

Under this principle of local knowledge perhaps de Man is justified, given his inevitable cultural myopia and the moment of his inscription, to see (in his other essay, "The Resistance to Theory") "historical and philological facts as the preparatory condition for understanding,"[27] and perhaps he is equally correct historically in seeing the link (via logic) between the trivium and the quadrivium to be "a clear instance of the interconnection between a science of the phenomenal world and a science of language conceived as a definitional logic, the pre-condition for a correct axiomatic-deductive, synthetic reasoning."[28] De Man would presumably have been quite comfortable on those promotion committees I have mentioned, sorting out the books from nonbooks and critical sheep from bibliographical goats. The logic of his own analysis thus plays out of this "definitional" precondition (in which foundational philology seems securely based) into

the larger claim that grammar-based systems (derived from the first component of the trivium) are nonthreatening because they are "in the service of
logic"[29] (the last component) and that perceived threats occur to the
relationship between theory and phenomenalism only when the tropical
dimension, that associated with rhetoric (the middle component) rather
than with grammar, begins to assert itself: in other words, when "text-
producing functions" rather than "extra-linguistic generalisation"[30] become the dominant mode of a theoretical discourse. It thus follows that, for
de Man's model of theory (a prereferential, text-based, linguistic one), "the
resistance to theory is in fact a resistance to reading"[31] and certainly to the
sort of circumscribed, nonreferential, "rhetorical" reading that Reuben
Brower practiced.

And for as long as scholarly editing and bibliography could be regarded primarily (or even solely) as analogous to grammatical rather than
to rhetorical modes of discourse, as productions that promoted the "logical" connection (i.e, the connection via logic) between the theoretical and
phenomenological worlds, then editing and bibliography could indeed be
"philological" in the restricted sense that Culler assumes for our traditional
practices. The problem with this formulation is (I believe) that, just as
criticism under poststructuralism became tropical and linguistic rather than
extralinguistic and referential, so too did the operations of textual criticism
become equally rhetorical and therefore just as "threatening" to the imputed prehermeneuticism that de Man and Culler, in their different ways,
observe for philology. Or, rather, as Gary Taylor has convincingly demonstrated, that the rhetorical medium in which textual criticism had always
conducted its business, despite a long-standing attempt to pass off its rhetoric as a grammar, now became available for rhetorical rather than (or as well
as) grammatical, or logical, analysis. As Taylor puts it: "the fact did not
change; we just saw it differently. Or rather, the problem did not change;
but we phrased it differently."[32]

Taylor uses this description of change to draw textual criticism into the
Kuhnian model of changes in scientific perception, itself simply one version
(via Kuhn's theory of discourse and reception)[33] of the history of the
transmission and reformulation of logical systems: "Revolutions in science,
like revolutions in editing, depend upon rhetoric, upon the ability of a
clique of adherents to persuade a majority of potential practitioners."[34]
The inevitable problem, which Taylor resolutely faces, is that this substitution of a rhetorical for a grammatical (i.e., linguistic rather than logical)
system at a specific moment in cultural history runs the risk of "turning a

discussion of the rhetoric which pervades our discourse into a defense of a particular point of view"[35]—that is, to mistake rhetoric for grammar, or (in the language of speech act theory) to confuse the performative with the constative. De Man had done no less in asserting, as a rhetorical necessity in his moment of theory, that philology had indeed been viewed as grammatical but that the prehermeneutic qualities of that grammar now rendered it (in the poststructuralist, linguistic dispensation) emblematically theoretical. It is this ploy that I am now rejecting and yet rejecting it via Taylor's caveat about rhetoric as imputed authority.

The institutional, cultural problem in my formulation for both Taylor's and de Man's assumptions about rhetoric and grammar is in that word *now*. For, in the decade or so following de Man's critique of philology and theory, it is tellingly, perhaps painfully, obvious that poststructuralism, and thus the *now* that went along with de Man's timing of his promotion of rhetoric over grammar, and linguistics over reference, is no longer the dominant discourse but, on the contrary, the constative and "extralinguistic" have intruded quite forcefully on our profession's deliberations.

This itself is not news. In the plangent tones of his MLA presidential address of 1986 ("The Triumph of Theory") J. Hillis Miller noted that his definition of "theory" (the very language-based structure endorsed by de Man and, for textual criticism, by Taylor) had been co-opted or invaded by these historicizing extralinguistic movements (cultural studies, gender studies, and so on) that to Miller seemed to have disenfranchised "theory." "Literary study in the past few years has undergone a sudden, almost universal turn away from theory in the sense of an orientation toward language as such and has made a corresponding turn toward history, culture, society, politics, institutions, class and gender conditions, the social context, the material base."[36]

If what Miller and a typical "literary" convention program in the 1990s have to say is true—and I think it would be foolish to deny it as a statistical reality—then the rhetoric-based vehicle of textual criticism that Taylor prescribed for us in 1988 has already been superseded, and we are back in that interstitial, logic-based location *between* the trivium and quadrivium, a position that in former days had given peculiar privilege to textual criticism as the arbiter between "the text itself" (the language-based trivium) and the phenomenological world (the nonverbal quadrivium of number [mathematics], space [geometry], motion [astronomy], and time [music]), whether in annotation, glossing, or in the establishment of authorial (or anybody else's) intention. But what does this shift in philological positioning mean at this *now*, and can we textuists take advantage of the shift to resituate ourselves as other than the "other," other than the "not-a-book"? Can we get promoted again now that cultural studies and gender studies have sent poststructuralism off with its prehermeneutic tail between its legs?

The local answer, using the text productions of local knowledge, is probably yes, the moment is propitious. Marion Wynne-Davies has, under feminist auspices, already produced a gendered edition of Chaucer's *Clerk's Tale* and *Wife of Bath's Tale*,[37] and Ann Thompson, now co–general editor of the "new" New Arden, has, in this current volume, laid down feminist protocols for the editing of Shakespeare.[38] And, as Brenda Silver, Gerald MacLean, William Andrews, Jonathan Goldberg, and Jonathan Bate and Sonia Massai forcefully demonstrate in the "discourse" section of this book, there are enormous challenges in thinking about textuality from one of the current constative, extralinguistic positions (such as race, gender, or class). And the same could be said for the much larger project of actually producing editions that embody the social textual criticism of McGann, McKenzie, and others, of which Gerald MacLean's forthcoming edition of Restoration poetry is just one possible manifestation.[39]

Now, it could be argued (I have argued it myself)[40] that these apparently concessive gestures to the nonlinguistic turn are just as rhetorical, and therefore just as nongrammatical, as were the supposedly prehermeneutic philologies espoused by de Man and carried out by (say) the text-centered productions of the Center for Scholarly Editions and the Center for Editions of American Authors. In fact, the rhetorical model, as long as it can be perceived as itself a social production (something that both de Man and the CEAA editors barely recognized) is observable at almost any stage in the history of editing and bibliography, from the decision of Callimachus to exclude the Torah on ethnic grounds from his otherwise "comprehensive" *Pinakes* (while including the menus and erotic delights of banquets given by Alexandrian courtesans)[41] to the MLA Variorum Shakespeare's decision to exclude the eighteenth-century reception history of Tate's happy ending to King Lear (in which Cordelia settles down to a respectable married life with Edgar and Lear is put out to senior citizenship pasture),[42] even though the very rationale for a critical variorum is social response over time and even though this version was the only one seen onstage for over a century. And, even in editions whose rhetorical colors do not flap quite so brazenly on their editorial mainmast, Murray McGillivray has shown, for example, that the "standard," "philological" Klaeber edition of *Beowulf* is fraught with political, Germanist assumptions about race, national origins, and social constraint.[43]

So the larger rather than the local answer may not be just to redirect our editorial and bibliographical practices to political, social, gendered, and racial ends that now happen to be fashionable (and about which we may feel at the very least suspicious and cautious) but, rather, to undertake the much more difficult job of both self-interrogation and proselytizing that will (1) persuade us that, while trying very hard not to persuade, that is in fact what we have been doing in our bibliographies and editions and (2) help us to convince others, particularly those whose professional position gives them the power to distinguish between the "real" book and the "nonbook," that editing can never be prehermeneutical because it is already embedded, as a cultural artifact, in the hermeneutic circle and that such apparently new movements as "personalist criticism"[44] are already documented in our editions, whether we still cling to their definitive pretensions or not. This latter tack will require some loss of face and loss of credibility for those philologists who still like to think of themselves as prehermeneutic; it will require that we abandon both James L. W. West III's hope for "invisibility"[45] and what Talbot Donaldson derisively called the "editorial death-wish;"[46] it will require that (in the words of Stanley Fish) philologists identify themselves as members of the species *homo rhetoricus* rather than *homo seriosus,*[47] but I cannot see that any other admission—an admission of sameness rather than of difference—is ever going to lead to the general reincorporation of textual and bibliographical study into the academic and scholarly world.

I have argued elsewhere[48] that this shift in Linnaean, or species, identification may be forced upon us anyway, for the recent unanimous Supreme Court Feist decision[49] allowing the resale of nonprotectable historical "fact" in the white pages of the telephone directory might well render the very claim of scholarly "grammatical" definitiveness a publishing liability rather than a virtue. Under Feist the more an edition (especially a clear-text edition of the typical CSE/CEAA type) promotes its historical definitiveness, the more it pretends to be prehermeneutic, the less protectable it becomes. One of the ironies of this decision might thus be that "inclusive text" editions (those in which the editorial "presence," "intrusion," or "constraint" are avowedly made part of the textual page—rather than seen as pudenda to be discreetly hidden in the back of the book) could be the more easily protectable because the "text itself" (historical fact) could not practically be photocopied separately from the editorial barbed wire (the "property" of the editor). By acknowledging our textual and bibliographical research as contingent, local, and ephemeral—in other words, as "personal criticism," or local knowledge—ironically, we may be better able not only to protect it under the copyright law's endorsement of Romantic originality but also to convince our colleagues and peers that what we produce really are books, not nonbooks or half-books. Hazlitt is reputed to have claimed that "it is utterly impossible to convince an Editor that he is a nobody"[50]—a challenge that the academy has clearly tried to meet, for of late we seem to have become nobodies producing nonbooks. But, if a combination of the Feist decision, personalist criticism, local knowledge, and the posthermeneutic dispensation can make us textually dangerous again,[51] then perhaps the loss of philological face will have been worth it.

NOTES

1. Paul de Man, "The Resistance to Theory" and "The Return to Philology," *The Resistance to Theory* (Minneapolis: University of Minnesota Press, 1986).
2. De Man, "Return to Philology," 23.
3. G. Thomas Tanselle, "The Editorial Problem of Final Authorial Intention," *Studies in Bibliography* 29 (1976): 167–211, esp. 179.
4. See my demurrals in *Theories of the Text* (Oxford: Clarendon Press, forthcoming).
5. Walter Jackson Bate, *Harvard Magazine,* September–October 1982; Alvin Kernan, *The Death of Literature* (New Haven: Yale University Press, 1990), esp. "The Tree of Knowledge: Literature's Presence in the Social World," in which Kernan claims that, because of the ravages of various contemporary "theoretical" dispensations, "literature is in the process of losing a place in the knowledge tree and therefore in danger of breaking up in the social world" (202).
6. Jonathan Culler, "Antifoundational Philology," in *On Philology,* ed. Jan Ziolkowski (University Park: Pennsylvania State University Press, 1990), 52.
7. Culler, "Antifoundational," 50.
8. The figure of an ideological/religious "schism" between literary criticism and bibliographical studies has become almost a staple of current discussion—indeed, overcoming it is the basic purpose of the series in which this book is published. Examples occur in Jerome J. McGann, "The Monks and the Giants: Textual and Bibliographical Studies and the Interpretation of Literary Works," in *Textual Criticism and Literary Interpretation,* ed. McGann (Chicago: University of Chicago Press, 1985); McGann, "Shall These Bones Live?" *TEXT* 1 (1984): 21–40; George Bornstein's introduction to *Representing Modernist*

Texts: Editing as Interpretation (Ann Arbor: University of Michigan Press, 1991); and Philip Cohen, ed., *Devils and Angels: Textual Editing and Literary Theory* (Charlottesville: University Press of Virginia, 1991).

9. MLA/Ford Foundation conference on the Future of Doctoral Study in English, Wayzata, Minn., 1986.

10. Richard Lanham, "Convergent Pressures: Social, Technological, Theoretical," in *The Future of Doctoral Studies in English,* ed. Andrea Lunsford, Helene Moglen, and James F. Slevin (New York: MLA, 1989), 110.

11. See, for example, John Miles Foley, "Editing Oral Epic Texts: Theory and Practice," *TEXT* 1 (1984): 75–94; Hans Walter Gabler, "The Synchrony and Diachrony of Texts: Practice and Theory of the Critical Edition of James Joyce's *Ulysses,*" *TEXT* 1 (1984): 305–26; and "The Text as Process and the Problem of Intentionality," *TEXT* 3 (1987): 107–16; Donald H. Reiman, " 'Versioning': The Presentation of Multiple Texts," *Romantic Texts and Contexts* (Columbia: University of Missouri Press, 1987); Gary Taylor and Michael Warren, eds., *The Division of the Kingdoms: Shakespeare's Two Versions of "King Lear"* (Oxford: Oxford University Press, 1988); Michael Warren, ed., *The Complete King Lear, 1608–1623* (Berkeley: University of California Press, 1989).

12. G. Thomas Tanselle, "Textual Scholarship," in *Introduction to Literary Scholarship in the Modern Languages and Literatures,* ed. Joseph Gibaldi (New York: MLA, 1981), 50.

13. G. Thomas Tanselle, "Bibliography and Science," *Studies in Bibliography* 27 (1974): 55–89; reprinted in *Selected Studies in Bibliography* (Charlottesville: University Press of Virginia, 1979). See my further commentary on this issue of the epistemological relations between bibliography and science in "Textual Forensics," *PMLA* (1996): 32–51, esp. 33–34.

14. See Gerald MacLean's essay in the present volume.

15. The citations of antibibliographical sentiment reprinted here date from the late 1970s, when I was presenting a paper on "Critics and Scholars" at various universities in Canada and the United States. The positions espoused could be replicated in critical reviews of editing and textual scholarship in a number of more recent publications. For example, Gerald Graff maintains that "the declining status of textual editing" (once "the staple of doctoral dissertations") is symptomatic of a general decline in positivist and "detailed" scholarship and is a result of its being "discounted as positivistic" ("The Scholar in Society," in *Introduction to Scholarship in Modern Languages and Literatures,* ed. Joseph Gibaldi [New York: MLA, 1992], 354). He commends an "alliance with theory . . . to reverse the downward fortunes of editing." I contend that this argument falls into the "territorial fallacy" (that theory and bibliography take place in different parts of the academic and intellectual map and must be imported or exported into each other's native *heimat*). See my critique in *Theories*). See also my account of nationalist antibibliography in "Getting Personal / Going Public," a review of Donald H. Reiman's book *The Study of Modern Manuscripts* (Baltimore: Johns Hopkins University Press, 1992), in *Review* 17 (1995): 225–52; my article "Textual Imperialism and Post-Colonial

Bibliography" (presented at the Society for Textual Scholarship conference, New York, April 1995); reprinted in *Textual Transgressions: Essays toward a Biobibliography* (New York: Garland, 1996).

16. C. H. Sisson, "Pound among the Pedants," *Times Literary Supplement*, 20 May 1979, 616, reviewing *Collected Early Poems of Ezra Pound*, ed. Michael John King (London: Faber, 1979).

17. Lewis Mumford, "Emerson behind Barbed Wire," *New York Review of Books*, 18 January 1968, 3–5, 23; Edmund Wilson, *The Fruits of the MLA* (New York: New York Review of Books, 1968).

18. *The Library of America* (New York: Literary Classics of the United States, 1982–).

19. John Gross, "The Wars of D. H. Lawrence," *New York Review of Books*, 27 September 1979, 17, reviewing *The Letters of D. H. Lawrence*, ed. James T. Boulton, vol. 1 (Cambridge: Cambridge University Press, 1979).

20. Paul Delany, "Letters of the Artist as a Young Man," *New York Times Book Review*, 9 September 1979, 44, reviewing Boulton, *Letters of Lawrence*.

21. Gross, "Wars of D. H. Lawrence."

22. Rosemary Dinnage, "Dodgson's Passion," *New York Review of Books*, 16 April 1979, 10, reviewing *The Letters of Lewis Carroll*, ed. Morton N. Cohen (Oxford: Oxford University Press, 1979).

23. Arnold, "The Function of Criticism in the Present Time"; "The Study of Poetry," in *The Complete Prose Works*, ed. R. H. Super (Ann Arbor: University of Michigan Press, 1960–77).

24. Netherlands State Institute for War Documentation, *The Diary of Anne Frank: The Critical Edition* (New York: Doubleday, 1989); *Diary of a Young Girl: The Definitive Edition*, by Anne Frank (New York: Doubleday, 1992). I am grateful to Laurie Bley for detailing the inadequacies of both editions ("The Many Many Diaries of Anne Frank: From Variorum to Monument" [seminar paper, CUNY Graduate School, spring 1995]).

25. Clifford Geertz, *Local Knowledge: Further Essays in Interpretive Anthropology* (New York: Basic Books, 1983), esp. "Local Knowledge: Fact and Law in Comparative Perspective," 167–234.

26. Saint Jerome, *Biblia Sacra iuxta Vulgatem Versionem*, ed. R. Weber et al., 2 vols. (Stuttgart: Würtembergissche Bibelanstalt, 1969); Shakespeare, *Works*, ed. Alexander Pope (London: 1723–25, 1728), *Works*, ed. Lewis Theobald (London: 1740); *Works*, ed. Samuel Johnson (London: 1765, 1768); James Joyce, *Ulysses: A Critical and Synoptic Edition*, ed. Hans Walter Gabler, with Wolfhard Steppe and Claus Melchior (New York: Garland, 1984); *Ulysses: Corrected Text*, ed. Gabler (New York: Random House, 1986); *The Dublin Edition of the Works of James Joyce*, ed. John Kidd (New York: Norton, forthcoming).

27. De Man, "Resistance to Theory," 4.

28. Ibid., 13.

29. Ibid., 14.

30. Ibid., 15.

31. Ibid.

32. Gary Taylor, "The Rhetoric of Textual Criticism," *TEXT* 4 (1988): 53. See also his essay "The Rhetoric of Reception," in *Crisis in Editing: The Texts of the English Renaissance,* ed. Randall McLeod (New York: AMS Press, 1994), 19–59, an account of the various "rhetorical" responses to the Taylor and Wells *Oxford Shakespeare.*

33. Thomas Kuhn, *The Structure of Scientific Revolutions,* 2d ed. (Chicago: University of Chicago Press, 1970).

34. Taylor, "Rhetoric," 53.

35. Ibid.

36. J. Hillis Miller, "The Triumph of Theory, the Resistance to Reading, and the Question of the Material Base" (MLA Presidential Address, 1986), *PMLA* 102 (1987): 281–91, esp. 283.

37. Marion Wynne-Davies, ed., *The Tales of the Clerk; and, the Wife of Bath,* by Geoffrey Chaucer (London: Routledge, 1992).

38. See Thompson's essay "Feminist Theory and the Editing of Shakespeare: *The Taming of the Shrew* Revisited," in the present volume. See also my discussion of Thompson and other feminist textual scholars in "Gender in the Text" (*Theories,* ch. 10).

39. Gerald M. MacLean, "What Is a Restoration Poem? Editing a Discourse, Not an Author," *TEXT* 3 (1987); and *English Poems Commemorating the Stuart Restoration,* forthcoming.

40. *Theories of the Text,* esp. 211–12.

41. See Rudolf Blum, *Kallimachos: The Alexandrian Library and the Origins of Bibliography,* trans. by Hans H. Welisch (Madison and London: University of Wisconsin Press, 1991), esp. 103. See my review in *Analytical and Enumerative Bibliography* n.s. 6 (1992): 132–36.

42. See the account of the *Lear* adaptation in Jonathan Bate and Sonia Massai's essay in the present volume, "Adaptation as Edition."

43. Murray McGillivray, "Creative Anachronism: Marx's Problem with Homer, Gadamer's Discussion of 'the Classical,' and Our Understanding of Older Literature," *New Literary History* 25 (1994): 399–413.

44. The term is widely used in much contemporary literary criticism, especially by feminist theorists (see esp. Nancy K. Miller, *Getting Personal: Feminist Occasions and Other Autobiographical Acts* [New York: Routledge, 1991]). It is adopted for bibliography by Donald H. Reiman in *The Study of Modern Manuscripts* (Baltimore: Johns Hopkins University Press, 1992), in order to "humanize the study of modern manuscripts by citing personal experiences and characterizing individuals involved in the anecdotes" (xi–xii).

45. James L. W. West III, "Novelist's Champion Vows to Keep the Flame Burning," *Chronicle of Higher Education,* 2 November 1994, A11.

46. E. Talbot Donaldson, "The Psychology of Editors of Medieval Texts," *Speaking of Chaucer* (London: Athlone; New York: Norton, 1970), 105.

47. Stanley Fish, "Rhetoric," in *Critical Terms for Literary Study,* ed. Frank Lentricchia and Thomas McLaughlin (Chicago: University of Chicago Press, 1991), 208; and *Doing What Comes Naturally: Change, Rhetoric, and the Practice of Theory in Literary and Legal Studies* (Durham: Duke University

Press, 1989), 482. Fish adopts the terms from Richard Lanham, *The Motives of Eloquence* (New Haven: Yale University Press, 1976), esp. 1, 4.

48. D. C. Greetham, "'Copy/Right,' or 'How to Do Things with Searle and Derrida'" (paper presented at conference on Literary Theory and the Practice of Editing, Liverpool, July 1993, and Canberra, April 1994).

49. *Feist Publications, Inc., v. Rural Telephone Serv. Co.,* 499 U.S. 340, 111 S.Ct 1282, 113 L.Ed.2d.358 (1991). The decision was handed down by the Supreme Court on 27 March 1991. See also *CCC Information Services, Inc., v. MacLean Hunter Market Reports, Inc.,* no. 1312, docket 93–7687, U.S. Court of Appeals, S.Ct., decided 5 December 1994. See my further arguments on Feist and subsequent cases in "Rights to Copy" (paper presented at MLA Conference, Chicago, December 1995); reprinted in *Textual Transgressions* and in "The Telephone Directory and Dr. Seuss: Scholarly Editing after *Feist v. Rural Telephone,*" *Studies in the Literary Imagination* (forthcoming).

50. Hazlitt, quoted in Joseph Epstein, "Too Relevant by Half," review of *The Columbia Dictionary of Quotations,* ed. Robert Andrews, *Times Literary Supplement,* 10 December 1993, 9.

51. Even the antibibliographical Sisson has to confess that "the future—even a little, with this [Pound] volume, the present—is with the indexers and the bibliographers" (616) and admits that, despite his reservations about editing in general, "this volume . . . is something which all under a compulsion to keep their Pound material up to date must certainly possess."

What's Class Got to Do with It?

Gerald MacLean

In this essay I ponder a number of questions that arise when editing early modern English printed texts while putting pressure on questions of class, gender, and national identity. Once excluded from editorial decision making and theorizing, such questions have nevertheless established philosophically cogent analytical and critical programs under various designations. Within the contexts of poststructuralist and postmodernist critique, the first section of this essay, "Class, Property, and Print Culture," outlines some theoretical concerns regarding class analysis and its relation to the fields of inquiry within which textual criticism is currently situated. By considering the keyword *class,* I offer some descriptive conditions for what seems to me to be the continuing importance of class analysis in social, historical, and literary research generally. The second section, "Class and Scholarly Editing," develops these arguments by linking class analysis with some specific concerns facing editors and scholarly critics of historical and literary printed texts. My examples are drawn from my work over the last decade editing and thinking about the vernacular poetry published in 1660 and 1661 on the Restoration of Charles Stuart to the English throne, but I trust that this specificity does not overly limit the applicability of my arguments.

CLASS, PROPERTY, AND PRINT CULTURE

Scholars and historians of the early modern period are unlikely ever to reach a consensus about class. There are certainly some social historians who would argue that class analysis belongs to an outmoded and peripheral sort of historiography that was long ago demolished by demographers and county historians; moreover, when applied to the early modern period, "class" is an empirically insupportable anachronism. There are also likely to be contemporary theorists wishing to argue that class is a category contaminated by its association with one of those master narratives that, according to a certain reading of Lyotard's important work, can no longer be used to account for our postmodern condition.[1] I nevertheless persist in considering class to be a useful and often necessary concept for examining and understanding the material and cultural conditions and developments of everyday life, rather than a reified historical category lockstepped into a unitary master narrative with explanatory and predictive authority. People enter history multiply situated, in complex relations not only with economic and productive forces but also with regard to such social categories as race, gender, sexuality, and nationality. The question of class, as I understand it, necessarily involves understanding human agency not simply in terms of relations to the development of the modes and forces of production but also complexly, in articulation with local, regional, national, racial, ethnic, religious, political, and sexual identifications and fantasies. Class identity cannot direct historical agency, since it cannot be shown to exist as such. Rather, historical agents discover themselves variously occupying and mobilizing various class positions.[2]

This view of class might be called "post-Marxist" in two respects. It is "post-" because it denies class a primary place in the determinations of social life. Yet it remains "Marxist" since it seeks to engage critically with questions arising from Marx's crucially important argument, the one he was developing at the point when *Capital,* volume 3, breaks off, that "What makes a class?" is not simply a question of "the identity of revenues and revenue sources" but also a more complex question involving

> the infinite fragmentation of interests and positions into which the division of social labour splits not only workers but also capitalists and landowners—the latter, for instance, into vineyard-owners, field-owners, forest-owners, mine-owners, fishery-owners, etc.[3]

For Marx "identity of revenues and revenue sources" is not a founding moment upon which class identities can be forged; rather, it is where the need for analysis of class relations begins, and it does so by recognizing how "social labour" brings about that "fragmentation of interests and positions." Not identities, but interests and positions.

Among the last things, we might say, that Marx had on his mind when he stopped writing his critique of political economy was this very question

of how class was a matter of position in relation to the historical development of productive forces in a specific place, not of identity. This is not very
surprising since, consistently for Marx, the relationship between property
and subjectivity was both direct and typically nationalistic or even tribal in
its variations.[4] The development of what has come to be termed "print
culture" has so mediated the relationship between property and subjectivity
over the last three hundred years that modernity may be characterized by
the interplay between reading subject and the reading public. In terms of
print culture the dislocation of property from its originary conception as
power in the productive capacity of the land would seem incapable of
accounting for the new forms of social agency emerging from those patterns of textual production and consumption that came of age during the
seventeenth century.[5]

Yet, if changes in property relations are conceived of as the condition
of subjectivity, class relations, and hence all social and political life during
the period, then they are clearly central to the development of seventeenth-
century print culture in England.[6] Nevertheless, in what sense *must* we
speak of the shifts in class relations during the period, especially those
introduced by print culture, in terms of shifts in the development of capitalist ground rent, merchant capital, and colonialism? In other words, how did
the commercial production of mechanically reproducible texts and images
suitable for personal/private consumption enter into the dislocation of
class formations from economic forces at the time?

The problem, in part, is that of the model itself, since Marx's analysis of
class relations in preindustrial societies is persistently blind to sex/gender
systems beyond casual glances at the "natural" family. Sexual differences
and the production of gender ideology could only with considerable
difficulty be analyzed in traditional class terms of relations of production.
Nevertheless, following Marx's lead with regard to class as a position and
not an identity, replacing mode of production analysis, complete with its
master narrative of the transition from feudalism to capitalism, by a relations of production model informed by recent developments in feminist
theory, shows that class analysis can account for the relative autonomy of
cultural forces in determining social life, without entirely abandoning the
centrality of property relations in the social formation of class positions.

The artisanal classes occupy the fault line in those tectonic shifts between the feudal and early capitalist modes of production and appropriation of "property" described for us in the narratives of Marxist historiography. It could be shown that the growth of the commercial printing industry

generated new class positions for both women and men and that it enfranchised them in new and formerly unimagined ways. During the early stages of unrest leading to the first civil war, the political consequences of printing were frequently deplored for helping to cause social unrest. One could describe how printing helped empower a section of the artisanal classes and, in such a description, show—following the example of Marx at the end of *Capital*—how class describes positionality, not identity of interest. I shall return to this question of class in relation to the Stationers' Company after elaborating more specifically some of the theoretical problems posed by shuttling back and forth between literary and more strictly historical concerns.

Textual Criticism and History

In arguing that we need class analysis in order to account for the agency of the printing industry upon property, conceived of (following Marx) as "the relation of the working . . . subject to the conditions of his production or reproduction as his own," the challenge is to develop an approach adequate to the emergence of relatively autonomous productive forces such as the printing industry, the consequent alterations in existing social relations attending the growing political importance of artisanal classes such as the men and women of the press, and the crisis in representation that attends the separation of state power from the interests of the dominant classes. From 1660 the printing industry enabled the legitimation of a (now culturally nonrepresentative, in some senses farcical) political form (monarchy) not simply by recalling the feudal principle of royal control over the land as the center of national production but also by developing Cromwell's most successful ideological and political practice—an aggressive imperialist foreign policy to promote British trade. Dryden expresses these nationalist ambitions in *Astraea Redux,* his Restoration panegyric addressed to the king:

> Our Nation with united Int'rest blest
> Not now content to poize, shall sway the rest.
> Abroad your Empire shall no Limits know,
> But like the Sea in boundless Circles flow.
> Your much lov'd Fleet shall with a wide Command
> Besiege the petty Monarchs of the Land:
> . . . .
> Their wealthy Trade from Pyrates Rapine free

Our Merchants shall no more Advent'rers be:
Nor in the farthest East those Dangers fear
Which humble *Holland* must dissemble here.
Spain to your Gift alone her Indies owes;
For what the Pow'rful takes not he bestowes.

(lines 296–301, 304–09)

To echo the *Eighteenth Brumaire,* the "farce" of the Restoration, following the "tragedy" of civil war, need not have happened and would not have happened in quite the ways it did were it not for the agency in 1660 of an established network of writers, printers, and booksellers with three decades of experience behind them, enabling them to set about the cultural work of legitimating monarchy not simply by asserting its divine authority but also by asserting their own power over the new king by insisting that Charles was the herald of a new age of empire.

Traditional literary history of the English kind, the model initiated by Dryden, and sustained into our own century, of a patriarchal descent from one great and usually male writer to the next, the model of Bloom and Frye, and of some feminist critics such as Gilbert and Gubar who substitute a matrilineage, needs to be rethought with regard to the conditions governing its own production and sustained legitimacy. Such a project of rethinking literary history from a perspective informed by feminist engagement with, and critique of, Marxist historiography falls within the broad "commitment to explore the social and historical dimensions of literary works" that Jerome McGann characterized in 1985.[7] He associates this commitment with an extreme (some might say postmodern) self-consciousness among scholars about their sociohistorical interests and with a general project that is "antithetical, in several respects, to the (equally various) tradition of formal, structural, and text-centered literary studies which have been so influential in the academy for two generations" (3). One of McGann's contributions to the theory of historically based literary studies is his assertion of the commensurability of Marxist and feminist theory with the poststructuralist displacement of referentiality. "Marxist and Marxist-influenced criticism," he writes, "has been an especially important factor in" the development of recent "sociohistorical critical work." This is largely

because the questions it poses are founded in a powerful and dynamically coherent tradition of critical enquiry. Feminist studies have also done much to expose the sociohistorical dimensions of literary work. Because both of these critical approaches necessarily practice a hermeneutics of a repressed or invisibilized content, both have found no difficulty in assimilating the basic poststructural programmatic. (4)

The philosophical distinction McGann makes to demonstrate the incommensurability of poststructuralist discourse-analysis and, say, the historicism common to what we might caricature as Whig, Tory, and Marxist accounts of seventeenth-century England seems to me a tendentious and interesting one. These kinds of problems are of special interest to literary historians of the "English" seventeenth century for numerous reasons. For one they allow us to frame the period as that in which the English language began to write itself as literature, a period that saw the installation of English as a nationalistic discourse that has helped shape attitudes and opinions and engender fantasies and expectations ever since.

In the seventeenth century this was a process enabled by print culture, but it was also caught up in larger sociohistorical determinations with direct bearing upon what I am calling print culture, such as the collapse of censorship in 1641, the change from Latin to English for keeping legal records after 1650, and the installation of liberal ideals of the subject based on changes in property relations and democratic practices. I would endorse the poststructuralist emphasis on the priority of discourse as the condition of our knowing anything that might be called "history" but without conceding that this position entails any necessary denial of the existence of a material referent. The past was peopled by real men and women who, during the seventeenth century, began to spend more and more time reading, writing, and printing their ideas, thoughts, and fantasies. For any literary history the field of inquiry is marked out by the texts left behind. The poststructuralist emphasis on the discursive functioning of texts, the argument that they don't simply refer to an otherwise knowable reality but that they engage with previous texts and discursive situations, may lead us away from any simple author-centric view of textual production, it may discourage us from making heroes and heroines of past writers whose views we would endorse, but, as far as I can understand, it need not and does not dismantle the material relations governing the production of literary history as a problem of gendered class relations.

CLASS AND SCHOLARLY EDITING

What have these considerations about class got to do with textual criticism and scholarly editing? I shall comment here on four aspects of this question:

(1) the class positions from which editorial work tends to be undertaken today; (2) the way editorial decisions are influenced by class concerns; (3) the way class necessarily involves considerations of gender, sexuality, and race; and (4), which is an extension of aspect 3, the way class analysis problematizes which texts get edited.

The Class Positions of Editorial Work

Questions of class, in the context of textual editing, will generally have less bearing on decisions concerning specific textual readings than they will on the way textual editors situate themselves professionally. Twenty years ago Alan Roper observed, "There's a middle-class solidity about editing, beside which the practice of criticism sometimes seems the mere dilettantism of a decadent minor aristocracy."[8] Not all textual editors started out, like Roper, as successful literary critics who were drawn to editing by professional and intellectual pressures. But, besides illustrating nicely my point that class is always relational, a matter of shifting positions and not fixed identities, Roper's perception that textual editors and literary critics might be said to occupy different "class" positions within the profession seems to me a telling one.

The division of labor that separates editing from criticism and theory certainly explains what I take to be common current values and practices within the profession; committees making hiring, tenure, promotion, and salary decisions typically seem to prefer candidates producing literary criticism to those who produce scholarly editions. In my own department it was recently proposed that any scholarly edition, complete with textual apparatus, critical and historical introduction, however many years it may have taken to produce, should count as worth half any single-authored book of critical analysis. How many of us, in these times, can advise doctoral candidates to undertake scholarly editions for their dissertation work and hope to find a job four, or however many, years from now?

A further effect of the division of labor is a problem familiar to scholarly editors interested in theorizing their work. As Michael Groden recently put it, literary critics and textual theorists have been asking similar questions for years, but, "as many people from both groups have noted, there has been relatively little contact between the two and not much recognition of common interests."[9] Groden reminds us of Fredson Bowers's 1958 Sandars Lecture, "Textual Criticism and the Literary Critic," which boldly polemicizes: "The relation of bibliographical and textual investigation to literary criticism is a thorny subject, not from the point of view of bibliography, but from the point of view of literary criticism."[10] There is every reason to be, like Groden, optimistic that there has been a steady improvement of relations since 1958, thanks largely to the heroic efforts of a familiar list of champions—Greetham, McGann, Shillingsburg, Tanselle, Taylor. But, even so, Groden admits the problem hasn't gone away, and he ends in the imperative mode: "literary critics should begin to recognize their obligation to analyze and assess" the work of textual critics and theorists (286). Textual scholars may be taking an active interest in the work of literary critics and theorists, but there is little enough reason to suppose that members of Roper's "decadent minor aristocracy" are listening.

Class and Editorial Decision Making

The question of how class influences the way editors make decisions very quickly returns us to the question of gender difference. But first I'd like to suggest ways in which class-specific activity is going on all the time that editors spend editing things. If, following the late Marx, class is about the interests and positions consequent upon a particular relation to the available modes of production, what are the class "interests and positions" of textual editors?

In such terms class relations can be seen to enter and even influence editorial practices. For the most part editors preparing traditional critical editions are initially concerned with uncovering a history of textual production—what the author wrote, how that gets altered by publication—and so tend to associate their work and purposes with those of authors and other primary producers. In doing so, they adopt a specific class position, together with its attendant perspectives, one from which the crucial problems presented by the evidence become apparent in terms of authorial production. Editors preparing translated or modernized texts, who are primarily aiming to satisfy the demands of specific readers, might be said to occupy a different class locale, one not circumscribed by a history of production. McGann addresses this point in his *Critique of Modern Textual Criticism* by imagining the

> practice of the nonspecialist or modernizing editor, whose choice of reading text is guided by what he judges to be most useful and important for a certain audience of readers.[11]

You really cannot get very far in talking about class before gender interrupts. The generic masculine pronoun here is historically symptomatic and not the author's fault; as Ann Thompson points out in her essay in this volume, editors usually were men back in the 1980s. Class is necessary but insufficient. McGann's modernizing editor who follows readers' needs thereby steps out of and challenges the position identified with authorial production. Instead, McGann suggests, such editors adopt a "point of view" from which "there is no such thing as final intentions, whether authorial or otherwise" (104). What we have, then, are specific class distinctions governing the interests and positions of textual editors in ways that will directly affect the kinds of text they are likely to produce: critical editors are most likely to define their tasks in relation to an ideology of authorial production, while modernizing editors are most likely to theorize "production" in terms of historically specific reading publics.

Editors don't operate outside of class interests and positions, whether or not they admit to it. When I started graduate studies at the University of Virginia in 1977, Fredson Bowers had already retired from teaching. Shortly after my arrival I was told that he had for many years been a breeder of champion dogs and a dog show judge. I was not surprised. Editors are surely animated by a fascination with ways of thinking about ancestry and bloodlines not entirely dissimilar to that found among horse breeders and trainers: "F1 by Q4 out of Q2," that sort of thing. In 1987 I was thinking of this tendency among textual editors to use class metaphors when I claimed that the editorial rationale for the magnificent seven-volume Yale edition of *Poems on Affairs of State* (*POAS*) "arranges extant texts according to their social status as defined by the condition of their production."[12] My point was that the editorial principles adopted for the Yale *POAS* reproduced a specific class structure when they arranged the variety of extant texts by preferring any single manuscript to any manuscript version from a scribal miscellany, while preferring any scribal version to any printed version. At issue here is the way an implicit class hierarchy, based on the division of labor in the production of a text, reinforces a historical elevation of the author and scribe over any printer, thereby directly influencing the choice and treatment of copy-text. As I wrote in 1987:

> Good-breeding and blood-lines count for a great deal here. The unique manuscript has closer direct ties to its progenitor than the text from an often promiscuous manuscript collection which is usually of a later generation anyway, having been reproduced at the hands of scribes. But the interference of the scribe is still preferable to that of the printing-shop compositor since, by this stage, the text has been

thoroughly corrupted by a phase of mechanical reproduction that removes it even further from its origins in the author's genius, fancy or intention. (321)

My own metaphors only faintly suggest it, but I was concerned at the time with arguments being made by a variety of feminist theorists about gender differences in the constructions of class interests and positions. I went on to examine the case of a manuscript poem on the Stuart Restoration attributed to Katherine Philips, a poet with a contemporary reputation as the English Sappho, since this immediately focused on the further distinction between gender and sexuality. What might a lesbian poem on the events of 1660 look like?

Class, Sexuality, Gender, Nationality

Which brings me to my third connection between class analysis and scholarly editing; the place within editorial theory and practice for theorizing the specific historical links between class, gender, sexuality, and race. I have already addressed the need for revising rather than discarding Marxist class analysis so will turn to the question of why I think about what I am doing in the ways I do.

One simple answer is that the poems I am editing invite their readers to think in terms of class, gender, sexuality, and national identity, though seldom in terms of racial difference. Moreover, the circumstances in which these poems appeared was a crucially important moment in the history of the press, itself a site where questions of class and gender were being renegotiated. The return of monarchy was, in part, accomplished through large-scale social reorganization that required a great deal of cultural work, including the writing and production of texts of all sorts. So crucial had the commercial press become by 1660 that, during the months immediately preceding and following Charles's return, all manner of commemorative and celebratory publications appeared that set about giving symbolic and cultural meaning to the social and political changes in British life.[13]

The return to monarchy was the first time that the commercial press in Britain played so direct and central a role in establishing the terms of a national political settlement. There had, of course, been previous occasions when the press had flexed its political muscles in opposition: we might think of the Marprelate controversies of the late 1580s or the insurgent pamphleteering of the early 1640s.[14] But the Restoration was the first time that the commercial press helped to bring in and legitimate a new government and, in so doing, helped to define and set conditions for the terms of the political settlement. By 1660 the social agency of the press had produced an irreverent, secularizing, commercial, literary culture that had already captured much of the political high ground once claimed by the authorized discourse of the established church.[15] The poems celebrating Charles's return are central to any explanation of this phenomenon, and all of these poems, in some way or other, specifically advise their readers about what it means to be newly subject to a king, a member of that imagined community—a monarchy.

I shall give one brief and inadequate instance of this complex articulation of class with sexuality, gender, and regional identity. The relation between the returning monarch and his subjects is frequently figured in the poems by sexual metaphors of a virile groom ravishing and restoring his languishing bride; as it is in the manuscript poem attributed to, but almost certainly not by, Katherine Philips. "Thou art now a Bride, a Royall Queene," the nation is told, "noe more, / A wretched widdow growling on the flore" (lines 7–8). But the question of gender was not always sexualized when used to locate a precise position of enunciation for the subject welcoming the king's return. Writing from Newcastle, Ralph Astell, uncle and tutor to Mary Astell, author of *Some Reflections on Marriage* (1700), constructed the persona of a "black Northern Lass" (line 35) who reflects critically upon how different her poem is from those "High-born Strains of Poetry" (line 24) being produced in London and at Court. Astell's regionalist satire on the courtly panegyrics written by "Southern Ladies" (line 17) directly thematizes not only its own conditions of production but also the massive production of poems on the Restoration in terms of class, gender, and regional claims to speak for the nation as a whole.

In general it seems to me that scholarly editing necessarily involves understanding the cultural conditions of the original production of the texts we edit, and I think it important that we recognize the extent to which those cultural conditions are crosshatched by the complex articulation of class, gender, sexuality, and national or racial identity. By 1660 the commercial press provided certain women and men with access to specific kinds of class privilege, public authority, and social status. Put the other way, class and gender provide keys to understanding the specific conditions of public writing and commercial printing, bookselling and publishing, in Restoration England. Within the Stationers' Company the general trade crisis of the 1640s and 1650s produced a reversal in the previous relation between production and distribution; the number and authority of master printers within the company displaced the traditionally greater power of the book-sellers. Throughout the period wives and widows of freemen of the Stationers' Company could take active part in company business; a widow could inherit Company Trade Stock and was licensed to carry on her husband's business. It would seem that they were also empowered to bind apprentices.[16] Maureen Bell has only begun to publish her research on the remarkable degree to which women were active in the London book trade of the seventeenth century.[17] The 1640s and 1650s were also, of course, decades when increasing numbers of women took to writing their ideas and seeing them into print.

But amid the general antifeminist backlash of the 1660s male-authored satires on women who dared to break their traditional injunctions to silence focus entirely on women writers, entirely ignoring women involved in other stages of textual production. Sometimes gender distinctions disappear beneath those of class. Certainly, the satires on printers and booksellers in Dryden's *MacFlecknoe* and Pope's *Dunciad* ignore women as they direct class contempt upon the Stationers. Dryden calls them "Yeomen" (line 104), but Pope specifies the conditions of their labor:

> With Authors, Stationers obey'd the call,
> The field of glory is a field for all;
> Glory, and gain, th'industrious tribe provoke;
> And gentle Dulness ever loves a joke.[18]

Tribe, Johnson reminds us, was "often used in contempt" but is rather vague otherwise: "a distinct body of the people as divided by family or fortune, or any other characteristic."[19]

For the seventeenth century the ironies of Pope's "industrious tribe" were partly accurate and potentially misleading; the men and women who made their living from printing and the book trade were certainly industrious, and many almost certainly thought of their employment as glorious as well as gainful. But it is less clear that they constituted a coherent class. Rather, the class divisions, relative to conditions of labor, operating across the book trade of seventeenth-century England can be specified with some apparent ease. At one end we find the itinerant sellers of ballad, chapbook, and almanac, the uncountable and often female "mercuries" who distributed popular books throughout the provinces.[20] At the other end we find the monarch who nominally owned and so controlled the press. Formally, it was by the grant of royal patents that the university presses were permitted to operate. The crown also licensed the Stationers' Company, permitting members of the company to maintain monopoly rights over certain kinds of book. For its own part the Stationers' Company was keen to establish its own authority to prevent imported and pirated books from crowding the market. It also supervised apprenticeships and operated a joint-stock company, the "English Stock," with limited shares paying dividends on specific groups of best-selling books. The company was made up of printers and booksellers, but not all booksellers were free of the company, and all print sellers were outside its purvey.

In his studies of the Stationers' Company, Cyprian Blagden has demonstrated just how rash it would be to think of the company as a stable or coherent class interest, much less as a unified class agent. The picture of the company in the seventeenth century that emerges from Blagden's reading of its records is rather one of constant trade and class struggle that suggests the heterogeneity and historical variability of the industrious tribe rather than its tendencies to operate in the interests of anything worth calling a class identity. "In the eyes of central government [the Stationers' Company] was the organization through which the King or the Archbishop of Canterbury or the Parliament or the Army or the Protector hoped to control the press; it had some usefulness. In the eyes of the City of London, however, it was still a young company . . . unimportant in City politics and . . . poor."[21]

For the Stationers' Company the seventeenth century was a history of internal struggle along internal class divisions that separated printers and booksellers, apprentices with and without capital, those who possessed shares in the English Stock, those called upon to pay for banquets, those called on to collect annual dues. The social composition of apprentices measured by their fathers' trade and class altered significantly in the early seventeenth century; more and more sons of gentlemen and esquires were bound to companies; many freemen would become very wealthy men. But the Stationers' Company was never very important in city politics during the seventeenth century. Stationers did not control the printing or selling of pamphlets or prints, both of them inflammatory political forms; they possessed monopoly rights on some profitable groups of book and other regulatory controls that were seldom obeyed.[22]

But the stationers thought rather differently of themselves. In 1643 one "A. W. Stationer of *London*" castigated other members of his guild for not realizing fully the special importance and high seriousness of their calling:

> And to you my brethren of my society, for to you especially do I intend my exhortation, I beseech you consider, that you have more means, by reason that your calling is oftner to have to do with good books, then many other callings have; and yet alas brethren, I feare we have been more profane, and wicked, then such as are of many other callings.[23]

The trade in books evidently encouraged diverse forms of social and cultural self-importance among its members that were—to primary producers such as Dryden and Pope—in excess of their position in the division of labor; that is part of Pope's complaint.

Class and the Texts That Get Edited

Finally, to return to scholarly editing, it seems to me that class attitudes are invariably part of the structures by which we decide which texts are and are not worth editing. Again, I shall risk elaborating this generalization from problems arising in the course of my own work.

Among the clichés to be found amid the literary histories of the Restoration period is that the king's return was accompanied by an unprecedented number of celebratory publications. When first looking through the actual documents twelve years ago, I became aware that, in terms of the number and variety of poems published in 1660, this generalization was truer than anyone who had repeated it was likely to have understood. And it was true precisely because these poems represented the need for a great deal of cultural work to be done to ensure both the king's return and the interests of those who brought it about—and not some spontaneous outpouring of popular support for the monarchy. This recognition, hardly a discovery, was among the initial impulses that spurred me to edit these poems, so that we might have a better understanding of the literary reception of the Restoration. The point I want to make here is that the principles that I have developed over the years, though I still think them sound and practical in themselves, might nevertheless be contributing to certain class-specific distortions of the very cultural field I wish to document.

One of the key principles of inclusion has been that poems directly address the facts and effects of Charles's return by writing about the king; thus are excluded several poems on General Monck and members of the royal household and satires on the now defeated revolutionaries, regicides, and Rump members. Also excluded are poems in languages other than English. There are obvious practical considerations at work here; even with these exclusions the edition will still be large, containing 128 primary title entries, some of which are collections of poems by several hands. There simply isn't any room for more. Nevertheless, these exclusions are class specific and worth considering as such.

For the most part the excluded foreign language poems are found in collections issued by the Universities of Oxford, Cambridge, and Edinburgh.[24] Leaving out what the dons had to say in Latin and Greek but also Hebrew, Anglo-Saxon, Persian, "Syrian," and Celtic is in some respects a considerable loss that significantly limits my edition's claims upon being representative of the poetic response to 1660 as a whole.[25] Even the Latin and Greek poems were available only to a fairly circumscribed elite readership and as such might well be said to constitute a "minority" discourse belonging to a specific class of language professionals. Leaving out what they had to say, in print, in the coded ambiguities of foreign lanugages and foreign scripts, is clearly to silence a significant minority.

But, as I fondly imagine that my editorial labors are drawing to an end, I find myself more concerned about excluding those anti-Rump satires. In leaving out this last group of poems, almost entirely broadside ballads, I shall be omitting what are, arguably, some of the most immediately significant poems to have appeared: the popular satiric broadside ballads. Here is Lucy Hutchinson writing about the day when Charles came back:

> Indeed it was a wonder in that day to see the mutability of some, and the hypocrisy of others, and the servile flattery of all. Monk, like his better genius, conducted him, and was adored like one that had brought all the glory and felicity of mankind home with his prince.
> The officers of the army had made themselves as fine as the courtiers, and everyone hoped in this change to change their condition, and disowned all things they had before advised. Every ballad singer sung up and down the streets ribald rhymes, made in reproach of the late commonwealth, and of all those worthies that therein endeavoured the people's freedom and happiness.[26]

In terms of how ballad production entered debates on the Restoration settlement, vilifying members of the Rump government was evidently as important as celebrating the person of the king. By including only ballads celebrating the king's return, my edition will not only be leaving out a historically important group of poems, the anti-Rump satires, but in doing so it will misrepresent the class significance of the ballad market. And the point about the ballad market, as Tessa Watt argues, is that people of all classes heard, bought, and read ballads. The ballad market was class "inclusive," in Watt's term,[27] because it linked the formally illiterate, who could only admire the woodcuts and listen to others singing or reading the words, with readers and collectors like Antony à Wood, Samuel Pepys,[28] Lucy Hutchinson, and the gentlewoman from Birmingham, Frances Wolfreston.[29] "The buyers," Watt writes,

> remained socially variegated: in the early seventeenth century gentry collectors were still copying ballads into their commonplace books; probably the same ballads which were to be found on the walls of "honest alehouses," in "the shops of artifices" and in "the cottages of poor husbandmen."[30]

It may well be that any one of the excluded anti-Rump ballads is more culturally significant in terms of my own rationale for the edition than, say, Henry Oxinden's *Charls Triumphant,* a massive 1,033-line heroic poem that even his best friend advised him to cut, which hardly anyone is likely to have endured reading at the time and which failed to achieve its purpose, getting Oxinden a church living.

I agree with Roger Chartier that it is not "possible to establish exclusive relationships between specific cultural forms and particular social groups";[31] there is no simple identity between a cultural form, such as the broadside ballad, and a specific social class. Again, the limitation built into my edition is not simply the exclusion of the anti-Rump satires as such but also what that might mean in terms of the possible misrepresentation of the ballad, a crucial poetic form that traverses class differences. In my own defense let me add that the edition will include a bibliographical checklist of any excluded poems from 1660, broadsides included, known to me, and I am currently preparing to write about the anti-Rump satires for the section of the historical introduction on the ballad market.

Yet it is partly because I agree with Chartier that I remain concerned about those excluded ballads, especially those I know I haven't found, which may never be edited. It would take dedication and some years to track them all down, to sort through the complex textual problems characteristic of broadsides, and then a few more years to situate and explicate the topical references, those very features that make ballads so crucial an indicator of the relation between the commercial press and the construction of public knowledge and opinion. It sounds like an exciting and worthwhile project to me but one beyond the scope of my present project. But perhaps I think that because I too have become infected by dilettantism.

If we are to understand the cultural conditions of the original production of the texts we edit, and I hope we can agree to that, then I think it important that we recognize the extent to which the historical field of our inquiry is already traversed by class discourse, a discourse that is directly linked to concerns of gender, sexuality, and nationality.

NOTES

Sections of this essay were presented at the Committee on Scholarly Editions session at the MLA Convention in New York, 1992; my thanks to David Greetham for that occasion and for critical encouragement since. Some of the archival research reported here was undertaken with funds supplied by the National Endowment for the Humanities through the Center for Seventeenth- and Eighteenth-Century Studies at UCLA during the autumn of 1989; my thanks to John Brewer and Susan Staves. And my thanks, as always, to Donna Landry for checking more than my spelling.

1. Obviously, these are extreme positions. See Robert Mayer's "Nathaniel Crouch, Bookseller and Historian: Popular Historiography and Cultural Power in Late Seventeenth-Century England," *ECS* 27, no. 3 (1994): 391–419, for a recent example of how questions of class continue to provide scholars working in the bibliographic archives with a necessary analytical vocabulary for understanding the materials to be found.

2. With Donna Landry I have written in more detail on the poststructural account of class relations developed by Ernesto Laclau and Chantal Mouffe in *Hegemony and Socialist Strategy: Towards a Radical Democratic Politics,* trans. W. Moore and P. Cammack (London: Verso, 1985); see Landry and MacLean, "Re-Reading Laclau and Mouffe," *Rethinking Marxism* 4, no. 4 (Winter 1991): 41–60; and, more generally, *Materialist Feminisms* (Oxford: Basil Blackwell, 1993).

3. Karl Marx, *Capital: A Critique of Political Economy,* trans. David Fernbach (Harmondsworth and London: Penguin, 1981), 3:1025–26.

4. In the *Grundrisse* Marx writes: "*Property,* then, originally means—in its Asiatic, Slavonic, ancient classical, Germanic form—the relation of the working (producing or self-reproducing) subject to the conditions of his production or reproduction as his own" (*The Marx-Engels Reader,* ed. Robert C. Tucker, 2d ed. [New York: Norton, 1978], 261–62).

5. See, among other works on these themes: Richard Helgerson, *Forms of Nationhood: The Elizabethan Writing of England* (Chicago: University of Chicago Press, 1993); Raymond Williams, *The Country and the City* (New York: Oxford University Press, 1973); Peter Hulme, *Colonial Encounters: Europe and the Native Caribbean, 1492–1997* (London: Methuen, 1987); Benedict Anderson, *Imagined Communities: Reflections of the Origin and the Spread of Na-*

tionalism (London: Verso, 1983); and Partha Chatterjee, *Nationalist Thought and the Colonial World: A Derivative Discourse* (1986; reprint, Minneapolis: University of Minnesota Press, 1993).

6. A different approach is that of literary historians such as Joseph Loewenstein and Arthur Marotti, who work on questions involving literature as property. See Loewenstein, "The Script in the Market Place," *Representations* 12 (Fall 1985): 101–14; and Marotti, *Manuscript, Print, and the English Renaissance Lyric* (Ithaca, N.Y.: Cornell University Press, 1995).

7. Jerome J. McGann, intro. *Historical Studies and Literary Criticism,* ed. Jerome McGann (Madison: University of Wisconsin Press, 1985), 3.

8. "A Critic's Apology for Editing Dryden's *The History of the League,*" in *The Editor as Critic and the Critic as Editor* (essays read at a Clark Memorial Library Seminar, 17 November 1971, by J. Max Patrick and Alan Roper), 43–72 (Los Angeles: William Andrews Clark Memorial Library, 1973), 51.

9. Michael Groden, "Contemporary Textual and Literary Theory," in *Representing Modernist Texts: Editing as Interpretation,* ed. George Bornstein, 259–86 (Ann Arbor: University of Michigan Press, 1991), 259.

10. *Textual and Literary Criticism* (Cambridge: Cambridge University Press, 1959), 1.

11. Jerome J. McGann, *A Critique of Modern Textual Criticism* (1983; reprint, Chicago: University of Chicago Press, 1985), 104.

12. "What Is a Restoration Poem? Editing a Discourse, Not an Author," in *TEXT* 3, ed. David Greetham and W. Speed Hill, 319–46 (New York: AMS Press, 1987), 321.

13. See Carolyn Edie, "Right Rejoicing: Sermons on the Occasion of the Stuart Restoration, 1660," *Bulletin of the John Rylands Library* 62 (1979–80): 61–86; and "News from Abroad: Advice to the People of England on the Eve of the Stuart Restoration," *Bulletin of the John Rylands Library* 76 (l984): 382–407; Gerald M. MacLean, "An Edition of Poems on the Restoration," *Restoration* 11 (1987): 117–21; and *Time's Witness,* 256–67; see also Jonathan Sawday, "Re-Writing a Revolution: History, Symbol, and Text in the Restoration," *Seventeenth Century* 7, no. 2 (1992): 171–99.

14. See Christopher Hill, "From Marprelate to the Levellers," *Collected Essays Volume One: Writing and Revolution in Seventeenth Century England* (Brighton: Harvester, 1985), 75–95.

15. I develop this argument in my introduction to *Culture and Society in the Stuart Restoration: Literature, Drama, History* (Cambridge: Cambridge University Press, 1995), 3–27.

16. See my article "Literacy, Class, and Gender in Restoration England," in *TEXT* 7, ed. David Greetham and W. Speed Hill (Ann Arbor: University of Michigan Press, 1995), 177–95.

17. See Maureen Bell, "Hannah Allen and the Development of a Puritan Publishing Business, 1646–1651," *Publishing History* 26 (1989): 5–66.

18. Pope, *The Dunciad,* ed. James Sutherland (London: Methuen, 1943), "A" text, bk. 2, ll. 27–30, p. 99.

19. *A Dictionary of the English Language,* 4th ed. (London, 1770).

20. See Margaret Spufford, *Small Books and Pleasant Histories: Popular Fiction and Its Readership in Seventeenth-Century England* (Athens: University of Georgia Press, 1981). Johnson writes that *mercury* "is now applied to the carriers of news" (*Dictionary;* see also *OED* 6).

21. "The Stationers' Company in the Civil War Period," *Library* 13 (1958): 1.

22. See Cyprian Blagden, ibid.; and "The English Stock of the Stationers' Company: An Account of Its Origins," *Library* 10 (1955): 163–85.

23. *The Young-Mans Second Warning-peece* (1643), 8.

24. Although I shall include epigraphs and occasional foreign tags, with English translations, when they occur in what are otherwise English poems, the substantial omissions will be very few, since there were, in fact, surprisingly few foreign language poems. In addition to the academic volumes, notable omissions will include Thomas Bisham's *Iter Australe* (Oxford, 1660), and Edmund Castell's *Sol Angliae Oriens* (1660), which contains verses claiming to be in a variety of "Eastern" languages including Hebrew, "Chaldean, Syrian, Arabic, Samariticum, Aethiopicum, Arabicum, Persian, Greek," all with Latin translations. Rachel Jevon, one of the few women to publish verses praising Charles on his return, understood the prestige value of Greek and Latin; the Latin version of her panegyric is given a Greek title, *Carmen* FRIAMBEUTIKON, and the English version appears with a Latin title, *Exultationis Carmen*.

25. There were also numerous foreign language publications, not all of them poetic, in French, Spanish, Italian, and German.

26. *Memoirs of the Life of Colonel Hutchinson,* ed. C. H. Firth, 2 vols. (London: Nimmo, 1885), 2:245.

27. *Cheap Print and Popular Piety, 1550–1640* (Cambridge: Cambridge University Press, 1992), 3.

28. On Pepys and Wood and the habits of early collectors, see ibid., 267–68.

29. For more on Wolfreston, see Paul Morgan, "Frances Wolfreston and 'hor bouks': A Seventeenth-Century Woman Book Collector," *Library,* 6th ser., 11 (1989): 197–219; and Watt, *Cheap Print,* 315–17.

30. Watt, *Cheap Print,* 3.

31. *The Cultural Uses of Print in Early Modern France,* trans. Lydia Cochrane (Princeton: Princeton University Press, 1987), 3.

Editing "Minority" Texts

William L. Andrews

In the fall of 1974, when I was an assistant professor at Texas Tech University, Alex Haley came to our campus to lecture on the extensive genealogical research he had been engaged in while writing a book he planned to call "Roots." It was my good fortune to be invited to have dinner with Haley during his campus visit. Ever since I had studied *The Autobiography of Malcolm X* (1965) in a graduate school course on black American autobiography, some questions had lingered in my mind about how Haley and Malcolm had collaborated to produce that book. In particular I wondered what sort of text the *Autobiography* was, since Haley made clear in the epilogue to the *Autobiography* that he, not Malcolm X, had written it. What did the ambiguous phrase on the title page, "With the Assistance of Alex Haley," mean? More particularly, I wondered about what the manuscript of the *Autobiography* had looked like.

From reading Haley's epilogue I understood that the narrative evolved out of Haley's interviews with Malcolm but that Malcolm had read Haley's typescript and had made interlineated notes and often stipulated substantive changes, at least in the earlier parts of the text. As the work progressed, however, according to Haley, Malcolm yielded more and more to the authority of his ghostwriter, partly because Haley never let Malcolm read the manuscript unless he was present to defend it, partly because in his last months Malcolm had less and less opportunity to reflect on the text of his life because he was so busy living it, and partly because Malcolm eventually resigned himself to letting Haley's ideas about effective storytelling take precedence over his own desire to denounce straightaway those whom he had once revered.[1] It seemed to me that Haley's epilogue more than hinted at interesting tensions, and perhaps even pivotal struggles for control of the text, between the writer and the subject of Malcolm's memoir.

At dinner with Haley I waited until the initial pleasantries had been completed and the food had been served before posing a question that I hoped would draw out the rather guarded author as to the creative and editorial process that had eventuated in the publication of his famous book. Having no experience in interviewing, I'm afraid my opening question turned out to be about as subtle as a thumb in the eye. "Mr. Haley," I announced, "there's something I've always wondered about *The Auto-biography of Malcolm X.* Whatever became of the manuscript—the one you composed and Malcolm edited?" Alex Haley glanced at me briefly, his face utterly impassive, and then turned to the person across from him at the table and said, "Pass the salt, please."

That was my big chance to learn something, firsthand, about the evolution of perhaps the most influential text of "minority" literature in the twentieth-century United States. In the absence of access to Haley's notes or the manuscript itself, I suppose readers and students of the *Autobiography* will have to be satisfied with Haley's version of how the *Autobiography* was constructed—that is, with Haley asking questions of Malcolm about his life, Malcolm answering them, Haley working the answers into narrative form, and then Malcolm reading drafts of chapters, editing them, and, according to Haley, ultimately approving them all.[2] But, even if we grant the unlikelihood of the process of composition following that neat, step-by-step process, I still wonder what to make of the fact that Malcolm yielded so much of the authority, both literal and figurative, for his life story to Alex Haley, leaving for himself a steadily diminishing role as editor. Can we regard the curiously inverted relationship of Haley and Malcolm in *The Autobiography of Malcolm X* as in some sense a metaphor of the complex interdependence of author and editor, utterance and script, self and other, in the generation of so-called minority autobiography in the United States?

These questions came up for me a few years after my dinner with Haley as I began to do some serious research into the nineteenth-century prece-dents for Malcolm's "as told to" autobiography. I refer, of course, to the many reputedly "edited" narratives of fugitive slaves over which more than a few literary skirmishes were fought by pro- and antislavery forces during the crisis decades in the middle of the American nineteenth century.[3] In the case of the well-received *Life of Josiah Henson* (1849), the narrator of which Harriet Beecher Stowe claimed was her model for the title character in

Uncle Tom's Cabin (1852), the evidence suggests that the relationship of Josiah Henson and Samuel A. Eliot, the white man identified on the title page of the *Life* as Henson's "editor," was probably very similar to that of Malcolm and Haley.[4]

In other words, Haley was not making up his role as Malcolm's "assistant" as he went along. He was working within and in accordance with a well-established tradition in African American autobiography. Since the beginning of this tradition in English, many white editors felt free, and sometimes obliged, to order and select, "improve" and "correct," the oral and written narratives of black people to the point that editing sometimes amounted to ghostwriting.[5] Because of the authorial powers often granted to or demanded by the editors of early African American and American Indian written narratives,[6] the line distinguishing author and editor in highly influential minority texts, such as Harriet Jacobs's *Incidents in the Life of a Slave Girl* (1861), John Neihardt's *Black Elk Speaks* (1932), and *The Autobiography of Malcolm X,* has been a matter of considerable dispute. In the case of *Incidents* we are fortunate to have a paper trail that enables us to trace the roles of author and white editor in the generation of that text.[7] Maybe one day we will have an equally cogent basis for deciding how we should answer the question Malcolm put to Haley early in the creation of his autobiography: "Whose book is this?"[8] In the meantime, however, those of us who are trying to edit minority texts today need to reflect critically on the kind of authority we assume as editors and whether and how that authority may be justified.

In the past decade we have seen more editing and publishing of heretofore unknown and/or out-of-print works by writers of color than probably ever before in a comparable period of time in United States history. To help appraise where we have been and where we are going in the editing of minority writers, let me survey briefly some noteworthy points in the history of the scholarly editing of African American texts. Although I do not wish to leave the impression that the editing of Hispanic or Asian American texts has been of lesser value or consequence, I will focus in this essay only on the African American tradition, mainly because it is what I know best but also because it has been the most visible, it seems to me, in the movement over roughly the last half-century to restore writers of color to respectable textual status within the canons of reading in contemporary America.

In 1950 the first of what would become a five-volume edition of the published writings of Frederick Douglass appeared under the editorship of the distinguished historian Philip S. Foner.[9] This crucial event in the Douglass revival, when a white editor selected a left-wing press during the McCarthy era to help promote the reputation of a Lincoln defender and onetime wheelhorse of the Republican Party, reminds us that even the scholarly editing of minority texts in this country has a well-established political history in this century. Foner's *Life and Writings of Frederick Douglass* may be justifiably viewed as a breakthrough in the editing of African American literature, if for no other reason than that it made abundantly clear, after decades of neglect, that Frederick Douglass was a prolific man of letters as well as an exponent of human rights. The 1950s also saw the publication of annotated editions of diaries by two very different representatives of the free Negro class in antebellum America, Charlotte Forten and William Johnson, in texts that by their very existence testified to the fact that forgotten nineteenth-century African American writing repaid close attention from scholars and modern readers, especially those who wanted access to firsthand accounts of American history in the making.[10]

With the boom in the publication of black texts touched off by the rise of black studies in the 1960s, many classic works of African American literature came back into print. Most of the editing in this field undertaken during the 1960s was what we would call today "noncritical." The purpose was usually limited to the reproduction of an established text, often through facsimile reprint, as in the case of the lengthy series overseen by the Arno Press and the Negro Universities Press, but sometimes through republication in handy paperback formats, such as that Macmillan devised for its multivolume African/American Library under the general editorship of Charles R. Larson. The beginning and end of the decade saw the happy results of two highly influential projects of editorial recovery and reconstruction: Benjamin Quarles's annotated edition of *Narrative of the Life of Frederick Douglass* and Floyd J. Miller's reconstitution of Martin R. Delany's *Blake; or, the Huts of America,* a serial novel published on the eve of the Civil War that featured a black nationalist hero better suited to the tenor of the 1960s than to any era since the time of his original creation.[11]

While students of African American literature struggled in the 1960s to get individual classic texts reprinted in fairly modest noncritical editions, leading scholars of classic nineteenth-century white American writers got busy on full-blown, multivolume, well-funded, high-profile editions of the sort customarily associated with what we call textual, or critical, editing. In the 1970s the reputations of Ralph Waldo Emerson, Nathaniel Hawthorne, Herman Melville, Stephen Crane, and Mark Twain, to name a few of the most highly regarded "major" authors of that time, glowed with unprecedented luster in the eyes of American literary scholars, in no small part due to the burnishing these writers received from teams of indefatigable editors at research universities, where textual editing was becoming increasingly professionalized.[12] The granting of the imprimatur of the Center for Editions of American Authors and later the Committee on Scholarly Editing represented the final phase of canonization for nineteenth-century pretenders to literary respectability such as Melville, Twain, and Crane.

To be sure, ambitious editions of the writings of Booker T. Washington and W. E. B. Du Bois also got under way during the 1970s, and the end of the decade saw the first volume of the ambitious Yale edition of *The Frederick Douglass Papers*.[13] But these editions of Washington, Du Bois, and Douglass, conceived and overseen by historians, incorporate a view of documentary editing that treats the text "primarily as a vehicle for meaning rather than form."[14] The historian's editorial emphasis places a premium on "ensuring the reader's convenience" in negotiating the text rather than on ensuring that whatever problematic the text may present *as* text is fully accounted for.[15] Insofar as the editing of African American literature was concerned, the preeminence of historians over scholars of literature continued into the 1980s. Not surprisingly, texts that most historians regarded as having scant documentary significance or reliability, such as Jacobs's *Incidents in the Life of a Slave Girl*, had to wait until very recently to reappear in new editions.

In the last fifteen years, however, the success of editions of unpublished, forgotten, and pseudonymous works by such key figures as Jean Toomer and George Schuyler, along with landmark annotated texts of *Incidents in the Life of a Slave Girl* and Harriet Wilson's *Our Nig* and the Library of America editions of Du Bois, Richard Wright, Frederick Douglass, and Zora Neale Hurston, indicates that scholarly editing of African American literature by and for the community of literary readers, black and white, has finally arrived.[16] Without slighting the excellent work done by the editors of these and other African American writers, we might still ask why so few writers of color have been accorded the kind of sustained textual and bibliographical grooming that editors are now lavishing on the likes of Theodore Dreiser and Willa Cather.[17] If a writer once considered as unassimilable as Dreiser can now be regarded as worthy of meticulous textual reconstruction and republication in massive scholarly tomes, why can't such classic writers of the African American tradition—

Phillis Wheatley, Charles W. Chesnutt, Langston Hughes, and Richard Wright, for example—also qualify for complete textual editions in formats comparable to those that are sealing a hallowed place in American literary history for a Harold Frederic or a Charles Brockden Brown?[18]

The answer, of course, is that, although Wheatley, Chesnutt, Hughes, and Wright do merit such editorial attention, thus far scholars most familiar with them have found other editorial tasks more compelling than that of the wholesale textual editing of the full corpus of a Wheatley or a Hughes. It is not that we lack serious scholarly editions devoted to Wheatley, for instance, or that the preponderance of the editions we have of Chesnutt, Hughes, and Wright have perpetrated misconceived or unreliable texts on an eager but naive public.[19] What we *do* lack, however, is focused and purposeful discussion about just how important exhaustive, multivolume textual editions might be to the establishment of the African American vein of minority writing in the canons of American literature. To my knowledge, the Modern Language Association's Committee on Scholarly Editions, which I have been a member of for the past three years, has never received an inquiry about the advisability of undertaking a major editorial project on behalf of an African American or, for that matter, any other writer of color.

Given the traditional but I hope now discredited scholarly relegation of most eighteenth-, nineteenth-, and early-twentieth-century African American writing to merely documentary rather than aesthetic value, we could hardly expect questions about the need for textual editions of black American writing to arise before the last ten or fifteen years. There may be, moreover, some good reasons why the trend in African American editing continues to be in favor of noncritical editions, in which the editor's responsibility is primarily to provide a readable reproduction of a particular edition, prefaced by a serviceable historical, biographical, and interpretive introduction, and often appended by some judicious annotating of the text itself. Obviously, the best way to bring back into print an ignored or neglected book by a writer of color is not to propose a full-bore textual edition of it. The audience for such a book is not likely to want or need all the textual apparatus. The profit margins of publishers would be squeezed unnecessarily by the costs of printing such apparatus.

A few years ago the University of Illinois Press received a thorough-going textual edition of an unpublished manuscript novel by Charles Chesnutt, which it sent to me for review. I was glad to recommend the publication of "Mandy Oxendine," but in so doing I also conveyed my opinion, perhaps heretical in this context, that what a work of that kind needs the most to maximize its appeal and use these days is a reliable and informative introduction and judicious annotation, not a list of textual variants, emendations, line-end hyphenations, and the rest of the panoply of textual description one finds in a thoroughgoing critical (or in this case genetic) edition. This does not mean that classic African American writers, such as William Wells Brown, would not benefit greatly from the kind of critical editing that enables us to trace the evolution of a text through multiple revisions and printings of the sort that Brown's novel, *Clotel*, went through from its initial publication in 1853 to its final reprise in 1867.[20] Nor do I wish to imply that the tools of the textual editor would not be valuable in revealing what happened to key African American texts such as *Up from Slavery* and *The Souls of Black Folk* when they made the transition from magazine publication, either serially or in separate articles, to publication in a book, which then underwent multiple reprintings in succeeding years, during which time, in Du Bois's case, the author engaged in further revisions.[21] The more one learns about African American literature the more one sees ample need for targeted textual *editing*—if not all-encompassing textual editions—of central texts and representative textual phenomena that can help us understand the origin, evolution, and fate of minority texts in a "majority" literature.

Let me close this essay by noting some of the more pressing issues facing anyone interested in the kind of targeted textual editing of minority writing that I am recommending as more needful right now than full-blown, multivolume, high-priced textual editions. It seems to me that, because today's editor of minority writing is often in the vanguard of the effort to reconstruct American literature, the editing of minority texts involves a great deal more than what has been traditionally associated with editing. To put it simply, minority texts must be reclaimed—and sometimes rehabilitated—before they can be preserved. Given today's market-driven publishing world, even in the university book trade, editors of minority texts must first become advocates of a text before they can edit it or feel confident that the edition will ever find its way into print. Even the editors of the most respected writers of color do not have the luxury to publish what and as they see fit.

There can be little doubt that those called upon to compile and edit the prestigious Library of America editions of Du Bois, Wright, Hurston, and Douglass, even as they must have been very gratified to know they could devote a substantial volume, or even two, to establishing their authors' claim to permanent canonical status in U.S. literary history, faced agonizing editorial dilemmas that had to be resolved before they did any tinkering with a text. On what basis was a selection of Du Bois's essays and articles made for inclusion in the Library of America volume? Who made the decision to publish only Douglass's *Narrative, My Bondage and My Freedom,* and the 1892 *Life and Times of Frederick Douglass* in the Library of America volume devoted to that author? Do longer, better-known works by a Douglass, Wright, or Hurston receive preference over shorter and lesser-known works, even though the longer ones are likely to be readily available while the shorter ones may need reprinting in the Library of America to have any chance at all of being perceived as more than topical and ephemeral?

It is the nature of canon-making enterprises like the Library of America to confer authoritative status on only a handful of texts, whether minority or otherwise. In the general publishing world economic and pedagogical factors such as compactness, accessibility, permissions costs, and adaptability to fashionable critical and theoretical approaches tend to do a lot of the sorting that results in some texts' becoming standard and steadily better known while others by the same author lapse into secondary and merely supplementary status. Thus editors who propose to rescue good work by notable minority writers may find it difficult to publish editions that seem to challenge the priority of already canonized texts by the same author. This was my experience when I decided in 1985 that Douglass's second autobiography, *My Bondage and My Freedom* (1855), deserved a properly annotated paperback edition designed for classroom use in literature and history courses. My preferred publisher, the University of Illinois Press, needed a bit of convincing, despite its outstanding record in African American studies, before it was willing to invest in a text that had nothing like the critical status or pedagogical popularity of Douglass's *Narrative*. And, when I urged the press to get the price on the edition as low as possible (to compete more effectively against the *Narrative*), the suggestion came back that the best way to do so would be to take out the text's appendix, so to speak—a string of salient excerpts from Douglass's better-known speeches appended to the narrative portion of the 1855 edition. For all anyone knows this anthology of Douglass's greatest rhetorical hits may have been tacked onto the autobiography by its original publisher for the same market reasons that my publisher was invoking to argue its elimination, namely, to help sell the book. I could not agree to edit *My Bondage and My Freedom* in this fashion, of course.[22] But I have seen proposals for anthologies of minority texts that, evidently in the interest of both the politics and sales,

pack in more writers by quietly distorting (through deletions and trunca-
tions) texts in ways that unwary publishers or readers might never detect.

Editors must therefore take seriously the fact that in today's hothouse
market for ethnic literature and multicultural texts, in which real profits can
accrue to those who have the skills, the prestige, and the experience to edit
under the auspices of major trade publishers, the editing of minority texts
can sometimes present Faustian bargains. Editions can actually foreclose,
rather than open up, opportunities for further editing of a writer. In light of
this it seems to me that editors of minority texts need more interchange and
mutual consultation on the intellectual, social, and financial politics of the
kind of editing they do. We need a mechanism, such as the Committee for
Scholarly Editions, whereby prospective editors can consult with more
experienced editors about everything from how to propose an edition to a
publisher to how to deal with copyeditors over questions having to do with
regularizing spelling and language usage in a given text. We need more
coordination of our efforts so that at the very least editors in a given field
can know what other editors are doing. We need forums that will help us
consider the larger implications of the choices and decisions we make with
regard to writers and texts that we want to revive or reconstruct. Assuming
the goals of such editing are shared among scholars in more than one
minority field, it is more important now than ever before, now that we have
unprecedented clout with publishers and status within our profession, for
editors to articulate coherent methods and agendas that will ensure a future
of sustained and purposeful productivity in the editing of minority texts.

NOTES

1. *The Autobiography of Malcolm X,* ed. Alex Haley (New York: Ballantine, 1973),
   387, 414.
2. For Haley's comments on his working relationship to Malcolm, see *Autobiography of Malcolm X,* 387, 406–7, 412, 414, 422.
3. For discussions of the editing of slave narratives, see James Olney, "'I Was
   Born': Slave Narratives, Their Status as Autobiography and as Literature," in
   The Slave's Narrative, ed. Charles T. Davis and Henry Louis Gates Jr. (New
   York: Oxford University Press, 1985), 158–66; and William L. Andrews, *To
   Tell a Free Story: The First Century of Afro-American Autobiography, 1760–
   1865* (Urbana: University of Illinois Press, 1986), 19–22, 32–39, 61–63, 81–
   90, 267–70.
4. Josiah Henson, *The Life of Josiah Henson, formerly a slave, now an inhabitant of
   Canada, as narrated by himself,* ed. Samuel A. Eliot (Boston: A. D. Phelps,
   1849).

5. Andrews, *To Tell a Free Story*, 32–39.
6. For an overview of important edited texts in American Indian autobiography, see Arnold Krupat, ed., *Native American Autobiography* (Madison: University of Wisconsin Press, 1994), 149–235, 321–98.
7. See the exemplary edition of *Incidents* fashioned by Jean Fagan Yellin (Cambridge, Mass.: Harvard University Press, 1987).
8. Haley, *Autobiography of Malcolm X*, 414.
9. *The Life and Writings of Frederick Douglass,* ed. Philip S. Foner, 5 vols. (New York: International, 1950–75).
10. Charlotte Forten, *The Journal of Charlotte L. Forton,* ed. Ray Allen Billington (New York: Dryden, 1953); and William Johnson, *William Johnson's Natchez: The Ante-Bellum Diary of a Free Negro,* ed. Edwin A. Davis and William R. Hogan (Baton Rouge: Louisiana State University Press, 1951). Forten's diary has been published in an enlarged edition, *The Journals of Charlotte Forten,* ed. Brenda Stevenson (New York: Oxford University Press, 1988). In 1993 Johnson's diary was also reissued with a new introduction by William L. Andrews.
11. Frederick Douglass, *Narrative of the Life of Frederick Douglass* (Cambridge, Mass.: Belknap Press of Harvard University, 1960); and Martin R. Delany, *Blake; or the Huts of America,* ed. Floyd J. Miller (Boston: Beacon, 1970).
12. The Emerson edition, under the general editorship of William H. Gilman, Ralph H. Orth, and others, was launched by the Harvard University Press in 1969. The Hawthorne edition, under the general editorship of William Charvat, Claude Simpson, and others, was published by the Ohio State University Press, 1963–88. The Melville edition, under the general editorship of Harrison Hayford, Hershel Parker, and G. Thomas Tanselle, was published by the Northwestern University Press and the Newberry Library, 1968–. The Crane edition, under the general editorship of Fredson Bowers, was published by the University Press of Virginia, 1969–75. The Mark Twain edition, currently under the general editorship of Robert Hirst, has been published by the University of California Press since 1972.
13. *The Booker T. Washington Papers,* ed. Louis R. Harlan, 14 vols. (Urbana: University of Illinois Press, 1972–89). *The Complete Published Works of W. E. B. Du Bois,* ed. Herbert Aptheker, 36 vols. (New York: Kraus-Thomson Organization, 1982–86). Additional volumes of unpublished materials, including the correspondence of Du Bois, were edited by Aptheker and published by the University of Massachusetts Press from 1973 to 1989. *The Frederick Douglass Papers,* ed. John W. Blassingame, 5 vols. to date (New Haven: Yale University Press, 1979–).
14. D. C. Greetham, "Textual Scholarship," *Introduction to Scholarship in Modern Languages and Literatures* (New York: Modern Language Association, 1992), 116.
15. Greetham, "Textual Scholarship," 116.
16. See *The Collected Poems of Jean Toomer,* ed. Robert B. Jones and Margery Toomer Latimer (Chapel Hill: University of North Carolina Press, 1988); *The Jean Toomer Reader,* ed. Frederik L. Rusch (New York: Oxford University

Press, 1993); George S. Schuyler, *Black Empire,* ed. Robert A. Hill and R. Kent Rasmussen (Boston: Northeastern University Press, 1991); Harriet E. Wilson, *Our Nig,* intro. Henry Louis Gates Jr. (New York: Random House, 1983); and the Library of America editions of the *Writings* of Du Bois (1986), the *Works* of Wright (2 vols., 1991), the *Autobiographies* of Douglass (1994), and the *Novels and Stories* and *Folklore, Memoirs, and Other Writings* of Hurston (1995).

17. The University of Pennsylvania Dreiser Edition, published by the University of Pennsylvania Press, and the Willa Cather Scholarly Edition, published by the University of Nebraska Press, began publishing volumes in 1988 and 1992, respectively.

18. Since 1977 the Major Works of Harold Frederic, under the editorship of Norman Hostetler and Robert Bergstrom, has been published by the University of Nebraska Press. In the same year the Bicentennial Edition of the Works of Charles Brockden Brown, edited by Sydney J. Krause and S. W. Reid, was launched by the Kent State University Press.

19. Valuable annotated editions of Wheatley, which involve thorough review of manuscript sources and variant versions of texts, have been fashioned by William H. Robinson, ed., *Phillis Wheatley and Her Writings* (New York: Garland, 1984); John C. Shields, ed., *The Collected Works of Phillis Wheatley* (New York: Oxford University Press, 1988); and Julian D. Mason, ed., *The Poems of Phillis Wheatley* (Chapel Hill: University of North Carolina Press, 1989). Examples of recent reliable editing of Hughes and Chesnutt are *Collected Poems of Langston Hughes,* ed. Arnold Rampersad (New York: Knopf, 1994); and *The Journals of Charles W. Chesnutt,* ed. Richard H. Brodhead (Durham, N.C.: Duke University Press, 1993).

20. William Wells Brown, *Clotel, or the President's Daughter* (London: Partridge and Oakey, 1853), usually dubbed the first African American novel, was revised and republished in the United States three times under the titles *Miralda; or the Beautiful Quadroon* (1860–61), *Clotelle: A Tale of the Southern States* (1864), and *Clotelle: or, the Colored Heroine* (1867).

21. For the composition and publishing history of *Up from Slavery,* see Harlan's introduction to *The Autobiographical Writings, Booker T. Washington Papers,* 1; xiii–xxx, 207. For notes on the evolution of *The Souls of Black Folk,* including revisions that Du Bois asked for when that book was reprinted in 1953, see Du Bois, *Writings,* 1306–8.

22. My edition of Douglass's *My Bondage and My Freedom* was published by the University of Illinois Press in 1987 and, fortunately, has gone through three reprint editions since then.

Whose Room of Orlando's Own? The Politics of Adaptation

Brenda R. Silver

The establishment of a canonical text, whether of Shakespeare or anything else, is only incidentally an objective and scientific matter. It involves much more basically doctrinal and political elements.
—*Stephen Orgel, "The Authentic Shakespeare"*

At the end of his exploration of "what . . . we mean by authenticity, and what [we will] accept as evidence of it," Stephen Orgel concludes that the desire for authenticity is for something "behind" or "beyond" the text:

> The assumption is that texts are representations or embodiments of something else, and that it is that something else which the performer or editor undertakes to reveal. What we want is not the authentic play, with its unstable, infinitely revisable script, but an authentic Shakespeare, to whom every generation's version of a classic drama may be ascribed.[1]

Virginia Woolf, you may be thinking, is not Shakespeare; not only did she not write plays (at least those performed in public), but her novels, the works that have more than anything else made her "canonical," are fictions that have long been considered inimical to "performances" in any other format or medium than those she gave them. In terms of name recognition, if people in the general public know "Virginia Woolf," it has been, until recently, more likely in conjunction with "who's afraid of" than for anything she wrote. Nonetheless, it is the authentic Virginia Woolf that I want to explore in this essay, the Virginia Woolf whose "canon" emerges from the "something else" of Orgel's formulation as much a historical and political construction as Shakespeare and his plays. More specifically, it is the authenticity of two particular works that concern me here: *A Room of One's Own* and *Orlando*. By virtue of their recent and, in the case of *Orlando*, multiple adaptations for television, theater, and/or film, both works have become the subject of extended battles over who will define the authentic Virginia Woolf and hence the "meaning" of her texts; as Orgel notes, authenticity is always "a matter of authentication, something bestowed, not inherent" (5). What is at stake in these battles is a politics of adaptation—an intersection of text, adaptor, audience, and institutions of production and dissemination—that is inseparable from the politics of gender being played out at every level of our culture today.

In outlining what I believe are the issues raised by the recent performances of *A Room of One's Own* (hereafter referred to as *Room*) and *Orlando*, I am making some assumptions about adaptations that are rooted in current debates within textual criticism. My primary assumption is that, rather than being subsidiary or marginal to the "original," adaptations should be conceived as versions of the work: texts with the same status as any other text in the ongoing, historical construction of a composite, palimpsestic work. In this reading the adaptation, whatever the medium or even when it crosses media, becomes one of those "*primary* textual documents and states of major texts" that Donald Reiman argues permit "readers, teachers, and critics [to] compare for themselves" the "distinct ideologies, aesthetic perspectives, or rhetorical strategies" inscribed in the different versions.[2]

The pertinent concept in this reading, as for Shakespearean critics, is performance: both performance, as of a play, and performance as event or act. In this construction all versions of a work, all its constituent texts, become performances, which, rather than existing in a hierarchical relationship to one another—original and adaptation, for example—exist in a fluid, shifting one, an intertextual cluster,[3] with each new performance an encoding of the particular historical, cultural moment that alters the configuration. Shakespeare's plays provide a model. As Shakespearean critics have increasingly argued and illustrated, it is impossible to divide the written texts of his plays into originals and copies; instead, all we have are copies, and these copies are almost always linked to performance. In Laurie Osborne's formulation: "With the new interest in the material production and historicity of the Shakespearean text, it becomes clear that the edited texts of the plays are closely akin to their individual theatrical productions, which more overtly participate in an immediate context of enactment. . . . The productions of Shakespeare's plays reveal the flaw in our scholarly view of a fixed and immutable canon of his work, since every enactment, whether text or performance, represents a version, not the play itself."[4]

If we substitute the phrase "work itself" for "play itself" in Osborne's formulation, we are of course on similar ground to that covered by Jerome McGann, among others, who has argued that a "work" is a series of texts, or "a series of specific acts of production":[5] a polytext. As Joseph Grigely glosses this formulation, "the work is not equivalent to the *sum* of its texts . . . , but instead is an ongoing—and infinite—manifestation of textual appearances, *whether those texts are authorized or not.* . . . Nor," he adds, once again using Shakespeare as his example, "is it necessary to exclude performances from this formulation," so that the work becomes "a non-tangible idea represented by a sequential series of texts—whether these texts are inscribed or performed, whether they are authorized or not."[6] This statement is part of the larger argument about "textuality" suggested by Grigely's title, "The Textual Event": that texts are more than objects, particularly literary objects; instead, "they are also (to take one position) signifiers," which raises the question of whether "performances have texts, or *are* . . . texts" (170).

Grigely's further contention that a work can be represented as an infinite series of texts and a specific text can be represented as an infinite series of performances supports, with only a very slight sleight-of-hand, my proposition that every version, every text, is an act, a performance, and that these performances involve very particular choices on the part of the per-formers, whether they be "author," editor, adaptor, director, or actor. *Editor* is the term I want to emphasize here, positing its congruence with *adaptor.* For Orgel editions of Shakespeare's plays are as much perfor-mances as those performed onstage, both "concerned with fixing the text, in both senses, in the interests of particular interpretations" (14). Osborne has a somewhat different take: "As with scholarly editing, performances also represent a kind of editing of Shakespeare's plays that involves cutting, rearranging, and otherwise altering a play in important ways" (40). And these choices, she adds, tell us a great deal about not only the theatrical practices and performance possibilities of the period but also the more intangible historical contexts and pressures, including attitudes toward gender and sexuality (48). If we expand our interpretation of what an editor does from "one who prepares the literary work of another person . . . for publication, by selecting, revising, and arranging the materials" to in-corporate the act of editing defined as "to garble, 'cook' (e.g., a war-correspondent's dispatch, etc.),"[7] and, if we then add to this semantic crossover between the editing of texts and the editing of news the role of the "editorial" in shaping public opinion, we can begin to see the politics at work in the "editing" of Woolf's printed texts for public performances on/ in television, theater, and film.

An adaptation, then, becomes a form of editorializing, but it does more than comment on or interpret an original, which is one way of describing the status of an adaptation. Neil Sinyard, for example, proposes this relationship when he writes that "the best adaptations of books for film can often best be approached as an activity of literary criticism," an interpretation, which through the process of selection and focusing "can throw new light on the original."[8] What this formulation ignores is any acknowledgment of how an adaptation, like a critical essay, claims legitimacy for its perspective, its own political agenda, through the construction of its text. It also ignores the reality that, in our culture today, many people come to the film or television version of a work before they know (if they ever do) the "original," and that this version will be the "original" against which other versions are measured or illuminated. (Publishers capitalize on this phenomenon when they reissue a novel-made-into-a-film with photographs of the film actors on the cover, usually with great success.) I am more convinced by Peter Shillingsburg's notion of a variety of potential versions, variously constituted by their potential function ("Is it for a magazine; is it a chapter in a book; is it a play adaptation, a translation, a revised edition aimed at a new market?").[9] This allows us to argue that when a novel or an essay—*Orlando* or *Room,* say—becomes a play or a film, it is functionally "translated" from one medium to another, using the definition of *translate* that associates it with the tailor trade, with the taking apart and remaking of a garment.[10] When the novel or essay is translated, then, it is metaphorically "refashioned" or "re-dressed" in the clothes (stage practices, cinematic conventions) currently fashionable or possible for that medium. In this sense we can say that clothes make the version, and the determination of how it is marketed and what sells becomes a question of style.[11]

There is yet one more factor to introduce here: the role of what Shillingsburg, in his carefully articulated taxonomy of the terms and concepts associated with work, text, version, etc., calls the "Reception Performance," a performance that makes "the reader . . . the 'functional authority' for the Work and its Versions" (74). This reception performance, it should go without saying, will be just as much a function of historical contexts and pressures as what he terms the creative or production performances of texts.

At this point I would set out my argument as follows. The multiple adaptations of *A Room of One's Own* and *Orlando* for television, theater, and film over the past five years can be read as versions of the works that play a performative role in constructing not only what we understand when we talk of these works but in shaping current cultural debates about feminism, androgyny, gender, and sexuality. It is no accident that these versions have received the mainstream and commercial attention we usually reserve for more accessible or popular texts, while the opera version of *Mrs. Dalloway*, even when we take into account the relatively smaller audience, quickly came and went with nary a ripple: they speak directly to some of the most hotly debated issues of our time. In addition, the conflicting meanings attributed to these versions, meanings produced by the congruence of creative, production, and reception performances, suggest that these versions are more than interpretations of an original or authentic text; to the extent that all works are a series of texts and these texts are a series of performances, a work can be said to exist only in its performance.[12] But this vision of the unstable work, of a series of texts constructed through repeated performances, should not be read as an endpoint: as an uncritical acceptance of a pluralism of versions, interesting only because they differ one from the other; for the various versions exist as materially as the bodies that are gendered through performative acts, and the way they are enacted, received, and policed can have a material impact on the way we teach and write and live. As Orgel cogently illustrates, because "the history of realizations of the text . . . is the history of the text," it is imperative to ask "what is being realized in such representations" (14).

WHAT EVER HAPPENED TO JUDITH SHAKESPEARE?

I began by noting that Virginia Woolf is not Shakespeare, or, more accurately, that you might not think the analogy apt. But you would in fact be wrong. While it was once fashionable to consider Woolf the reembodiment of Judith Shakespeare—William's "wonderfully gifted sister" imagined by Woolf in *A Room of One's Own*, who rather than writing plays and becoming Britain's greatest writer ended up pregnant and a suicide (for "who shall measure the heat and violence of the poet's heart when caught and tangled in a woman's body?")[13]—more recently, she has become for many the embodiment of Shakespeare himself. Just look at the *New York Review of Books* (*NYRB*), that self-styled arbiter of what constitutes legitimate/respectable cultural artifacts, icons, and styles. For most of the 1980s their "special offer to . . . readers" featured T-shirts emblazoned with David Levine's caricatures of either Shakespeare or Woolf; the ad began, "Here is your chance to sport your literary preferences," and pictured both writers.[14] But from 29 March 1990 on, Woolf's image has reigned alone. What this suggests is a transformation, an elevation perhaps, that shifts Woolf's iconic representation from the gendered body of Judith Shakespeare to the androgynous mind of William: a concept she simultaneously imagines in her 1929 text. There are, it seems, as many "Virginia Woolfs" as there are "Shakespeares," and the battles to assert which one is "authentic" are inseparable from battles over what constitutes a legitimate feminist critique or gender politics or literary canon: battles that have been fought through the various performances of her texts.

A Room of One's Own has long been a central work in these battles. It is no exaggeration to say that for twenty-five years almost every work of feminist criticism and theory was almost certain to include a quotation from Woolf's essay in its epigraph, its introduction, and/or its text to support or authorize arguments of every conceivable persuasion. By the end of the 1980s, however, the reception of the work had begun to change. Challenged, on the one hand, from within feminist discourse for the limitations of its class or racial positions, it was reclaimed, on the other, by non- or antifeminist critics, who used it against what they still insisted on defining as a monolithic feminist project: in their version the consideration of women writers as *women* and the field of women's studies that encouraged this consideration. In the opinion of the conservative columnist Jeffrey Hart, writing in the *National Review* about a "feminist criticism" that in 1988 still consisted for him entirely of Sandra Gilbert, Susan Gubar, and Elaine Showalter, if feminists had "let Woolf be Woolf," had listened to her words in *A Room of One's Own*, none of this—that is, feminist criticism— ever would have happened.[15]

The question is, which words? and, more to my point, in which text?— a question that became more complicated with the 1992 publication of the manuscript version, *Women & Fiction*,[16] which differs from what we know of the talks Woolf originally delivered at Cambridge in 1928, from the article published as "Women and Fiction" in March 1929, from the extant typescript, and from the book that appeared in October 1929. But the version that concerns me here—the version that enacts or performs the political and doctrinal elements at work in Hart's claim to the authentic Woolf—is the dramatic version of *A Room of One's Own* "edited" by Patrick Garland and performed by Eileen Atkins both on television and the stage, first in London (1989) and then in the United States (1991). Both the editorial choices made by Garland for the performance text and the reception the play received from critics and commentators illustrate how powerfully even the smallest shifts can alter the perception of Woolf's meaning and Woolf herself and how closely aligned these perceptions are to politicized cultural agendas.

In the case of *Room*, calling Patrick Garland an editor seems less problematic than usual, given that all the words spoken by Atkins during the play are found in the book produced by Woolf, even if they do not constitute *all* the possible words, and even if they are not always presented in the same order.[17] As Grigely argues, glossing Jacques Derrida's "Signature Event Context," an utterance, once the original moment is past, is "'grafted'" or "recontextualized: . . . language deceives us as to how its iterable presence (written word, marks, inscriptions) do [*sic*] not translate to an iterable intention, or meaning" (172). The implication, he notes, is that editions are always "re:construct[ed]" texts, "texts that are a part of the social institution of professionalized literature . . . , and these texts serve all kinds of social, economic, and political purposes" (174). When the text is a theatrical performance, meant to be heard once only, the potential impact of its various agendas becomes greater; unlike other kinds of texts—books, for example, or films on video—it does not grant the addressee the ability to slow down, to repeat, to analyze, to control. "Performance," Harry Berger Jr. writes, "does not allow us the leisure to interrupt, challenge, or question. And since we can't flip the moments of a performance back and forth the way we can the pages of a book, we are prevented as spectators from carrying out our central interpretive operations that presuppose our ability to decelerate the text, to ignore sequence."[18] As a result, both the choice of words and their sequence in a theatrical performance have the power to shape the hearer's perceptions of the work's meaning far more than in other textual formats.

This is certainly the case with the play version of *Room*, which almost without exception critics declared to be not just "faithful" to the original but representative of the "real Woolf." In the few reviews in which critics acknowledge the (extensive) cuts, they either shrug them off as inconsequential or prefer the new version; with one exception no one analyzes *what* was left out. No one seems to have noticed one of the major editorial decisions made by Garland: the change of sequence that alters the last words of the play and, hence, its perceived meaning, although the impact of the change is apparent in almost every rendering of Woolf's message. Performance in this case truly seems to create its own depth and substance: Garland's version becomes the work itself. The result is the willing construction of a Virginia Woolf and a *Room* for the 1990s that tells us a great deal about battles to determine what constitutes the proper or improper study of women and literature, gender and art, with significant implications for the status of feminism and feminist critique.

The place to start is with Garland's editorial choices. As I noted earlier, almost every movement in feminist and now gender criticism—as well as those opposed to this criticism—has claimed the work as its own, a situation made possible by the multiplicity, the complexity, of Woolf's argument. To a great extent the complexity and the controversy arise from Woolf's positing of a divided consciousness when it comes to gender and art. The narrator, that is, speculates, with Coleridge, that "a great mind is androgynous": that each of us has two powers in our soul, male and female, and that, when a fusion, or marriage, occurs between them, "the mind is fully fertilised and uses all its faculties." Only then, perhaps, does it become "resonant," "porous," "incandescent," "undivided" (98)—and produce, as William Shakespeare did, great art. As another interrelated thread in this strand of the argument asserts, the best writers are not conscious of their sex when they write; it is, in fact, "fatal for any one who writes to think of their sex," whether that anyone is man or woman (104).

But, as strongly as the book posits the potential of the androgynous mind (and the concept itself has been interpreted in radically different ways as definitions of androgyny have changed), it also repeatedly asserts how and why women's writing, women's creativity, has been and will remain different from men's: that it has been, and will remain, no matter how unconsciously (and in fact the art is better when it *is* unconscious [93]), sex inflected, and what a loss it would be if this were *not* the case. "For we think back through our mothers if we are women," the narrator states in one of the most widely cited passages (76); women's texts, she speculates, from their sentences to their genres, have "somehow to be adapted" to their bodies (78). Finally, much to the delight of recent queer theorists, the text also seems to be making an argument for dismantling the binaries that lead to either sameness or difference, men or women, for putting into play the categories that underlie gender not by embodying them in a single (androgynous) figure but by multiplying gender's permutations and possibilities: "for if two sexes are quite inadequate, considering the vastness and variety of the world, how should we manage with one only?" (88).

This summary does not do justice to the complex counterpoint of seemingly dissonant motifs in the book, but it is a great deal more inclusive then Garland's dramatized version. Garland's choices construct a text that gives us not a multiplicity of voices and perspectives that leave literature firmly, if lightly, attached to sex and its cultural politics but, rather, a single note: the transcendent universality of art. It gives us William, we could say, a William in whom Judith, his gifted sister, is subsumed, but not Judith herself. This is not to say that Judith is entirely absent: the story of her genius and death is told, and her ghostly presence permeates the play's exposition of the difficulties confronting women who wanted to write in the past. Her legacy is also felt in the more subtle representation of the difficulties confronting women who wanted to write in what was Woolf's present (1929): the inequalities within the educational system and the dominance of "experts" such as Professor von X who set out to define what women are. But Woolf's present is now our past, and the Judith who emerges from Garland's text as a model for women today can be perceived either as already beyond the politics of gender and its discriminatory practices—to have entered, that is, into a disembodied, mental world of art—or as the recipient of an admonishment to do so as quickly as she can. The words, then, even the sentences, of Garland's *Room* might be more or less identical to those in the 1929 book, but the "extralinguistic (dialogic) aspects" of the utterance, the historical and social circumstances in which they are uttered, will alter the message that is being communicated.[19]

Taken as a whole, Garland's *Room* leaves intact those parts of the argument that posit androgyny as an erasure of gender consciousness and anger necessary for art even as it erases those parts of the argument that bring gender back into art. Audiences can hear the speaker, who is presented as Woolf herself,[20] say loudly and clearly that "it is fatal for a woman to lay the least stress on any grievance; to plead even with justice any cause; in any way to speak consciously as a woman"—the words that Jeffrey Hart cites in his article to illustrate the wrongheadedness of "feminist criticism," with its emphasis on women writing as women—but they won't hear any of the counterpoint that shows how gender permeates art, men's and women's alike. Gone are the descriptions of what it means to think back through one's mothers or what it means to write as a woman or even what it means to *be* a woman, with the multiple perspectives that entails. Gone are the text's construction of a female narrator whose explicit assumption of anonymity and multiplicity stands in direct contrast to the male authorial "I," and gone are the critiques of "virile" and fascist literature by men. Gone are the long passages detailing the marks of women's creativity; and gone are Chloe and Olivia, the two protagonists of the contemporary women's novel the narrator evokes, who for the first time in fiction not only like each other but also, in liking each other, open the door for women to explore those areas of their experience for which no language yet exists. Also gone is the narrator's invocation of Sir Chartres Biron as the man lurking behind the curtain, who, if he heard her say that Chloe liked Olivia, might well censor her speech; what Woolf's audience in 1929 would have known immediately was that Biron was the presiding magistrate at the obscenity trial of *The Well of Loneliness*. In other words, gone is any reference to, any hint of, lesbianism.

In the end, though, it is the ending of the play that serves most effectively to assimilate Judith to William: not by erasing her but by rearranging the scenes to give her the penultimate rather than the final word. The book ends with a vivid image of Judith and her rebirth: the narrator's assertion that "the dead poet who was Shakespeare's sister will put on the body which she has so often laid down" if "we [women] worked for her" (114). In the play this vision of women's communal inheritance and struggle is followed by the reiteration of a passage already spoken in conjunction with the past: the narrator's assertion that "it would have needed a very stalwart young woman in 1828" to ignore the snubs and chidings of the male experts and to say that "literature is open to everybody. I refuse to allow you, Beadle though you are, to turn me off the grass. Lock up your libraries if you like; but there is no gate, no lock, no bolt that you can set upon the freedom of my mind." Powerful as these words are, their sole appearance in the book (75–76) is followed immediately by the narrator's exposition of what she calls the more important impediment facing women writers in the nineteenth century—that there was no tradition of women's writing for them to look back to, no literary mothers—and they do not appear again. Taken out of context and placed at the end, these words give the play a structure different from that constructed by the book: a structure, and hence a meaning, that hinges on its ungendered, individualist, humanist last word.

Laurie Osborne has argued that changes in the sequence of scenes in late eighteenth-century performance texts of *Twelfth Night* indicate as much an "anxiety or unease" about gender relationships (in that case the potentially homoerotic relationship between Sebastian and Antonio) as they do changes in theatrical conventions (55); the same holds true, I would argue, in this translation of the work from one medium to another. The changes in Garland's performance text of *A Room of One's Own* can be attributed as much to anxiety or unease about what happens when Judith Shakespeare is allowed to have a last word unmediated by William, as has been the case in much feminist criticism, for example, as it can to the need for the play to present a more focused narrative line. Ironically, had feminist criticism not been so successful in making Woolf's work in general, and *Room* in particular, canonical, a "classic" work, the struggle over who gets to speak for Judith, to define what her creator meant—to fix or contain her meaning by having the last word—would not be taking place. The acclaim for Garland's version, indicated by rave reviews on both sides of the Atlantic and the awards it garnered, suggests that Garland is not alone in his vision of a *Room* and a Virginia Woolf for the 1990s: a *Room* and a Woolf that are construed to rise above the politics of gender at the same time that, through its inclusions, exclusions, and rearrangements, the play creates a gender politics of its own.

The cultural pressures inscribed in Garland's editorial/performance choices and their implications for gender politics were not lost on critics, whether or not they acknowledge that choices were made. Most critics content themselves with saying that the adaptation is "faithful," without explicating any further; no one, as I said before, comments on the altered ending, though we can hear its impact in their rendering of what the play means. Thus, Sylvie Drake in the *Los Angeles Times,* who, after noting that the play was a "faithful adaptation" concludes that "ultimately 'A Room of One's Own' the play, like 'A Room of One's Own' the book, celebrates the one thing we all possess: the inviolable freedom of the mind, the only region of our being to which we exclusively hold the key."[21] Similarly, for Sid Smith, writing in the *Chicago Tribune,* the play "builds a passionate, cleanly logical argument for intellectual freedom. . . . In the end, Woolf magnificently argues that sex must be forgotten and humanity alone remembered to achieve any genuinely creative act."[22]

Others were more explicit about what they perceive as the play's—and Virginia Woolf's—agenda and its significance for current cultural battles. Rosemary Dinnage, writing in the *Times Literary Supplement,* provides the one analysis I have found in the reviews of what has been left out and why, only to renounce her insight by recuperating Garland's Woolf: "But it follows the main sweep of Woolf's leisurely but tightly controlled argument." In her view the cuts constitute "some digressions, and some sections that are perhaps not fashionable: the argument, for instance, that it would be a pity if women were, or wrote like, men (and that in fact we need a few more sexes)."[23] *Fashionable* is the crucial word here, foregrounding the fact that this is a translation, a re-dressing, of the earlier text and of its author in accord with contemporary pressures and anxieties. If Dinnage betrays some sadness over the loss of women's writing, of Judith's distinctive voice, it doesn't seem to be a matter of great concern to her, a response I read as a reflection of the less material impact feminist criticism has had in Britain than in the States: the struggle to "own" Woolf and her text is not as central to assertions of cultural authority, and men seem less anxious to reclaim her for the canon.[24] In contrast, a number of male critics writing in the United States are vehement in their defense of the text, the Virginia Woolf, and the meanings constructed by Garland's editorial choices. Stefan Kanfer, writing for the *New Leader,* makes no bones about his preference for Garland's version: "It hardly matters that adaptor-director Patrick Garland has omitted massive portions of the original work. Other than Woolf's long-suffering husband Leonard, the writer never had a more sensitive editor." The result is to transform what, he argues, should have been "relegated to the status of a charming but badly faded antique," whose theme, he says, "is being sung by more strident and effective voices" in the media and the academy today, to a statement for our times: "the freshest 63-year-old in town."[25]

Kanfer is not alone; others feel much the same and for the same reasons: the play has given them a way to use Woolf and her now "classic" feminist work against what they, like Hart, present as a monolithic contemporary feminism, to claim her for their own ends. Howard Kissel's review in New York's *Daily News* is instructive here. Commenting that Garland, in his adaptation, "has done a splendid job of focusing on Woolf's sharpest ideas, her most pungent images," Kissel writes that "Woolf stresses that women must be able to take the large view generally associated with male writers. This concern with literature as something beyond special pleading," he adds, "is what raises Woolf above most of her feminist successors."[26] Another equally explicit comment on the political and cultural stakes appears in John Simon's enthusiastic review in *New York* magazine, which acknowledges that Garland has "abridg[ed] and knead[ed]" the book even as it asserts that he "nowise betray[s] its essence and tone." His one critique is leveled at what he sees as Atkins's betrayal of Woolf:

Under Garland's apt direction, this true-blue actress delivers that reddest of red jellies Woolf was after. The blood of all squelched, trampled-on women, writers and nonwriters, courses through this evening and keeps us, women and men, laughing blithely, compassionately, androgynously. At times Miss Atkins may be a shade too didactic, with effects a pennyworth or scruple too heavy, pauses a mite too conspiratorial. But this is only a mole on a beloved face, not so much black mark as beauty mark.

Woolf knew what today's feminists don't: that humor and wit are more powerful polemics than shrillness and fanaticism.[27]

The desire to rescue Virginia Woolf from "today's feminists"—what Kanfer calls "the Sisterhood"—attests more strongly than anything else to the inroads feminisms (and I insist on the plural) have made in our culture: the prominence they have given to gender and gender politics, whether in classrooms, syllabi, the canon, or media events. For Simon, it is clear, as for Hart, *A Room of One's Own,* having demonstrably entered the literary canon and public consciousness, must be recuperated, reclaimed; rather than furthering our understanding of the interventions of gender and gender politics at every level of the production and reception of texts, they would dismiss the topic, leaving in place the supposedly "universal" realm of art and education that produced the gender inequalities Woolf's text undertook to address in the first place. (The fact that Jeffrey Hart was appointed to the board of the National Endowment for the Humanities [NEH] by President Reagan, and that he uses the politically visible and volatile Carol Iannone as his expert witness in his essay, makes his views more than "academic" in terms of cultural politics.) Garland's *Room,* it would seem, provides them with the means to mount this argument once again. To the extent that it privileges the androgynous mind associated with William Shakespeare, it threatens to erase Judith's gendered body. But odd things happen in the reception performance so integral to the construction of a text's meaning, even when the creative and production performances seem to move toward one conclusion only; slippages can and do occur. Thus, despite the power of the final words of the play as Eileen Atkins performs them, with their emphasis on the freedom of the mind, and despite the status they gain from being the last word, a number of *women* reviewers, including Rosemary Dinnage, still present their readers with a text, a climax, and a message that ends with Judith Shakespeare " '[putting] on the body which she has so often laid down' " before.

REFASHIONING ORLANDO

> *But I'm always true to you, darlin', in my fashion,*
> *Yes, I'm always true to you, darlin', in my way.*
> —Cole Porter, *"Always True to You in My Fashion,"*
> Kiss Me, Kate

If the gendered body constitutes the return of the repressed in the reception of Garland's *A Room of One's Own*, threatening an androgyny presented as a supposedly ungendered mental construct and linked to "great art," it is the ungendered, androgynous body—or sexuality—that dominates recent performances of *Orlando*, threatening to undo both a mind-set and social/cultural institutions that have traditionally been grounded in gender difference and heterosexuality. The association of androgyny with a deconstruction of gender binaries that would make possible multiple sexualities, possible in Woolf's *Room* but excluded from Garland's, constitutes the central figure in Woolf's *Orlando*. The two texts were published within a year of each other (*Orlando* in 1928; *Room* in 1929) and have long been perceived as companion pieces. From this perspective *Orlando* becomes an exploration of what would happen if we extended the idea of androgyny from the mind of the artist to the body (in terms of sexuality, not sexual organs): if we took seriously the speculation put forward in *Room* that we could happily do with more than two sexes.

Given the interconnectedness of the two works, it is not surprising that they should have generated a nearly simultaneous spate of adaptations, or versioning, in what has been called, conflictually, this "postfeminist" or "queer" moment. The most visible *Orlando*, at least in the United States, is Sally Potter's 1992 film; having won raves at a number of festivals, it became a box office hit in Europe and England before opening here, amid great anticipation and publicity, in the summer of 1993.[28] But Potter's film is only one of three recent adaptations of the work. Robert Wilson created a stage version that premiered in Berlin in 1989 and has since been performed in Switzerland, France, and Denmark; performances in Great Britain and Australia are scheduled for 1996. Robin Brooks's theatrical adaptation played at the Edinburgh Fringe Festival and in London in the summer and fall of 1992.[29] (Even earlier Ulrike Ottinger, the avant-garde German filmmaker, drew upon the novel in two of her explorations of sexuality and power, fantasy and reality: the 1977 *Madame X—An Absolute Ruler*, which features both a character and a ship named Orlando, and the 1981

Freak Orlando.) Despite, or because of, the apparent sameness of the historical moment in which the adaptations of Woolf's two texts appeared, the differences between the textual and reception performances of Garland's *Room* and Potter's *Orlando* provide vivid markers of the historical pressures at work in the claim to represent the authentic Woolf.

What is it about *Orlando* that lends itself to reiterated performances not only in terms of texts but also of gender and its realizations? Subtitled *A Biography* and dedicated to Vita Sackville-West, *Orlando* has been called "the longest and most charming love letter in literature";[30] its connection with Vita, whose family history and ancestral estate bear a close resemblance to Orlando's, has ensured from the beginning that *Orlando* would have a following among those knowledgeable about its encrypted lesbianism. But *Orlando*, like its title character, is never one thing only; it is also an exploration, often ironic, of time, biography, history, English literature, literary criticism, imperialism, the "spirit of the age," and, as noted earlier, an androgyny that undoes rather than enforces sameness by multiplying the genders. From this latter perspective the premise is fairly straightforward: Orlando begins the novel as a sixteen-year-old, a "he," an aristocrat, and a would-be writer during the reign of Elizabeth I; sometime toward the end of the seventeenth century, aged thirty, while ambassador to Constantinople, he wakes after a long sleep to discover that he has become a "she." At the end of the novel Orlando the woman, now thirty-six, having married, borne a son, and published an award-winning poem, has arrived at Woolf's present: October 1928. Others in the novel prove equally mutable and hence uncategorizable (and live as long); Orlando, particularly during the eighteenth century, pleasurably engages in relationships with both men and women.

During the course of the journey both Orlando and the narrator, whose presence is as central to the text and as unstable as Orlando's own, meditate on what it means to be a man or a woman, often tying the question of what constitutes our sex or gender to the powerful role of clothes. The book, that is, explicitly evokes the cultural significance of clothing and its relation to subjectivity and to gender, whether in psychosocial or juridical discourses. It is not surprising, then, that *Lesbians Talk Queer Notions* (1992), to take just one example, places one of *Orlando*'s most widely cited passages—"In every human being a vacillation from one sex to the other takes place, and often it is only the clothes that keep the male or female likeness, while underneath the sex is the very opposite of what it is above"—immediately after the dictionary definitions of *queer*.[31]

Significantly, one of the central questions raised by the intersections of gender and clothes—what, if anything, substantial or essential lies beneath or beyond this covering?—can be read as an apt analogy for the status of adaptations (clothes) and their relationship to the authentic work or the authentic Woolf. This is particularly true in the case of the *Orlando* adaptations, none of which is constructed solely from Woolf's words, however artfully and pointedly rearranged, as Garland's *Room* is. In both Potter's and Brooks's versions few of the words spoken are transcribed directly from Woolf's text, making translation rather than iteration the pertinent concept. Peter Shillingsburg speculates that adaptations, like translations, can be read in terms of George Steiner's "real presences": every word might be different, but there is a real presence that remains essentially the same.[32] But to the extent that translations themselves can be understood as a form of refashioning or re-dressing—the taking apart of a garment and making it anew—and to the further extent that the clothes make or define the essence or substance, then the adaptation, rather than capturing or preserving a prior essence, creates one by its fashioning of the body of the text. In this reading the "something else" that Orgel argues the performer or editor wants to capture or fix in his or her particular performance, or realization, is an effect of the representation or embodiment realized in the performance itself, not an origin or a cause, and tells us more about the values and politics of the historical moment of the performance than about an authentic Shakespeare or Woolf.

For my purposes what characterizes this moment is the centrality of the questions posed by *Orlando:* questions of what constitutes gender, sex, and/or sexuality and their relationship to "identity." These questions have generated some of the most hotly contested debates in our culture today, debates that are occurring not only in the academic inquiries associated with women's studies, gender studies, gay, lesbian and bisexual studies, and queer theory, but also in activist communities and organizations; in popular culture; in the medical profession; and in the public policies governing the acceptance or restriction of gays and lesbians in the military, the government, and the public schools. The power of these issues, it could be argued, as well as the stakes, would be enough to explain why Potter's film has enjoyed the widespread attention it has garnered and why it has generated so much controversy.

But there is more at work here. Unlike Garland's refashioning of *Room*, a refashioning that dresses antifeminism in the garb of androgyny for what has been called the postfeminist moment in gender politics, Potter's refashioning of *Orlando* projects it into the arena of queer. Or, to put this somewhat differently, whereas Garland's refashioning evokes an intellectual androgyny that can be recuperated from "feminists" in the name of Virginia Woolf for a universality that leaves intact a sex/gender system grounded in difference, Potter's refashioning of *Orlando*, which dresses androgyny in the concepts of cross-dressing, gender bending, masquerade, camp, and/or "genderfuck," appears to undo not only the difference between the genders/sexes but also the stability of gender itself. In this way the film's representation of gender could be read as a mirror image of its status as an adaptation: a performance that undoes any claim to stability, oneness, or an authentic text.[33] Ironically, however, despite its potential to undo the concept of authenticity, Potter's *Orlando* and its reception illustrate how powerfully the desire for authenticity, both as trope and political strategy, continues to operate, even, or especially, in a queer age.

Nothing could be a more powerful statement of the timeliness, the cultural moment highlighted by Potter's *Orlando*, than the extent and nature of its reception.[34] Everyone got into the act, from Ruth Bader Ginsburg to fashion magazines. Given the starring role of the parodic albeit accurate period piece costumes in the film, the latter is not surprising; what is surprising is that, rather than focusing on the clothing, the fashion magazines featured the film's evocations of "androgyny." It was left to the mainstream press to talk about the costumes themselves.[35] This crossover occurred at all levels. *Marie Claire*, the British fashion magazine, commissioned a diary from Quentin Crisp, repeatedly referred to by Sally Potter as "the *true* queen of England," who plays Queen Elizabeth I in the film; the *New Yorker* printed nude photographs of Tilda Swinton, who performs Orlando, taken by Richard Avedon, and trashed the film.[36] In a Britain that was distinctly unimpressed by Robin Brooks's biographical refashioning of *Orlando*, with its explicitly lesbian scenes between Virginia and Vita/Orlando, Potter's *Orlando* received almost nothing but praise, while the reception in the United States, where British films tend to do better than they do at home, was far more mixed. One newspaper reported that the film was being marketed in the States to "women and homosexuals," but responses among gays and lesbians here have been decidedly ambivalent, with many lesbians declaring that it was not a lesbian film.[37] Meanwhile, the harshest critiques of the film came from women writing in explicitly feminist publications, on the one hand, and from identifiably conservative journalists and journals, on the other. This reception alone would seem to support the contention that we are in a decidedly "queer moment."[38]

At the risk of reducing the film and its reception to their performance of gender/sexuality (a response Potter lamented even as many commentators accused her of doing the same to the novel), I want to focus on what should be the most unsettling moment—the transformation of Orlando from man to woman—as an illustration of the fractured politics inscribed in the constructions of an authentic Woolf. Sally Potter, interviewed extensively, has been unequivocal in her claim that her version is true to the "spirit" if not the details of Woolf's text: that her "translation," which several writers refer to as a "refashioning," retains its essence.[39] She is also clear on what this "essence" is: the "essential self," a self that transcends the false impositions of genders dictated by society that have nothing to do with the "essential human being." For her that essence is captured at the moment of Orlando's transformation when she/he looks at him-/herself in the mirror and says, "Same person, just a different sex." When it comes to one of the major alterations she made—providing a motivation for the change of sex: Orlando's refusal to participate in the killing associated with war—Potter argues in part that it provides the "narrative muscle" necessary in film but not the novel to make the premise "psychologically convincing" and in part that, pushed to the limits of masculinity, Orlando rejects it, just as Orlando rejects the limits of femininity at the end. She is also clear about the choice she made when confronted with the need to have a person, with a body, visible on the screen: that is, not to try to make Tilda Swinton a convincing man but, instead, to create a "suspension of disbelief." As she notes, and others confirm, this self-consciousness was reinforced in the opening scenes by the presence not only of Quentin Crisp as Queen Elizabeth I but also of Jimmy Somerville, the gay pop singer known for his extraordinary falsetto, serenading the queen. Finally, she is also quoted as saying that *Orlando* should not be seen as a "feminist" film, just as it wasn't an openly political novel; the word, she argues, has become too "debased" and dated, associated, at least in Britain, "with a movement with a rather limited appeal," and she insists that men must struggle as well as women. In the same vein she is wary of identifying the film with the current gay and lesbian visibility, which, she worries, apropos of "lesbian chic," is being represented "as if it were all just *fashion*."[40]

Potter, of course, can no more fix the reception of her film—the perception of its or its protagonist's essence—than she can fix the definition of the authentic Woolf. Writing in *Mirabella*, Ruby Rich attributes the popularity of Woolf's novel not only to "the centrality of sexuality to its story and the fillip of gender playfulness in its plot" but also to the "eternal corps of Woolfians who preserve and celebrate everything by their author with near-religious fervor."[41] The last phrase, which recalls Orgel's evocation of the "doctrinal" aspect of authentication, seems particularly appropriate when listening to some of the critiques of how, in Jane Marcus's words, those involved in the production "desecrated" Woolf's novel, a denunciation that comes as strongly from those writing in recognizably conservative journals (John Simon in the *National Review,* e.g.) as it does from those writing in recognizably feminist journals (Marcus in the *Women's Review of Books* or Robin Morgan in *Ms.,* who catalogs Potter's "disastrous" violations of the book).[42] For Simon, as for Marcus and Morgan, the film fails for not being faithful to its source (it "is not even as faithful to its sources as Classic Comix are to theirs" [53]); for Stanley Kauffman, in the *New Republic,* the desecration comes from the very attempt to adapt a novel by Woolf for the movies, a response that paradoxically claims Woolf for "high art" (the comparison is to *Finnegans Wake*) even as it insists that Woolf is not as good a writer as Joyce and dismisses the novel as "a lesser work than some claim." Potter, he asserts, "didn't quite grasp the inevitable. Woolf's work is in the form that it's in because that's what it *is*."[43]

The disconcerting crossover of self-defined feminists and self-defined conservatives revealed by the assumption of, and claim to speak for, an authentic Woolf extends to their shared view of what is being desecrated: their reading of the film's undoing of gender categories as a challenge to the idea of "difference." Simon, for example, the same John Simon who so admired the androgynous mind in *Room*, balks when it comes to the androgynous sexual persona. While he acknowledges that Woolf's novel includes a "guarded plea for lesbianism" as a concomitant to the androgynous artist's "bisexual" amours (53), he wants his sexes clearly demarcated; Tilda Swinton, he writes (and he is not alone in this observation), "never made me believe her as a man, or respond to her as a woman" (54), the assumption being that he (and his readers) know what a man and a woman *are*. Robin Morgan also laments the film's treatment of gender, its "trendy 'gender fuck'" message "that there is no meaningful difference. The result is a sort of period-piece parody of *The Crying Game*" (79). Morgan, though, attributes this as much to Potter's statement in the *New York Times* that women have hard lives but men do too—her postfeminism—as she does to battles over sexuality or sexual identity.

Given that a number of other critics either lament that the film does not go far enough in undoing gender stereotypes and difference ("all the big moments fall along classic gender lines" [Dargis]), that it eliminates the lesbian sexuality, that it eliminates sexuality altogether (except for the straightest kind), that it is either too camp or not camp enough, too feminist or not feminist enough, or praise the film for its critique of gender politics and its daring portrayal of "the new androgyny," we can begin to assess the complexity of the historical moment Potter's *Orlando* represents.

But a question remains: Is this performance, this translation or re-fashioning, only a matter of the moment, a moment, as Sedgwick suggests about the queer moment, that may already have exceeded itself "in the short-shelf-life American marketplace of images"?[44] Is it, that is, only a question of style with no real import? I would say yes and no. Yes, to the extent that the work is an event, a performance, that enacts the cultural anxieties and desires of its time. No, because it would be a mistake to dismiss this or any performance of Woolf's novel, as of Shakespeare's plays, as only fashionable performance. For one thing, performance and style can be highly subversive; moreover, performance, in both its productive and reception modes, constructs its own substance and hence meaning in and through its act, and we would do well to understand what this perceived meaning is and why it matters. Politicians and others in public life such as Ruth Bader Ginsburg, who used Potter's *Orlando* as a representation of a legal philosophy grounded in gender sameness and equality rather than difference(s),[45] know what textual scholars would do well to learn: that performances are acts or events that not only realize a historical moment but also have a substantive impact on every aspect of our lives and that none of these are immune to attitudes about gender and sexuality. The politics of adaptation translates into a desire for a Shakespeare or Woolf whose performance, however unfixable, mutable, or unstable, creates an all too material authority of its own.

NOTES

My thanks to David Greetham for his invitation to speak on the MLA panel that sparked this book and for his excellent editorial help; to Peter Shillingsburg, an admirable interlocuter, whose suggestions and comments in the early stages made this piece possible; to my colleagues Jonathan Crewe and Lynda Boose for their Shakespearean input and to Jonathan for his generous readings; and to Jonathan Eburne, whose creative research is evident throughout.

1. Stephen Orgel, "The Authentic Shakespeare," *Representations* 21 (Winter 1988): 2, 24; hereafter cited in the text.
2. Donald Reiman, *Romantic Texts and Contexts* (Columbia: University of Missouri Press, 1987), 169.

3. In "The Shakespearean Editor as Shrew-Tamer" Leah Marcus suggests "that we start thinking of the different versions of *The Taming of the Shrew* intertextually—as a cluster of related texts which can be fruitfully read together and against each other" (*English Literary Renaissance* 22, no. 2 [Spring 1992]: 198).

4. Laurie Osborne, "The Texts of *Twelfth Night*," *ELH* 57, no. 1 (Spring 1990): 40; hereafter cited in the text.

5. Jerome McGann, *A Critique of Modern Textual Criticism* (Chicago: University of Chicago Press, 1983), 52.

6. Joseph Grigely, "The Textual Event," in *Devils and Angels: Textual Editing and Literary Theory*, ed. Philip Cohen (Charlottesville: University of Virginia Press, 1991), 176–77; hereafter cited in the text.

7. *The Compact Oxford English Dictionary* (Oxford: Oxford University Press, 1971).

8. Neil Sinyard, *Filming Literature: The Art of Screen Adaptation* (New York: St. Martin's Press, 1986), 117.

9. Peter L. Shillingsburg, "Text as Matter, Concept, and Action," *Studies in Bibliography* 44 (1991): 71.

10. "To change in form, appearance, or substance; to transmute; to transform. . . . Of a tailor, to renovate, turn, or cut down (a garment)" (*Compact Oxford English Dictionary*); the relevant example comes from Shakespeare's *A Midsummer's Night Dream* (III.i.122): "Blesse thee Bottome, blesse thee; thou art translated." I owe this reference to Ann Rosalind Jones and Peter Stallybrass, who explore the use of the term in different versions of the "Patient Griselda" story: "By translation, Petrarch had something quite radical in mind. 'Translatio' could refer not only to a linguistic metamorphosis but also to a specific metamorphosis through clothing (thus Chaucer, translating Petrarch's version of the tale, describes Griselda as being '*translated*' by her new clothes). . . . Petrarch announced in a letter to Boccaccio which accompanied his translation that, having written in another style, . . . he had, perhaps, 'beautified it by changing its garment.'" See "(In)Alienable Possessions: Griselda, Clothing and the Exchange of Women," forthcoming in *Worn Worlds: Clothes and Identity in Renaissance England and Europe*. I am grateful to Jones and Stallybrass for sharing this essay with me.

11. For Dudley Andrew, studying the adaptation of a work from one medium to another involves an awareness not only of the use of "'matching'" or equivalences between one (semiotic) system and another but also of the adaptation's particular historical moment. "The stylistic strategies developed to achieve the proportional equivalences necessary to construct matching stories," he adds, "not only are symptomatic of a period's style but may crucially alter that style" (*Concepts in Film Theory* [Oxford: Oxford University Press, 1984], 101–2, 104). Jane Gaines borrows these ideas in her analysis of "Costume and Narrative: How Dress Tells the Woman's Story," bringing the theory back to "fashion" (in *Fabrications: Costume and the Female Body*, ed. Jane Gaines and Charlotte Herzog [New York and London: Routledge, 1990], 191).

12. If this formulation sounds suspiciously like those put forward by theorists such

as Judith Butler in their radical deconstruction of gender and sexuality—both in their argument that there is no original or foundational gender or sexuality, no original and copy but only copies, and in their argument that gender/sex and the gendered/sexed subject are performative—it is meant to: theories of textual editing are no more immune to the cultural contexts and pressures of their moment than any other form of criticism or scholarship. Listen, for example, to Jonathan Goldberg on Shakespeare's texts: "we have no originals, only copies. The historicity of the text means that there is no text itself" or "if texts, even lexically identical texts, are never the same because of history, history, as the principle of difference, cannot be a principle of identity"; and to Judith Butler on gender and identity: "gender is not a performance that a prior subject elects to do, but gender is *performative* in the sense that it constitutes as an effect the very subject it appears to express" or "and if the 'I' is the effect of a certain repetition, one which produces the semblance of a continuity or coherence, then there is no 'I' that precedes the gender that it is said to perform; the repetition, and the failure to repeat, produce a string of performances that constitute and contest the coherence of that 'I' " or "*gender is a kind of imitation for which there is no original*; in fact, it is a kind of imitation that produces the very notion of the original as an *effect* and consequence of the imitation itself." See, respectively, Goldberg, "Textual Properties," *Shakespeare Quarterly* 37, no. 2 (Summer 1986): 214, 216; and Butler, "Imitation and Gender Subordination," in *Inside/Out: Lesbian Theories, Gay Theories*, ed. Diana Fuss (New York and London: Routledge, 1991), 24, 18, 21. In *Bodies that Matter: On the Discursive Limits of "Sex,"* Butler further describes "performativity" as "that reiterative power of discourse to produce the phenomena that it regulates and constrains" ([New York and London: Routledge, 1993], 2). For a further discussion of the issues, see *Performativity and Performance*, ed. Andrew Parker and Eve Kosofsky Sedgwick (New York and London: Routledge, 1995).

13. Virginia Woolf, *A Room of One's Own* (San Diego: Harcourt Brace Jovanovich, 1989), 46, 48; hereafter cited in the text.

14. See, for example, 18 January 1990: 43. During this same period the journal either ignored the majority of feminist critical studies that had catapulted Woolf to this eminence or found a "legitimate"—that is, nonfeminist—critic to review them negatively. Nevertheless, the connection is so strong that Nicholas von Hoffman, writing about the *NYRB* on its thirtieth anniversary, commented, "Mention *The Review*'s name among the nonacademic literate and you may hear someone groan, 'Oh, no, not Virginia Woolf again!' " (*New York Observer*, 11 October 1993, 17).

15. Jeffrey Hart, "Wimmin against Literature," *National Review*, 30 September 1988, 60; Hart was ostensibly talking about *The Norton Anthology of Literature by Women* (1985), edited by Sandra Gilbert and Susan Gubar.

16. Virginia Woolf, *Women & Fiction: The Manuscript Versions of A ROOM OF ONE'S OWN*, ed. S. P. Rosenbaum (Oxford: Blackwell, 1992).

17. Patrick Garland, dir., *A Room of One's Own*, with Eileen Atkins, Lamb's Theatre, New York, March 1991. The play also includes some voice-overs from Woolf's diaries.

18. Harry Berger Jr., "Text against Performance in Shakespeare: The Example of *Macbeth*," in *The Forms of Power and the Power of Forms in the Renaissance*, ed. Stephen Greenblatt (Norman: University of Oklahoma Press, 1982), 163.

19. Mikhail Bakhtin, *Speech Genres and Other Late Essays* (1986); cited in Grigely, "Textual Event," 181.

20. This is confirmed by the care taken by Eileen Atkins—and noted by almost all the reviews—to project Woolf's gestures, clothing, and facial expressions; photographs of Woolf adorned her backstage dressing room in New York. Since then Atkins has adapted, and performed with Vanessa Redgrave, a selection of letters between Virginia Woolf and Vita Sackville-West, which is far more explicit about lesbian sexuality and bisexuality: *Vita & Virginia*, dir. Zoe Caldwell, Union Square Theatre, New York, December 1994.

21. Sylvie Drake, "A Visit to the Mind, Spirit of Woolf," *Los Angeles Times*, 17 October 1991, F9.

22. Sid Smith, "'Room' adds some feeling to one woman's fight for literary freedom," *Chicago Tribune*, 9 October 1991, 22.

23. Rosemary Dinnage, "Creative Collaboration," *Times Literary Supplement*, 16 June 1989, 666.

24. It would be hard to imagine the *London Review of Books*, for example, making Woolf their cover girl as the *New York Review of Books* has done. Instead, London's Channel 4 broadcast a program on Woolf in its *J'Accuse* series, in which cultural icons were brought to trial and found wanting (*J'Accuse: Virginia Woolf*, written by Tom Paulin; dir. and prod. Jeff Morgan, Fulmar Productions for Channel Four, London, 29 January 1991).

25. Stefan Kanfer, "A Trio of Solos," *New Leader*, 11–25 March 1991, 22–23.

26. Howard Kissel, "A 'Room' of great dimensions," *Daily News*, 5 March 1991.

27. John Simon, "Two from the Heart, Two from Hunger," *New York*, 18 March 1991, 76.

28. *Orlando*, dir. Sally Potter, with Tilda Swinton as Orlando, Sony Pictures Classics, 1992.

29. *Orlando*, by Darryl Pinckney and Robert Wilson, features a single actress and a radically pared-down text. The German version was performed by Jutta Lampe at the Schaubühne Theater in Berlin, fall 1989; the French version, performed by Isabelle Huppert, opened in Lausanne in 1993. Miranda Richardson will perform the piece at the Edinburgh Festival in 1996. Robin Brooks's *Orlando* treats the novel as autobiography, a play-within-a-play, placing Vita Sackville-West, Virginia Woolf, Violet Trefussis, and Harold Nicolson on the stage in their own persons as well as in their *Orlando* guises.

30. Nigel Nicolson, *Portrait of a Marriage* (New York: Bantam, 1974), 218.

31. Cherry Smyth, *Lesbians Talk Queer Notions* (London: Scarlet Press, 1992), 5.

32. Peter Shillingsburg, "Texts, Cultures, Mediums, and Performers: *The French Lieutenant's Woman*," MS.

33. See note 12.

34. Not surprisingly, many articles and reviews compared it to *The Crying Game*; several even noted that the same woman, Sandy Powell, designed the costumes for both films.

35. See, for example, Tina Gaudoin, "Prisoner of Gender: Is androygyny the new sexual ideal?" *Harper's Bazaar,* June 1993, 114–17, 158. One exception was *Vogue,* which featured an interview with Sally Potter by Mira Stout accompanied by photographs of Tilda Swinton in costume taken by Karl Lagerfeld in his eighteenth-century Parisian apartment ("Raising Orlando," *Vogue,* July 1993, 26, 138–43). A *Los Angeles Times* article devoted to Sandy Powell and her costumes notes Lagerfeld's praise for the costumes and states that they are "getting equal time with Donna Karan and Giorgio Armani in American fashion magazines" (Betty Goodwin, "Renaissance Woman," *Los Angeles Times* 2 July 1993, E3).

36. Quentin Crisp, "Playing the Virgin Queen," *Marie Claire,* December 1992, 32, 34. Potter's comment about Crisp appears, among other places, in B. Ruby Rich, "Sexual Personae," *Mirabella,* May 1993, 40–45, which illustrated the clothing but talked mostly about film and sexual politics. The Avedon photographs appeared in the *New Yorker,* 8 March 1993, 72–75; Terence Rafferty's review appeared on 14 June 1993 (96–97).

37. The information about Sony Pictures Classics targeting "women and homosexuals" in the United States appeared in Lauren David Peden, "Big Little Movies Stand Up to Summer's Blockbusters," *New York Times,* 22 August 1993, sec. 2, 10. Like the reviews in general, reviews in the British gay and lesbian press applauded it more enthusiastically than the American reviews. The critiques of the film's failures of nerve in terms of lesbianism occur either in private conversations or in more mainstream journals, including *Ms.* and the *Women's Review of Books;* see also Alexis Jetter writing about the new lesbian visibility in the same *Vogue* that featured *Orlando:* "While *[Orlando]* the book was an homage to Woolf's married lesbian lover, Vita Sackville-West, you wouldn't know that from watching the movie" ("Goodbye to the Last Taboo," 87).

38. I am borrowing, freely, Eve Kosofsky Sedgwick's 1992 formulation in "T Times," the introduction to *Tendencies,* in which she argues both that we seem to be in a queer moment and that queer is grounded in the concept of "across": "*across genders, across sexualities, across genres, across 'perversions'*" (*Tendencies* [Durham: Duke University Press, 1993], xii). See also Alexander Doty's exploration of the multiple "positions within culture that are 'queer' or non-, anti-, or contra-straight" and that operate in the production/reception of mass culture (*Making Things Perfectly Queer: Interpreting Mass Culture* [Minneapolis and London: University of Minnesota Press, 1993], 3).

39. For interviews with Potter, see Walter Donohue, "Immortal Longing," *Sight and Sound* 3, no. 3 (March 1993): 10–12; Pat Dowell, "Demystifying Traditional Notions of Gender," *Cineaste* 20, no. 1 (July 1993): 16–17; David Ehrenstein, "Out of the Wilderness," *Film Quarterly* 47, no. 1 (Fall 1993): 2–7; and Gary Indiana, "Spirits Either Sex Assume," *Artforum* 31, no. 10 (Summer 1993): 88–91. For "refashioning," see Sheila Johnston, "Woolf in Chic Clothing," *Independent* (London), 12 March 1993.

40. For the "essential human being" and "suspension of disbelief," see Donohue, "Immortal Longing"; Dowell, "Demystifying"; and Ehrenstein, "Out of the Wilderness." On the reasons for the sex change, see Indiana, "Spirits," for the

quotations (90); Stephen Holden, "Films from New Directors Taking Literary License," *New York Times,* 19 March 1993, C24; and Manohla Dargis, "Sally Potter: A Director Not Afraid of Virginia Woolf," *Interview,* 23 June 1993, 42. On her rejection of the term *feminist,* see Dargis, "Sally Potter"; Dowell, "Demystifying"; Ehrenstein, "Out of the Wilderness"; and Bernard Weinraub, "How Orlando Finds Her True Self: Filming a Woolfian Episode," *New York Times,* 15 February 1993, C11. Potter's response to "lesbian chic" appears in Ehrenstein, "Out of the Wilderness," 6.

41. Rich, "Sexual Personae," 42.
42. Jane Marcus, "A Tale of Two Cultures," *Women's Review of Books* (January 1994): 11; John Simon, "A Rheum in Bloomsbury," *National Review,* 5 July 1993, 53–54 (hereafter cited in the text); Robin Morgan, "Who's Afraid of Sally Potter?" *Ms.* (July–August 1993): 78–79 (hereafter cited in the text).
43. Stanley Kauffman, "Unafraid of Virginia Woolf," *New Republic,* 28 June 1993, 26.
44. Sedgwick, "T Times," xii.
45. In an essay on Ginsburg's legal philosophy, Jeffrey Rosen recounts that she sent a letter to Katha Pollitt praising Pollitt's critique of difference feminists and enclosed with it "a clipping about the movie *Orlando*" ("The Book of Ruth," *New Republic,* 2 August 1993, 20).

Feminist Theory and the Editing of Shakespeare: *The Taming of the Shrew* Revisited

Ann Thompson

In the second half of 1992 I committed myself to two developments in my career that seemed to some of my friends incompatible. I went as visiting professor to the Center for Women's Studies at the University of Cincinnati for three months to teach a graduate course in Feminist Theory, and I signed a contract to become joint General Editor (with Richard Proudfoot) of the new Arden Shakespeare series, Arden 3. Women's Studies are still, even in the United States, a marginal, controversial area, existing precariously within academic institutions and vulnerable to financial cutbacks. Shakespeare Studies are at the center of English Studies, arguably one of the more conservative disciplines.

Insofar as the academic study of "English" has begun to change, with pressure from various quarters to enlarge the canon of texts, women's writing is seen as a direct threat to Shakespeare—for example, in the debate about "political correctness" in the teaching of English that followed the publication of a survey of English degree syllabi in British Polytechnics and Colleges of Higher Education early in 1992.[1] This survey was widely reported in a distorted form in the right-wing popular press, which seized on the fact that Shakespeare was compulsory in only 50 percent of the institutions covered. A. N. Wilson's article on "Shakespeare and the Tyranny of Feminism" (London *Evening Standard,* 4 February 92) can be taken as representative of the generally hysterical reaction with its claim that the novels of Margaret Atwood, Toni Morrison, and Alice Walker are compulsory reading for more students in British higher education than the plays of William Shakespeare. This is of course a ludicrous exaggeration, and the survey itself made no assumptions about any necessary antagonism between Shakespeare and women writers, but, while the same abbreviation serves (confusingly, in my notes) for both, W.S. (women's studies) is the opposition, W. S. (William Shakespeare) the establishment.

So what can feminist theory have to do with the editing of Shakespeare? Even within women's studies the role of feminist theory is problematic. There is still considerable hostility to it for two basic reasons:

1. It is seen (in its institutionalized form) as the exploitation, appropriation, and even de-radicalization of the women's liberation movement. Through women's studies, feminism becomes co-opted into the white male establishment, and its energies are misdirected into narrow scholastic battles.
2. It is seen as elitist because it is inaccessible to most women. It is in conflict with the popular and historical feminist stress on the personal, the experiential.

The first of these objections was discussed by Mary Evans in her 1982 essay "In Praise of Theory."[2] She argued that feminist theory has not been appropriated or co-opted because women's studies cannot merely be "added on" to the existing academic agenda without challenging and changing everything else. She quoted Maurice Godelier's paraphrase of Marx:

We might say that the dominant ideas in most societies are the ideas of the dominant sex, associated and mingled with those of the dominant class. In our own societies, a struggle is now under way to abolish relations of both class and sex domination, without waiting for one to disappear first. ("The Origins of Male Domination," *New Left Review* 127 (1981): 3–17)

Feminist theory challenges patriarchal ideology and questions how "ideas" themselves are produced, assessed, and distributed in our society. Given the overwhelming dominance of the male sex in the editing of Shakespeare, Evans's argument implies a prima facie case for feminist intervention.

The second of the objections was the focus of Sarah Fildes's 1983 essay "The Inevitability of Theory."[3] She traced the emphasis on the personal element in popular feminism to the absence of other discussions of women's lives: feminists have been obliged to make use of sources such as diaries, autobiographies, even novels, as the only available forms of data on the experiences of women, which were otherwise ignored by the traditional academic disciplines. (One might also mention the importance of the personal in the influential consciousness-raising movement.) But the personal can be claustrophobic, a dead end in which feeling is privileged over analysis or action. Theory opens onto a larger, more objective picture. Moreover, it is not optional but inevitable: there is no escape from theory, as there is no escape from ideology. While you accept the status quo, theory can remain unconscious, implicit, but, once you begin to resist or challenge, theory has to become conscious and explicit. In the present context it is clear that a major aspect of women's responses to Shakespeare over time has been the personal one, in particular the desire to identify with female characters and to praise or blame the author accordingly.[4] Without detracting from the validity of such responses, feminist theory can facilitate an analysis of how Shakespeare has been mediated and reproduced for women readers (and audiences) through the male editorial tradition.

For, as Gary Taylor says, "Women may read Shakespeare, but men edit him."[5] Apparently, no edition of the complete works has ever been prepared entirely by a woman. Mary Cowden Clarke wrote in the preface to her 1860 edition of Shakespeare's works, "I may be allowed to take pride in the thought that I am the first of his female subjects who has been selected to edit his works," but she did most of the work in collaboration with Charles Cowden Clarke (who was incidentally her husband, not her brother, as Taylor calls him both here [196] and in *Reinventing Shakespeare*).[6] In fact, the first edition published in New York by Appleton was ascribed simply to "M. C. C.," but the 1864 London edition published by Bickers was ascribed to "Charles and Mary Cowden Clarke," as were subsequent reprints. In any case the claim was a mistaken one: the distinction of first female editor must unfortunately go to Henrietta Bowdler, whose edition of the works (far from complete, by definition) was first published anonymously in 1807 and then under the name of her brother, Thomas Bowdler, in 1818. The most important female editor in the twentieth century was undoubtedly Alice Walker, who succeeded R. B. McKerrow on the old-spelling edition sponsored by Oxford University Press in the 1930s "under the condition that her work be vetted by a board of male scholars headed by W. W. Greg";[7] she never finished it.

The situation is not much different today. A survey of current editions of single plays reveals the following statistics: in the New Arden series (henceforth to be known as Arden 2), which has published all the plays except *The Two Noble Kinsmen*, only one play has been edited by a woman: Agnes Latham's *As You Like It* (1975). In the Penguin series, which has published all the plays except *Cymbeline* and *Titus Andronicus*, only three plays have been edited by women: Anne Righter (Barton)'s *The Tempest* (1968), M. M. Mahood's *Twelfth Night* (1968), and Barbara Everett's *All's Well That Ends Well* (1970). In the Oxford series only one of the nineteen plays published so far has been edited by a woman: Susan Snyder's *All's Well That Ends Well* (1993). In the New Cambridge series only three of the twenty-five plays published so far have been edited by women: my own *Taming of the Shrew* (1984), Elizabeth Story Donno's *Twelfth Night* (1985), and M. M. Mahood's *Merchant of Venice* (1987). It is still the case, as Taylor says, that, "when they do edit, token women are almost always confined to the comedies, usually to plays which present few textual problems."[8] In addition, it is notable that none of these female editors, from Henrietta Bowdler in 1807 to M. M. Mahood one hundred and eighty years later, would have been publicly recognized as a feminist. (I include myself here, since I had not published anything relevant at the time my edition was commissioned.) Would it have made any difference? Would more female editors have produced editions significantly different from those produced by male editors? On the existing evidence one would probably have to answer this question in the negative, but I would want to draw a distinction between female editors and feminist editors—between what has happened in the past and what might happen in the future. Presumably no one today would dispute that more female editors are desirable (like more female judges or more female members of Parliament or Congress), but what specific contribution might feminist editors make?

It is clear that it is much more easy for a female Shakespearean scholar to identify herself as a feminist today than it was twenty or even ten years ago. Feminist criticism is widely recognized and respected. It has been a lively and quite extraordinarily prolific approach: in his 1991 annotated bibliography of *Shakespeare and Feminist Criticism*[9] Philip C. Kolin covered four hundred and thirty-nine items from the publication of Juliet Dusinberre's *Shakespeare and the Nature of Women* in 1975[10] to his cut-off point in 1988. I have even heard complaints that recent publications and conferences have been unduly dominated by the notion of "gender," which as usual (but curiously) seems to be something possessed by heterosexual women, lesbian women, and homosexual men but not by heterosexual men, who consequently feel excluded. Yet it can hardly be claimed that feminism has had a comparable impact on editing.

During this same period, however, the practice of editing has been beginning, cautiously, to open up to contributions to literary theory more generally that might (potentially at least) include feminist theory. A series of recent articles in *Studies in Bibliography* illustrates this development as well as some of the difficulties that have been encountered. In his 1989 essay "Textual and Literary Theory: Redrawing the Matrix"[11] D. C. Greetham argued that, despite the absence of an explicit debate between textual critics and literary critics, there has been some unacknowledged common ground between them. In particular, they have shared "a specific intellectual climate [that] made some critical and textual assumptions more likely or plausible at some times than at others." Beginning with the observation that it is "no accident that the current 'revisionist' textual view of certain Shakespeare plays occurred during a period of poststructuralist unease with the fixed, determinate text of literary criticism" (1), Greetham went on to demonstrate that there has been greater "filiation" between the two camps than has yet been realized in their approaches to writer-based, text-based, and reader-based theories. In the following year G. Thomas Tanselle focused more on potential divisions in "Textual Criticism and Deconstruction,"[12] which is essentially a belated review article on *Deconstruction and Criticism*, a 1979 collection of essays by Harold Bloom and others,[13] in which he deplored the lack of interest in "texts" (as understood by editors) on the part of the deconstructionists and their casual equation of "textual criticism" with "literary criticism." Greetham's reply to this essay, "[Textual] Criticism and Deconstruction,"[14] cleverly read Tanselle's argument as itself a deconstruction of the text he addressed. This allowed Greetham to reread *Deconstruction and Criticism* in order to deconstruct Tanselle's deconstruction, looking as before for "congruence rather than difference, common cause rather than dissension, between the deconstructors and the textual critics" (14). He put special stress on the mistrust or suspicion of "authoritative" texts, long practiced by textual critics and now taken up by deconstructors, claiming "textual criticism has anticipated and domesticated the agenda of the deconstructors" (20).

Further contributions to the 1991 volume of *Studies in Bibliography* by Peter L. Shillingsburg ("Text as Matter, Concept and Action") and G. Thomas Tanselle again ("Textual Criticism and Literary Sociology")[15] pursued and extended these arguments, making it apparent that at least some textual scholars are prepared to engage with theoretical debates and to attempt to articulate the thinking behind their own practice within the frameworks made available by the theorists. It is indeed impressive to me how thoroughly these scholars have acquainted themselves with the ideas, terminology, and characteristic procedures of the deconstructionists in particular, down to the level of Derridean playfulness with the signifier and jokes that cannot help being somewhat ponderous in this context: for anyone who finds both textual scholarship and literary theory hard going, *Studies in Bibliography* taking on Derrida has the air of a scholarly equivalent of "Godzilla Meets King Kong!"

These writers are not Shakespeare scholars; Greetham, for example, works on medieval texts, Tanselle on Herman Melville. Nor are they feminists, though Greetham does briefly raise the question of whether a feminist approach might challenge the traditional hierarchical structures of the presentation of texts in his essay "The Manifestation and Accommodation of Theory in Textual Editing."[16] They sometimes complain that their overtures are not being reciprocated: it has become obligatory for everyone in the profession to be aware of literary theory, while it is not yet obligatory to be aware of the finer (or even the cruder) points of textual editing. Nevertheless, I see this debate as an enabling one for feminist editors of Shakespeare. As feminists, we too have had to engage with theory (though our encounter has taken place in a different part of the forest from that inhabited by the deconstructionists), and we can surely take courage from the notion that textual critics as well as feminist critics are likely to be receptive to our work.

But what, in detail, is our work going to be like? I shall now attempt a brief survey of how a feminist approach to editing might make specific differences in the three main areas of an editor's responsibility: the text, the introduction, and the commentary.

THE TEXT

Editors of Shakespearean texts have always had to choose between possible readings, and it is arguable that a feminist editor might make a different set of choices. In the case of plays that survive in two or more early printed versions, editors have to choose which version they sees as more "authoritative." This choice will depend on a number of factors including of course an argument about the provenance of each text, but an awareness of gender issues can contribute to such a choice in the present and help to explain the reasons behind editorial decisions made in the past. At the most obvious level editorial choices can strengthen or weaken the roles of female characters. As long ago as 1965, Nevill Coghill argued in "Revision after Performance"[17] that, if the folio text of *Othello* is an authorial revision, one of the author's aims was to make the role of Emilia more important, particularly toward the end of the play. This did not have much impact at the time, but it was taken up again in 1982 by E. A. J. Honigmann, who added the observation that several of the folio-only passages are more "sexually specific" than the equivalent passages in the quarto, "that is, they add images or turns of thought that throw new light on sexual behaviour or fantasy, notably reinforcing the play's central concern with normal and abnormal sexuality."[18] D. C. Greetham would say that the intellectual climate in 1982 was more receptive to revisionism than that in 1964 partly because of the work of the literary theorists. I would add that the higher level of gender awareness was partly due to the work of feminists.

Another example of discussion of the potential for editorial choice in this area is Steven Urkowitz's essay "Five Women Eleven Ways: Changing Images of Shakespearean Characters in the Earliest Texts,"[19] in which he demonstrates that the parts of Queen Margaret in *2* and *3 Henry VI*, Anne Page in *The Merry Wives of Windsor*, Juliet and Lady Capulet in *Romeo and Juliet*, and Gertrude in *Hamlet* differ significantly between the early quartos and the folio. Also relevant is Beth Goldring's essay, "Cor.'s Rescue of Kent,"[20] in which she argues that *Cor.* as a speech prefix at a crucial point in the opening scene of *King Lear* could stand for Cordelia and not, as editors have assumed, for Cornwall.

Othello, King Lear, and the *Henry VI* plays are all textually complex, but editors of apparently straightforward, folio-only plays also have to make choices. They are sometimes confronted with passages of speech that seem at first sight meaningless and need to be reassigned, relineated, repunctuated, or more substantially emended before they can be made to yield any sense. In addition to their reliance on relatively objective criteria (such as theories about the provenance of the folio copy and the degree of likely scribal and compositorial error), editors must of course attempt to understand the context of each letter, word, sentence, or speech and to relate what is happening at the microlevel of the language to larger patterns of coherence at the macrolevels of plot, character, theme, or message. We have all learned from the literary theorists that such an understanding is bound to be limited and subjective: we cannot stand outside the ideological baggage we carry, though we can at least attempt to be aware of the preconceptions and prejudices that may affect our interpretations.

In "Textual and Sexual Criticism"[21] Gary Taylor discusses a crux in *The Comedy of Errors* that he claims has defeated past editors, partly because they were men who accepted the double standard of sexual behavior that the speaker (Adriana in 2.1) is complaining about. Thus, a gender-conscious male editor, sympathetic to the aims of feminism, can expose the sexist assumptions of previous male editors. It seems to me highly likely that feminist editors will discover many more examples of this phenomenon, and I am personally indebted to Taylor's work, but I am less happy about the last section of his essay in which he represents the process of editing itself through sexual metaphors, claiming that male editors favor "lightning strikes of ingenuity" rather than slow, painstaking efforts. He concludes:

> Editors always engage in a particular kind of intercourse with an author's discourse: they engorge the text, and simultaneously intrude themselves into it. The male editorial tradition has preferred cruxes which offer opportunities for a quick, explosive release; if an emendation does not provide such a quick fix, it leaves editors feeling dissatisfied. But a crux like this one presents us with "falshood and corruption" which can only be overcome by "often touching": prolonged exploratory attentiveness. Neither of these methods should have a monopoly on the text. A good editor, like a good lover, should be capable of both. (221)

While this is clever in its use of phrases quoted from the passage under discussion ("falshood and corruption," "often touching") and, I believe, the author is at heart well-intentioned toward feminist scholarship, it leaves us, like Taylor's more famous metaphor of editors as "the pimps of discourse," with the impression that texts are female and editors (still) male.[22]

THE INTRODUCTION

Male editors who have misunderstood the nature of the problem in the passage from *The Comedy of Errors* discussed by Taylor have also of course failed to pay any attention in their introductions to the larger issue of the double standard of sexual behavior in the play, which is endorsed most strongly by the female characters (Luciana in 3.2, the Abbess in 5.1) and which has been highlighted by feminist critics. Male editors have solemnly assured their readers that Prince Hal in the *Henry IV* plays undergoes a "comprehensive" education through his visits to the Boar's Head tavern, which enable him to achieve a "universal" or "representative" knowledge of his subjects, not noticing that this has involved an extremely limited experience of women. (Hal himself remarks on this deficit when he is required to become a wooer at the end of *Henry V*—one instance among many of Shakespeare being less blind to women's issues than his editors.) Male editors assume that sex is Ophelia's only problem: one remarked in 1982 that "her tragedy of course is that Hamlet has left her treasure with her" and that she has nothing left to do but "bewail her virginity."[23] A successor quoted these remarks approvingly in 1987, adding complacently that as a virgin Ophelia dies "unfulfilled."[24]

A feminist editor of Shakespeare will in fact usually find that in their introductions her male predecessors have neglected, distorted, and trivialized topics that are of interest to women. She must interrogate the assumptions made about gender in the text itself and in the previous transmission and elucidation of the text, drawing on feminist studies of the ways in which Shakespeare has been reproduced and appropriated by patriarchal cultures. An interesting example of this is Elaine Showalter's essay "Representing Ophelia: Women, Madness and the Responsibilities of Feminist Criticism."[25] She sets out to "tell Ophelia's story" not so much from the text of *Hamlet* but from the "afterlife" of the character as represented in painting, literature, and psychiatry as well as in stage history. Ophelia has become the type, or icon, of female insanity, and her story changes independently of theories about the play insofar as it is determined by attitudes toward women and madness more generally. Hence, Showalter's focus is on "the Ophelia myth" that has accrued around the play and that affects our interpretation of it.

One could adopt a similar strategy in an edition of *Cymbeline* by investigating "the Imogen myth," whereby the play's heroine became, during the Victorian period, "the most lovely and perfectly delineated of all Shakespeare's characters"[26] and "the immortal godhead of womanhood."[27] What precisely was it about Imogen that brought forth these superlatives at a time when the play as a whole was not held in very high esteem? It turns out, briefly, that she is specifically praised for her total femininity, which cannot be concealed under male disguise, for the domesticity of her figurative language (she refers twice to her needle) and her actions such as cooking for her brothers and Belarius: as the actress Helen Faucit put it, "For the first time, the cave is felt to be a home."[28] She is also commended for her purity (unlike the problematic Isabella in *Measure for Measure,* she calls out for help as soon as she recognizes the language of seduction), her complete obedience to her husband even when he orders her death, and for the magnanimity with which she gives up her right of succession to the kingdom once her long-lost brothers are found.

"Conjugal tenderness" is said to be her dominant quality, and she is often described as "matronly": perhaps it is not surprising that three of the most celebrated performers of the role—Helen Faucit, Ellen Terry, and Peggy Ashcroft—all played Imogen when they themselves were fifty or more.

This approach could also inform and enliven a stage history, often a rather dull section of an introduction consisting of a dutiful list of names, dates, and places with little to interest nonantiquarian readers. With *Cymbeline*, for example, one can trace how the idealization of the heroine could only have been achieved by radical cutting and expurgation of the text, beginning with David Garrick's version in 1761. Explicit sexual references and references to all but the most "innocent" parts of the human body were routinely omitted. In the wager scene (1.4), for example, it became standard for Iachimo to assert that he would "win the love" of Imogen rather than that he would enjoy her "dearest bodily part," and in the scene in which he returns to Rome (2.4) it became standard to omit Posthumus's blunt challenge to him to prove "that you have tasted her in bed." Posthumus's misogynistic soliloquy at the end of this scene was often cut, as were Iachimo's references to prostitutes in his scene with Imogen (1.6). The purpose of Cloten's pursuit of the heroine was altered insofar as references to his intent to rape her were omitted. After his fight with Cloten (4.2), Guiderius usually entered carrying Cloten's sword, not his head, and Imogen's speech on awakening from her drugged sleep later in this scene was shorn of its references to the body's leg, foot, thigh, and so on. She certainly did not daub her cheeks with the dead man's blood. Despite all this, Imogen's part remained central to the play, though the dynamics of it shifted according to whether the actor-manager of the time was playing Posthumus (like Garrick and John Philip Kemble) or Iachimo (like Macready and Irving). In thus attempting a gender-conscious approach to the study of stage history, a feminist editor can also build on the work of Irene Dash, whose book *Wooing, Wedding, and Power: Women in Shakespeare's Plays*[29] considered the ways in which female roles in a number of texts have been altered and abridged in a male-dominated theatrical tradition.

THE COMMENTARY

Mary Cowden Clarke took a swipe at the male editorial tradition when she dismissed most footnotes as "mere vehicles for abuse, spite and arrogance." Any editor who has plowed through the eighteenth-century commentaries will have some sympathy with the charge. As in the introduction, so in the commentary, a modern feminist editor can generate a refreshing amount of interesting new material simply by performing a critique of her male predecessors' work. The typical rhetorical stance of the male editor is aloof, patronising and overtly or covertly misogynistic. The feminist editor will again find that the editors are frequently more sexist than the text, both in what they discuss and in what they fail to discuss. I shall limit myself to two examples of each category.

To begin with sins of commission, toward the end of *The Comedy of Errors* the Abbess questions Adriana about the possible cause of her husband's apparent madness and establishes that it is due to "the venom clamors of a jealous woman" (5.1.69),[30] Adriana having dared to complain to her husband about his relationship with a prostitute. This conclusion is reached after some very leading questioning, in which Adriana is made to convict herself of excessive and violent scolding. Her sister Luciana objects to the Abbess's verdict and defends Adriana, asserting, "She never reprehended him but mildly" (87), and she asks her, "Why bear you these reproofs and answer not?" (89), to which Adriana replies, "She did betray me to my own reproof" (90). This last line is paraphrased by a 1972 editor[31] as meaning "She tricked me into recognizing my own faults"—a paraphrase that is quoted without comment (and presumably approvingly) by a 1987 editor.[32] Surely this is simply incorrect? The line means, "She tricked me into criticizing myself," and the context (not to mention the rest of the play) establishes that the criticism is not justified. Adriana is not "recognizing her own faults" but accusing herself of faults she does not possess. This misreading can, like Taylor's textual example, be attributed to the unthinking sexist assumption on the part of male editors that Adriana is indeed the one who is at fault in this context. The way they present their reading as an apparently straightforward paraphrase means it will all too easily be accepted by readers who are themselves conditioned by patriarchal attitudes and who assume the editor speaks with authority in such a matter.

My other example is from *Othello*. (Can one imagine anyone advising *him* not to criticize his wife for her infidelity but, rather, to put up with it quietly and even accept that it is all his own fault? Can one imagine male editors finding it natural to endorse such a position?) The problem here is with Desdemona's sensuality, and it was, sadly, a female editor in 1957 who, as Gary Taylor demonstrates,[33] rejected the quarto reading of 1.3.251, in which Desdemona says her heart is subdued to the "utmost pleasure" of Othello, preferring the less physical folio reading "very quality." The same editor argued in her commentary that, when Desdemona complains that if Othello goes to Cyprus without her, "The rites for why I love him are bereft me" (1.3.257), *rites* has nothing to do with conjugal rites. A male editor in the following year, whose textual theory committed him to following the quarto, printed "utmost pleasure" in 1.3 but explicitly expressed his approval of a later quarto reading at 2.1.80, in which Cassio prays that Othello's "tall ship" may soon arrive in Cyprus so that he can "swiftly come to Desdemona's arms."[34] This editor commented unfavorably on the more physical folio reading that Othello may "Make love's quick pants in Desdemona's arms" on the grounds that it is "out of character for Cassio and his usual attitude to Othello and Desdemona." Both these editors seem to use their authority in their commentaries to take as much sex out of the play as they can.

As for sins of omission, I'll begin with *As You Like It*, in which it has always struck me that the famous "seven ages of man" speech (2.7.137–66) conspicuously excludes women. After the Duke's introductory reference to "this wide and universal theatre" and Jacques's opening "All the world's a stage, / And all the men and women merely players," the speaker limits his focus to just one half of mankind—"each man in his time plays many parts"—and proceeds to delineate the schoolboy, the specifically male lover, the soldier, the justice, and so on. No editor remarks on this. Indeed, all eight pages of commentary on the speech in the recent New Variorum edition[35] celebrate Shakespeare's ability to portray "representatives of the entire human race." A feminist editor might note the invisibility of women here and perhaps relate it to the absence of actual women on the English Renaissance stage, a convention about which this play is notably self-conscious, especially in its epilogue.

My other example is from *King Lear*. At the beginning of 4.3 in editions that conflate the quarto and folio texts, a Gentleman explains that the army that has arrived from France to support Lear is being led by Cordelia, not by the king of France, whose absence is rather vaguely explained by "something he left imperfect in the state," (3) which needs his attention. Editors do have something to say about this passage (which is in the quarto text but not in the folio), the standard explanation for the king's absence being that Shakespeare is cautious about making what is after all French military intervention look too much like a foreign invasion. This issue has been debated by recent textual critics who have disputed Shakespeare's need to "censor" his work in this way: see, for example, Gary Taylor's essay "Monopolies, Show Trials, Disaster and Invasion: *King Lear* and Censorship."[36] But a feminist editor might add that it is also crucial for the emotional effect of Lear's reunion with Cordelia in 4.7 and 5.3 that her husband not be present. One might even express concern at the way in which the play's ending encourages us to endorse Lear's appropriation of Cordelia regardless of her wishes or her other ties, ignoring our sense that she was right to refuse just such an appropriation in the opening scene.

Finally, it is hard to know whether to laugh or cry when one comes to examine the traditional editorial procedures for dealing with obscenity in Shakespearean texts, an area that gives rise to sins of both kinds. Some editors simply try to evade the issue altogether, from Pope, who cut many of the lines Shakespeare gave to the sexually outspoken Princess in *Love's Labour's Lost*,[37] to modern editors of *As You Like It*, who fail to comment on the sexual innuendo in Rosalind's speeches.[38] In both cases the fact that a woman is speaking is significant: Shakespeare's heroines (including Desdemona in my earlier examples) are more frank and enthusiastic about sex than his male editors think "ladies" should be.

Frequently, editors use coy phrases such as "bawdy quibble," "double entendre," or the even more quaint "sexual equivoque" without spelling out what precisely is going on. They go to extraordinary lengths to avoid using "rude" words themselves, as can be illustrated from the English lesson scene in *Henry V* (3.4). One 1965 editor informed his readers that *le foot* and *le count* are "similar in sound to the French equivalent of English 'four-letter' words."[39] A 1968 editor volunteered the information that *foutre* means "coition" and that *con* means "female organ."[40] The year 1976 saw a regression from this brave outspokenness with an editor who remarked that the scene in general exhibits "some gentle humour in a number of mispronunciations" and that *foot* and *count* are "close approximations to obscene words."[41] A modern feminist editor would surely make less of a fuss about printing *fuck* and *cunt* and commenting on the kind of humor that is being generated in this scene between two women.

The sexual politics of *The Taming of the Shrew* have always been controversial. It is the only one of Shakespeare's plays to have provoked a theatrical reply or sequel in his lifetime in the form of John Fletcher's *The Woman's Prize, or The Tamer Tamed* (c. 1611), in which Petruchio, now a widower, marries again and has the tables turned on him by his second wife. (The implicit homage of such a sequel may have been one of the factors in Shakespeare's decision to collaborate with Fletcher in his last three plays from around 1612–14: *Cardenio*, *Henry VIII* and *The Two Noble Kinsmen*.) While *The Shrew* has been a popular play in the theater for four hundred years, its stage history offers numerous examples of ambivalence on the part of adaptors and producers toward its subject matter. As early as *The Taming of a Shrew*, the problematic quarto text published in 1594 and generally known as *A Shrew*, Katherina is given an aside in the wooing scene (the equivalent to 2.1 in the traditional treatment of the folio version):

> *She turnes aside and speakes*
> But yet I will consent and marrie him,
> For I methinkes have livde too long a maid,
> And match him too, or else his manhood's good.
>
> (sc. 5, 40–42)[42]

Thus, it is made explicit, as it never is in *The Shrew*, that Katherina can see some positive advantage in marrying and that she is going to enjoy competing with her partner. But later the brutality of the taming is played up when, in the equivalent of 4.3, we get the stage direction "*Enter Ferando* [Petruchio] *with a peece of meate uppon his daggers point.*"

Similarly, Catherine has an aside in the midst of the exchange of insults in this scene in Garrick's version (which held the stage from 1754 to 1844 in England and to 1887 in the United States):

> A Plague upon his Impudence! I'm vexed—
> I'll marry my Revenge, but I will tame him.
>
> (14)[43]

And at the end of the scene she confirms this hint of a reversal of roles and adds further motivation in a closing soliloquy:

> Sister Bianca now shall see
> The poor abandon'd Cath'rine, as she calls me,
> Can hold her Head as high, and be as proud,
> And make her Husband stoop unto her Lure
> As she, or e'er a Wife in Padua.
> As double as my Portion be my Scorn;
> Look to your Seat, Petruchio, or I throw you.
> Cath'rine shall tame this Haggard;—or if she fails,
> Shall tye her Tongue up, and pare down her Nails.
>
> (16–17)

Garrick has here transferred some of Petruchio's taming metaphors to Catherine in an attempt to redress the balance between hero and heroine, but it also seems that it was he who first made a whip an obligatory stage property for Petruchio. Thus, from the beginning the theatrical tradition has simultaneously apologized for and exaggerated the play's misogyny.[44]

Male editors have also felt uneasy about *The Shrew*. In 1904 one found Petruchio's order to Katherina in the last scene to take off her cap and tread on it particularly offensive: "Though not intended to humiliate her, but rather to convince his sceptical friends, it always strikes me as a needless affront to her feelings . . . offered at the very moment when she is exhibiting a voluntary obedience."[45] Another in 1928 wrote, "There have been shrews since Xantippe's time . . . and it is not discreet for an editor to discuss, save historically, the effective ways of dealing with them . . . but . . . one cannot help thinking a little wistfully that the Petruchian discipline had something to say for itself." He immediately withdrew this by remarking that Petruchio's method "was undoubtedly drastic and has gone out of fashion. . . . Let it suffice to say that *The Taming of the Shrew* belongs to a period, and it is not ungallant, even so."[46] A more recent editor writing in 1981 revealed his embarrassment about the play by having a great deal to say in his introduction about shrews as little furry animals and almost nothing to say about sexual politics. Both this editor and another one in 1982 contrived to take no notice whatever of feminist critics, who had by then already produced some stimulating new readings of the play.[47]

It is not an exaggeration to say that being commissioned to edit *The Taming of the Shrew* around 1979 and the experience of working on the play over the subsequent three or four years contributed to my becoming a feminist in a public, professional sense as well as in a private capacity. (I was simultaneously beginning to develop the first courses on women writers and feminist criticism at the University of Liverpool.) I don't want to dwell on the final product, which was published in 1984, but I did try, especially in my introduction and commentary, to consider issues neglected by other editors and in particular to treat *The Shrew* as a "problem play" whose darker side has been acknowledged, consciously or unconsciously, throughout its stage and critical history. Perhaps I did not, by today's standards, go far enough. I was present at a paper given by Annabel Patterson at the World Shakespeare Congress in Tokyo in August 1991 during which, after some positive remarks about my edition, she said as much. I reflected then that some of the defects could be attributed to my lack of self-assurance, both as an editor and as a feminist, while others were due to the need to compromise with the wishes of the general editors of the series and behind them the publishers. Rather than conduct a backward-looking autocritique, what I shall do in the final section of this essay is consider briefly what I would do differently if I were editing *The Shrew* today, ten years after it was published.

I doubt if I would want to make any changes in the text itself, though I would of course need to engage with the choices and arguments of subsequent editors, notably those of Stanley Wells and Gary Taylor in the Oxford *Complete Works* and *Textual Companion*.[48] The 1594 quarto text of *A Shrew* is so different at the level of linguistic detail from *The Shrew* that no editor of the latter play would be likely to emend the text with readings taken from the former, but I would want to reexamine my position on *A Shrew* itself and on the relationship between the two versions in the light of work published recently by Graham Holderness and Bryan Loughrey in the introduction to their reprint of *A Shrew*[49] and by Leah Marcus in her essay "The Shakespearean Editor as Shrew-Tamer."[50] These discussions challenge the orthodox position, established by all three of the 1980s editions, that *A Shrew* is a later text than *The Shrew* and is to some extent derived from it. They also argue that *A Shrew* is a more "progressive" text than *The Shrew* in its sexual politics. Marcus contrasts the continuing use of the additional Christopher Sly episodes in the stage history of *The Shrew* with their suppression by editors and traces a depressing history of a virtual conspiracy to associate the greater realism and the greater commitment to patriarchy of *The Shrew* with the "authentic Shakespeare," while *A Shrew* with its "significant ideological differences" is banished from the canon.

I think the ideological differences are less clear-cut than these authors claim, and their textual arguments for the chronological precedence of *A Shrew* are not immediately convincing. A substantial counter argument is advanced in Stephen Roy Miller's unpublished Ph.D. thesis, *A Critical, Old-Spelling Edition of "The Taming of A Shrew, 1594,"*[51] which seems to me, after a very thorough analysis of the evidence, forcefully to reestablish the view that *A Shrew* is a deliberate (though not always totally competent) adaptation of *The Shrew*. Marcus misrepresents the editorial tradition when she says that editors have suppressed the additional Sly episodes when all recent editions print them, albeit in appendices. Nevertheless, her work and that of Holderness and Loughrey is interesting, perhaps especially to literary theorists, in representing a poststructuralist and postrevisionist attitude to the fundamental indeterminacy of all texts. The solution proposed by Marcus for editors—that they should print complete versions of both texts—is not likely to appeal to publishers of regular Shakespeare series (Routledge, the Arden publishers, are not prepared to contemplate two versions even of *Hamlet* or *King Lear*), but the text provided by Holderness and Loughrey will allow those interested to read the plays intertextually. In an ideal world we would also have a published version of Miller's edition, and perhaps the current interest in "not-after-all-so-bad-quartos" (textually challenged quartos?) will make that possible.

In line with what I have said here, I might wish to be even more explicit in my commentary about obscenity in the play, especially in the wooing scene (2.1) and in the final scene (5.2), though I was gratified to read in a recent essay by Thomas L. Berger that my commentary was the most explicit on these matters of the six editions of *The Shrew* he examined.[52]

But the major changes would come in the introduction. Many things would need updating, but I would want to do that along specifically feminist lines. In discussing more recent stagings, for example, I'd pay particular attention to those that have made some distinct point about the play's sexual politics. Two such productions were those at the Everyman Theatre in Liverpool in 1987 and at the Royal Shakespeare Theatre in Stratford-upon-Avon in 1992. (The latter production transferred to the Barbican Theatre in London in 1993.) The Liverpool production, directed by a woman, Glen Walford (who incidentally used my text), gave the play a North African setting, which was apparently intended to emphasize the restrictions on the women who appeared partially veiled. While this was effective to some extent, it also allowed the overwhelmingly white British audience to feel a sense of racial and religious superiority, complacent in their assurance that the Western Christian tradition is more progressive in these matters than the Eastern Islamic tradition. The Stratford production, directed by Bill Alexander, was (I would say significantly) more interesting for its treatment of the Induction and the subplot than for its treatment of the main plot. (Leah Marcus should have seen it.) It used an extended and thoroughly modernized version of the Christopher Sly episodes featuring a group of thoughtless yuppies who remained onstage right through the play and participated by being required to play minor roles from time to time, usually as servants. In the subplot Tranio became a potentially serious rival to Lucentio in the wooing of Bianca. The main plot was disappointingly conventional (apart from the casting of a blonde Katherina and a small Petruchio), with hero and heroine falling in love fairly obviously at first sight, though the playing of the scene on the road back to Padua (4.5) as a straight love scene was novel. In general, however, this production seemed more interested in class issues than in gender issues—the first postfeminist *Shrew*?

Turning to the critical tradition, I would be delighted to find much more material now than ten years ago. In the early 1980s I was able to treat feminist criticism as relatively univocal, partly because the field was then dominated by the North American approach, which had developed out of psychoanalytic criticism and which was exemplified by Coppélia Kahn's essay "*The Taming of the Shrew*: Shakespeare's Mirror of Marriage"[53] and Marianne Novy's essay "Patriarchy and Play in *The Taming of the Shrew*."[54] Now I would want to explore the pluralism of feminist approaches and, in particular, the extent to which they have been influenced by American New Historicism and British cultural materialism. This would involve a more historical treatment of the play itself: I'd put it in the context of actual sexual politics in the 1580s and 1590s, drawing on recent work by critics such as Karen Newman in her chapter "Renaissance Family Politics and Shakespeare's *Taming of the Shrew*," in *Fashioning Femininity and English Renaissance Drama*,[55] and Lynda E. Boose in her essays "Scolding Brides and Bridling Scolds: Taming the Woman's Unruly Member"[56] and "*The Taming of the Shrew*: Good Husbandry and Enclosure."[57] At the same time I'd want to pay more attention to the history of women's responses to the play over the last four hundred years, drawing on my own recent work in this field and on books such as *Women's Re-Visions of Shakespeare*, edited by Marianne Novy.[58]

While feminist critics have been becoming more historical, they have accused New Historicist critics in particular of treating issues of sexuality almost entirely in terms of power to the exclusion of gender: see Lynda E. Boose, "The Family in Shakespeare Studies; or—Studies in the Family of Shakespeareans; or—The Politics of Politics";[59] Carol Thomas Neely, "Constructing the Subject: Feminist Practice and the New Renaissance Discourses";[60] and my own essay "Are There Any Women in *King Lear*?"[61] A contemporary edition of *The Shrew* would need to take on these debates as they impinge upon critical discussions of the play. It would also need to engage with the ongoing debate within feminist criticism itself between what one might call "apologist" critics, who want to "save" Shakespeare or even co-opt him as a protofeminist, and the more negative, or pessimistic, critics, who see him as quite irredeemably patriarchal. (In the former camp one might put Irene Dash[62] and Linda Bamber, author of *Comic Women, Tragic Men*;[63] in the latter camp one might put Peter Erickson, author of *Patriarchal Structures in Shakespeare's Drama*,[64] and Marilyn Williamson, author of *The Patriarchy of Shakespeare's Comedies*.)[65]

There are of course anxieties that focus around this latter position: If we conclude that Shakespeare's views on gender would class him with the reactionaries were he alive today, does that mean we shall stop reading or teaching him? This brings me back to "Shakespeare and the Tyranny of Feminism": feminism as censorship. The very fact that criticism of *The Taming of the Shrew* has enjoyed a positive renaissance in recent years mainly because of the contributions of feminist critics, while other early comedies such as *The Two Gentlemen of Verona* and *The Comedy of Errors* remain relatively neglected, does not bear out the charge. (One might also cite the feminist-inspired debates that are revivifying study of more problematic misogynists such as John Milton and D. H. Lawrence.) Personally, however, I am prepared to admit I have no intention of reediting *The Taming of the Shrew:* having toyed with *Cymbeline* for a while, I'm now working on the Arden 3 edition of *Hamlet.*

NOTES

1. The survey was carried out by Tim Cook of Kingston University for *PACE,* the newsletter of SCEPCHE, the Standing Conference on English in Polytechnics and Colleges of Higher Education. SCEPCHE subsequently merged with CUE, the Council for University English, to become CCUE, the Council for College and University English, and the publication is now known as the CCUE newsletter.
2. *Feminist Review* 10:61–74.
3. *Feminist Review* 14:62–70.
4. See my essay "Pre-Feminism or Proto-Feminism?: Early Women Readers of Shakespeare," in *The Elizabethan Theatre* 14 (1996), 195–211.
5. "Textual and Sexual Criticism: A Crux in *The Comedy of Errors,*" *Renaissance Drama* 19 (1988): 195.
6. *Reinventing Shakespeare* (New York: Weidenfield and Nicolson, 1989), 206.
7. "Sexual and Textual Criticism," 197.
8. Ibid.
9. *Shakespeare and Feminist Criticism* (New York: Garland, 1991).
10. *Shakespeare and the Nature of Women* (London: Macmillan, 1995).
11. *Studies in Bibliography* 42:1–24.
12. *Studies in Bibliography* 43:1–33.
13. *Deconstruction and Criticism* (New York: Seabury Press, 1979).
14. *Studies in Bibliography* 44:1–30.
15. *Studies in Bibliography* 44:31–82, 83–143.
16. In Philip Cohen, ed., *Devils and Angels: Textual Editing and Literary Theory* (Charlottesville: University Press of Virginia, 1991), 78–102.
17. In his book *Shakespeare's Professional Skills* (Cambridge: Cambridge University Press, 1965).

18. "Shakespeare's Revised Plays: *King Lear* and *Othello*," *Library* 4 (1982): 162.
19. In *Images of Shakespeare*, ed. Werner Habicht, D. J. Palmer, and Roger Pringle (London: Associated University Presses, 1988), 292–304.
20. In *The Division of the Kingdoms*, ed. Gary Taylor and Michael Warren (Oxford: Clarendon Press, 1983), 143–51.
21. As cited in note 5.
22. Taylor uses the phrase "pimps of discourse" in the general introduction to the Oxford *Textual Companion* (Clarendon Press, 1987), 7. It becomes more explicitly gendered on p. 60, where he gives an analogy from Harold Pinter's *The Homecoming* in which Lenny the pimp talks of a woman "falling apart with the pox": when a listener asks "How did you know she was?" Lenny replies, "I decided she was." Taylor continues, "An editor, in emending, decides a text is diseased."
23. The Arden *Hamlet*, ed. Harold Jenkins (London: Methuen, 1982), 152, 151.
24. The Oxford *Hamlet*, ed. G. R. Hibbard (Oxford: Oxford University Press, 1987), 51.
25. In *Shakespeare and the Question of Theory*, ed. Patricia Parker and Geoffrey Hartman (London: Methuen, 1985), 77–94.
26. Louis Lewes, *The Women of Shakespeare*, trans. Helen Zimmern (London: Hodder Brothers, 1895), 340.
27. A. C. Swinburne, *A Study of Shakespeare* (London: Chatto and Windus, 1880), 227.
28. *On Some of Shakespeare's Women, by One Who Has Impersonated Them* (London: Blackwood, 1885), 251.
29. *Wooing, Wedding, and Power: Women in Shakespeare's Plays* (New York: Columbia University Press, 1981).
30. Quotations and references are from *The Riverside Shakespeare*, ed. G. Blakemore Evans (Boston: Houghton Mifflin, 1974).
31. The New Penguin *Comedy of Errors*, ed. Stanley Wells (Harmondsworth: Penguin, 1972), 176.
32. The New Cambridge *Comedy of Errors*, ed. T. S. Dorsch (Cambridge: Cambridge University Press, 1987), 99.
33. "Textual and Sexual Criticism," 199. The edition in question is the New Shakespeare *Othello*, ed. Alice Walker (Cambridge: Cambridge University Press, 1957).
34. The Arden *Othello*, ed. M. R. Ridley (London: Methuen, 1958).
35. The New Variorum *As You Like It*, ed. Richard Knowles (New York: Modern Language Association, 1977).
36. In *Division of the Kingdoms*, 75–119.
37. See Dash, *Wooing, Wedding, and Power*, 14–20.
38. See Juliet Dusinberre, "As *Who* Liked It?" *Shakespeare Survey* 46 (1993): 9–21.
39. The Signet *Henry V*, ed. John Russell Brown (New York: New American Library, 1965).
40. The New Penguin *Henry V*, ed. A. R. Humphreys (Harmondsworth: Penguin, 1968).
41. The Macmillan *Henry V*, ed. Brian Phythian (London: Macmillan, 1976).
42. Quotation and reference from the text given in Geoffrey Bullough, ed., *Narra-*

tive and Dramatic Sources of Shakespeare (London: Routledge and Kegan Paul, 1964), 1:77.

43. *Catharine and Petruchio* (London: Cornmarket Press Facsimile, 1969), 14.

44. For further discussion of these and other examples, see "*The Taming of the Shrew* on Stage," in the introduction to my edition (Cambridge: Cambridge University Press, 1984), 17–24.

45. The Arden *Taming of the Shrew,* ed. R. Warwick Bond (London: Routledge, 1904), lviii.

46. The New Shakespeare *Taming of the Shrew,* ed. Sir Arthur Quiller-Couch (Cambridge: Cambridge University Press, 1928), xxxvi–xxxvii.

47. The 1981 editor was Brian Morris, the Arden *Taming of the Shrew* (London: Routledge); the 1982 editor was H. J. Oliver, the Oxford *Taming of the Shrew* (Oxford: Oxford University Press).

48. *Complete Works* and *Textual Companion* (Oxford: Clarendon Press, 1986 and 1987).

49. *A Shrew* (Hemel Hempstead: Harvester-Wheatsheaf, 1992).

50. *English Literary Renaissance* 22 (1992): 177–200.

51. Miller's thesis was approved for the doctorate of the University of London (King's College) in 1993.

52. Berger's essay "Looking for Sex in All the Wrong Places," a contribution to the seminar on editing at the International Shakespeare Conference at Stratford-upon-Avon in August 1992, is as yet unpublished.

53. *Modern Language Studies* 5 (1975): 88–102.

54. *English Literary Renaissance* 9 (1979): 264–80.

55. *Fashioning Femininity and English Renaissance Drama* (Chicago: Chicago University Press, 1991): 33–50.

56. *Shakespeare Quarterly* 42 (1991): 179–213.

57. In *Shakespeare Reread,* ed. Russ McDonald (Ithaca: Cornell University Press, 1994): 193–225.

58. For my own work, see note 4. See also *Women Reading Shakespeare, 1660–1900* by Ann Thompson and Sasha Roberts, forthcoming from Manchester University Press (1996). Novy's book was published by the University of Illinois Press (1990).

59. *Renaissance Quarterly* 40 (1987): 707–42.

60. *English Literary Renaissance* 18 (1988): 5–10.

61. In *The Matter of Difference,* ed. Valerie Wayne (Hemel Hempstead: Harvester-Wheatsheaf, 1991), 117–28.

62. Dash, *Wooing, Wedding, and Power.*

63. *Comic Women, Tragic Men* (Stanford: Stanford University Press, 1982).

64. *Patriarchal Structures in Shakespeare's Drama* (Berkeley: University of California Press, 1985).

65. *The Patriarchy of Shakespeare's Comedies* (Detroit: Wayne State University Press, 1986).

Under the Covers with Caliban

Jonathan Goldberg

My task here is to consider the gay text, and I begin with a caveat; if by "gay text" one designates a text in terms of the presumed sexual identity of its writer or of characters represented, the term functions as a kind of legislative, normative category, and the task for the critic is reduced to questions of how the author's sexuality affects the text or to find the gay character in the text. In these acts of discovery a regulatory definitional apparatus always is in place. Moreover, to think of a gay text this way constitutes a marginalizing gesture: only texts that fit the criteria can properly be called gay texts, and what this inevitably means is that most texts aren't. Instead, I take Eve Kosofsky Sedgwick's stunning program in *Epistemology of the Closet* to be a far more productive route in asking what a gay text is; in her cogent formulation there is no question of knowledge in modernity that is not structured by the homo-hetero problematic, and this means that the question of the gay text is not to be reduced to one of identity.[1] Rather, it is always a relational question, and it figures everywhere. This formulation is vital especially in the situation that concerns me here, the consideration of a text produced in an era that handles the homo-hetero divide quite differently from our own, since those identity categories are unavailable in the Renaissance (but the range of sexual experiences is not)—a consideration, of course, by a critic who writes now and whose task must be shaped by modern protocols of knowledge. Indeed, the aim of these pages is not merely to read *The Tempest* but also to ponder its editorial and critical production, that is, to measure its status as a modern text. In exploring questions of sexuality in *The Tempest* enabled by recent work in feminist and gay/lesbian studies and in engaging with earlier accounts of the play produced from other vantage points, my critical stance does not entail charges

105

of blame or ignorance; instead it measures future possibilities. I should add immediately that this piece does not pretend to cover all of the sexual elements in the play but, rather, to tease out, largely on the basis of textual evidence of the bibliographic kind, some implications occasioned by, although not limited to, the figure of Caliban.

Caliban first appears in the text of *The Tempest* when his birth is recounted in the dialogue between Prospero and Ariel in 1.2. To Alden T. Vaughan and Virginia Mason Vaughan, I owe my awareness that this moment is accompanied by a hitherto uncommented upon crux in the Folio text of the play, its sole authoritative source. They print the lines as follows:

> Then was this Island
> (Save for the Son that [s]he did littour heere,
> A frekelld whelpe, hag-borne) not honour'd with
> A humane shape

depending on the Folio text and, for the bracketed *s* in *[s]he*, on an emendation, which, they note, Rowe first supplied.[2] This bibliographic information will, of course, be found in most modern texts of the play (e.g., Frank Kermode's New Arden edition, Stephen Orgel's recent Oxford text), and it undoubtedly was the context in which the lines are cited in *Shakespeare's Caliban* that made the Folio text and Rowe's emendation suddenly seem urgent: the Vaughans are considering the question of whether or not Caliban is regarded as human in the play; they take these lines as establishing that he (unlike his mother, presumably) is the first "humane shape" to inhabit the island.[3] What is striking in this context is the fact that, at least as printed throughout the seventeenth century, this moment in the play ascribes his birth to a mother who has—and only for these lines describing the moment of parturition, since elsewhere there is no question of the gender of Sycorax—become male in gender. If Caliban is born human, he is born from a mother who is not merely inhuman (littering is not a human form of giving birth) but whose inhumanness the text would seem to be underscoring by the impossible gender change that takes place at this moment. Were one to take the male pronoun seriously, it would necessarily call into question at least one biblical definition of the human—man, born of woman. Caliban's humanity would not be assured if his mother were not a woman.

That it is possible to take the Folio line seriously (i.e., not simply to regard *he* as a printer's error that Rowe corrected) is attested by the textual history of the play in the seventeenth century. For, if this is merely a mistake, it is remarkable that it was not until Rowe's 1709 edition of Shakespeare that it was caught. As is argued by Matthew W. Black and Matthias A. Shaaber, "the three later folios are not imperfect reprints of F1, F2, and F3 respectively, but critical editions in exactly the same sense that Rowe's is a critical edition."[4] The anonymous editors of 1632, 1664, and 1685 each consulted the previous folio for the basic copy-text, much as Rowe based his text on F4. Each, moreover, was unlikely to have had much, if anything, in the way of authoritative textual material in support of emendations to the previous texts. That is, in most cases changes in the subsequent folios (when they are not new errors) are emendations, many of which modern editors happily accept, that can be chalked up to common sense, to what Black and Shaaber refer nicely as "the fitness of things" (25). Which is to say that a "mistake" of the kind that appears at this moment in the first folio text of *The Tempest* is exactly what one might have supposed would have been caught in one of the seventeenth-century folio printings of the play, which, Black and Shaaber argue, are especially good at correcting obvious typographical errors (even if some new ones inevitably were also introduced) as well as correcting the kind of solecism the misgendering of Sycorax would seem to represent.

The fullest modern collation of these lines occurs in Kermode's edition: "282. son] Sunne F2; Sun F3, F4. she]Rowe; he F, Ff,"[5] and it suggests something that an examination of the seventeenth-century texts further reveals: that these lines were not printed unchanged from edition to edition (the pronoun *he* remains constant); that, instead of correcting the "obvious mistake," a possible new mistake was introduced in the lines, the replacement of F1's *Son* with the *Sunne* of F2 modernized in spelling to *Sun* in F3 and F4. A possible mistake, that is, unless the change from *son* to *sun* was an attempt to locate birth from a male at an appropriately mythological level, where such an event could happen (Zeus gives birth to Athena, e.g.); if so, the response to the lines would seem less to register the "wrongness" of the gender as to want, somehow, to accommodate it. This is, of course, mere speculation on my part, and it is possible that *son/sun* is an indifferent variant (although, given the insistent modernization of the text from edition to edition, this is not all that likely). What is clear, at any rate, is that changes in punctuation (which serve, in fact, to confuse the sense of the lines, another sign that the "obvious" mistake of *he* for *she* was not perceived as such), in capitalization, and in the spelling of *frekelld, hagborne,* and *humane,* to bring the text in line with modern orthographic practices, make it evident that these lines were not merely reset from folio to folio; in every instance there is change, and, therefore, in every instance there was the opportunity to change *he* to *she*.[6] That Rowe first did it, then, is not quite to be ascribed to common sense, nor is it the case that Rowe was the first editor to have felt that these lines needed to be changed. He was simply the first who thought that *he* should read *she*. (Actually, not quite: while Rowe first made the change in a Shakespeare edition, Dryden and Davenant have *she* in their *The Tempest: Or the Enchanted Island* [1670].)

How, then, to account for the persistence of this "error" in seventeenth-century editions of *The Tempest*? Perhaps by appealing to the "fitness of things" that Black and Shaaber invoke, the fitness, that is, that necessitates that the monstrous offspring of a witch (in these lines bestially born, whelped and littered, and freakishly marked, freckled, a maculate conception) must be prodigiously and unnaturally mothered. But perhaps, too, by seeing that this gendered change has its counterparts elsewhere in the play. Stephen Orgel has described some lines from Prospero's narration of the past to Miranda earlier in this scene as articulating a birth fantasy on his part.[7] In these lines, if one follows Orgel's reading of them, Miranda's saving presence on board their vessel of exile is turned by Prospero into the instrument by which he gives birth:

> *Miranda.*   Alack, what trouble
>   Was I then to you!
> *Prospero.*   O, a cherubin
>   Thou wast that did preserve me. Thou didst smile,
>   Infused with a fortitude from heaven,
>   When I have decked the sea with drops full salt,
>   Under my burden groaned, which raised in me
>   An undergoing stomach to bear up
>   Against what should come.
>
>   (Orgel, 1.2.151–58)

Burden, Orgel notes, "is the contents of the womb," while groaning "is a lying in." In these lines, as is the case throughout the play, as Orgel argues in the introduction to his edition and in his crucial essay "Prospero's Wife," which preceded it, Prospero does his best to efface and denigrate women and to appropriate their powers to his own; in this he would seem to mirror the monarch of the time, whose misogyny was accompanied by proclamations of his female creative powers as "nourish-father" to the nation.[8] James I's formulation makes him, at once, nursing mother (*nurse* derives etymologically from Middle English *nourrish*) and father; Prospero's lines to Miranda place him even less equivocally in the female position, as the one with a burdened and delivered womb, while (and perhaps in some tension with the erasure and appropriation of the female) Miranda is in the angelic position, spirit to his matter, strength and fortitude to his tears; she seems not merely responsible for "infusing" him but also for his final erection, as he reports himself "raised" and bearing "up." The lines, therefore, much as they appropriate femaleness (or, more specifically, maternal function)[9] from the woman, also would seem to be giving and taking maleness to and from Miranda. As Orgel remarks, concluding the section of "Prospero's Wife" on "The Marriage Contract," "The women of Shakespeare's plays, of course, are adolescent boys" (57), and, he continues, this may help to explain Shakespeare's identification with nominally female characters; so, in this instance, these gender dislocations might be relocated by remembering the fact that Miranda was played by a boy, that these exchanges between genders are nonetheless exchanges between persons of the same gender.

In the context of such an argument the gendering of Sycorax as male at the moment of her delivery of Caliban mirrors Prospero's seizure of female territory and mirrors as well the stage that Orgel reminds us only appears to offer a world of *he*s and *she*s. Rowe's emendation, then, especially as it is printed by the Vaughans, *[s]he,* nicely brackets and subordinates the female to the male. Their proper bibliographic form is Prospero's plot in small.

And yet: nowhere save in the line Rowe emended is Sycorax anything but female. If the line in the first folio is not a mistake, its "fitness" would not lie along the naturalizing lines that would remind us that under the covers (beneath their costumes) all of Shakespeare's actors were genitally male but, rather, in "fitting" monstrous birth to monstrous womb. Orgel's suggestion that Prospero indulges in a birth fantasy and, by extension, encroaches on female/maternal powers, is borne out and not merely in the lines from 1.2 cited previously. It can be seen in many of the assumptions of his power, whether he is delivering Ariel from a tree (something Sycorax, he claims, could not do, and in which he acts as a midwife in a scene reminiscent of the birth of Adonis from Myrrha, his incestuous mother—"It was mine art, / When I arrived and heard thee, that made gape / The pine and let thee out" [Orgel, 1.2.291–93])—or uttering lines originally spoken by

Ovid's Medea in the monologue in 5.1 that marks his closest moment of identification with Sycorax. If, then, the male gendering of Sycorax is to be explained, one route would lie through the identification of magicians in the play, cutting across the denials that structure Prospero's assumptions (or those of Kermode's Arden introduction, with its detailed discriminations of black and white magic). But it has to be remembered that Prospero has two seemingly opposing but actually congruent gender strategies in the play: one involves strongly marking gender difference and denigrating females (this is especially the case with Sycorax, but it is there when Prospero turns on Miranda and calls her his foot); the other is through the erasure of gender difference, the subsumption of women into his part, as in the lines we have already considered, in order to produce identification. Much as a critic such as Peter Hulme struggles in *Colonial Encounters* to drive a wedge between Prospero's play and *The Tempest*, so too to read the crux about the gender of Sycorax in the lines we have been contemplating as a further instance of the appropriation of female under the sign of male and the erasure of gendered difference is to fold one play into another and thereby to subscribe to a patriarchal phantasm.[10] If, then, one were to treat F1's mistake as not mistaken, it would be with the aim of preserving and exploring what is monstrous in this moment rather than seeing it as part of the way in which Prospero's seamless power overrides all opposition, including gendered difference. A simpler but, I think, equally important point to be made would also be this: the genital identification between adult male actor and boy actor is not necessarily a bottom line; that boys could play women's parts has everything to do with the fact that there was a strong gender identification of boys and women. Boys are only genitally male, although the fact that they are not genitally female must also have meant that their identification with or as women was not based in genital equipment. In other words, it is not a simple matter of looking under the covers to sort the genders in Shakespeare and to reduce them to one. It may be more to the point that the Shakespearean stage offers three genders, that the boys playing women are neither simply male nor simply female.[11]

Sycorax's violation of the biological function that differentiates males and females cannot then be equated with Prospero's violation of that same boundary from the opposite direction. The interchangeability of genders that is the result of the one-gender model that Thomas Laqueur has detailed (and which stands behind the historicizing of gender in a number of New Historicists' thinking, including that of Orgel and Stephen Greenblatt) works, as it were, only in one direction.[12] If, under the covers (beneath the appearance of external difference), women "really" are men (genitally), it is the cover that ensures difference, the social trappings of gender and, in the case of women, the very flesh, that cannot simply be removed (women and men are only the same in the one-gender model at the level of anatomical drawing, at a level of abstraction that does not ramify to the social distinctions maintained between genders). If, at the moment that Sycorax performs the uniquely female act of giving birth and encroaches, in so doing, on territory that Prospero claims for himself, her monstrosity is registered as gender change and recorded in the form that her offspring takes. Were Sycorax to serve as a mirror of Prospero at this moment, it would not be, therefore, in order to bolster the assurance of male power, the subordination and incorporation of the female within the male, but, rather, to suggest something that is quite different. Not the opposite of female monstrosity (for that opposition is included in the masculinist plot) but a monstrosity gendered here as male at the maternal site and even more equivocally in the shape of what is delivered, Caliban. *Is* he human? Is he *properly* male?

I don't know whether such questions vexed Sir Arthur Quiller-Couch and John Dover Wilson in their editorial labors for their 1921 Cambridge edition of the play, but Dover Wilson is quite adamant about the inappropriateness of the lines we have been considering. Here are the lines in the Cambridge edition:

> Then was this island,
> (Save for the son that she did litter here,
> A freckled whelp, hag-born) not honoured with
> A human shape.
> *Ariel.*   Yes: Caliban her son.
> *Prospero.* Dull thing, I say so: he, that Caliban
> Whom now I keep in service.

And here is Dover Wilson's comment on them:

> (1) This passage is a violent digression. (2) Omit it and the context flows straight on. (3) The F. has a comma after "in service," which is absurd. . . . Is it possible to avoid the conclusion that these five lines are an addition, a piece of patchwork, designed to compensate for a rent elsewhere in this section? The reason for their introduction is not far to seek; Caliban is to enter at l. 321, and this is the first mention of his name! (83)

Dover Wilson, as his well-known, argued (unconvincingly to most subsequent editors) that F preserves a text of *The Tempest* reworked for court performance and that this is especially apparent in 1.2, in which Prospero's prolix narrations replace an earlier play that dramatized what he narrates. Nonetheless, this is the only passage that Dover Wilson explicitly and vehemently declares not merely to be awkwardly covering over the earlier text but also to be spurious and in need of excision. All this, I would add, without even addressing the *she/he* problem that is dutifully noted elsewhere in the edition. That is, I assume that it is the monstrous birth of Caliban in this passage that exercises Dover Wilson, an eruption that unnaturally secures his presence at this moment in the dialogue and creates a moment of awkwardness between Prospero and Ariel as they describe the conditions of the island when Prospero arrived to find Ariel confined in a tree. The "violent digression" provokes a violent response: "Omit it," Dover Wilson suggests, make up for "a rent elsewhere" by making another cut here. And to what end? So that the discussion will flow "straight on," and the relationship between Prospero and Ariel will not be interrupted, and (as I have already suggested), even worse, be echoed when the birth of Caliban parallels the birth of Ariel from the tree. So that one might not hear in Prospero's threat to "rend an oak / And peg thee in his knotty entrails" (Orgel, 1.2.294–95) not merely a repetition of Sycorax's act but also of her mode of delivery: the tree to which Prospero would return Ariel is gendered male, and the spot in which Ariel would be confined is "his knotty entrails."

What exercises Dover Wilson here is perhaps more evident in the gloss supplied for 2.2.163–64 (Cambridge edition lineation): "*An abominable monster!* Exclamation perhaps caused by a glimpse of Caliban from behind, as he bends to kiss Stephano's foot." The Vaughans, we might recall, cited the lines describing Caliban's birth in order to argue that, however monstrous Caliban is, he is nonetheless human, and they detail for pages the various configurations that haunt this claim: Caliban as tortoise or fish as well as the more general claims about his bestiality, monstrosity, demonic origins, and the like, not to mention the stage traditions in which Caliban has appeared in various non- or subhuman forms. Nowhere, however, does the play seem to suggest that Caliban is particularly monstrous when seen from the rear, and, although what Dover Wilson presumably has in mind is the degradation and abasement of his offer of service to Stephano (as compared, presumably, with the propriety, in the Cambridge editor's eyes, of his service to Prospero), this political abjection is described in charged physical terms. This is Dover Wilson's fantasy, his glimpsing of a monstrosity that I would, now, be willing to credit—not as a "fact" but, rather, as a consequence of the line of associations that I have been pursuing here: Caliban born from a male mother, a witch, born monstrously and as a monster, born in a manner that is echoed in the threatened return of Ariel to his origins in the entrails of a tree. Caliban, in short, as sodomite.

To make this case one wishes that the conjunction of witchcraft and sodomy had been the subject of sustained historical scrutiny. Arthur Evans's *Witchcraft and the Gay Counterculture*[13] is the only book with these ambitions, and it is deeply flawed by its desire to prove a transhistorical identity between witches and homosexuals as part of an ages-long subversive counterculture. While there is little to be said for this thesis, some of Evans's references to moments in which the two crimes coincide are indisputable, as when, for example, the inquisitors in Avignon in 1582 condemned fornication between men and succubi, women and incubi, as sodomy.[14] As Jeffrey Richards notes in his recent survey of sexual dissidence in the Middle Ages, by the mid-thirteenth century "homosexuality became an inevitable concomitant of accusations of heresy and witchcraft," no doubt thanks in part to the papal bull, *Vox in Rama* (1233), from which he quotes this description of the witches' sabbath: "those present indulge in the most loathsome sensuality, having no regard to sex. If there are more men than women, men satisfy one another's depraved appetites, women do the same for each other."[15] E. William Monter, in his several studies of the Inquisition in various locales during the sixteenth and seventeenth centuries, has supported these linkages, noting, for instance, that of fifty-eight witches convicted in Fribourg in the early seventeenth century eight were condemned as sodomites (there seems to have been no distinction between male witches and sodomites); accusations of witchcraft, sodomy, and infanticide, Monter further concludes, circulate differentially, as ways of policing the category of the "unnatural."[16] What makes this connection easy can be gleaned from one description of a sodomite as someone "committing heresy with his body,"[17] for it suggests how the bodily act of witchcraft that preoccupies Prospero and many other commentators—sex with the devil—might easily overlap with the category of sodomy (not least because witchcraft was most usually a charge leveled against women, sodomy against men). Paul Brown has commented on Prospero's sexual obsessiveness and his desire to regulate others' sexuality, and this feature of the character—the way in which his "project" plays out in the realm of sexual behavior—perhaps bears comparison with the fevered imaginations of those who described the supposed goings-on at the sabbath; as G. R. Quaife summarizes, these scenes regularly included "anal and oral sex, homosexuality, bestiality, mutual masturbation, group sex and incest."[18]

These connections do not exist solely on the Continent and in practices sponsored by the Catholic Church. As Retha Warnicke has pointed out, the first person condemned under the sodomy statute passed in England in 1533 (the statute that made sodomy a felony rather than a matter of church control), Walter Lord Hungerford, was found guilty not only of having sex with his male servants and with his daughter but also of having plotted against the king with the help of witches.[19] This particular configuration is, in certain respects, no surprise: sexual crimes in the period are always linked to state crimes; heresy, in Reformation England, translated into papacy (so much so that the law against sodomy was repealed during Mary's reign), and this, in turn, translates into treason. Warnicke summons up the 1540 case against Hungerford in the context of her study of the fall of Anne Boleyn, and it is her argument that it was the queen's delivery of a monstrous, abortive fetus that sent Anne Boleyn to the block; Warnicke details the "sexual heresy" that surrounded these events, in which charges of incest, adultery, and sodomy (between the queen's supposed lovers), followed upon this monstrous birth. The fetus, that is, represented not only the queen's infidelity to the king—and therefore her treason; the other sexual charges followed upon it and served to explain the monster. We are close here, I think, to the imagination that links the witch Sycorax with the monstrous Caliban.

Here, as with charges of heresy on the Continent, we are not dealing exactly with an equation so much as a relay from witchcraft to sodomy, and indeed with a point of some contention in the literature on witchcraft. For, while the witches' sabbath was often viewed as a feverishly sexual event, there was much debate about whether actual physical union between a (mortal) witch and the devil was possible and, if so, whether such unions were capable of producing offspring. (Reginald Scot, in arguing against these sexual possibilities in *The Discoverie of Witchcraft* [1584], nonetheless provides a fair sampling of the arguments made on both sides.) Even such a debate about the impossibility of such sexual acts must necessarily traffic with notions of sodomy—because they involve acts that frustrated sexual reproduction within marriage (witches were regularly assumed to have the power of causing impotence, often by making a man's penis vanish; the sodomitic wasting of seed or its implantation in improper vessels links to accusations of witchcraft, since it was argued by those who thought that the witch could not have intercourse directly with the devil that human male semen was conveyed by the devil to the witch) or because the sex acts of witches, like those of sodomites accused of bestiality (the charges are not usually distinct), were thought capable of resulting in monstrous births.

In *Homosexuality in Renaissance England* Alan Bray pursues the consequence of these (non)connections, pointing both to the ways in which sodomy overlapped with demonism (in terms of assumptions about destructiveness, heresy, and the like), especially in the "persistent motif that the child of the witch's diabolical union is a sodomite," but also to the ways in which witchcraft and sodomy diverged.[20] One of his main examples for the latter point is, significantly for the discussion here, Michael Drayton's *Moone-Calfe*. The term, of course, is applied repeatedly to Caliban in *The Tempest* to indicate his monstrous, abortive nature. In Drayton's poem the familiar topos of the world, the flesh, and the devil is presented in an allegorical narrative in which the devil fathers on the world monstrous offspring, twins who are masculine-feminines, androgynes and hermaphrodites.[21] The male twin is explicitly a sodomite, and the devil, frightened by the monster (l. 170), appears to share the divine disgust at the sin of Sodom (ll. 317–24). Bray argues that, in so doing, Drayton's devil is expressing a commonplace, that sodomy could be viewed with horror by the devil because it seemed to go beyond even his domain. That is, insofar as demonic offspring were nonetheless the product of heterosexual unions, sodomy suggested a form of sexual relationship that exceeded what was already a kind of demonic parody of proper sex. Strange as this point might seem, it is, in fact, made in the *Malleus Maleficarum,* that handbook of beliefs about witchcraft, in which it is claimed that "nowhere do we read that Incubi and Succubi fell into vices against nature," for sodomy, the writers claim, is a sin of such "very great enormity . . . that all devils, of whatsoever order, abominate and think shame to commit such actions."[22] Sodomy and witchcraft cannot be equated; they touch at a border of abomination and of the unspeakable.

In this context it is worth recalling too that the pregnant wombs of condemned witches were opened to reveal within them horrific and deformed spawn. These assumptions are most fully in play around the trial of Anne Hutchison in early-seventeenth-century New England, in which charges of heresy materialize in her body as well as in her followers', who also are revealed as witches in their abortive and monstrous offspring (one of whom, like Caliban, is described as having horns, claws, and scales). "Mistris Hutchison . . . brought forth not one . . . but . . . 30. monstrous births or thereabouts, at once; some of them bigger, some lesser, some of one shape, some of another; few of any perfect shape, none at all of them (as farre as I could ever learne) of humane shape."[23] Next to this puritan minister's description, Sycorax's "littering" is almost demure and the declaration that her offspring bears a human shape almost humane. Yet he is also insistently called monster and "mooncalf" as she is never anything but a witch—whose crime Prospero cannot name.

If Dover Wilson's recoil at the "abominable monster" is then a recoil at what is most abominable—the sin beyond all others—he turns from ass kissing (metaphorically, to spell out what foot licking means in this scene) to even more unspeakable acts—literalizing in his presumed view of Caliban's bottom the horror that he sees him performing. Ass kissing is of course the devil's kiss, the sign the witch makes of her devotion to her master. It is the sign of a political allegiance, just as Caliban's is. There is, however, another moment in the play that prepares and makes "fit" Dover Wilson's reaction to the abominable monster. Here is how Prospero describes what Antonio did:

>   bend
> The dukedom yet unbowed—alas, poor Milan!—
> To most ignoble stooping.
>
>   (Orgel, 1.2.114–16)

Dover Wilson's gloss on Caliban inadvertently glosses these lines, and the implications here are complex, not least because "Milan" is at once the name of Antonio and of Prospero in the substitution that has as yet not quite differentiated one from the other (as the rightful holder of the name, it is in Prospero's interest not to make that distinction). The lines thus represent the submission of Milan to Naples as either Antonio's voluntary or Prospero's enforced violation. Here Dover Wilson's reading of Caliban's abject position finds a more immediately plausible object; this scene of "ignoble stooping" invites a view from the rear, indeed, suggests that Milan has been taken from behind, mastered anally. Moreover, the connections between sodomy and treason make this implication utterly unexceptionable (not that any editor, so far as I have found, has ever commented on the lines describing Antonio's behavior).[24]

Dover Wilson's reading of the scene of Caliban's submission to Stephano thus ramifies to one way in which betrayal of political propriety is registered in the play as sodomitic submission. It also connects back to the scene of Caliban's origins with which we began. Finally, it connects to the episode in the play that readers of *The Tempest* will recognize as alluded to in the title of this essay, a scene in which Caliban is represented as anally receptive and as anally productive. In 2.2 Trinculo creeps under Caliban's gaberdine. "Misery acquaints a man with strange bedfellows" (Orgel, 2.2.38), he remarks as he does so, using the word that refers to same-sex sleeping partners. Stephano comes across this four-legged figure and assumes that "this is some monster of the isle" (63). Yet the monstrosity here (the term is used over and again in the scene), while initially registered by Trinculo in terms of the animal/human nature of Caliban and by Stephano in terms of the Mandevillian man of Ind, lies in what Stephano finally sees, Trinculo and Caliban making the beast with two backs, "an incarnation of the monstrous in lovemaking" (41), as David Sundelson comments, not distancing himself from what he takes Stephano's attitude to be.[25] Stephano euphemizes the situation when he regards the four-legged creature before him as doubly mouthed, though he marks one mouth as forward and the other as backward. The exchange of mouth and anus here fits nicely with a figure whose name respells *cannibal* and with the colonialist tradition that regarded New World inhabitants as cannibals and sodomites.[26] At the moment when Trinculo emerges at Stephano's command to "come forth" (98; the line echoes Prospero's delivery of Ariel as well as his first command to Caliban [1.2.315]), Stephano asks: "How cam'st thou to be the siege of this mooncalf? Can he vent Trinculos?" (101–2). The excremental vision of birth here also would seem to imagine that Caliban has swallowed Trinculo and now is delivering him whole (Jonah and the whale; Rabelais's experience inside the body of Gargantua). The alimentary canal and the birth canal meet in the fantasy of anal delivery that we have already seen in Prospero's threat to return Ariel to the entrails of the tree from which he was delivered. It is this scene that realizes the mistake about Caliban's origins that the seventeenth-century folios repeated and that Rowe corrected. Here a male mother, the mooncalf who is the abortive and monstrous child of the witch, gives birth anally. Orgel is one of the few editors to at least record that *siege* means excrement and *vent* to defecate. Only George Steevens, in a note to the line in his 1778 edition of the play, registers (phobically, to be sure) any sense of what is going on here: "siege] *Siege* signifies *stool* in every sense of the word, and is here used in the dirtiest."

The scene of male delivery in 2.2, therefore, stages what is implicit in the gendering of Sycorax as male at the moment she is described giving birth to Caliban. While it is not my point here that future editors of *The Tempest* ought to follow the Folio reading, mere notation of Rowe's emendation seems an inadequate response to what, if my argument is convincing, is, at the least, a highly overdetermined error in the Folio text. To simply print *she,* and to adopt Rowe's reading as what the line was supposed to have read, has consequences. For, as I have been suggesting, Prospero traffics in fantasies of male birth, too. That the play realizes these fantasies, doubly, on the body of Caliban (as the one who gives birth and as the one who is so born) represents the kind of deflection and displacement to be found throughout the play: the location of abomination anywhere but in the figure of Prospero.

To suggest some of the further ramifications of the crux that has occasioned this essay, I want to turn now to a *recognized* crux in the play (one that involves textual and sexual issues) and to place beside the problematic *he/she* of 1.2. "a reading whose time has come," to cite the final words of the "bibliographic coda" to Orgel's "Prospero's Wife" (64). Having teased out "the absent, the unspoken," in his essay—instances centering on the suppression of women in the play (and it is my concern now to consider those silences next to the unspeakable terrain that this essay has been exploring)—Orgel ends his essay by endorsing the bibliographic evidence presented by Jeanne Addison Roberts, that Ferdinand's lines during the masque in 4.1., "So rare a wondered father, and a wise, / Makes this place paradise" (the reading to be found in all previous twentieth-century editions of the play), originally read "So rare a wondered father and a wife / Makes this place paradise" (this is the reading adopted in Orgel, 4.1.123–24).[27] Orgel summarizes Roberts's findings in his note to line 123: "early in the print run, the cross-bar of the f broke, transforming 'wife' to 'wise.' Several copies of the Folio show the letter in the process of breaking"; this explains why most copies of the Folio read *wise,* why the variant *wife,* when recorded, has seemed merely a variant, and hence why most modern editions of the play read *wise.* Orgel's endorsement of Roberts's work is made not merely on the bibliographical grounds that *wife* is what the Folio text read originally and authoritatively; it is also part of a "collaborative" effort of the kind that he remarks on throughout his essay, the understanding that what makes for the "rightness" of a reading is never simply the facts but also the climate in which they are available and visible.

Orgel's reading marks a time, then, in which feminist readings allow one to see things that were formerly invisible, and the restoration of *wife* in these lines thus restores Miranda to the scene of celebration. It marks her presence, whereas the traditional reading had absented her from Ferdinand's rapt response, which begins, after all, "Let me live here ever" (4.1.122).

I thoroughly support this reading and find Roberts's bibliographic evidence compelling; nor would I, for a moment, wish to dispute the feminist impulses arguably to be found in her essay (it is not an explicit thematic) and affirmed in Orgel's. Nonetheless, the crux that these lines represent, especially in the context of the argument that I have been presenting here, requires some further consideration. In "Prospero's Wife" Orgel claims that the variant *wife* was lost before Roberts found it: "after 1895 the wife became invisible: bibliographers lost the variant, and textual critics consistently denied its existence until Roberts pointed it out" (64). This is not, in fact, quite true, and therefore there is a question of choice in twentieth-century editions, for the variant *is* recorded (e.g., in Morton Luce's 1901 Arden edition; in Northrop Frye's Penguin text);[28] it is simply not adopted. Kermode has it both ways: he places a question mark after noting the variant and recommends "further inquiry" but ends his gloss by commenting that "the true reading may be *wife* after all." Kermode does not have before him the evidence that Roberts did; he relies, instead, on the easy mistake of *f* and long *s* in the printing process and, lacking hard evidence, can only allow *wife* in his note, not in the text. Furness in the 1892 variorum edition of the play cites with approval one Grant White who opines that to print *wife* here would "degrade the poetical feeling of the passage" and then goes on to make the revealing comment that in his own copy of F he cannot tell by looking whether the line reads *wife* or *wise;* how he comes to print *wise* fully supports Orgel's contention that we see only what we are prepared to see. "Personally," Furness writes, "seeing that I much prefer *wise*, I incline to believe that it is 'wise' in my copy." Presumably, editors after Furness who print *wise* have shared his preference.

What preference is this, however? Not the one Kermode records in his note: "we may think that in this Adam-like situation, Ferdinand must have said *wife*," nor the preference to be found in all eighteenth-century editions, from Rowe on, which, in fact, print *wife*. Rowe probably did not emend the line on the basis of consultation of a folio text that read *wife;* his emendation was made on what Orgel in "Prospero's Wife" calls "logical grounds" (63), the logic, presumably, that Kermode suggests: that it is difficult to believe that at the moment of his betrothal, and in the context of a declaration of a desire to live in paradise forever, Ferdinand would not include Miranda in this sentiment.

It is this logic, however, coupled with the fact that eighteenth-century editors invariably print *wife,* that must lead us to ask what time has come when the line reads *wife* in Orgel's edition. Eighteenth-century editors, who assumed that Shakespeare wrote *wise,* were not restoring his intended meaning but were, instead, modernizing the text, indeed, in ways that I would argue parallel the normalizing of gender that Rowe first performed in assigning a feminine pronoun to Sycorax at the moment of her delivery of Caliban. The eighteenth-century readings of the play, that is, are not feminist interventions; they put *wife* there to ensure the domestic relationship and the propriety of Ferdinand's remarks. They make the wife present in order to police the male-male relations between Ferdinand and Prospero; Ferdinand's celebration of his "father" is only saved from excess within the context of marriage. This must be granted at least as a caveat against the assumption that restoring *wife* restores the woman to the text; *wife* is not Miranda's name but her function. While she has been given the illusion that she has freely chosen Ferdinand, she marries him as part of her father's designs. (Ferdinand is Prospero's choice, and it is his desire that his daughter enacts and legitimizes.) As Orgel astutely argues, Prospero's aim in marrying them serves to legitimize what Antonio did, placing Milan beneath Naples; now Milan will not fall to "ignoble stooping" because of the marriage alliance. What this further ensures is the propriety of male-male relations and manages the hierarchy between Naples and Milan by having the woman come between the men. What Rowe and his followers presumably heard in Ferdinand's lines as they were presumed to appear in the folio was the admission that Ferdinand's desire for Prospero repeated Antonio's for Alonso.

This "danger" is not entirely removed when the correct reading is restored. "And a wife" is, at best, an addition, and "so rare a wondered" seems primarily, if not exclusively, to refer to Prospero; as "wife," Miranda is in the lines but not named, and she is clearly in a subordinate relationship to her husband-to-be and to her father. Moreover, as Orgel notes, as do other editors as well, *wondered,* as an adjective describing Prospero, echoes Miranda's name, which is subject to such punning elsewhere in the play. If *wondered* means someone who can produce wonders, then Prospero's magic show and his magical daughter are equated: they are both wonders that he produces. What Ferdinand is celebrating in the lines is Prospero's art and his production of a child, his male maternity. Miranda is, as it were, already in the phrase "rare a wondered," and her separation out in "and a wife" is almost as redundant and self-referential as the line would be if it read "and a wise." Putting the wife in the line—as presumably Shakespeare did—hardly ensures her independence or her existence outside of patriarchal arrangements being celebrated here as Prospero hands her over to his chosen son-in-law.

The difference between eighteenth-century texts and the original Folio reading "and a wife" is that Rowe and his followers presumably believed that, by supplying the wife, the intensity of the male-male bond had been diluted and made acceptable, whereas F does not quite have those guarantees. In the sex/gender system in which Shakespeare writes, the choice between male and female lovers is not an exclusive one, as it comes to be in the eighteenth century; the fact that in these lines these two relations come together as one, and that the emphasis is on the father (he gets the adjectives, he comes first in Ferdinand's utterance), is marked too by the verb form *makes:* father and wife are here a single entity. Rowe and subsequent eighteenth-century editors emend *makes* to *make;* this separation, this grammatical propriety of making father and wife two subjects, furthers the work of heterosexual propriety. Shakespeare's more fluid grammar cannot be taken unequivocally to be making father and wife a single subject, but it cannot be ruled out either.

Hence, the modern reinsertion of *wife* in this line does not by itself mean that some time of enlightened gender relations has necessarily come when the woman is put back in the lines. Now, of course, that is not Orgel's argument either; it is only within a certain climate of reading that the line would have feminist force. But, to my mind, it is not enough simply to get Miranda back into this line; a feminist reading of the lines might well involve a critique of the limits under which the woman appears here (as that appendage called wife) and might seek to underscore the work that heterosexual arrangement is being called upon to do: that is, to make acceptable male arrangements that might otherwise give (homophobic) critics pause. The lines, of course, also have a caution for the gay critic; to note that F here marks the difference between the properly homosocial and the overcharged and dangerously sodomitic (which it seeks to situate everywhere but in Prospero's relations with men) through the body of a woman means that one cannot simply celebrate Shakespearean sexuality for the ways in which it takes male-male and male-female relations in stride, as complementary and not as mutually exclusive. There are hierarchies of power in these lines, between father and children, between men and women. To Ferdinand's ecstatic lines Prospero replies, "Sweet, now, silence!" a gentle and affectionate command at which some editors have balked (Dover Wilson assigns the line to Miranda), although Orgel quite usefully points out that men do call one another sweet in Shakespeare.

Dover Wilson refuses to print this display of male-male affection, but like all other modern editors, he prints *wise* here too (the "variant" *wife* does not appear in the Cambridge edition). This returns us to a question raised earlier: why modern editors have preferred *wise* to *wife;* not, presumably, because it allows the eros of the situation between Prospero and Ferdinand to be registered. Indeed, when Grant White claimed that printing *wife* would constitute a "degradation" of "poetic feeling," I think that one can see that the presence of *wife* for him would necessarily introduce a sexual element and thus mar poetic feeling between men, which presumably cannot ever be supposed to have an erotic component. Here Kermode's remark on the Adam-like situation of Ferdinand-in-paradise could be further glossed. In his line Prospero is, as it were, the sole source of Miranda, just as in the biblical myth woman comes from man. This is the paradisial version of what, were Sycorax male, would be the abomination of Caliban's monstrous birth, and it is a component of the version of misogyny that led Marvell to write that "Two Paradises 'twere in one / To live in Paradise alone" ("The Garden," ll. 63–64) and, indeed, of the ages-long Christian tradition that lays the blame of the Fall on woman and yearns for the time before the creation of Eve when Adam's only playmate was his creator. White's recoil at *wife* is a response to these yearnings for a paradise of male solitude. Kermode's more tempered remark about Ferdinand in paradise participates in eighteenth-century normativizing heterosexualization. The time that has come when *wife* appears in these lines certainly disputes the virulent misogyny of White; it remains in danger, however, of simply reproducing heterosexuality, thus also insisting upon limits for women (they were meant for marriage) and for men (their relations could not ever be sexual ones).

It thus seems necessary to recognize the limits of interventions in the name of feminism or of gay affirmation that can be made by way of the Shakespearean text; nonetheless, within its modest limit as a political move, Orgel's restoration of *wife* and his declaration that it is a reading whose time has come would utterly unexceptionable. Could anyone after Orgel print *wise?* The answer, of course, is yes. As a brief bibliographic coda to this essay, I turn to the single-volume Shakespeare produced for Oxford by Gary Taylor and Stanley Wells at the same moment that Orgel was preparing his Oxford edition of *The Tempest*. In that edition, 4.1.123 of *The Tempest* reads *wise,* and John Jowett provides the explanation for that decision in the 1987 textual commentary for the edition. His note is worth reprinting here:

> Roberts . . . showed that there was progressive damage to the crossbar of "f" during printing. Error is none the less so easy that the matter does not end there. Whereas previous critics were divided as to what F actually read, almost all preferred "wise" as the more convincing reading. F's pararhyme is suspicious; *wise/paradise* is a Shakespearian rhyme. "Wife" gives trite sense and demands two grammatical licences: that "So rare a wondered" is extended to qualify "a wife," and that "Makes" has a plural subject.[29]

This is an extraordinary note. Though it starts seemingly by accepting Roberts's findings, it immediately introduces an unspecified sense of "error." One presumes that Jowett has in mind something like Kermode's note on how easily *f* and long *s* can be confused in the printing process; what's extraordinary here, then, is that Jowett appears to accept the fact that F originally read *wife* but also wants to entertain the possibility that it did so in error (presumably as a compositor's error). Thus, even though what Roberts saw really did happen, that is beside the point.

I assume here that what would normally be accounted a strong bibliographical demonstration on Roberts's part is being policed precisely because of the context that Orgel adduces—that this was bibliographic work done with a feminist agenda (it hardly needs to be pointed out that the field of bibliography has been and remains still heavily male dominated). Although Jowett's category of error is the closest he comes to making a bibliographic objection to Roberts, the logic of his claim would lead to an undermining of any bibliographic protocols. If any reading of a text could be in error (and, of course, any can), then the textual/bibliographic evidence, even when it is uncontrovertible (as it is that F originally read *wife*), only can be subject to interpretation. It is, then, presumably (though this is unstated) the "bias" in Roberts's presumed interpretive stance that leads Jowett on.

Having established *wife/wise* as variants (rather than *wife* as the reading, *wise* as a variant produced by mechanical breakdown), Jowett appeals to "previous critics." Here, as with "error," who or what is involved goes unspecified; it is not really a matter of criticism that is being determined here but of editorial practice, and the overwhelming numbers ("almost all") mobilized on the side of *wise* represent only twentieth-century editors. Here, then, Jowett relies upon editors who have seen the folio with their own eyes, one supposes, editors with proper bibliographic training. With one hand, in his opening sentence, he has removed any support for bibliography as some kind of standard in making editorial decisions; now he relies on "proper" modern editors as giving him support for *wise* as the more convincing reading. *Convincing* is, of course, a question-begging term; convincing in terms of the bibliographic evidence? Surely not, unless the fact that more copies of F read *wise* than *wife* (which must be true) is taken as constituting a bibliographic fact. Convincing from some critical predisposition? Presumably, but that is not where the note concludes. Rather, on questions of what is genuinely Shakespearean at the level of writing practice.[30] Yet one must suspect any claims to know what is Shakespearean, especially, as here, when the rhyme is so heavily loaded semantically. *Wise* and *paradise* presumably rhyme for Jowett because they are not trite words nor off-rhymes; Jowett's "pararhyme" is a technical term that sneaks in *para;* it makes Jowett's explanation rhyme. What Jowett wants is that things alike be joined. Wives are trite. In the high masculine world of wise thoughts and enclosed gardens (the male world of the textual/ bibliographic police), wives and women have no place. Let Jeanne Roberts beware. Shakespeare or the police: no grammatical licences allowed here.

The licences, however, are extraordinary; on the one hand, Jowett is probably right that "rare a wondered" does not extend to *wife*—this is the only moment where Jowett's reading coincides with my own, and it points to the limits, as I've remarked, of reclaiming the line and *wife* in the name of feminism (indeed, here one could say that Jowett won't have *wife* because, if the word were there, it would show that Shakespeare did not have a properly modern, egalitarian view of women). The point about *makes,* I have addressed already. It's amazing that a Shakespearean editor has not noticed how often Shakespeare's subjects and verbs do not agree; has not noticed, that is, that Shakespeare had not learned eighteenth-century grammar. For, of course, what is remarkable about Jowett's note is that it goes beyond the eighteenth-century editors (who presumably don't count when he conjures up the previous critics) in demanding from the lines grammatical propriety of the kind Rowe and his followers provided by making *makes* into *make.* In short, much as Jowett's reading is motivated by an animus against Roberts and the collaborative efforts that Orgel endorses in positing the time that has come, his eighteenth-century editorial procedures (he does not rely on F as his copy-text here; he relies on the weight of tradition; he expects Shakespeare to use modern grammar) are *also* aimed at a propriety of gendered relations. Because a wife should be praised at least as much as a father-in-law and should be an independent subject (and not just grammatically), the line must read *wise*. Otherwise, Shakespeare might have been a misogynist and a patriarchal poet. Jowett's reading, then, is *also* a product of the time that has come.

The question, then, of the reading whose time has come is complicated if, as I've been demonstrating, Jowett's regressive reading of "So rare a wondered father, and a wise" and Orgel's progressive reading of "So rare a wondered father, and a wife" founder on the divisions that I've been tracing. But these also suggest the resources of the present, the possibility of mobilizations that would not be available were the present a self-identical moment and were futurity therefore impossible except as some continuation of a monolithic present. That even Jowett's reading is legible as a kind of feminism is, however troubling, also an encouraging sign, for it translates the site of contention to divisions within feminism and thus to a terrain upon which a rethinking of social relations is possible. The masculinist bias in his preference for *wise* returns us, I would conclude, to the complex divisions between homosocial relations that Jowett's reading affirms and to homosexual possibilities, relegated, once again, to the margins but now, I would hope, not therefore to remain under the covers.

NOTES

1. See Eve Kosofsky Sedgwick, *Epistemology of the Closet* (Berkeley: University of California Press, 1990), chap. 1, 75–76.
2. Alden T. Vaughan and Virginia Mason Vaughan, *Shakespeare's Caliban: A Cultural History* (Cambridge: Cambridge University Press, 1991), 10. Rowe's edition of Shakespeare appeared in 1709.
3. Yet, as Peter Hulme points out in *Colonial Encounters* (London: Routledge, 1986), the lines admit Caliban's humanity by way of "an eminently misreadable double negative" (114); as Hulme notes, in addition to Caliban's bestial/demonic/human forms in various descriptions of him, he figures as "a man and not a man according to Miranda's calculations" (107).
4. Matthew W. Black and Matthias A. Shaaber, *Shakespeare's Seventeenth-Century Editors, 1632–1685* (New York: Modern Language Association, 1937), 95.
5. Frank Kermode, ed., *The Tempest* (London: Methuen, 1954); I cite the lemma to 1.2.282. The original Arden edition, ed. Morton Luce (London: Methuen, 1901), fails to record the *he/she* emendation.

6. Here are the texts in question:

> Then was this island
> (Save for the Sunne that he did littour heere,
> A frekelld whelpe, hag-borne) not honour'd with
> A humane shape.

(F2 1632)

> Then was this Island
> (Save for the Sun that he did littour here.
> A frekelld whelp, hag-born) not honour'd with
> A humane shape.

(F3 1664)

> Then was this Island
> (Save for the Sun that he did littour here.
> A frekel'd whelp, hag-born) not honour'd with
> A human shape.

(F4 1685)

7. See Stephen Orgel, intro., *The Tempest*, ed. S. Orgel (Oxford: Clarendon Press, 1987), 18–19; as well as his essay "Prospero's Wife," in *Rewriting the Renaissance*, ed. Margaret Ferguson, Maureen Quilligan, and Nancy Vickers (Chicago: University of Chicago Press, 1985), 54.

8. James I, *Basilikon Doron*, as discussed in Jonathan Goldberg, *James I and the Politics of Literature* (Baltimore: Johns Hopkins University Press, 1983), 141–43.

9. For a pertinent critique, within the context of historical/critical accounts of witchcraft in the Renaissance, of a dehistoricizing reduction of questions of femininity to questions of the mother in psychoanalytically inflected feminist criticism, see Karen Newman, *Fashioning Femininity and English Renaissance Drama* (Chicago: University of Chicago Press, 1991), chap. 4.

10. It is just such a fantasy of male genius that governs Peter Greenaway's *Prospero's Books*, during which Gielgud (as Prospero) recites everyone's lines.

11. For an argument congruent with this one, see Ann Rosalind Jones and Peter Stallybrass, "Fetishizing Gender: Constructing the Hermaphrodite in Renaissance Europe," in *Body Guards*, ed. Julia Epstein and Kristina Straub (New York: Routledge, 1991), which concludes that fixing gender on genitals is an eighteenth-century development and that, in the Renaissance, gender could be located elsewhere—their final examples include other body parts such as the mouth (which will be important for the argument that follows) or clothing as sites of gender identification.

12. See Thomas Laqueur, *Making Sex* (Cambridge: Harvard University Press, 1990); and the use of Laqueur's model in Stephen Greenblatt, *Shakespearean Negotiations* (Berkeley: University of California Press, 1988), chap. 3; and in Stephen Orgel, "Nobody's Perfect: Or Why Did the English Stage Take Boys for Women?" *SAQ* 88 (1989): 7–29.

13. Arthur Evans, *Witchcraft and the Gay Counterculture* (Boston: Fag Rag Books, 1978).

14. Evans depends here on Henry Charles Lea, *Materials toward a History of Witchcraft*, ed. A. C. Howland, 3 vols. (Philadelphia: University of Pennsylvania Press, 1939), 2:485: "vos viri cum succubis and [*sic*] vos mulieres cum incubis fornicati estis, Sodomiam veram et nefandissium crimen misere cum illis tactu frigidissimo exercuistis."

15. Jeffrey Richards, *Sex, Dissidence and Damnation* (London: Routledge, 1991), 143.

16. E. William Monter, *Witchcraft in France and Switzerland: The Borderlands during the Reformation* (Ithaca: Cornell University Press, 1976), 136, 198. A similar view of the relationship between sodomy and witchcraft accusations is offered by Guido Ruggiero (*The Boundaries of Eros: Sex Crime and Sexuality in Renaissance Venice* [New York: Oxford University Press, 1985], 140), who regards the two crimes as parallel instances of the policing of "the normal and the abnormal"; in a note he further speculates on the relationship and distribution of these accusations (196 n. 135).

17. Cited in William Monter, *Frontiers of Heresy: The Spanish Inquisition from the Basque Lands to Sicily* (Cambridge: Cambridge University Press, 1990), 280. Monter details executions for sodomy and for witchcraft in separate chapters of this study but does not draw connections between them.

18. Paul Brown, "'This thing of darkness I acknowledge mine': *The Tempest* and the Discourse of Colonialism," in *Political Shakespeare*, ed. Jonathan Dollimore and Alan Sinfield (Ithaca: Cornell University Press, 1985). G. R. Quaife, *Godly Zeal and Furious Rage: The Witch in Early Modern Europe* (London: Croom Helm, 1987), 99; Quaife continues by referring to one claim that the devil had a three-pronged penis, thus "permitting him to engage in coitus, sodomy and fellatio simultaneously." In his reviews of previous scholarship he notes those who have thought of witchcraft prosecutions as policing nonheterosexual relations, whether among women or among men. For further documentation of witchcraft involving anal sex with the devil, see Jeffrey Russell, *Witchcraft in the Middle Ages* (Ithaca: Cornell University Press, 1960), 391. John Boswell (*Christianity, Social Tolerance, and Homosexuality* [Chicago: University of Chicago Press, 1980], 235) has a passing consideration of the witchcraft/sodomy/heresy nexus.

19. Retha M. Warnicke, *The Rise and Fall of Anne Boleyn* (Cambridge: Cambridge University Press, 1989), 194.

20. Alan Bray, *Homosexuality in Renaissance England* (London: Gay Mens Press, 1982), 21; Bray turns to Drayton on the following page.

21. Michael Drayton, "The Moone-Calfe," ll. 178, 190, in vol. 3 of *The Works of Michael Drayton*, ed. J. William Hebel, 5 vols. (Oxford: Basil Blackwell, 1932).

22. Heinrich Kramer and James Sprenger, *Malleus Maleficarum*, trans. Montague Summers (1928; reprint, New York: Dover, 1971), 30.

23. Thomas Weld, a minister, cited by Carol F. Karlsen, *The Devil in the Shape of a Woman* (New York: Vintage Books, 1989), 17–18. As Karlsen comments and goes on to cite Weld further to this point, the monstrous births were seen as the

analogues to the monstrous beliefs of Hutchison and her followers. Such accusations against witches are a particular instance of the phenomenon that Marie-Hélène Huet studies in *Monstrous Imagination* (Cambridge: Harvard University Press, 1993), in which the monstrous imagination of the mother is said to be responsible for deformed offspring. This phenomenon is also discussed in Audrey Eccles, *Obstetrics and Gynaecology in Tudor and Stuart England* (Kent, Ohio: Kent State University Press, 1982), who also notes that sodomy and bestiality were among the supposed causes of deformed offspring (65).

24. David Sundelson, in "So Rare a Wonder'd Father: Prospero's *Tempest*," in *Representing Shakespeare,* ed. Murray M. Schwartz and Coppélia Kahn (Baltimore: Johns Hopkins University Press, 1980), does, although the lines are adduced in the context of Prospero's "impotence" in Milan (35); Sundelson does note how, once on the island, Prospero assumes paternal and maternal powers.

25. Sundelson, "So Rare a Wonder'd Father," 41. As he continues to explicate this scene, he reads the greedy mouth as making a female demand and the scene of venting as a parody of childbirth and an expression of female loathing; while the latter point is not to be denied, I don't think one can simply collapse this scene onto a female body.

26. On the former point, see Hulme, *Colonial Encounters;* for the latter, see Jonathan Goldberg, *Sodometries* (Stanford: Stanford University Press, 1992), pt. 3.

27. See Jeanne Addison Roberts, "'Wife' or 'Wise'—*The Tempest* 1.1786," *Studies in Bibliography* 31 (1978): 203–8.

28. Frye notes at 4.1.123 that "some copies of F read 'wife'" (Baltimore: Penguin Books, 1959).

29. Stanley Wells and Gary Taylor, with John Jowett and William Montgomery, *William Shakespeare: A Textual Companion* (Oxford: Clarendon Press, 1987), 616.

30. One could compare here the note in Luce's 1901 Arden edition, which, as ambivalent as Kermode's, prints *wise* and yet seems in the note to prefer *wife;* one of the arguments in the note is that "the rhyme of Paradise with wise is a blemish, and it could hardly have been intentional."

Adaptation as Edition

Jonathan Bate and Sonia Massai

Recent scholarly editions of Shakespeare's works generally reveal a peculiar interest in those aspects of a playtext that are specifically theatrical, such as the position of stage directions, the legitimacy of the traditional five-act division, the dramatic potentiality of the dialogue, and the influence of stage conventions on the reception of a play. This interest in performance as an essential element in the interpretation of a play is unprecedented in the history of the textual-critical approaches to Shakespeare of the last few centuries. A shift from stage to page was crucial to the development of Shakespearean editing in the early eighteenth century: Restoration "acting editions," which, as Jay Halio has noted,[1] made the comparison between scripts and texts very simple, were replaced by "scholarly texts" and "school editions," which for two hundred and fifty years predominated over, if not altogether effaced, theatrically inspired editions.

Though the recent shift away from "armchair" back to "theater-centered" criticism has helped to dispel this deep-rooted prejudice against the influence of the stage on play writing, theatrical adaptation, the most visible consequence of the necessity for a dramatic text to submit and conform to mutable stage conventions, still remains a relatively unexplored area within Shakespearean studies. What concerns or mythologies keep adaptations at the margin of contemporary critical discourse? Our impression is that a certain, now questionable, concept of authorship is the most likely reason why critics find it so difficult to include adaptations within the scope of their analyses. The figure of the author is still very powerful, and the further a text departs from the author's holograph, the more marginal and negligible it becomes to the critic's attention. Editing is particularly affected by this prejudice, in that the editor's task is generally identified with the recovery of a partially lost original: a transcendental drive leads editors to try and fill the gap left by the disappearance of the natural author at the center of his work.

Yet, as recent theorists have repeatedly argued, the concept of a single, God-like author is particularly inappropriate when applied to a Renaissance playtext.[2] Within the realm of fiction, drama is the textually least stable genre: play writing does not derive from a solitary act of creation but is, instead, the result of a collaborative effort between the playwright and his company, which reaches its natural completion only through performance. The fruition of a playtext takes place through an endless process of rewriting, revision, and adaptation, carried out by editors, adaptors, and directors. The existence of the text is perpetuated and modified in theaters and educational institutions long after its author is no more.

Once the lopsided, restrictive conception of authorship is overcome, or at least substantially qualified, there remains no reason why editors should defer exclusively to early documents and previous scholarly editions, at the expense of what may then be seen as only superficially "marginal," derivative texts. This essay will be devoted to a demonstration of the practical advantages that might derive from a close, systematic investigation of theatrical adaptations.

It has already been convincingly argued that derivative texts can help critics to increase their awareness of the original, in that adaptors, by rearranging the play to impose their own perspective on it, make Shakespeare's own perspective more evident by contrast. Norman Rabkin, for example, defines theatrical adaptation/redaction as the dramatic alter ego of critical exegesis. Jay Halio, despite setting himself the "conservative" task of seeking a rationale for the assessment of the extent to which "Shakespeare's adaptations can be said to be still Shakespeare's," admits that theatrical adaptations have an important role in the general interpretation of a playtext: "By shifting the focus and removing some parts of the text, directors may help us to see more clearly some aspects of the play that otherwise may remain hidden or obscure." Similarly, Alan C. Dessen acknowledges that the changes introduced by directors and adaptors "can serve as major clues to what separates us from the age of Shakespeare and can even help to pinpoint the distinctive vision of a particular play."[3] But theatrical adaptations may be of great help to textual critics too: adaptors, like editors, at least up to the early 1980s, had to deal with two conflicting early texts of such plays as *King Lear* and decide which variant passages are better and, therefore, worth retaining; adaptors, like editors, when faced with highly variant passages, have to make "editorial" decisions to create their own "scripts."

One might object that, while the editor's aim is to restore what the author originally wrote, adaptors tend to impose their own readings on the play and that their choices therefore have no authority whatever. The problem with this objection is that, despite great advances in methods and technical equipment, editing still remains a tendentious practice: any edition is a translation, a rewriting, whether or not there is an overt claim to be restoring the author's original intentions. As Margreta de Grazia has argued, the theoretical assumptions underlying any textual practice—that is, the "apparatus"—inevitably affect the way in which a text is received by its audience and, ultimately, the very quality of the text itself; the apparatus is precisely what makes reproduction possible by

> retrieving or translating the alien past of a text's inception into the familiar present of its reception. The apparatus makes it possible for a text to come back—to make a comeback—on conditions it both prescribes and instantiates. In reproducing a text, in making it again available and accessible, the apparatus dictates the terms of its reception. . . . In determining the text's identity the apparatus predisposes the reader to specific modes of reading and understanding.[4]

Editors and adaptors, usually considered as two distinct figures, are in fact very similar: they both actively interact with a playtext to adjust it to the different exigencies of the receiving audience—respectively, a theater audience and a small group of Renaissance scholars and cultivated readers. The former expect good playscripts and good drama, the latter "authoritative" texts. Neither text, however, necessarily coincides with what the author originally wrote.

One might then raise a second objection: adaptors rely on no more solid ground than their own taste, or their own theatrical sensitivity, to choose between two variant readings. This objection is again easily met: even the assumedly objective methods first introduced by the New Bibliographers in the early 1940s, such as paleographical or "type-recurrence" studies, have fallen short of the great expectations they aroused when first applied to playtexts such as *King Lear*. By now scholars are well aware that "the textual bibliographer," as Paul Werstine puts it, cannot "assume the role of Neoplatonic philosopher, intent on stripping away the veil of print from the extant texts of *Lear* to reveal the manuscripts behind these texts in their pristine forms."[5] Too many years have elapsed since the original texts were released to the press: very few copies have survived, and too little information about their origins has come down to us. Any sure link is definitively lost. The editor's critical judgment has always been, and remains, the primary element in the editing of variants. Later adaptations and adaptors' editing of quarto/folio (Q/F) variants may therefore contribute to improving our awareness of the different theatrical potentialities of Q and F texts, thus helping editors to exert their own judgment more critically.

The greatest virtue of the 1986 Oxford Shakespeare was the way in which Stanley Wells, Gary Taylor, and their associates edited with a much sharper sense of the plays as theatrical working scripts than nearly all their predecessors had done. Their willing acknowledgment of textual revision was the most obvious manifestation of this sense: the moment a text is seen as raw material for performance rather than the finished product of a literary genius, the idea that it is provisional rather than definitive, that it is open to reworking, becomes a matter of common sense. It will, however, be our contention here that, despite their strictures against the "anti-theatrical prejudice" of previous editors, Wells and Taylor are not without a particular antitheatrical prejudice themselves.

This prejudice may be seen in a remark of Gary Taylor's in the general introduction to the *Textual Companion* to the edition: "The editing of Shakespeare began with the publication of the first editions of his work in the 1590s, but literary historians usually regard Nicholas Rowe as Shakespeare's first editor, perhaps because he is the first we can confidently name."[6] The account then proceeds with a familiar genealogy of editions: Rowe, Pope, Theobald, Warburton, Johnson, Capell, Steevens, Malone. The implication is that it was the succession of eighteenth-century editors for the closet who established our inherited sense of what is involved in the transmission of Shakespearean texts. In this account, as in all others of which we are aware, it is assumed that the activities that editors still undertake began with the line that ran from Rowe to Malone: the modernization of spelling, the introduction of stage directions in the many places in which they are lacking in the early printed texts, the drawing up of a list of dramatis personae,[7] and, that highest of all editorial activities, the collation of quarto and folio variants, in which alternative readings are scrupulously weighed and the "better" of them is enshrined in the edited text.

But all these activities are apparent in editions printed before that of Rowe. And one can "confidently name" some of the editors: they include Friedrich Menius, Edward Ravenscroft, Nahum Tate, John Dryden, William Davenant, and Colley Cibber. The English names are, of course, familiar—but as *adaptors* rather than editors. And that is why they have been neglected in accounts of the editorial tradition: they were only theatrical hacks, they "butchered" the texts, so we needn't pay any attention to them. But is it not the theoretical consequence of Wells and Taylor's arguments about the theatrical nature of the early texts that the rigid distinction between edition and adaptation no longer stands? Are not all editions adaptations? Is it not likely that some part of the revision of *King Lear* was made by Shakespeare's company in the theater when he was not present? If so, is the difference between the Q to F revision and the Q/F to Tate revision then one of degree, not of kind? And, even if we wish to retain our faith in the possibility of providing an edition of some kind of "original" text, whether a version of the author's foul papers or of the promptbook of the play's first performance, then at the very least, if an emendation that seems to recover some feature of that text was first made by a Restoration adaptor, why should the textual apparatuses of scholarly editions continue to ascribe that innovation to Rowe or some other eighteenth-century editor?

The first textual note in J. C. Maxwell's Arden edition of *Titus Andronicus* refers to the dramatis personae and says, "First given imperfectly by Rowe." And yet the verso of the title page of Edward Ravenscroft's *Titus Andronicus, or The Rape of Lavinia,* which predates Rowe by some twenty-two years, gives us the extremely serviceable list that is reproduced here (fig.1). It is serviceable not least in its English heading—"The Persons Names" is a great deal more "modern" than the Arden's "Dramatis Personae"—and in its method of organization. As in many modern theater programs, it is arranged by "team," Romans versus Goths, which helps one to see the basic structure of the play. It puts Tamora in her proper place at the head of the Goth team, whereas in the tradition that runs from Rowe to Maxwell's Arden she's down at the bottom with all the other women, below even Messenger, Clown, and anonymous Goths and Romans. Ravenscroft's list is also informative about family relations, rank (note its careful enumeration of military captains, senators, tribunes, plebeians, and imperial guards), and dramatic function (Alarbus is noted as "A Mute"). The spelling of names is also true to the earliest edition: the figure whom we call Aaron is Aron, as he always is in the quartos and sometimes is in the folio;

The Perfons Names.

ROMANS.

Saturninus, }	} Sons of the Deceas'd
Baffianus, }	} Emperour.
Titus Andronicus,	An Old Roman General.
Marcus Andronicus,	A Tribune, Brother to Titus.
Emillius,	A Tribune.
Lucius, }	
Mutius, }	
Martius, }	The Sons of Titus.
Quintus, }	
Junius,	Son of Lucius, a Child.
Lavinia,	Daughter of Titus.

A Roman Captain, Other Captains, Senators, Tribunes,
Plebeans, and Guards. A Dead Son of Titus.

GOTHS.

Tamora,	Queen of Goths.
Alarbus, }	A Mute.
Chiron, }	The Queens Sons.
Demetrius, }	
Aron,	{ A Moor in favour with Tamora,
	{ and her General.
	A Common Souldier.

A Goth,
His Wife.
A Blackamoor Infant.
   All brought Captives to Rome by Titus.

The Scene ROME.

Fig. 1. *Dramatis Personae* in Ravenscroft's adaptation of *Titus Andronicus*
(1687).

Emillius is Emillius, as in quartos and folio, not Aemilius, as he became in Rowe and all subsequent editions. The Arden third edition restores Emillius;[8] there was a strong editorial temptation to restore Aron too, but in the end folio's Aaron (itself a kind of modernization of spelling) was retained in order to assist the modern reader to hear the wordplay in such lines as "*Aaron,* I see thou wilt not trust the *air* / With secrets."[9] Certain features of Ravenscroft's list pertain to his rewriting: Titus's grandson is renamed Junius to avoid the confusion of having two generations of Luciuses, the Goth and his wife mentioned by Aaron as potential foster parents for his child are actually brought onstage, the invading Goth army is excluded (possibly for similar political reasons to those which led Tate to exclude the invading French army from his *Lear*). But, even if these alterations are viewed as excrescences, that does not invalidate the list as a whole.

Turning to the text of the play itself, careful examination of Ravenscroft's version reveals that he based it on thorough collation of Q2 and F1, with a marked preference for the readings of Q2. This may be demonstrated from the very first stage direction: "*Enter* Saturninus *and his Followers:* Bassianus *and his, at another door. With Drums and Trumpets.* Senators *above in the Capitoll.*"[10] The quartos do not indicate a door for Bassianus and his followers; the folio has "at the other," the source of Ravenscroft's "at another door." But the folio has "Drum and Colours"; Ravenscroft's "Drums and Trumpets" are from the first or second quarto (third quarto is ruled out since it has a singular *drum*). The opening speech of the play also conflates the early texts: line five follows the quartos' "I am his first borne sonne" (with spelling modernized to "first-born Son") rather than folio's "I was the first borne Sonne," whereas line 6 follows folio's "Wore the Imperial Diadem" rather than the quartos' *Ware*.

Later variants reveal that Ravenscroft used a copy of the second quarto, not the first.[11] The rarity of the first quarto is probably a mark of its popularity: it appears to have been virtually read into disintegration until a single copy turned up in Sweden in 1904, revealing, among other things, that the last four lines of the play in every edition from Rowe's until then were an editorial addition. A responsible modern edition must omit Q2's concluding moralization,

See iustice done on Aron that damn'd Moore,
By whom our heauie haps had their beginning:
Than afterwards to order well the state,
That like euents may nere it ruinate.

Occasionally, where Q2 was corrupt, Rowe and later editors conjecturally emended to readings, which were then confirmed as correct by the discovery of Q1. But Rowe was not the first in this. For example, in Titus's image of "Looking all downwards to behold our cheeks, / How they are stained like meadows yet not dry" (3.1.125–26), Q2, Q3, and F had "in Meadowes," but Ravenscroft (30) by good conjecture altered his copy-text's *in* to *like*.

A clutch of emendations that textual apparatuses traditionally attribute to Rowe and other later editors were in fact anticipated by Ravenscroft.[12] But where his adaptation is most valuable is in the area of stage directions. And that, of course, is exactly because he was preparing a text for the stage. It is in this area that the conventional valuation of closet editions above theater ones seems particularly factitious.

To take one example. The staging of the first scene of the play is extraordinarily complex and sophisticated in its movement between the "aloft" space of the gallery and the main stage. Exactly who comes down or goes upstairs at what point is often very difficult to reconstruct. Consider, for example, the moment at which Marcus offers Titus the white gown of the *candidatus*. It is clear from the dialogue that he attempts to give it to him to put on and that Titus refuses it. But in the closet editions, including both the single-volume Oxford of Eugene Waith and the complete Oxford of Stanley Wells, at this point Marcus is above with the tribunes, and Titus is below on the main stage. Are we to assume that the gown is thrown down from the upper stage to the lower? David Bevington, a modern editor unusually sensitive to the theater, saw the problem but resolved it rather clumsily by bringing on an attendant with the gown. Ravenscroft had a much better solution: he follows the early texts in initially having Marcus above with the other tribunes but brings him on below when he speaks the line "Long Live Lord *Titus* my beloved Brother" (6)—a line that is surely better delivered with an embrace rather than from the distance of the aloft space. He is then in place below to attempt to put the robe on his brother. By having him come down alone at this point, rather than with the other Roman officials, who descend a little later in the scene, the dramatist makes him into a link between the Roman people and the Andronici, a role he will sustain throughout the play. The new Arden edition abandons the closet tradition and follows Ravenscroft here, on the supposition that, with his sharp sense of theater, he intuited the original staging.

Ravenscroft is especially valuable in his indications of Lavinia's gestural language, which in the third act is beautifully counterpointed against

Titus's verbal elaborations: "*Lavinia makes signs of sorrow lifting up her eyes & then hanging down her head & moving her stumps,*" "*Lavinia turns up her eyes & then hangs down her head as weeping*" (30–31). His stage directions are full of other incidental dramatic detail. He includes a direction for the moment at which the raped girl turns to face Marcus during his "Who is this?" monologue, a direction that is necessary to make sense of his gradual recognition of her injuries. He maps out the business with Marcus's handkerchief in the third act. He carefully blocks the sitting and standing in the scene when the Nurse is stabbed by Aaron. He notices, as no subsequent editor seems to have done, that Titus must pull off Lavinia's veil before killing her.

One other direction he introduces seems to be wrong, but it is of value in that it suggests that the corresponding direction in the closet tradition is also wrong. Shortly after Shakespeare's grisliest stage direction, "*Enter a Messenger with two heads and a hand*" (3.1.234SD), there is the following dialogue in which the Andronicus family is alone onstage:

> *Marcus.* Now let hot Etna cool in Sicily,
> And be my heart an ever-burning hell!
> These miseries are more than may be borne.
> To weep with them that weep doth ease some deal,
> But sorrow flouted at is double death.
> *Lucius.* Ah, that this sight should make so deep a wound
> And yet detested life not shrink thereat!
> That ever death should let life bear his name,
> Where life hath no more interest but to breathe!
> *Marcus.* Alas, poor heart, that kiss is comfortless
> As frozen water to a starved snake.
> *Titus.* When will this fearful slumber have an end?
>
> (3.1.242–53)

Titus's next utterance is that wonderful line "Ha, ha, ha"; after this catharsis of laughter he asks the way to Revenge's cave, and the counteraction of the drama is initiated. This sequence is the very cusp of the play, which makes it all the more imperative to visualize the text's intentions for its staging.

There is an implied stage direction at this pivotal moment. Neither quartos nor folios include one, but there must be a kiss to prompt Marcus's "Alas, poor heart, that kiss is comfortless / As frozen water to a starved snake." Dr Johnson therefore introduced the direction "*Lavinia kisses him*," meaning "*Lavinia kisses Lucius*"; the nineteenth-century Cambridge editor changed this to "*Lavinia kisses Titus*," and all modern editors include one or other of these directions. But in Ravenscroft's adaptation there is a different direction: "*Lucius kisses one head.*" This cannot be right, since Marcus's "poor heart" must be addressed to Lavinia. But the fact that Ravenscroft's direction is different from that in the editorial tradition alerts us to the fact that there is a crux here. It opens the way for the modern editor to perceive what may well be the correct stage direction: "*Lavinia kisses the heads.*" Deprived of a verbal reaction like those of Marcus and Lucius, the tongueless girl kisses the severed heads of her brothers. Perhaps she first picks them up between her stumps, in a movement paralleling her subsequent bearing off of Titus's hand between her teeth. Only the combination of mutilated sister and decapitated brothers can make sense of Marcus's image of a physical impediment that denies comfort. The word *comfortless* should have indicated to editors that Lavinia is not kissing Titus, for earlier in the scene a kiss between father and daughter is associated with comfort: "Gentle Lavinia, let me kiss thy lips / Or make some sign how I may do thee ease" (3.1.121–22). The emended stage direction also makes more sense of Titus's next line: like Marcus, he is a spectator, not a participant, at this moment. What he is looking at, the scattered remains of his family, his tongueless daughter kissing his sons' severed heads, would be any father's fearful nightmare. Lavinia's motivation for the kiss may well be an attempt to communicate her brothers' innocence of Bassianus's murder, a response to Marcus's perplexity earlier in the scene, "Perchance she weeps because they killed her husband, / Perchance because she knows them innocent" (3.1.115–16).

Because Ravenscroft was writing for the stage, he came up with a theatrical solution to the implied crux; although it was not quite true to the intention of the original text, it intuited something about the moment that Johnson and his followers, editing in and for the study, failed to see. The Ravenscroft-inspired conjecture about the kiss of the severed heads was made fairly early in the process of re-editing *Titus* for the third Arden edition. Very late in the process, support for the emendation was found in a source that has extraordinary force but which has been extraordinarily neglected. Reputable editions of *Titus Andronicus* will supply the information that a German play published in 1620 bears some resemblance to Shakespeare's tragedy. But Eugene Waith is typically dismissive when he says that it merely provides "a tantalizing glimpse of what might be part of the early stage history of the play";[13] like other editors, he relates the German version to the red herring of a probably nonexistent *Ur-Titus*. The assumption shared by all modern editors that the German text has only an indirect bearing on Shakespeare accounts for the fact that examination of it was almost an afterthought in the work for the third Arden *Titus*. But, once one has read the play through, it is hard to be so readily dismissive of it.

Titus Andronicus was not only the first of Shakespeare's plays to be printed in England; it was also the first to be printed in Germany. In 1620, possibly in Leipzig, there was published a volume of 384 unnumbered pages called *Englische Comedien und Tragedien*, described as "the plays acted by the English in Germany."[14] It included, for example, a *Fortunatus* that is manifestly based on Dekker. The eighth play in the collection was *Eine sehr klägliche Tragaedia von Tito Andronico und der hoffertigen Kaiserin, darinnen denckwürdige actiones zubefinden* (A most lamentable tragedy of Titus Andronicus and the haughty empress, wherein are found memorable events). The "reporter" responsible for the text was one Friedrich Menius. If it is examined without prejudice, the obvious conclusion about its nature is that it is a translation of Shakespeare's play into plain German prose, with heavy cutting and a reduction of the cast to twelve parts (with some doubling possible) and a couple of all-purpose silent extras (who serve as soldiers, carriers on of the table for the bloody banquet, and so on).

The scenic structure is in all essentials identical to that of Shakespeare's play minus the fly-killing scene (which was a later addition, not included in the quartos). There are some very minor adjustments of order. The cuts are the obvious ones that a company would make in reducing the size of the cast. There is no Bassianus in the opening scene, no rivalry for rule of Rome, no opposing factions requiring large numbers of soldiers. This greatly streamlines the complex opening, which in the original requires a huge cast of twenty-five. The crown is offered to Titus, since he has saved Rome in war; he refuses it and gives it to the emperor, who is "next in line"; Bassianus appears briefly and merely as "Husband" in act 2,[15] in which he is killed. There is no killing of Alarbus; this might suggest that the text derives from a version before Alarbus was added,[16] but it need not, since it is an obvious self-contained cut. Quintus and Martius do not actually appear while alive: this reduces the cast size and avoids the difficult-to-stage pit scene; we are told that they have been imprisoned for unspecified crimes, and then their heads are brought on in the central scene in the third act, in which Titus is tricked into cutting off his hand in the hope that it will save his sons' lives.

Many scenes, however, such as the one in which the sons of the new empress vie over the charms of Titus's daughter and the Moor intervenes, and the one in which the Moor kills the nurse, are hardly altered at all. And many vestiges of the language of the English play are quite clear. For instance, when the empress and her sons come to Titus in disguise, he "*looks down from above*" and says, "Who are you who calls out to me in this way?" which is obviously a prose version of Titus's line spoken from above in the original, "Who doth molest my contemplation?"[17]

The whole structure of classical allusion that underpins the play is removed. A bucket of sand and a stick—easy props for a touring company—replace the sophisticated business of turning the pages of a text of Ovid's *Metamorphoses*. A "lower" audience than Shakespeare's is implied, one that requires a strong concentration on spectacle and action rather than ornate rhetoric. This is only to be expected in view of the language problem: in the 1590s the English actors in Germany performed in English, so much of the audience would have been entirely dependent on the visual; after 1600 they increasingly used German, but since it was not their first language they tended to use it as a vehicle for narrative, not for literary display.

There is one notable difference from the Shakespearean original, and that is in the names of some of the characters. Instead of Tamora, Queen of Goths, and her two sons, Chiron and Demetrius, there are Aetiopissa, Queen of Ethiopia, and her two sons, Helicates and Saphonus. This is what has led scholars to contemplate some other source for the German play, but surely there is a more obvious explanation. In the Renaissance Goths were synonymous with Germans; if you are an English company touring in Germany, you would be ill advised to have a barbarous Gothic/German queen and her rapist sons, and, therefore, you turn them into more distant barbarians, namely Ethiopians (this also means that you avoid the scandal of miscegenation between the empress and the Moor, a change that is in accordance with a certain moral cleansing of the text appropriate to Luther's Germany—Lavinia writes *hunt* with her stumps instead of *rape*). Certain other names are changed in the German version, and there is likely a different explanation for this. Menius must have either witnessed a performance or had access to material such as a promptbook. If his text was a memorial reconstruction or if it was based on a promptbook that had only the actors' names, not the characters', he might well have forgotten or not had access to the names of the lesser characters. He therefore makes them up: so it is that Lavinia becomes Andronica and Lucius Vespasian. It was the latter renaming that led scholars to the red herring of Henslowe's lost *Titus and Vespasian*. But Menius had a classical education, and, if he had needed to supply a name for the son of a Roman called Titus, Vespasian would have been the first to come to mind.

But, despite the changes in name and the various simplifications of the action, the sustained structural similarity, together with the many verbal reminiscences, strongly suggests that the German text is a cut-down touring version of Shakespeare. A modern-day small company wanting to perform a "reduced" *Titus* could learn a lot from it.

And so can a modern editor. As a performance from within, or very shortly after, Shakespeare's own lifetime, it has a kind of authority that is rare indeed. If its staging is not Shakespeare's own, it is that of a company as close to him as one is ever likely to get. So its directions are of enormous interest. Probably because it was a performance for a foreign audience, there is a great deal of visual business—one is reminded of the Frenchman's remark on seeing a private performance of *Titus* at Burley-on-the-Hill in 1596 that "the spectacle has more value than the matter."[18] The bloody banquet is especially vivid: Titus wears a blood-spattered apron and carries a knife in his hand, he "*Goes to the pasties, cuts and places portions of them before the Emperor and the Empress,*" then "*walks mournfully up and down before the table,*" every bit in the manner of Brian Cox in the wonderful 1987 Deborah Warner production at the Swan Theatre in Stratford-upon-Avon. But it is two bits of business in the great central scene of the third act that are most fascinating. At the end of that scene the Andronici make an oath that they will right one another's wrongs. Eugene Waith's edition introduces the stage direction "*He pledges them*" and adds a footnote to the effect that what is needed is "*a simple ritual, such as handshaking*" (140). In the circumstances this suggestion seems mildly unfortunate: one can only say with Titus, "O, handle not the theme, to talk of hands, / Lest we remember still that we have none." Menius's description of the English actors in Germany suggests that "ritual" is right but that something more elaborate is needed:

Now Titus Andronicus *falls upon his knees and begins to chant a dirge, all the others sitting down by the heads. Titus takes up his hand, holds it up and looks to heaven, sobs and repeats the oath softly; he beats his breast and at the conclusion of the oath sets the hand aside. Then he takes up one head and then the other, swearing by each one in turn. Finally he goes to [his daughter], who is kneeling, and swears by her also, as he did with the others, whereupon they all rise again.* (36)

This seems in keeping with the high formality of the occasion. It would be fascinating to see it staged, though one suspects that a general editor would take a lot of persuading to accept it into a text such as the Arden edition. But what the third Arden edition of *Titus* does incorporate is the following, a little earlier in the scene: shortly after the Moor brings on his cargo of dismembered parts, Titus's daughter "*walks to the heads and kisses them*" (34). To have one's conjectural emendation confirmed by a record of a performance so close to Shakespeare's lifetime affords an editor a certain satisfaction. It suggests that, if we attend seriously to the rich tradition of early adaptations, if we treat them as editions and not aberrations, we may still have discoveries to make.

Of all Shakespeare's plays *King Lear* has become most notorious for its theatrical instability. But modern editors have interested themselves in revisions of quarto into folio, not in the more remarkable revision of the play that held the stage for over a century and a half: Nahum Tate's extraordinarily popular 1681 version, *The History of King Lear*.[19] Editors of *Lear*, despite the wide range of recent studies on the nature and origins of its texts, are still very much in need of evidence and information to support their critical judgment. Tate's *History*, it will be argued, provides some intriguing insights into some of the editorially most challenging passages in the original play. By using *History* as a touchstone, we think it can be shown that even Taylor and Wells's revolutionary 1986 Oxford edition of *King Lear* is occasionally affected by old prejudices. Some specific emendations are not entirely in keeping with the theoretical assumptions that have led the new generation of scholars, of whom Taylor and Wells are eminent representatives, to advance the hypothesis of revision.

One such doubtful intervention on the text occurs in the second act, in a passage that Greg defined as "one of the major cruxes in the play."[20] The corrected and the uncorrected versions of the first quarto (hereafter Qa and Qb) and the first folio (hereafter F) offer three alternative readings: Qa reads "the deare fate, / Would with the daughter speake, come and tends service"; Qb offers a much more straightforward alternative, "the deare father / Would with his daughter speake, commands her service" (Q 1167–68). F follows neither Qa nor Qb: "The deere Father / Would with his Daughter speake, commands, tends, service" (F 1377–78).[21] Taylor and Wells decided that F preserves the authorial reading, whereas Qa and Qb represent, respectively, a compositorial misreading and a failed attempt on the part of the Q corrector to restore what must have been in the copy text. Neither Qa nor Qb is therefore retained in their Q edition of *King Lear;* Q is emended to read like F.[22]

Tate, on the other hand, must have been quite satisfied with Qb. His editing of other Q/F variants in Lear's speech clearly indicates that he was using F here as his source text: he retains F's extra line, "Are they informed of this? My breath and blood!" (*History,* 2.5.48), which does not appear in either Qa or Qb, and adopts F in the following line, "Fiery! the fiery duke! . . ." (2.5.49). Nevertheless he preferred to go back to Qb for the most difficult line in this variant passage. His rewriting of Lear's speech therefore reads as follows:

> The king would speak with Cornwall, the dear father
> Would with his daughter speak, commands her service.
> Are they informed of this? My breath and blood!
> Fiery! the fiery duke! Tell the hot duke—
>
> (2.5.46–49)

Tate's editing of this passage could be denied any authority simply by objecting that normalization of style and imagery might be the only reasons why he adopted Qb.[23] It will, however, be argued that his treatment of this passage is more coherent than that of Taylor and Wells.

Let's start by examining the evidence that has usually been used to reject Qb. The most common argument against it is based on the principle of the *difficilior lectio:* both F and Qa, when duly emended, offer a more sophisticated reading than Qb. In Qb "commands her service" emphasizes what the king has already expressed in the preceding line: the king would like to speak with his daughter; he bids her perform the service a dutiful daughter cannot deny to a loving father. What Taylor and Wells regard as the authorial reading in F provides a more complex interpretation: "commands, tends service" reflects the paradoxical position of the king at this point of the play. Since Lear has abdicated his royal titles, he is no longer king but subject to his queen-daughters; he therefore "tends" (i.e., offers) his service to Regan. But though no longer a king, Lear is still a father, and, as a father, he "commands" (i.e., claims) his daughter's respect. When Regan refuses to obey his orders, Lear realizes that being obeyed as a king did not necessarily imply being loved as a father; as soon as he divests himself of his power as a king, he is precipitated into a position of absolute dependency and emotional vulnerability.

Another argument against Qb is that, if Qb actually restored what must have been in Q copy-text, it would be rather difficult to justify the unusual reading offered by Qa as a compositorial misreading; *tends* is quite unlikely to be mistaken for *her*. The arguments in favor of Qa and F are quite plausible, but are they strong enough to reject Qb once and for all, especially in a modern critical edition of the play, such as Taylor and Wells's, which is explicitly intended to reflect the substantial differences between Q and F? Several arguments can be used to defend Qb and to demonstrate that F is neither necessarily authorial nor necessarily better than Qb and that Taylor and Wells's corrective editing of the passage is the result of an old editorial prejudice against Q and is not in keeping with the general purpose of their edition.

The first argument to support Qb is purely bibliographical: if, as it has been argued against Qb, *her* is unlikely to be mistaken for *tends*, it is however possible that *service*, which is usually associated with the verbs *to do, to command* or *to offer*, misled the compositor. If *her* and *tends* are not likely to be confused because they have got a different physical shape, it is undeniable that *tends* is semantically appropriate in the context of Qa. Moreover, Shakespeare never used *attend* or *tend*, the aphetic form of *attend*, with *service* elsewhere. There are two examples in which *attend* means "to escort, follow, or accompany for the purpose of rendering service or giving assistance" (OED, 7a): one occurs in *The Merry Wives of Windsor*, "Destiny, I attend your office and your quality" (5.5.40), the other in *Antony and Cleopatra*, "I must attend my office" (4.6.26). But neither *attend* or *tend* are ever associated with the word *service*, which occurs quite frequently in Shakespeare (228 times in the whole canon). Since *tends* is semantically correct but was never used by Shakespeare himself, it is perhaps safer to conclude that it is compositorial rather than authorial; and, if *tends* can be accounted for as a compositorial misreading, there is no reason to suspect that Qb might not be a successful correction of Qa. Besides, whereas *come and* may have originated from a compositorial misreading of the original *commands*, it is unlikely that the corrector was able to replace Qa without consulting his copy.

The weight of the internal evidence suggests that the Q corrector consulted his copy-text while checking this line and therefore that he managed to restore the reading he found there. This theory is further reinforced by Blayney's reconstruction of the printing of Q1. In *The Texts of King Lear and their Origins,* he concluded that, despite its evident shortcomings, Q was not worse than the other quartos printed by Nicholas Okes; "the only essential difference," in fact, "between the *Lear* variants and those in most of the other quartos is the frequency with which the *Lear* copy *does* appear to have been consulted." Moreover, Blayney continues, even if the copy-text was not always consulted by the proofreader, there is enough evidence to demonstrate that "when [outer E]," the forme containing the variant analyzed here, "was corrected at press, reference was made to the copy."[24]

If Qb is then taken to represent a successful attempt to restore what was in the copy-text, how can we account for the origin of F's variant reading? Taylor and Wells's editing of the passage implies that F provides the authorial reading, which both the Q compositor and the Q corrector failed to reproduce. Paradoxically enough, their theory—a single authorial reading underlying both texts—seems to be more in keeping with the old theory of the lost original than with the new hypothesis of revision.

It is worth keeping in mind that the revision of *King Lear* seems to have been initially carried out on a copy of the first quarto and that the original copy-text for Q might not have been available to the reviser; therefore, all the latter had to work on was a copy of the first quarto, either corrected or uncorrected. In order to identify F with the authorial reading we must consequently assume that the reviser was the author himself and that, after a relatively long time,[25] he managed to emend either of the two readings he found in his copy of Q1 and restore his original intentions. Is it not safer to assume that the F reading was not in the copy-text for Q but that it is the result of a later rewriting of the passage? Even if this theory does not exclude the possibility that the F version might be the result of a later *authorial* intervention on the text, carried out without the support of the copy-text originally used for Q, a closer examination of the passage within which this line is included shows that F is in fact more likely to derive from a compositorial conflation of Qa and Qb.[26]

The main problem with this theory is that it leads to the conclusion that, whereas the more common reading might be authorial, F's reading, usually regarded as more sophisticated, might be the result of a later, not necessarily authorial, conflation of the second quarto and the revised promptbook. This theory is disturbing because it confirms that playtexts are not the result of the author's personal creation but of a collaborative effort. This principle is by now quite widely recognized among textual scholars, but its consequences are hardly ever approved of. Despite recent contributions of deconstructionist theories to establishing the concept of textual instability, old prejudices about the corrupting influence of the theater and the printing house still have a strong hold on editors.

The arguments used up to this point are based on purely typographical evidence; bibliographical and typographical analyses, however, seldom provide the key to disentangle textual cruxes once and for all. The extant texts of a play such as *Lear* offer but scattered pieces of evidence, and, in trying to reconcile them, textual scholars and editors have to make inferences and be content with more or less probable theories, never objective certainties. Although the evidence analyzed here calls into question the legitimacy of the corrective editing Taylor and Wells applied to this passage in Q, the argument advanced can claim no higher status than an alternative hypothesis.

Since textual criticism based on traditional evidence hardly ever manages to go beyond the limits of mere probability and likelihood, a wider-scoped analysis of the evolution of the text through later rewritings, revisions, and adaptations should take over whenever it is likely to provide some useful extra insight and information on a particular complex textual crux such as the one discussed here. Traditional methods, for example, aim at assessing the nature and the origin but not the theatrical quality of a variant reading; by examining the way in which the earlier passage has been adapted to the stage, it will be possible to show that F, far from necessarily authorial, is not even necessarily better—that is, theatrically more effective—than Q.

We can start by noticing that adaptors have generally preferred Qb to F. All the theatrical adaptations examined have retained Qb's reading "commands her service."[27] It might be objected that adaptors simply complied with an old tradition first established by Tate, as the title page in Elliston's adaptation of *Lear* seems to suggest ("Printed chiefly from Nahum Tate's edition, with some restoration from the original"). This is however not the case, at least insofar as the most notable adaptation after Tate's is concerned. When David Garrick rewrote the first act of his *King Lear, A Tragedy,* he mainly used F as his copy-text: seven times out of ten he followed F; on two occasions he preferred Tate to either Q or F, and only on one occasion did he resort to Q.[28] But, although Garrick generally used F, at least more often than Tate did, he adopted Qb's "commands her service" instead of F's "commands, tends service." More generally, he did not simply accept Tate's editorial choices acritically, when he was not satisfied with F.[29]

Tate chose to adopt Qb "commands her service" despite the fact that he was clearly using F as his copy-text; it is worth stressing that he left the rest of the passage unaltered, except for this single line, for which he deferred to Q at the expense of what he regarded as the better text.[30] His editing of this passage is clearly in keeping with the overall strategy of his revision: as usual, he chose the reading that was more immediately comprehensible onstage. F may provide the "slit-eyed" reader, to use Harry Berger's phrase,[31] with deeper insights, but Qb is probably more actable. Tate's editing of this variant throws light on the different theatrical potentialities of Q and F and provides further evidence for rejecting Taylor and Wells's editorial choice as inappropriate. Even if no general consensus has been reached so far on the actual identity of the reviser, revisionists generally agree on the nature of the revision: the literary early version of the play was adapted to conform to theatrical values such as "contrast, concision and surprise."[32] Between Qb and F, Qb is the reading that conforms most closely to these theatrical values, as Tate's rewriting of the passage would seem to suggest. A brief analysis of later theatrical adaptations seems therefore to confirm our conclusions about the origins of this variant passage: in this case F is more likely to represent a later conflation of Qa and Qb than an authorial intervention on the text, in keeping with the general purpose of the revision in F.

An important theoretical principle follows from this hypothesis. Editorial shibboleths such as the rule of the *difficilior lectio* derive from the editing of classical texts, in which an editor is attempting to recover the authorial text behind an intermediate scribal hand: in these circumstances it is always likelier that the scribe will have cut the gordian knot of a difficult reading by introducing an easier one. But a Renaissance playtext is not a classical manuscript: in this case it may be more likely that the simpler reading will be the correct one because it is the more stageable, the more readily accessible in the brief instant of theatrical audition. Tate's handling of this variant in *Lear* suggests that editors of playtexts should give some consideration to what might be termed the rule of the *facilior lectio*.

In conclusion let us consider two other cases in which Taylor and Wells's editing is clearly prejudiced against Q and in which a comparative analysis of Tate's theatrical adaptation reveals such editorial predilection for F. In act 4, scene 5, Q reads, "through tottered raggs, smal vices do appeare" (Q 2370); F's slightly inconsistent equivalent line, "Thorough tatter'd cloathes great Vices do appeare" (F 2606–7) is left unaltered by Taylor and Wells. Q clearly makes better sense than F: Lear is drawing our attention to the different treatment reserved for poor and powerful people.

The former are severely punished for small crimes, whereas the latter are condoned even great vices. F undercuts the effect of this image by replacing *small* with *great*. Tate's alert theatrical sensitivity led him to prefer Q.

But in a similarly variant passage in act 5, scene 3, in which Q is logically inferior to F, Taylor and Wells did not hesitate to emend Q. In Q Edgar's moralizing comment on Edmund's deserved defeat in the combat reads, "The Gods are just, and of our pleasant *vertues*. / Make instruments to scourge us" (Q 2830–31), whereas F logically emends, "The Gods are just, and of our pleasant *vices* / Make instruments to plague us" (F 3131–32; emphasis added). Taylor and Wells justified their intervention in Q by saying that "Q could represent a compositorial antonym substitution";[33] the same argument could, however, have been used to emend F in the previous example. But, whereas in the one case Q was emended, in the other F was left unaltered.

The few variants analyzed here should be enough to show how, despite being in many respects revolutionary, Taylor and Wells's edition of *King Lear* is still burdened by prejudices of the past. Not only do they resort to traditional methods such as paleographical reconstruction or the rule of the *difficilior lectio,* but they also emend Q whenever there is not enough evidence to prove its authority, a symptom of their clinging to a concept of authorship that is visibly at odds with the theory of revision. Paleographical reconstruction may be useful on many occasions, but it is hardly ever definitive. Old methods should be supported by new ones, such as the comparative analysis of Q and F and later theatrical adaptations of the play, as suggested here. Neither old nor new methods can provide definitive evidence; they are not exclusive but complementary strategies of analysis, and editors should avail themselves of both.

It is by now commonly agreed that Renaissance playtexts should be accorded no higher status than "working scripts."[34] Why, then, should editors refrain from resorting to later adaptations of the play, which represent later stages in the endless process of rewriting of a playtext? Adaptations, far from being at the margins of the orthodox editorial tradition of Shakespeare's works, rightly belong to its mainstream. In the past editors did not hesitate to analyze Shakespearean sources to decide whether some variants might be authorial. Now that emphasis has shifted from the author to the text, we should start devoting our attention to a playtext's "afterlife" in the theater, and not simply the process through which it came into being. It is high time for textual scholars to consider the stage not as a corrupting agent external to the text but as the privileged place in which the text is perpetually revived.

NOTES

Sections 1 and 3 of this essay are by Sonia Massai, section 2 by Jonathan Bate, but we have each revised the other's work.

1. Jay L. Halio, *Understanding Shakespeare's Plays in Performance* (Manchester: Manchester University Press, 1988), 14.
2. See, for example, Stephen Orgel, "What Is a Text?" *Research Opportunities in Renaissance Drama* 26 (1981): 3–6.
3. Norman Rabkin, "Tragic Meanings: The Redactor as Critic," *Shakespeare and the Problem of Meaning* (Chicago and London: University of Chicago Press, 1981), 63–117; Halio, *Understanding Shakespeare's Plays*, 2; Alan C. Dessen, "Modern Productions and the Elizabethan Scholar," *Renaissance Drama* n.s. 18, (1987): 209.
4. De Grazia, *Shakespeare Verbatim: The Reproduction of Authenticity and the 1790 Apparatus* (Oxford: Clarendon Press, 1991), 11.
5. Werstine, "Folio Editors, Folio Compositors, and the Folio Text of *King Lear*," in *The Division of the Kingdoms: Shakespeare's Two Versions of "King Lear,"* ed. Gary Taylor and Michael Warren (Oxford: Clarendon Press, 1983), 247.
6. *William Shakespeare: A Textual Companion*, ed. Stanley Wells and Gary Taylor (Oxford: Clarendon Press, 1987), 53.
7. A handful of folio plays list "Names of the Actors" (with *Actors*, meaning what we would call "characters").
8. *Titus Andronicus*, ed. Jonathan Bate, Arden Shakespeare, 3d ser. (London and New York: Routledge, 1995).
9. 4.2.171–2. All quotations are from the new Arden text.
10. Edward Ravenscroft, *Titus Andronicus, or The Rape of Lavinia* (1687, reprint [facs.] London: Cornmarket, 1969), 1.
11. For example, at 1.1.165, Q2, Q3, F, and Ravenscroft all have "the earth" where Q1 has "this Earth."
12. For example, the punctuation of 1.1.14, *fault* for Qq, F's *faults* at 2.2.291, *him* for Qq, F's *them* at 2.3.27 (all traditionally attributed to Rowe), and the repetition of *arm* to improve the rhythm of 4.4.61 (traditionally attributed to Warburton).
13. Eugene M. Waith, ed., *Titus Andronicus* (Oxford: Oxford University Press, 1984), 7.
14. The standard account of the Elizabethan and Jacobean touring companies in Germany remains Emil Herz, *Englische Schauspieler und englisches Schauspiel zur Zeit Shakespeares in Deutschland* (Hamburg and Leipzig: Theatergeschichtliche Forschungen, 1903).

15. In this description of the German play, for convenience, the act and scene divisions of the Shakespearean are followed.

16. There is some evidence that he may not have been in the first draft of the play.

17. German version of 1620, translated by Ernest Brennecke in *Shakespeare in Germany, 1590–1700* (Chicago: University of Chicago Press, 1964), 46. *Titus*, 5.2.9. Some features of the language suggest the characteristics of actors' simplification or reporter's memorial reconstruction: Aaron's "Madam, though Venus govern your desires, / Saturn is dominator over mine" (2.2.30) becomes "No, lovely Empress, although Venus is tempting you strongly to indulge in her gay sport, Mars has taken possession of me and rules me now" (29)—the parallel structure of gods is retained, but Venus/Saturn is replaced with the more commonplace Venus/Mars.

18. See Gustav Ungerer, "An Unrecorded Elizabethan Performance of *Titus Andronicus*," *Shakespeare Survey* 14 (1961): 102–9.

19. Nahum Tate, *The History of King Lear*, ed. James Black (London: Edward Arnold, 1976); hereafter referred to in the text as "*History*."

20. W. W. Greg, *The Variants in the First Quarto "King Lear": A Bibliographical and Critical Inquiry* (London: Bibliographical Society, 1940), 161.

21. Q and F line numbering refers to *The Parallel "King Lear,"* ed. Michael Warren (Berkeley, Los Angeles, and London: University of California Press, 1989).

22. William Shakespeare, *The Complete Works*, ed. Stanley Wells and Gary Taylor (Oxford: Clarendon Press, 1986); *The History of King Lear* [Q], sc.7.264–5; *The Tragedy of King Lear* [F], 2.2.273–4.

23. Tate actually normalized the original text on many occasions. In act 1.1, for example, when faced with the perplexing variant line in Edmund's speech, which reads, "a stale dull lyed bed" in Q (Q 312), and "a dull stale tyred bed" in F (F 347), he did not take the trouble to decide which text provides the better reading; he simply omitted the variant adjective and reduced the original reading to his more neutral "stale marriage-bed" (*History*, 1.1.10). Another good example of his normalization of the original text occurs later on in the same scene: Q reads, "As much a child ere loved, or father friend"(Q 54), whereas F reads, "As much as Childe ere lov'd, or Father found" (F 64). Taylor and Wells left these two variant readings unaltered. Tate bypassed the obstacle by rewriting the whole line: "As much as child can love the best of fathers" (*History*, 1.1.81).

24. Peter W. M. Blayney, *The Texts of "King Lear" and their Origins*, (Cambridge: Cambridge University Press, 1982), 1:219, 208.

25. Taylor himself, in his article "*King Lear:* The Date and Authorship of the Folio Revision" (in Taylor and Warren, *Division of the Kingdoms*), argued that the revision cannot have taken place before 1608–9.

26. The passage within which this variant line is included seems to represent the result of the collaborative effort of the revising author and the compositor. The extra line, "Are they inform'd of this? My breath and blood:" which appeared in neither Qa nor Qb, and which therefore is unlikely to have been in the original copy-text for Q, was evidently added later on. The line is interesting in that it anticipates and heightens the effects of Lear's progressive decline into a state of

utter bewilderment; on the other hand, it is not essential to the economy of Lear's speech as a whole. This line is therefore more likely to be a later improvement than a necessary restoration.

27. David Garrick, *King Lear, A Tragedy* (1756), in *The Plays of David Garrick,* ed. H. W. Pedicord and F. L. Bergmann, vol. 3: "Garrick's Adaptations of Shakespeare, 1744–1756" (Carbondale and Edwardsville: Southern Illinois University Press, 1981). George Colman, *The History of King Lear* (1768; reprint, London: Cornmarket, 1969). Robert Elliston, *Shakespeare's Tragedy of King Lear* (1820; reprint, London: Cornmarket, 1970). *King Lear, A Tragedy in Five Acts by William Shakespeare* (text of Edmund Kean's 1823 production; reprint, London: Cornmarket, 1970). Charles Kean, *Shakespeare's Tragedy of King Lear* (1858; reprint, London: Cornmarket, 1970).

28. Tate also adopted Q while editing the passage where this variant is included, so here Garrick might have consulted only F and Tate's adaptation, but it is clear from a brief scrutiny of the variants in act 2 that he had a copy of Q and used it: at 2.3.149–56 he retains a Q-only passage that Tate had heavily abridged:

> Let me beseech your Grace not to do so.
> *His fault is much, and the good king his master*
> *Will check him for't.* [*Your purposed low correction*
> *Is such as basest and the meanest wretches*
> *For pilf'rings and most common trespasses*
> *Are punished with.* The king] must take it ill
> That he, so slightly valued in his messenger,
> Should have him thus restrained.
> (Garrick, ed. cit., italics indicate Q-only lines; lines between brackets were omitted by Tate)

29. It might be objected that Garrick's copy preserved the uncorrected version "come and tends service" and that, since he was satisfied with neither Q nor F, he decided to follow Tate. Even if Garrick had not the chance of choosing between Qb and F, it is however indicative that he preferred "commands her service" to F's "commands, tends, service."

30. From a brief analysis of Tate's editing of the Q/F variants, it appears that he initially preferred Q to F. In act 1 he used Q almost as often as F. In act 2 the number of Q/F variants taken over from Q and F is almost the same. From act 3 onward, however, Tate seems to rely more on F than on Q, perhaps due to impatience with the poor quality of Q's composition.

31. Berger, *Imaginary Audition: Shakespeare on Stage and Page* (Berkeley, Los Angeles, and London: University of California Press, 1989), xiv *et passim.*

32. Stephen Urkowitz, *Shakespeare's Revision of King Lear* (Princeton: Princeton University Press, 1980), 70–76.

33. *Textual Companion,* 526.

34. Jonathan Bate, "Shakespeare's Tragedies as Working Scripts," *Critical Survey* 3 (1991): 118–27.

Part 2
The Margins of the Book

"Opening Titles Miscreate": Some Observations on the Titling of Shakespeare's "Works"

Thomas L. Berger

I don't know when it was I started to worry about titles. It may have had to do with naming more than titling, but it began, like so much begins, with Adam. I discovered that it was Adam, a male, who did the naming in the Garden of Eden. Living in a prelapsarian, pre-copyright world, it was he who affixed "titles" to biological entities. I worried more than I should have how we would look at the animals if, for example, Adam, speaking the King's English, had called a lion a giraffe or, say, an elephant a python. My concern deepened when I pondered, as still I do, the language lesson in *Henry V*. It seems to make a good deal of difference to the Princess Catherine what words are applied to what parts of the body/bawdy: "d'Hand, de Fingre, de Nayles, d'Arme, d'Elbow, de Nick, de Sin, de Foot, le Count."[1] Language for the Princess, for most of us, is what things are called. What we call a work, what a work is called, very much determines the way we think about that work, the way we read it. We all know better, of course; we all know that it's the contents that count. But, then, isn't the title, the work's nomination, very much a part of the contents?

Let me give a few examples culled from a highly informal, deeply unscientific survey of friends and colleagues. Does it make any difference if the title of a recent gay novel published in the United States is *Martin and John*,[2] whereas its British counterpart is called *Fucking Martin*?[3] Well, yes, I very much think it does. Robert James Waller's best-selling romance (and recent "major motion picture" starring Clint Eastwood and Meryl Streep) is titled *The Bridges of Madison County* in the United States.[4] It has as its British title the somewhat confusing, if not miscegenationally misleading, *Love in Black and White*.[5] Margaret Drabble's novel about an unwanted pregnancy was titled *The Millstone* on one side of the Atlantic,[6] *Thank You*

All Very Much on the other side.[7] Both titles are ironic, each in its own way, but each title leads "the careful reader" (a largely mythical beast) in a different direction.[8] The title of John Ashbery's poem "The Cathedral Is" becomes part of the poem's one-line "text": "Slated for demolition."[9]

More specifically thought provoking are the titles that *The Oxford Shakespeare* assigned to the texts it presented as *The Complete Works*.[10] My first reaction was a conservative one, the same one that the general academic community had about the entire project, one of horror, dismay, and rejection, not only at, over, and of the titles of various works, but also of the editions of texts that followed those titles. What was I to make of *The History of Henry the Fourth (1 Henry IV)*, of *The Comical History of the Merchant of Venice, or Otherwise Called the Jew of Venice*, or of *All is True (Henry VIII)*? My horror, ever attuned to a heady strain of self-righteousness—which should never, ever, be confused with self-interest—increased as I was asked to review *The Complete Works, The Original Spelling Edition,* and *The Textual Companion*. And review them I did.[11] Since that time I have had the opportunity to consider with more leisure what the Oxford editors might have been thinking about and what might have guided (or clouded) their judgments in titling the playtexts as they did. What follows, then, are some ruminations on the titles of Shakespeare's plays and on the titles of some of the plays of his fellow dramatists.

The real villains in the piece (if one is inclined to look for villains, and I am) are not the editors of *The Oxford Shakespeare* (who, grudgingly, are almost heroic) but the "editors"[12] of the First Folio of 1623, whoever they may have been. Let me "name" those editors, let me call them John Heminge and Henry Condell, Shakespeare's colleagues in the King's Men.[13] It was the purpose of the capitalist cartel of Shakespeare's colleagues and members of the London book trade to turn Shakespeare from a play-maker into an author, to turn the plays into works, a process achieved in the arrangement of the preliminaries to the folio edition.[14] Just as the works of Samuel Daniel and Ben Jonson used the generic qualities of the literary "pieces" as part and parcel of the creation of their authorships, so too were Shakespeare's plays divided into literary genres: comedies, histories, tragedies.[15]

I want to look first at the histories, whose titling in the folio most clearly exemplifies the desire to make Shakespeare into a coherent author of a body of works.[16] A glance at the folio table of contents, its "CATA-LOGVE" (fig. 1), reveals that Shakespeare's history plays are all tidied up in chronological order for folio presentation, beginning with *King John* and

A CATALOGVE

of the feuerall Comedies, Histories, and Tragedies contained in this Volume.

Fig. 1. Table of Contents, or "Catalogue," of the First Folio of Shakespeare, 1623, Sig. A6. Reproduced with kind permission of the Folger Shakespeare Memorial Library.

ending with *Henry VIII*. Let me skip to the second tetralogy; from the wonderfully descriptive *The First part of the Contention betwixt the two famous Houses of Yorke and Lancaster, with the death of the good Duke Humphrey; And the banishment of and death of the Duke of* Suffolke, *and the Tragicall end of the proud Cardinal of* Winchester, *with the notable Rebellion of* Iacke Cade; And the Duke of Yorke's first claime unto the Crowne on the title page of the 1594 quarto, we are left with *The Second part of King Hen. the Sixt* in the folio catalog, expanded, revealingly, as a head title to *The second Part of Henry the Sixt, with the death of Good Duke HVMFREY.* Much the same obtains for what we, and the folio catalog, call *The Third part of King Henry the Sixt* and what the play's head title gives as *The third Part of Henry the Sixt, with the Death of the Duke of YORKE.* This is a far cry from the 1594 octavo's title, *The true Tragedie of Richard Duke of Yorke, and the death of good King Henrie the Sixt, with the whole contention betweene the two Houses Lancaster and Yorke, as it was sundrie times acted by the Right Honourable the Earle of Pembrooke his seruants.*[17] *1 Henry VI*, probably written after the two plays whose titles I have just described, never got a quarto (or even an octavo) edition. It is simply, in the folio catalog and on its head title, *The First part of King Henry the Sixt.*

To complete the tetralogy—and I hope it is apparent that such a term, *tetralogy*, is quite creative—is *Richard III*. Again, the folio levels; to encompass the play generically, to create an author of a body of work, the folio catalog and the text's running title read, *The Life & Death of Richard the Third*, while the head title of the text, demonstrating instability even in titles, reads more like the title of the 1597 quarto: *The Tragedy of Richard the Third: with the Landing of Earle Richmond, and the Battell at Bosworth Field*. That 1597 title is even more revealing: *THE TRAGEDY OF King Richard the third. Containing, His treacherous Plots against his brother Clarence: the pittiefull murther of his iunocent nephewes: his tyrannicall vsurpation: with the whole course of his detested life and most deserued death. As it hathe beene lately Acted by the Right honourable the Lord Chamberlaine his seruants*. This title, more or less intact in six quartos through 1622, survived the First Folio and appeared more or less the same in Q7 of 1629 and Q8 of 1634.

That quarto and octavo title pages were printed separately and were used to advertise plays and to inform prospective readers where they might purchase same are facts of commercial printing in early modern London, just as glossy covers, embossed lettering, and bountifully bosomed heroines (in certain genres of prose fiction) are in late postmodern paperback publishing. What is of interest to me is our continued willingness to follow the folio's titles and thus to discard the earlier, more "authentic" titles of the quartos and octavos. Such a practice permits us to continue nominating (and thus conceiving and thus criticizing and thus theorizing Elizabethan and Jacobean conceptions of history and the historical and thus finding connections where none may exist) the plays *1, 2,* and *3 Henry VI* and *Richard III* as though they were a tetralogy.[18] There is, I understand, nothing at all wrong with this. We are readers, the receptors, the audience. We're in charge. If we want to make these four plays into a tetralogy, then we can. But we do so, receptively, at our peril(s). These four plays can and should be looked at from a variety of perspectives, each yielding, I would venture to say, some really interesting readings. I have never read, much less taught, *The First Part of the Contention* and *The True Tragedy of Richard Duke of York* as exclusively self-contained artifacts, much less as two parts of a single artistic conception. Nor have I ever seem them in production as two parts of a single dramatic entity. Excepting the 1994 Royal Shakespeare Company *Henry VI* (*3 Henry VI*), I have never seen either alone in production. If they are produced, they are always part of a trilogy or a tetralogy. I have never read, much less taught, *1 Henry VI* as a "prequel" (as opposed to a sequel) to the issues raised in *The First Part of the Contention* and *The True Tragedy of Richard Duke of York.* If I were to do that, I might find *1 Henry VI* to be a deftly experimental play. Again, I have not seen the play produced all by itself, bereft of its older siblings. *Richard III,* tragedy or history, is a grand piece of theater, all by its lonesome or as the culmination of a tetralogy. The titles of all four of these plays, titles we have inherited from the folio's need, the folio's determination, to contain Shakespeare's plays as works within generic boundaries, have at the very least robbed the plays of a multiplicity of readings.

If the four plays that constitute what we have been led to believe is the second tetralogy give us problems of entitulation, so too do those in the so-called first tetralogy. What the folio calls *The Life & Death of Richard the second* began its life in a 1597 quarto as *THE Tragedie of King Richard the second. As it hath beene publikely acted by the right Honourable the Lorde Chamberlaine his Seruants* and remained that way in four more quarto editions to 1615. When the play appeared in a quarto edition of 1634, basing its text not on the preceding quarto of 1615 but on its most immediate predecessor, the Second Folio of 1632, it took as well that folio's title, *The Life and Death of King Richard the Second.*

The First part of King Henry the fourth, so-called in the folio catalog, is expanded in the head title to add *with the Life and Death of HENRY Surnamed HOT-SPVRRE.* The first quarto of 1598 is a fragment, but the second quarto of the same year (and subsequent quartos) give the title as *THE HISTORY OF HENRIE THE FOVRTH; With the battell at Shrewsburie, betweene the King and Lord Henry Percy, surnamed Henrie Hotspur of the North. With the humourous conceits of Sir Iohn Falstaffe.* This title remained intact in the quartos of 1604, 1608, 1613, 1622, 1632, and 1639, the latter two editions uninhibited by the folio title. Nowhere is there mention that this is the first part of a two-part play. It is, its title maintains, complete in itself.

The Second part of K. Henry the fourth, as the folio catalog and its running titles nominate it, is expanded in its head title to add *Containing his Death: and the Coronation of King Henry the Fift.* This head title is remarkably like that of the first, and only, quarto, published in 1600; the 1600 title goes on to add *With the humours of sir Iohn Falstaffe, and swaggering Pistoll. As it hath been sundrie times publikely acted by the right honourable, the Lord Chamberlaine his seruants. Written by William Shake-speare.* Here, then, is a play in an early, pre-folio edition that attempts to capitalize on its predecessor and seeks, like Marlowe's *1 and 2 Tamburlaine,* to be two parts of a single, unified whole.[19]

The Life of King Henry the Fift, as it is titled in the folio, began its life in 1600 as a "bad" quarto: *THE CHRONICLE History of Henry the fift, With his Battell Fought at Agin Court in France. Togither with Auntient Pistoll. As it hath bene sundry times playd by the Right honorable the Lord Chamberlaine his seruants.* There may be some attempt at linkage with *2 Henry IV* in the mention of *Pistoll* on the quarto title page. This earlier title remained in effect in the second and third (also "bad") quarto editions of 1602 and 1619.

These four plays are more frequently taught, more frequently discussed and analyzed, and more frequently produced than those histories dealing with the reigns of Henry VI, Edward IV, and Richard III, or the reigns of John and Henry VIII. Aesthetically, perhaps, they give us reason to tetralogize them. There certainly are links among all four plays that seem too obvious to pass up. What distresses me is what I do with *1 Henry IV,* and I just did it by titling it *1 Henry IV,* making it into at least a two-part play. When I teach *The History of Henry IV* I am usually teaching it in a survey course to first- and second-year college students who are being exposed to Shakespeare for the first time as undergraduates after what was, most likely, some not-all-that-pleasant Shakespeare instruction in high school. Yet I find myself spending altogether too much of my time "back-grounding" the play, placing it next to *Richard II* and preparing my students to read it against the earlier play about the rise of Bolingbroke, placing it next to *2 Henry IV* and talking about retribution, and placing it next to *Henry V* and talking about the education of a Christian prince, about Machiavelli, about everything but the play in question. Indeed, that is my problem, but it is one that the folio encourages. To amass vexations, why, in eight early quartos of the play to 1639, is there never, ever, any mention made of Prince Hal on any of the title pages? And why is my focus relentlessly on him?[20]

For *The Life and Death of King John,* the first of the history plays printed in the folio, we have only the folio title, and that title is consistent in the catalog, the head title, and the running title.[21] For the folio's *The Life of King Henry the Eight* (catalog and running title), expanded in the head title to *The Famous History of the Life of King HENRY the Eight,* the Oxford edition proposes *All is True,* as the play was called in an early reference. A day or so after that first reference it was called *Henry VIII.* Then *All is True.* Then *Henry VIII* again. Perhaps the title began as *All is True: or, The Famous History of the Life of King Henry the Eight.* What *All is True* does, in addition to annoying me, is to remind me that Shakespeare wrote this "history" play late in his career, at least a decade after *Henry V,* probably in collaboration with John Fletcher. To call the play *Henry VIII,* as the folio does, to place it at the end of the histories, as the folio does, may be seriously to misconstrue what Shakespeare was or was not doing near the end of his career.[22] Had we clipped the subtitle from *All is True,* had we *All is True* as our only title, how then would we view the play? As a historical romance, perhaps? Who knows? The folio has largely precluded our doing so.

The foregoing may sound like an apologia for the manner in which the Oxford Shakespeare titled the history plays. It is not. If I have not seen myself, then most certainly I have heard myself, laboring under the aegis of the folio, pontificating about the long sweep of English history that Shakespeare envisioned in his history plays, with *King John* as a prologue, *Henry VIII* as an epilogue, probing in a multiplicity of ways the very heart of monarchical England.

If I have fewer "problems" with the titles of Shakespeare's comedies and tragedies, it is not because the problems are fewer or absent; if anything, the problems are less apparent, more complex. The first observation I would make is that folio tragedies are *always* named after someone—

Hamlet, King Lear, Macbeth—and that folio comedies are *never* named after people. Comedies are less important; because they deal with people like you and me, the names of the characters do not figure in the titles. This tip of the generic hat to Artistotle, with a nod to Northrop Frye's *Anatomy of Criticism*, is violated quite freely by Shakespeare's contemporary playwrights, as *The Spanish Tragedy*,[23] *The Revenger's Tragedy*, *The White Devil*,[24] and *'Tis Pity She's a Whore*, among others, demonstrate. The same holds true for contemporary minions of Thalia, as *Mucedorus, Fair Em*,[25] *Friar Bacon and Friar Bungay*,[26] *Monsier D'Olive*, and *Volpone*[27] make clear.

Love's Labour's Lost is a play about language, its title a quibble ambiguously presented in the apostrophe-free quarto title: *Loues labors lost*. The folio's catalog drops the *s* in *labors*, but it is picked up again in the head title and running titles. The 1598 title puff, *A PLEASANT Conceited Comedie*, becomes in the 1631 edition *A WITTIE AND PLEASANT COMEDIE*. Why do Falstaff's "humourous conceits" remain in place in all of *1 Henry IV*'s early quarto editions? What has happened to the meaning of the word *conceited* over the course of thirty-three years?

The title of *The Merchant of Venice* is, I think, well treated by *The Oxford Shakespeare*. Shylock is included in the title, as the play is listed as *The Comical History of the Merchant of Venice, or Otherwise Called the Jew of Venice*. In this the Oxford edition adopts part of the Stationers' *Register* entry of 22 July 1598: *a booke of the Merchaunt of Venyce, or otherwise called the Jewe of Venyce*. Like *Love's Labour's Lost*, Oxford's title, unlike that in the Stationers' *Register*, is ambiguous. Who, or what, is otherwise called "the Jew of Venice," "the Comical History," or "the Merchant of Venice"?[28]

The Merry Wives of Windsor, called such even in *The Oxford Shakespeare*, derives from the folio, leading us to consider Mistress Ford and Mistress Page, the wives, as the central figures in the play, as indeed they are. But in both the Stationers' *Register* entry of 18 January 1602 and the first (and "bad") quarto of the same year, Falstaff is every bit as prominent as the two women: *A Most pleasaunt and excellent conceited Comedie, of Syr Iohn Falstaffe, and the merrie Wiues of Windsor. Entermixed with sundrie variable and pleasing humors, of Sir Hugh the Welch Knight, Iustice Shallow, and his wise cousin M. Slender. With the swaggering vaine of Auncient Pistoll, and Corporall Nym. By William Shakespeare. As it hath bene diuers, times Acted by the right Honorable my Lord Chamberlaines seruants. Both before her Maiestie, and else-where.* I can only speculate on what prompted the Folio editors to remove Falstaff from the title.[29] I have suggested an unwillingness to use proper names in comedies. I would note, too, that the title of the 1630 quarto edition conflates the 1602 quarto and the First Folio: *THE MERRY VVIVES OF WINDSOR. With the humours of Sir Iohn Falstaffe, As also the swaggering vaine of Ancient Pistoll, and Corporall Nym. Written by William Shake-Speare. Newly corrected.*[30]

The title *Twelfth Night* seems designed for explicating explicators, from those who explain the feast of the Epiphany to those who digress on the epiphanizings of various of James Joyce's heroes. Leslie Hotson has argued that the play was first produced on 6 January 1601.[31] The theory is in disrepute, which may be why I like it so much. Let me quote from the summary provided in *The Riverside Shakespeare*:

> [Hotson] believes that Shakespeare wrote the play at royal command in honor of the state visit of Don Virginio Orsino, Duke of Bracciano, and that it was first presented on Twelfth Night (January 6) in 1601. As it happened, news of Orsino's projected visit did not reach England until December 26, 1600. Hotson's theory implies that Shakespeare wrote the comedy, and that the Lord Chamberlain's Men somehow managed to learn their parts and rehearse for a performance at court, within a space of ten or eleven days. This seems hard to believe.[32]

I for one don't find it hard to believe. If Shakespeare was working on—nay finishing, nay rehearsing—a play he had, albeit tentatively, entitled *What You Will*, it would not have been that difficult to spruce it up with the odd allusion here, the odd name change there, and retitle it *Twelfth Night* for the Royals, who, apparently, liked that sort of thing.[33]

If genre and nomination hold, then *Pericles* can hardly be called a "comedy," for it has a proper name in/as its title. This, however, is not the reason that the play does not appear in the First Folio. I rather think that the project to institutionalize Shakespeare, to fix him as an author of works, would not admit a play such as *Pericles*, less perhaps for the dubious nature of its authorship than for its popularity, a popularity that would not enhance a folio edition nor be enhanced by a folio edition. What is interesting is that the play is not a comedy. Rather, it is a play: *THE LATE, And much admired Play, Called Pericles Prince of Tyre*. One does not know whether to applaud or abhor the generic cowardice, or discretion, of the entitulators of the 1609 quarto.[34]

Two Noble Kinsmen (never, ever, *Palamon and Arcite*) was excluded from the folio as well, achieving print for the first time in 1634. Its genre, too, is not of the sort that is up to snuff for the folio editors, as the Stationers' *Register* entry of 8 April 1634 reveals: *a tragicomedy called the Two Noble Kinsmen*.[35]

The first tragedy in the folio may be the most hilarious example of the problems inherent in naming plays. *Troilus and Cressida* never managed to make it into the catalog of the folio. The first issue of the first quarto of 1609 titles the play, *THE Historie of Troylus and Cresseida*, which the second issue of the same year improves to *THE Famous Historie of Troylus and Cresseid*, adding, *Excellently expressing the beginning of their loues, with the conceited wooing of Pandarus Prince of Licia*. The head title and the first two running titles in the folio call the play, *THE TRAGEDIE OF Troylus and Cressida*, the later running titles simply calling the play, wisely perhaps, *Troylus and Cressida*. Because it deals not with English history, it cannot be a history play, and so *Troilus and Cressida* remains stuck between history and tragedy, though most of us feel secure in calling it a "problem," which is to say, a "problematic" comedy. The things we do.

Titus Andronicus began life in the Stationers' *Register* as *a noble Roman historye of Tytus Andronicus*, only to become *THE MOST LAmentable Romaine Tragedie of Titus Andronicus* on the title page of the 1594 quarto. By 1611 *Roman* has been dropped. In the folio catalog the title is simply *Titus Andronicus*.[36]

Timon of Athens is listed among the folio tragedies, but its folio head title reads, *THE LIFE OF TYMON OF ATHENS*, very much like the titles of some of the history plays.[37] The tables turn with *Julius Caesar*, as the title in the catalog reads, *The Life and death of Julius Cæsar*, while the head title and running titles read, *THE TRAGEDIE OF IULIVS CÆSAR*.[38]

Hamlet began its life in the Stationers' *Register* as *a booke called the Revenge of Hamlett Prince (of) Denmarke, as yt was latelie acted by the Lord Chamberleyn his servantes*. It became *THE Tragicall Historie of HAMLET Prince of Denmarke* in both the first and second quartos, with the head titles and running titles leaning toward and then becoming fixed as *The Tragedie of Hamlet, Prince of Denmarke*. The title remains the same in later quartos and in the folios, where, as the Dane becomes more of a household cultural commodity, *Prince of Denmark* is dropped from the catalog and running titles.

The folio catalog, sneaky as ever, lists *King Lear* as just that, *King Lear*. Its head title and running titles expand that to *THE TRAGEDIE OF KING LEAR*. The 26 November 1607 Stationers' *Register* entry calls the play *a booke called Mr. William Shakespeare his history of Kynge Lear*, a title the 1608 quarto, retaining Shakespeare's name, changes to *M. William Shak-speare: HIS True Chronicle Historie of the life and death of King LEAR and his three Daughters. With the vnfortunate life of Edgar, sonne and heire to the Earle of Gloster, and his sullen and assumed humor of Tom of Bedlam.* *Historie* remains intact in the head title and the running titles. It was not in Thomas Pavier's "interest" to change the title for his 1619 reprint, nor did Jane Bell, the publisher of the 1655 quarto, feel compelled to change it in spite of the existence of two intervening folios. Hedging its bets, the folio catalog calls the play simply *King Lear,* but the head and running titles read, *The Tragedie of King Lear.* I suspect two-text *King Lear* would have had a much more difficult time getting off the ground had the 1608 quarto included the word *tragedy* somewhere, anywhere, on its title page.

Of some interest for lovers of *Cymbeline* is the fact that, while its having a proper name must mean that it is a tragedy, it is now a romance. It is called simply *Cymbeline King of Britaine* in the folio catalog but *THE TRAGEDIE OF CYMBELINE* in the head title and running titles. Why, when they do not regularly do so for other tragedies, do F2, F3, and F4 insist in their catalogs, unlike F1, that *Cymbeline* is indeed a tragedy?

Titles in the Stationers' *Register* and titles in the quartos and in the folio are one thing. What they are called outside the world of print is something else again (table 1). *1 Henry IV* is many things, with the possible exception of its printed title: *Sir John Falstaff, The Hotspur, The First Part of Sir John Falstaff,* even simply *Falstaff. Much Ado about Nothing* becomes *Benedict and Beatrice,* and *Twelfth Night* becomes *Malvolio.* What scares me and what would give a New Historicist or a Cultural Materialist pause is that *Othello* never gets his name. The play is consistently referred to as *The Moor of Venice,* as it is in the catalogs of F2, F3, and F4. Perhaps this is meaningless, merely descriptive. It does seem strange that in table 1 it is the only play whose title moves from a proper name to a subtitle/generic name. Perhaps robbing the moor of a nominative is not racist. Perhaps that is simply what they called the play.

I worry about fabrication, about nomination. I was taken to the Hirshhorn Museum in Washington, D.C., that round thing on the Mall, looking at some pictures, being forced to look at pictures, before I would be allowed to go to the Air and Space Museum, my favorite. I saw some great paintings, or certainly ones that caught my eye. "Gosh, that's really 'neat' (my artfully contrived critical term for something I like), but what does it mean?" Wait a second, there's a small card next to the painting. If I can just amble over to that card and find out what the artist titled the

TABLE 1. Shakespeare Onstage, 1591–1642

Date	Venue	Play
3 March 1591/92	Rose	*Henry VI*
7 March 1591/92	Rose	*Henry VI*
11 March 1591/92	Rose	*Henry VI*
16 March 1591/92	Rose	*Henry VI*
28 March 1591/92	Rose	*Henry VI*
5 April 1592	Rose	*Henry VI*
21 April 1592	Rose	*Henry VI*
4 May 1592	Rose	*Henry VI*
7 May 1592	Rose	*Henry VI*
14 May 1592	Rose	*Henry VI*
19 May 1592	Rose	*Henry VI*
25 May 1592	Rose	*Henry VI*
12 June 1592	Rose	*Henry VI*
19 June 1592	Rose	*Henry VI*
6 January 1592/93	Rose	*Titus* (= *Titus Andronicus*)
16 Janaury 1592/93	Rose	*Henry VI*
23 January 1592/93	Rose	*Titus Andronicus*
25 January 1592/93	Rose	*Titus* (= *Titus Andronicus*)
31 January 1592/93	Rose	*Henry VI*
6 February 1592/93	Rose	*Titus Andronicus*
5 June 1594	Newington	*Andronicus*
11 June 1594	Newington	*The Taming of a Shrew*
12 June 1594	Newington	*Andronicus*
28 December 1594	Gray's Inn	*Comedy of Errors*
7 December 1595	London	*King Richard* (= III? = II?)
1599	London	*Kayser Julio Caesar* (= *Julius Caesar*)
6 March 1599/1600	Hunsdon House, Blackfriars	*Sir John Oldcastle*
17 February 1600/1	Globe	*King Harry IV and of the killing of King Richard II* (= *Henry IV*? = *Richard II*?)
2 February 1601/2	Middle Temple	*Twelfth Night, or What You Will*
1603	Wilton	*As You Like It*
1 November 1604	Whitehall	*The Moor of Venice*
4 November 1604	Whitehall	*The Merry Wives of Windsor*
26 December 1604	Whitehall	*Measure for Measure*
28 December 1604	Whitehall	*The Play of Errors*
Between 1 and 6 January 1604/5	Whitehall	*Love's Labour's Lost*
7 January 1604/5	Whitehall	*Henry V*
10 February 1604/5	Whitehall	*The Merchant of Venice*
12 February 1604/5	Whitehall	*The Merchant of Venice*
1608?	London	*Pericles*
30 April 1610	Globe	*The Merchant of Venice*

TABLE 1—*Continued*

Date	Venue	Play
20 April 1611	Globe	*Macbeth*
1611	London	*Cymbeline King of England*
30 April 1611	Globe	*Richard II*
15 May 1611	Globe	*Winter's Tale*
1 November 1611	Whitehall	*The Tempest*
5 November 1611	Whitehall	*The Winter's Night Tale*
20 May 1613	Payment warrant for performances at Court	*Much Ado about Nothing* *The Tempest* *The Winter's Tale* *Sir John Falstaff* (= *Merry Wives of Windsor*?; = *2 Henry IV*?) *The Moor of Venice* *Caesar's Tragedy* *Cardenio* *The Hotspur* (= *1 Henry IV*) *Benedict and Beatrice* (= *Much Ado about Nothing*)
8 June 1613	Court	*Cardenio*
29 June 1613	The Globe	*All Is True* (= *Henry VIII*)
6 April 1618	Court	*Twelfth Night*
7 April 1618	Court	*The Winter's Tale*
20 May 1619	Whitehall	*Pericles, Prince of Tyre*
ca. 1619/20	probably considered for performance at Court	*The Winter's Tale* *The Two Noble Kinsmen* *The Tragedy of Hamlet* *Second Part of Falstaff*
2 February 1622/23	Court	*Malvolio* (= *Twelfth Night*)
19 August 1623	Revels License	*The Winter's Tale*
18 January 1623/24	Whitehall	*The Winter's Tale*
1 January 1624/25	Whitehall	*The First Part of Sir John Falstaff*
29 July 1628	Globe	*King Henry VIII*
5 August 1628	Globe	*King Henry VIII*[a]
21/22 November 1629	Blackfriars	*The Moor of Venice*
17 October 1630	Hampton Court	*A Midsummer Night's Dream*
6 January 1630/31	Court	*Sir John Oldcastle,* part 1 (= *1 Henry IV*?)
10 June 1631	Globe	*Pericles*
11/12 June 1631	Globe	*Richard II*
16/17 November 1633	St. James	*Richard III*
26 November 1633	Court	*The Taming of the Shrew*
1 January 1633/34	Court	*Cymbeline*

(continued)

TABLE 1—*Continued*

Date	Venue	Play
16 January 1633/34	Court	*The Winter's Tale*
April 1635	Blackfriars	*Falstaff* (= *Merry Wives of Windsor?* = *1 Henry IV?* = *2 Henry IV?*)
6 May 1635	Blackfriars	*The Moor of Venice*
8 December 1636	Hampton Court	*The Moor of Venice*
24 January 1636/37	Hampton Court	*Hamlet*
31 January 1636/37	St. James	*The Tragedy of Caesar*
29 May 1638	Cockpit-in-Court	*Oldcastle* (= *1 Henry IV?* = *2 Henry IV?*)
13 November 1638	Cockpit-in-Court	*Caesar*
15 November 1638	Cockpit-in-Court	*The Merry Wives of Windsor*

Source: Information derived from Joseph Quincy Adams, ed., *The Dramatic Records of Sir Henry Herbert* (New Haven: Yale University Press, 1917); E. K. Chambers, *William Shakespeare* (Oxford: Clarendon, 1930); David Cook, ed., "Dramatic Records in the Declared Accounts of the Treasurer of the Chamber, 1558–1642," *Malone Society Collections* 6 (1961): i–xxvii, 1–175; G. E. Bentley, *The Jacobean and Caroline Stage,* vii (Oxford: Clarendon, 1968), app. C: "Annals of Jacobean and Caroline Theatrical Affairs," 16–128; T. J. King, *Shakespearean Staging* (Cambridge, Mass.: Harvard University Press, 1971), 142; W. R. Streitberger, "Jacobean and Caroline Revels Accounts, 1603–1642," *Malone Society Collections* 13 (1986): ix–xxv, 1–182. Play titles have been modernized.

[a]See A. R. Braunmuller, " 'To the Globe I rowed': John Holles Sees *A Game at Chess*," *English Literary Renaissance* 20 (1990): 350.

painting, then I'll understand it; I'll be able to talk about it with wit and discernment. It turns out, and when has it not, that the small card inevitably reads "Untitled." Titles matter. Titles matter a lot.

NOTES

1. Ann Thompson, in her essay in this volume, relates how very long it took editors to gloss the last two words as the French equivalents of *fuck* and *cunt*.
2. New York: Farrar, Strauss, and Giroux, 1993.
3. London: Chatto and Windus, 1993.
4. New York: Warner, 1992.
5. London: Sinclair-Stevenson, 1992. In reviewing *Ancestral Truths* for the *New York Times Book Review,* Hugh Kenner observes that "when Sara Maitland's new novel was published in England last year it was called 'Home Truths.' A home truth? That's 'an indisputable fact or basic truth, esp. one whose accuracy may cause discomfort or embarrassment.' It hits you, so to speak, where you live; and if Ms. Maitland's New York publishers deemed such an idiom just too veddy British for American comprehension, let them ponder the voice behind the definition I've cited: that of the streetwise Random House Unabridged.

No, to change 'Home' to 'Ancestral' is to impart a majesty of phrasing both inaccurate and pointless. It's like judging that 'Moby Dick' ought to have been called 'Prince of Whales'" (13 March 1994, 12).

6. London: Weidenfeld and Nicolson, 1965.

7. New York: Signet, 1965.

8. Edgar Allen Poe titled his short story "The Visionary" when it first appeared in *Godey's Ladies Book* in 1834. When it reappeared in the *Broadway Journal* in 1845 it had become "The Assignation." *The Choice of Life* was Dr. Johnson's working title for what later appeared in print as *The History of Rasselas, Prince of Abyssinia*.

9. In *As We Know* (New York: Viking, 1979); reprinted in *Literature: An Introduction to Fiction, Poetry, and Drama*, ed. X. J. Kennedy (New York: Harper-Collins, 1991), 602. Can much the same be said for Pound's "In a Station of the Metro," in which the "text" ("The apparition of these faces in the crowd; / Petals on a wet, black bough") really needs the title to complete itself? Pound's poem first appeared in *Persona* (New York: New Directions, 1926); reprinted in Kennedy, *Literature*, 569. The editor of this volume (the one in your hands) has observed, astutely, that the "incipit" at the beginning of manuscripts and incunabula may well function both as part of a "title" and as a "reader-friendly" stage direction.

10. *The Complete Works of William Shakespeare* (Oxford: Clarendon, 1986); the titles in *The Original Spelling Edition* (Oxford: Clarendon, 1986) vary only in terms of spelling.

11. *Analytical and Enumerative Bibliography*, n.s. 3 (1989): 139–70.

12. The *OED* assigns the first use of this word to a *Spectator* paper of Joseph Addison in 1712.

13. Increasingly, I am coming to believe, without a shred of evidence, that at best Heminge and Condell assembled what texts they could and then turned the job over to a professional folio "editor," probably Ben Jonson.

14. If it can be called a process. *Mr. WILLIAM SHAKESPEARES COMEDIES, HISTORIES, & TRAGEDIES* on the title page of the First Folio became, on the last leaf of the preliminaries, *The Workes of William Shakespeare, containing all his Comedies, Histories, and Tragedies.* See my essay "New Historicism and the Editing of English Renaissance Texts," in *New Ways of Looking at Old Texts*, ed. W Speed Hill (Binghamton, N.Y.: Medieval and Renaissance Texts and Studies, 1993), 195–97.

15. Samuel Daniel's *Works* begin in 1601 with *Works; Certain Small Workes* appear in 1607 and again in 1611 and *The Whole Workes* in 1623, the year of Shakespeare's First Folio. Jonson's *Works* appear in 1615, a year before Shakespeare's death. As both Jonson and Daniel included nondramatic pieces in their "works," the layouts of the "contents" vary considerably from that of the First Folio. G. K. Hunter believes that Shakespeare's folio "is a company volume, and . . . that its division of plays into Comedies, Histories, and Tragedies reflects company understanding of the repertory, and . . . the understanding of the good company man, William Shakespeare." This is fanciful. See his essay "Truth and Art in History Plays," *Shakespeare Survey* 42 (1989): 15.

16. The damage that the folio category of "Histories" has done to studies of the genre of the "history play" is incalculable. Virtually eliminated from consideration as history plays are plays on classical subjects, such as *Troilus and Cressida* and any of Thomas Heywood's "Age" plays: *The Golden Age* (1610), *The Silver Age* (1611), *1* and *2 The Iron Age* (1611); plays on foreign topics, such as George Chapman's *Chabot, Admiral of France;* and biblical plays, such as George Peele's *David and Bethsabe.* If it ain't English, it ain't history.

17. While the 1994 Royal Shakespeare Company production of *3 Henry VI* was denied its octavo title, at least it did not have the disadvantage of its folio title. Director Katie Mitchell chose simply *Henry VI* for the program title, along with the subtitle, *The Battle for the Throne.* Perhaps, though, no one would have bought tickets to *3 Henry VI,* having missed the first two parts. Word got out that the production was of *3 Henry VI,* and many in the audience had raced to various texts to bone up on one or more parts of the trilogy. But the production/play/text explained itself very nicely, almost as if the playwright knew what he was doing when he wrote the play.

18. Or, failing that, a trilogy with a really long tail.

19. *1 and 2 Tamburlaine* were published at the same time, in the same edition, to take advantage one of the other. In each of the reprints—1593, 1597, and, even, the somewhat irregular 1605/1606—both parts appear together.

20. Scott McMillin observes that "one decisive change marks the stage history of *1 Henry IV,* and it occurred in the twentieth century. What had been a 'Falstaff' play or, on occasion, a 'Hotspur' play—a play about one or both of the most flamboyant characters—came in the twentieth century to be seen as a study of political power with Prince Hal as the central character. That change of emphasis required a change of fact. It takes both parts of *Henry IV* and *Henry V* to make Prince Hal into a fully fledged hero, or anti-hero, and it was not until the mid-twentieth century that an influential cycle of these plays—influential enough to be imitated in later productions—was staged in the English Theatre" (*Henry IV, Part One* [*Shakespeare in Performance*] [Manchester: Manchester University Press, 1991], 1).

21. Too complex for this essay is the play's relationship to *The Troublesome Reign of King John,* two parts in one, published in 1591.

22. The Folio title also renders John Fletcher's part in the play—indeed, Fletcher's role at the end of Shakespeare's "career"—negligible or nonexistent.

23. The names of Hieronimo, Don Horatio, and Bel Imperia appear on the title page(s) as well, but it is not until the seventh edition of 1615 that the play's title becomes *The Spanish Tragedie, OR Hieronimo is mad Againe.*

24. The first quarto of 1612 reads, *THE WHITE DIVEL, OR, the Tragedy of Paulo Giordano Vrsini, Duke of Brachiano, With the Life and Death of Vittoria Corombona the famous Venetian Curtizan.* The head title makes no mention of a white devil, reading *The Tragedy of Pavlo Giordano Vrsini Duke of Brachiano, and Vittoria Corombona.* The running title reads, simply, *Vittoria Corombona.* The same is true in the play's second edition of 1631. The head title and running title for the 1665 edition remain the same as those in 1612 and 1631, but the title has been changed to *THE White Devil, OR, VITTORIA COR-*

OMBONA A Lady of VENICE. By 1672 the title has been switched to *Vittoria Corombona, OR, THE WHITE DEVIL.*

25. The running title prefers *The Millers daughter of Manchester.*
26. The title page, head title, and running title insist, however, that the play is an *honourable history.*
27. The title of the first edition of 1607 reads, *BEN: IONSON, his VOLPONE Or THE FOXE,* with the head title and running titles reading *THE FOXE.* In the Jonson folios the catalogs call the play *The Foxe,* as do the running titles. The head title is *VOLPONE, OR THE FOX.*
28. My less able students often think that Shylock is the merchant, and I correct them. Perhaps I should not.
29. With Falstaff out of the title, are we more inclined to think of Shakespeare as having lost interest in Falstaff, as having written the play merely to please Queen Elizabeth?
30. Note that *conceited* is missing from the 1630 edition, as it is in the 1631 edition of *Love's Labour's Lost.*
31. *The First Night of 'Twelfth Night'* (New York: Macmillan, 1954).
32. Ed. G. Blakemore Evans (Boston: Houghton Mifflin, 1974), 403. See also Elizabeth Story Donno's New Cambridge edition of *Twelfth Night* (Cambridge: Cambridge University Press, 1985), 1–5.
33. This is not to deny but to temper such critics as Chris Hassel (*Renaissance Drama and the English Church Year* [Lincoln: University of Nebraska Press, 1979]) and Francois Leroque (*Shakespeare's Festive World: Elizabethan Seasonal Entertainment and the Professional Stage,* trans. Janet Lloyd [Cambridge: Cambridge University Press, 1991]), as they "read" the calendar and the festivities and holidays thereto appertaining into plays of the early modern period.
34. *Pericles* remains a "play" on its quarto title pages (1611, 1619, 1630, 1635) and on its folio head titles (1664, 1685) throughout the seventeenth century.
35. Shakespeare did not, could not, in the minds of the folio editors, write tragicomedies.
36. The folio head title is, nonsuperlatively, *The Lamentable Tragedy of Titus Andronicus;* the running title is *The Tragedie of Titus Andronicus.* Sometimes students think the play is like *Romeo and Juliet, Troilus and Cressida,* or *Antony and Cleopatra.* Stationers' *Register* entries for 1602, 1626, and 1630 refer to the play, schizophrenically, as *Titus and Andronicus.*
37. Its running title, *Timon of Athens,* like its catalog title, is noncommital.
38. *Coriolanus* remains a tragedy in its catalog title, head title, and running titles; the same obtains with *Macbeth,* a play whose very title strikes fear into the hearts of superstitious actors, directors, and producers (see Richard Huggett, *The Curse of Macbeth, and Other Theatrical Susperstitions: An Investigation* [London: Picton, 1981]). Stationers' *Register* entries for *Antony and Cleopatra* call it just that, with no generic fussing. The play becomes a tragedy in its folio head title and running titles, but it is "mistitled" as a gender bender, *Anthony and Cleopater,* in the catalog.

TABLE 2. A Summary of Shakespeare in Print, 1594–1700

1. * Greg 117   *Titus Andronicus:* 1594 / 1600 / 1611 / F1–F4
2. Greg 119   *2 Henry VI (The First Part of the Contention):* 1594 / 1600 / 1619 / F1–F4
3. Greg 120   *The Taming of a/the Shrew:* 1594(a) / 1596(a) / 1607(a) / F1(the) / 1631(the) / F2–F4(the)
4. Greg 138   *3 Henry VI (The True Tragedy of Richard Duke of York):* 1595 / 1600 / 1619 / F1–F4
5. Greg 141   *Richard II:* 1597 / 1598 / 1598 / 1608 / 1615 / F1–F2 / 1634 / F3–F4
6. Greg 142   *Richard III:* 1597 / 1598 / 1602 / 1605 / 1612 / 1622 / F1 / 1629 / F2 / 1634 / F3–F4
7. Greg 143   *Romeo and Juliet:* 1597 / 1599 / 1609 / F1 / n.d. / F2 / 1637 / F3–F4
8. Greg 145   *1 Henry IV:* n.d. / 1598 / 1599 / 1604 / 1608 / 1613 / 1622 / F1 / 1632 / F2 / 1639 / F3–F4
9. Greg 150   *Love's Labour's Lost:* 1598 / F1 / 1631 / F2–F4
10. Greg 165   *Henry V:* 1600 / 1602 / 1619 / F1–F4
11. Greg 167   *2 Henry IV:* 1600 / F1–F4
12. Greg 168   *Much Ado about Nothing:* 1600 / F1–F4
13. Greg 170   *A Midsummer Night's Dream:* 1600 / 1619 / F1–F4
14. Greg 172   *The Merchant of Venice:* 1600 / 1619 / F1–F2 / 1637 / 1652 (reissue of 1637) / F3–F4
15. Greg 187   *The Merry Wives of Windsor:* 1602 / 1619 / F1 / 1630 / / F2–F4
16. Greg 197   *Hamlet:* 1603 / 1604–5 / 1611 / n.d.[1625?] / F1–F2 / 1637 / F3 / 1676 / n.d. / 1683 / F4 / 1695
17. Greg 265   *King Lear:* 1608 / 1619 / F1–F2 / 1655 / F3–F4
18. Greg 279   *Troilus and Cressida:* 1609 / F1–F4
19. Greg 284   *Pericles:* 1609 / 1609 / 1611 / 1619 / 1630 / 1635 / F3–F4
20. Greg 379   *Othello:* 1622 / F1 / 1630 / F2 / 1655 / F3 / 1681 / F4 / 1687 / 1695
21. Greg 390   *The Tempest:* F1–F4
22. Greg 391   *Two Gentlemen of Verona:* F1–F4
23. Greg 392   *Measure for Measure:* F1–F4
24. Greg 393   *The Comedy of Errors:* F1–F4
25. Greg 394   *As You Like It:* F1–F4
26. Greg 395   *All's Well That Ends Well:* F1–F4
27. Greg 396   *Twelfth Night:* F1–F4
28. Greg 397   *The Winter's Tale:* F1–F4
29. Greg 398   *King John:* F1–F4
      Greg 101/102   *The Troublesome Reign of King John:* 1591 / 1611 / 1622
30. Greg 399   *1 Henry VI:* F1–F4
31. Greg 400   *Henry VIII:* F1–F4
32. Greg 401   *Coriolanus:* F1–F4
33. Greg 402   *Timon of Athens:* F1–F4
34. Greg 403   *Julius Caesar:* F1–F3 / 1684 / F4 / n.d. / n.d. / n.d. / n.d. / 1691
35. Greg 404   *Macbeth:* F1–F3 / 1673 / F4
36. Greg 405   *Antony and Cleopatra:* F1–F4
37. Greg 406   *Cymbeline:* F1–F4
38. Greg 492   *Two Noble Kinsmen:* 1634 / 1679 (Beaumont and Fletcher Second Folio)

Note: Greg = W. W. Greg, *A Bibliography of the English Printed Drama to the Restoration,* 4 vols. (London: Bibliographical Society, 1939–1959).
F1 = First Folio, 1623
F2 = Second Folio, 1632
F3 = Third Folio, 1663–64
F4 = Fourth Folio, 1685
F1–F4 = First, second, third, and fourth Folios
n.d. = no date

Questions of Entitlement: Some Eighteenth-Century Title Pages

James McLaverty

An interesting development over the last thirty years, though one little noted and seldom discussed, except perhaps with analysts, has been the increasing anxiety induced in scholars by *a, an,* and *the* in titles. Fifty, forty, thirty years ago, when, for example, that careful, even precise, scholar Geoffrey Tillotson was editing *The Rape of the Lock,* he consistently referred to the poem as "*Rape of the Lock*" or "the *Rape of the Lock*" in a relaxed way, even though his title was *The Rape of the Lock and Other Poems.*[1] But a modern scholar, for example, David Vander Meulen in his facsimile of *The Dunciad,* consistently writes *The Dunciad,* though his title is *Pope's "Dunciad" of 1728: A History and Facsimile.*[2] I believe Tillotson and Vander Meulen represent the general historical movement, but seeds of disquiet were evident even in the early years of the century. *Hart's Rules for Compositors and Printers at the University Press Oxford,* after explaining about *The Times* and the *Daily Telegraph,* says, "*The,* if it is part of the title of a book, should also be in italic," but a footnote explains in more detail:

> Henry Bradley and W. A. Craigie, joint editors of the OED, laid down the following rule: "When the writer's intention is to quote the exact title as it stands, the article should be printed *The;* but when a work or periodical is merely referred to either as well known to the reader or as having been already mentioned, then the article should be left in roman (without initial capital, if not at the beginning of a sentence)."[3]

Bradley and Craigie seem to be making a distinction leading in a different direction from the current rule in Hart. They are not guilty of tautology—simply saying you should be fussy when you are being fussy—their point is that only on special occasions, when the title is being quoted, does *The* have to be included: when you use the title, there is no need for conspicuous accuracy. The distinction resembles the philosophical one between use and mention, and it takes us to the heart of the dilemma about titles and title pages.

Scholars increasingly feel that titles should be right. If they are to be right, they must follow an authority. In spite of movements to the contrary, from New Criticism to Deconstruction, that authority cannot reside in the reader or the scholarly community; it cannot be found in what people generally say. Authority is sought in the book, in the title page. "The title should be given as it appears on the title-page," say the Modern Humanities Research Association (MHRA); "Always take the title from the title page," say the Modern Language Association (MLA). But no sooner has the direction been given than it has to be modified: "although very long titles may be suitably abbreviated," concedes MHRA; "Do not reproduce any unusual typographical characteristics," warns the MLA.[4] Just as the scholarly legislators approach the bibliographers, they veer away. In looking for an authority for the text, they find themselves looking at a book. And, faced with a book with all its physical particularity, all its social details, and all its blearings and smearings with trade, they turn away. It will be the argument of this essay that there is nowhere else to go.

If scholars in general, and particularly literary critics, find in title pages a repressed and niggling anxiety, bibliographers seem addicted to them, obsessively transcribing them in their specially devised code, and the sources of this neurosis are no easier to untangle. Few aspects of bibliography as it has been developed by Greg and Bowers are so repulsive to outsiders as quasi-facsimile title-page transcription. A representation that promises to resemble but does not, severe demands of accuracy, a set of complex rules of translation (and not translation, for some things must be left out), and an arcane symbolism all repel outsiders and suggest that no guide to literary interpretation will be found here. The basis of the practice seems to lie in bibliography's relation to bookselling and the need to distinguish editions, issues, and impressions. Yet when, in his booklet *Thoughts on the History and Future of Bibliographical Description*,[5] David Foxon argued that conventional title-page transcription failed to fulfill its purpose of distinguishing editions, suggesting that facsimiles were to be preferred and that, even in their absence, transcription could be dispensed with, he failed to shake the bibliographical establishment.

The question was taken up from a theoretical perspective by G.

Thomas Tanselle, who has recently summarized his arguments while discussing the role of bibliography as historical scholarship:

> It is well understood that historians who write narrative histories will expand or contract their treatment of certain subjects, depending on the aims and focus of the acccounts they are constructing; descriptive bibliographers must similarly shape their work into coherent accounts, since every historical reconstruction involves selection. Neglect of this point also underlies the controversy over whether photographic fac-similes of title pages can take the place of quasi-facsimile transcriptions . . . David Foxon's . . . argument does not spring from a conception of a bibliographical description as a verbal historical account—which may of course be supplemented, but not in part supplanted, by illustrations.[6]

The emphasis on history is attractive, more so than the argument, which subtly elides recognition of the historical nature of bibliography with a hidden stipulation that it is verbal (not pictures). The conclusion comes entirely from the stipulation. It is as strange as to conclude that, because histories of painting are mainly in words, it would be improper to allow a picture to intrude on the narrative and that some painting notation must be invented and used as well or instead. Bibliographical transcriptions and discussions traditionally lack any indication of why title pages are con-sidered important. David Foxon expects transcription to distinguish edi-tions and thereby help editors as well as book collectors, but what more we are to expect from it has not yet been clarified by its supporters. Perhaps the best practical defense of transcription was given by David Vander Meulen in his thesis, when he pointed out that it "provides a standard form of the title page that can be more easily re-used and transmitted," and that is how I shall use various forms of rough transcription in this essay.[7] Transcription has advantages of brevity, ease of reproduction, and cheapness. A more relaxed and positive attitude to it might facilitate the interpretation and analysis of title pages, and might suggest their potential importance in literary and historical studies.

The strange status of title pages—feared and needed by critics, revered and fetishized by bibliographers—probably stems from their curious tex-tual position, which in turn stems from the complex notational status of titles. Titles are a special form of notation. They are most obviously labels. We could devise a code that would sort all literary works, based, for example, on ISBNs or Library of Congress codes; sometimes such a library code almost succeeds in becoming the name of a work (Junius XI, the Caedmon poems). But a system of codes would not fulfill the same function as our present titles do: titles both describe (in a complex way I shall consider later), denote, and exemplify. In being given the title of a novel or poem, we are being given something of the work that will stand for the work itself. The title of the novel differs in this way from most titles of paintings, which, being in a different medium, are not integral to the work. The literary title is, then, like Nelson Goodman's paradigm illustration of exemplification, the swatch of cloth, "exemplification plus reference." But it is a complex case: "If I ask the color of your house, you may say 'red,' or you may show me a red paint-chip, or you may write 'red' in red ink. You may, that is, respond with a predicate, with a sample, or with a combined predicate and sample."[8] The title of a novel is a combined predicate and sample, whereas an incipit is a special form of sample and an ISBN is a label.

Title pages reflect the unusual status of the title. As a label, the title has to be given a special place, identifiable and separate from the rest of the text, but, as a sample, it has to be part of the text. Titles are an essential part of the work—modern works must have titles—but they are only known to be titles by their physical place in the book. Attention to titles leads in a materialist direction. Before the establishment of a print culture, works tended to be identified by their beginnings; a work was listed under its incipit. Latin prayers are known by their beginnings ("Pater noster," "Confiteor"); post-Reformation prayers may have titles (the "Lord's Prayer," the "General Confession"). Only in a book, and, perhaps, a generally available book, can there be this sort of identifying and participating label. There is no oral place for a title because there is no physical means of identifying it. In those curious sets of links and contrasts that have become so popular, between documents, texts, and works (Tanselle), events, texts, and works (McGann), and works and texts (Barthes), title pages stand on the boundary, or at the point of intersection, or, as Genette so accurately has it, on the threshold.[9] They are paratext, more narrowly epitext; they are textual para-/epitext; but they are inescapably text. The distinctions between works and texts and documents are necessary (there are variant texts of *The Rape of the Lock* and there are various instances of those variants), but they should not lead us into believing that literary works are not physical. Just as Rolls-Royces have engines, *Tom Jones* has a title page. The title page will appear in individual instances, and it may vary as different models of *Tom Jones* appear, but this does not require it to have a spiritual or linguistic existence apart from these instances. Critics are, of course, entitled to their own ontological commitments, but the belonging of the title to its page and the page to its book should encourage materialists, even though it will always fall short of providing a knockout blow to their Platonizing opponents.

The eighteenth century can validly be claimed as a point of transition for the title page, a time when its legal role and status became clarified and a time when something slimmer, more elegant, more defiantly textual (and symbolic), emerged. The origin of title pages seems to be crudely physical. The book grows ever outward, acquiring more and more onionlike layers; there is always a new wrapping to protect the text from, or attach it to, the outside world. At first, around 1500, something to protect the text, a short title on the outside of the sheets; then something more elaborate with first the author's (sometimes) and then the publisher's name; then the elaborate title page with frames and compartments, which needed protection from a blank leaf (around 1600) or a leaf with a short title on it (around 1700), which in turn needed protection from a blank leaf. The nineteenth and twentieth centuries have seen the continuation of this process, with edition bindings, elaborately designed jackets (or covers for paperbacks), and even additional bands for special promotions.[10] At the beginning of the eighteenth century this retreat within the citadel of epitext had only just begun; neither half title nor cover posed a threat to the authority of the title page, and it remained the site of the struggle between various competing roles for the book.

An important influence on the development of the book trade, and consequently on title pages, during the period was the legislation of 1709–10 and 1712: "An Act for the Encouragement of Learning" and the "Stamp Act."[11] These two acts reflected different roles for the state. The first responded to lobbying by the Stationers' Company and regulated trade. The idea was to protect the investments of the London traders by preventing printing and dissemination of their "copies"; there was an underlying argument that these copies represented a property that could be bought, sold, and owned like any other—you could have a title to it. The Stamp Act, on the other hand, represented a control on newspapers and pamphlets by taxation. Both reinforced established practices of the London trade, registration of copies, and the provision of imprints. The Act for the Encouragement of Learning provided exclusive rights of printing (twenty-one years for current books, fourteen for new ones) only if "the Title to the Copy of such Book or Books hereafter published shall, before such Publication, be entered in the Register-Book of the Company of Stationers, in such manner as hath been usual." The usual manner involved registering your title by entering the title. The clerk wrote the name of the claimant in one column, the extent of the claim (whole, half, etc.), and then "entered for his copy" and the title of the work:

> Lawton Gilliver The Whole Then Entered for his Copy The Dunciad Variorum with the Prolegomena of Scriblerus. Reced Nine Books. [signed] L. Gilliver

The practice differed little from that which had prevailed under the Licensing Act, which had lapsed in 1695.[12] The accurate representation of the title had been important because the book had to be identifiable as the one licensed by the appropriate authorities; now accuracy was important because it concerned property rights. In the case noted here Gilliver took the whole title from the title page, and this was general practice, even in cases in which the title was complex. *Robinson Crusoe,* for example, has a long and descriptive title, which is discussed later, but it was transcribed into the register on 23 April 1719 with the utmost care. It may be that, in the registering of property, a long title was advantageous as more adequately defining the book.

The Stamp Act also had its effect on the title page by reinforcing Stationers' Company rules about imprints. An ordinance of 1681 required every piece of printing to bear "the name of the printer or of a bookseller with a shop in London or the suburbs," and this was now backed up by a twenty pound fine on anyone publishing a pamphlet without an imprint.[13] The title page was, therefore, under legal control, and it had major importance in the current system of commercial protection.

The actual wording of the title page, unless the work was a collection or miscellany, was probably determined by the author, though this was an area in which the determined bookseller or printer would certainly have a say. Gaskell tells us: "the title page was set from copy, which might indicate roughly how it was to be set out. Details of the layout, however, and choice of type were commonly left to the compositor" (52). These were matters on which the interested, and proofreading, author was likely to be consulted. In some cases the involvement of the author was even more direct. Samuel Richardson was obviously in full control of his books, while Hellinga gives an example of manuscript layout in seventeenth-century Holland, and Julian Ferraro of Liverpool University has recently discovered a title-page draft by Pope in his usual imitation type.[14] The collection of Richard Chiswell's papers in the Bodleian, containing licensed manuscripts and title pages in manuscript and type, provides the opportunity for investigation of the transition from manuscript to print. I believe William Wake's *Exposition of the Doctrine of the Church of England* to be a representative case. The Chiswell papers contain a draft title page in Wake's own hand, with corrections made by the bookseller or printer:

> AN | EXPOSITION | of the | DOCTRINE of the | Church of | ENGLAND | IN | The severall Articles | proposed by Monsr de | MEAUX | ["Late Bishop of Condom." added] | In | His Exposition of | the doctrine of the | CATHOLICK | CHURCH: | To which is prefix'd a par- | ticular acc^t of m^r de M[caret and "Meaux his" added in margin]^s book. | ["ANNO DOM: M. DC. LXXXVI" in funny writing deleted] | ["London printed for Richard Chiswell | at the Rose & Crown in S^t. Pauls church | yard. MDCLXXXV" added].[15]

The compositor accepted most of the wording but rearranged it like this:

> [within a frame of double rules] AN | EXPOSITION | OF THE | DOCTRINE | OF THE | [black letter] Church of England, | IN THE | Several ARTICLES proposed by | Monsieur de *M E A U X,* | [black letter] Late Bishop of Condom, | IN HIS | EXPOSITION of the DOCTRINE | OF THE | [black letter] Catholick Church. | To which is prefix'd a particular account of | *Monsieur de Meaux*'s Book. | [full rule] | LONDON, | Printed for [+ black letter] Richard Chiswell [− black letter], at the *Rose* and *Crown* in St. *Paul*'s | Church-yard. MDCLXXXVI.

The bookseller or printer made the decision to be more explicit about Wake's antagonist by giving his name twice and naming his see, but most of the decisions are aesthetic. Little words are grouped together and put in smaller type so that the main elements of the title can be given a proper emphasis. The Church of England and the Catholic Church are given their own lines and are paralleled by being picked out in black letter. Meaux's name is given in italic spaced caps. The result is more varied and conveys its chief points more forcibly without departing from the author's intentions. Interestingly, the final result is more modern than the marked-up page in having "de Meaux's Book" instead of "de Meaux his book," but we cannot know whether this was the work of the compositor or of the author insisting on his preferred form. This case is likely to be typical of the relation between the printer and the active author. Moxon, who in his *Mechanick Exercises* (London, 1683–84) gives full advice on setting a title page, emphasizes that the compositor should

> read his Copy with consideration; that so he may get himself into the meaning of the Author and consequently consider how to order his Work the better both in the Title Page, and in the matter of the Book: As how to make his Indenting, Pointing, Breaking, Italicking, &c. the better sympathize with the Authors Genius, and also with the capacity of the Reader.[16]

Wake, at least, was lucky enough to find a printer and compositor able to fulfill Moxon's injunctions.

The typical title page around 1700 can usefully be divided into four parts: the title; the name of the author; the motto; and the imprint. Good examples would be *The Country Wife* (1675) and *Love for Love* (1695), whose title pages are currently reproduced in the Penguin edition edited by Gamini Salgado (1968). Each section is neatly divided off by a rule, as this transcription of *Love for Love* shows:

> LOVE for LOVE: | A | COMEDY. | Acted at the | THEATRE in *Little Lincolns-Inn Fields,* | BY | His Majesty's Servants. | [rule] | Written by Mr. *CONGREVE.* | [rule] | *Nudus agris, nudus nummis paternis,* | *Insanire parat certa ratione modoque.* Hor. | [rule] | *LONDON:* | Printed for *Jacob Tonson,* at the *Judge's-Head,* near the | *Inner-Temple-Gate* in *Fleetstreet.* 1695.

(The play printed with them, *The Man of Mode,* differs from this style in one respect: it has a license from Roger L'Estrange where the motto is usually found.) Two of these elements remained unregulated: the motto was entirely a matter of authorial choice, and there was no requirement to declare the author's name on the book, even though contemporary writers discussing copyright sometimes suggested there was.[17]

What a bare transcription does not reveal about these title pages is the relative sizes of the lines of type and their colors. These aspects were not solely determined at this date by the role of this page within its book. The eighteenth-century title page differed from its modern counterpart in one important respect: it was also a mini-poster or advertisement. Title pages were posted up in the shop or in the street to help sell the books. The title page, therefore, belonged to that world of publicity that we now think of as surrounding, but not being part of, the text. When in his *Epistle to Dr. Arbuthnot* Pope expresses his contempt for writing as a profession, he turns away from his attack on Addison (the false literary friend) to this aspect of the title page:

> What tho' my Name stood rubric on the walls?
> Or plaister'd posts, with Claps in capitals?
> Or smoking forth, a hundred Hawkers load,
> On Wings of Winds came flying all abroad?
> I sought no homage from the race that write . . .

John Butt explains, "Books were advertized by 'clapping' copies of title-pages to boards or posts in front of booksellers' shops. Pope's former publisher Lintot was especially fond of red-letter title-pages."[18] Pope's name on a title page, and a showy one at that, here stands for the poet's entrapment in the false values of literature as a trade. His claim is a familiar one: commercial success and the fame that it brings are unimportant; they merely offer a place among ungentlemanly scribblers. (It was perhaps unfortunate that Pope's strong antipathy towards Lintot dated only from the bookseller's attempt to deprive him of some of his anticipated profits from the Odyssey translation.)[19]

The point about the use of red in title pages is made again in the *Dunciad,* in which the province of Dulness is identified as the source of "Curll's chaste press, and Lintot's rubric post," and the note (it might be by Pope or Scriblerus or Sutherland) tells us, "the latter usually adorn'd his shop with Titles in red letters."[20] Nor is it a coincidence that the urinating contest in *The Dunciad* II begins at the site of this poor-quality publicity:

> First Chetwood leaned against his letter'd post;
> It rose, and labour'd to a curve at most
>
> (II, 163–64)

Pope himself, however, had little to complain of in Lintot's title pages— after 1728 he doubtless designed his own; perhaps he was remembering the way that his first venture with Lintot, the collection *Miscellaneous Poems and Translations. By Several Hands,* to which he had contributed the two-canto *Rape of the Locke* and some translations, had been reissued as "Particularly . . . By Mr. Pope." But Pope could hardly have claimed that Lintot's title pages had seriously damaged his gentility, even if he had to wait for independence and control of his printer and bookseller before being advertised as "Alexander Pope of Twickenham in Com. Midd. Esq;" on the title page of *The First Satire of the Second Book of Horace* in 1733, a change finally confirmed in 1735, when the second volume of his works became *The Works of Alexander Pope, Esq;*.

The role of the title page as advertisement, therefore, had a strong influence on a poet as sensitive of his dignity as Pope, but it also had an influence on layout. On the three title pages of Restoration comedies previously referred to, the stress each time is on "comedy". In *The Country Wife* and *The Man of Mode* the contrast is between upper and lower case for the title and capitals for "COMEDY"; in *Love for Love* the contrast is between capitals of 11 mm and capitals of 14 mm. The emphasis on genre is connected with eighteenth-century publicity conventions. *Bibliotheca Annua: or The Annual Catalogue for the Year, 1699* (London, 1700) lists books under the headings: Divinity, History, Law, Musick, Poetry, Plays, Miscellaneous, Physick, Mathematicks, Lit. Lat., and Livres François. The *Gentleman's Magazine* index later worked in much the same way, anticipating Bentham with a category "Poetry and Amusement." The customer was interested in comedies first, a particular play second, and the author a bad third. The same emphasis on genre can be seen in the title page of one of the most famous of all novels, *Robinson Crusoe:*

> The Life and Strange Surprizing Adventures of Robinson Crusoe, of York, Mariner: Who lived Eight and Twenty Years, all alone in an uninhabited Island on the Coast of America, near the Mouth of the Great River of Oroonoque; Having been cast on Shore by Shipwreck, wherein all the Men perished but himself. With An Account how he was at last as strangely deliver'd by Pyrates. Written by Himself. London; Printed for W. Taylor at the Ship in Pater-Noster-Row. MDCCXIX.

The emphasis is on "LIFE" (11 mm) rather than "*ROBINSON CRUSOE*" (5 mm), though "*Written by Himself*" is highlighted by its italics and by being separated from the rest of the text by two rules, the only two within the page (fig. 1). There can be no doubt that, whatever the sophistication of Defoe's narrative, the work is presented in this title page as a true story. The italic capitals of "*YORK*" ground this life in a known

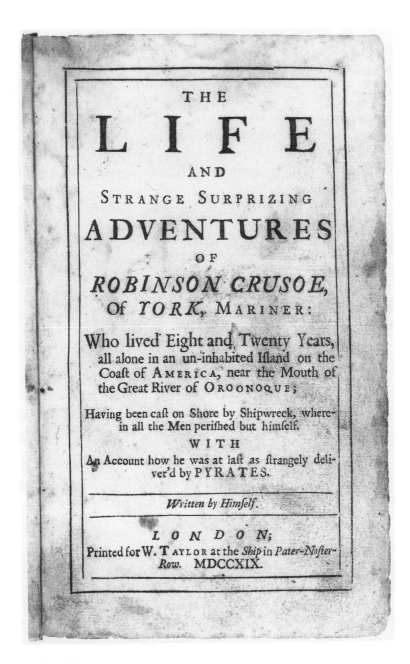

THE
L I F E
AND
STRANGE SURPRIZING
ADVENTURES
OF
ROBINSON CRUSOE,
Of *YORK,* MARINER:

Who lived Eight and Twenty Years,
all alone in an un-inhabited Ifland on the
Coaft of AMERICA, near the Mouth of
the Great River of OROONOQUE;

Having been caft on Shore by Shipwreck, wherein all the Men perifhed but himfelf.

WITH

An Account how he was at laft as ftrangely deliver'd by PYRATES.

Written by Himfelf.

L O N D O N;
Printed for W. TAYLOR at the *Ship* in *Pater-Nofter-*
Row. MDCCXIX.

Fig. 1. Title page of *Robinson Crusoe.* (Reproduced by kind permission of
the Bodleian Library [Don. e. 442].)

reality and set up a comparison with the (much smaller) caps. and small caps. of "AMERICA" and "OROONOQUE." In this context "*Written by Himself*" seems to guarantee authenticity. The modern title, *Robinson Crusoe*, expunges this possibility by making Crusoe himself the subject of the work; the consequences of the change become apparent if we imagine the *Apologia* entitled *John Henry Newman* or *The Prelude* entitled *William Wordsworth*. The modern title brings the work into line with fictions rather than autobiographies.

Significant numbers of long, descriptive titles like that to *Robinson Crusoe* have been abbreviated for both popular and academic use, usually to the name of a person, often with unsatisfactory results. The most striking example is *Roxana*. Roxana differs from *Robinson Crusoe* and *Moll Flanders* because a short title has been supplied, probably by Defoe, and subsequently ignored: "The Fortunate Mistress: Or, A History of the Life and Vast Variety of Fortunes Of Mademoiselle de Beleau, Afterwards Call'd The Countess de Wintselsheim, in Germany. Being the Person known by the Name of the Lady Roxana, in the Time of Charles II." This time there is no reference to authorship at all (*Moll Flanders* follows the pattern of *Robinson Crusoe*, reading "*Written from her own* MEMORANDUMS" between rules), but there is a short title offered ("THE *Fortunate Mistress*," with swash *F* and *M*), which gives the novel a thematic emphasis. It has frequently been remarked that, though the action is set in the time of Charles II, this may merely serve as a disguise for contemporary references, but there has been less emphasis on either the irony or the social specificity of the offered short title. The whole title seems less of a description than that of *Robinson Crusoe* and *Moll Flanders* and more of an attempt to set up a set of reference points: mistress; France, Germany, Charles II. Of these the greatest weight is given to "*GERMANY*," set in italic caps., with spacing between letters for emphasis, which may indeed point in the direction of George I.

In comparison with what now seem conventional titles, like *Far from the Madding Crowd* or even *Middlemarch,* Defoe's are summaries or descriptions rather than single symbols standing completely for the whole. The contrast between the title that is a description and one that seems to be merely a label (though, in the best works, one potentially rich in meaning and in a special way a sample) relates to the debates about proper names in philosophy. The best introduction to the relevant issues is provided by John Searle in *Speech Acts,* and, although the questions raised are too profound and various to be discussed here, a summary may prove useful. The view that proper names are not descriptions is a traditional one:

proper names do not have senses, they are meaningless marks; they have denotation but not connotation (Mill). The argument for this view is that whereas a definite description refers to an object only in virtue of the fact that it describes some *aspect* of that object, a proper name does not *describe* the object at all.[21]

Searle then offers three reasons for rejecting this commonsense view: proper names are used in existential propositions when the name cannot refer ("Cerberus does not exist"); proper names can be used to make identity statements that convey factual information ("Everest is Chomolungma"); and a description is necessary for identification. Searle's resolution of this clash between common sense (though it has strong philosophical support) and philosophical argument is to find a way between:

> My answer, then, to the question, "Do proper names have senses?"—if this asks whether or not proper names are used to describe or specify characteristics of objects—is "No." But if it asks whether or not proper names are logically connected with characteristics of the object to which they refer, the answer is "Yes, in a loose sort of way." (170)

Searle believes his point can be clarified by reference to what he calls "degenerate proper names," for example, "the Bank of England," in which the connected characteristics emerge on the surface (173).

Literary titles seem to play with these poles of definite description and meaningless mark, many of them following the Bank of England into degeneracy of proper name. The most obvious way in which they approach the status of meaningless mark is derivatively. It is theoretically possible for novelists to give their novels random identifying marks, though habits of reading make it well-nigh impossible, and apparent random marks rarely prove to be so (e.g., Berger's *G*). (The rock star Prince has recently set an example by declaring himself to be denoted by a symbol, thus evading the general connotations of his name and those created by his career, but this gambit has had a poor take-up, as this sentence shows.) Eighteenth-century novelists set a pattern, which hardened in popular novels of the nineteenth century, of naming their novels after the near meaningless marks within them, that is, after the names of their characters. This provides a minimal identification of the content of the novel while preserving much of the freedom a random mark would offer. The most famous eighteenth-century novels all seem to fit this pattern: *Pamela, Joseph Andrews, Clarissa, Tom*

Jones, Humphry Clinker, Evelina. Closer examination, however, reveals more complicated arrangements.

Richardson's *Pamela,* perhaps the most famous of the character-labeled novels, is in fact a belt and braces job, combining a character name with almost as much description as Defoe's novels use. But Richardson's description is less concerned with identification than with evaluation. Volume 4 of the first edition provided the account that remained current until at least 1801 (fig. 2):

> Pamela; or, Virtue Rewarded. In a Series of Familiar Letters From a Beautiful Young Damsel to her Parents: And afterwards, In her Exalted Condition, between Her, and Persons of Figure and Quality, upon the most Important and Entertaining Subjects, In Genteel Life. [rule] Publish'd in order to cultivate the Principles of Virtue and Religion in the Minds of the Youth of Both Sexes.

Richardson was a printer and knew his business, and this is more of a puff than any of Defoe's works was given. *Pamela*'s title page describes not the work but the moral intentions of the author. It initiates criticism of the novel but on its own terms, attempting to control both the ground of the debate and the judgment of the reader. The first volume was, if anything, even more explicit in its efforts to control the nature of critical exchange:

> A Narrative which has its Foundation in TRUTH | and NATURE; and at the same time that it agree- | ably entertains, by a Variety of *curious* and *affecting* | INCIDENTS, is intirely divested of all those Images, | which, in too many Pieces calculated for Amusement | only, tend to *inflame* the Minds they should *instruct.*

Small changes between the first and fourth volumes reflect differences in emphasis in this attempt to write not only the novel but also its critique. New material (Pamela's exalted condition and persons of Figure and Quality) has to be accounted for, but Richardson takes the opportunity to emphasize "Entertaining Subjects" while significantly downgrading the importance of Pamela's beauty by moving the word back a line and reducing it by about 1.5 mm. (A change from ":" to ";" after "PAMELA" I cannot account for.) Richardson points to the novelist's dilemma by offering through his title and subtitle—his protagonist and his theme—something like Searle's name and connected characteristics. A printer's skill

PAMELA;

OR,

VIRTUE Rewarded.

In a SERIES of

FAMILIAR LETTERS

From a Beautiful

Young DAMSEL to her PARENTS:

And afterwards,

In her EXALTED CONDITION,

BETWEEN

HER, and Perfons of *Figure* and *Quality*,

UPON THE MOST

Important and Entertaining Subjects,

In GENTEEL LIFE.

Publifh'd in order to cultivate the Principles of
VIRTUE and RELIGION in the Minds of
the YOUTH of BOTH SEXES.

VOL. IV.

LONDON:

Printed for S. RICHARDSON:
And Sold by C. RIVINGTON, in *St. Paul's Church-
Yard* ; And J. OSBORN, in *Pater-nofter Row.*

M.DCC.XLII.

has been used to ensure the right balance of emphasis, with the spaced capitals of "Pamela" only 1 mm higher than those of "Virtue" in "Virtue Rewarded." Fielding's first novel presents us with a neat and probably deliberate contrast: "The History of the Adventures of Joseph Andrews, and of his Friend Mr. Abraham Adams. Written in Imitation of The Manner of Cervantes, Author of Don Quixote." There is little of the puff here, and only a minimum of description; readers are given interpretive and evaluative freedom. I suspect that by this stage "The History of the Adventures of" does little more than convey information that this is a novel (though "history" may have a special importance for Fielding). What is unusual in this title page is its self-conscious literariness; we are a long way from "Written by Himself." The reference to a literary predecessor gives a generic indicator and also initiates the work of general critical analysis that Fielding is to continue in his preface and novel.

The movement towards brevity of title provides greater freedom for both writer and reader, but it risks the flatness of the mechanical. *Virtue Rewarded,* like *Sense and Sensibility* or *Pride and Prejudice,* may provide too neat a summary of its work and too strongly determine its reading—a reading Fielding famously resisted—but the advantage of the openness of a character name is offset by its unimaginative neutrality. Wordsworth, with his early emphasis on the literal and his resistance to artificial representation and symbolization, found titles peculiarly difficult. *The Prelude,* of course, was unpublished and untitled. *Lyrical Ballads,* which now seems to have powerful connotations, is in many ways strikingly neutral. The first title page had "Lyrical Ballads, with a Few Other Poems," which is almost haphazard, and that of the fourth edition had "Lyrical Ballads, with Pastoral and other Poems," which is hardly an improvement. Within the volumes, titles on the page sometimes differed from those listed in the contents. Wordsworth's attempts to avoid a symbolizing title take different forms. Sometimes he avoids a title by using an incipit; often he refers to matters that would normally be thought contingent to the meaning of the poem—what it was written on, where it was written, when it was written. Sometimes he does settle on a symbolic object, as in "The Thorn," but in what is probably the most successful poem about an object, the ruined sheepfold, he takes a trick from the novelist and calls the poem "Michael." The movement towards brevity in titles should not therefore be thought of as unqualified advance; it seems that an oscillation between revelation and concealment is always desirable.

Titles on title pages, therefore, which might be expected to serve primarily as names, as near meaningless marks, actually do much more: sample, summarize, advertise, moralize, criticize, evade. As they present so much information, it is tempting to raise the question of their truthfulness, but, although title pages may be evasive or misleading, it would be difficult to convict one of a lie. We have already seen examples of cases in which the claims made on the title page are not to be taken at face value: *Robinson Crusoe* is not "written by himself"; *Moll Flanders* is not "written from her own memorandums"; and *Pamela* is not truly free from "all those images" that tend to "inflame the minds they should instruct." Whether the title page is lying or false is, however, as Genette suggests, a matter of what illocutionary act you attribute to the author (15–16). Some title pages raise the question very directly—for example, Pope's *A Full and True Account of a Horrid and Barbarous Revenge by Poison, on the Body of Edmund Curll, Bookseller; With a Faithful Copy of his Last Will and Testament,* which is neither full nor wholly true nor faithful. But, although the account itself is false in relation to events, the title accurately represents the work's view of itself; the duty of a title page seems to be to its book rather than to its reader. This is in part justifiable because the title page is entitled to derive its illocutionary status from the book. If the book is ironic, the title (e.g., *Sober Advice from Horace*) is entitled to be; if the book is a fiction, the title (e.g., "Memoirs of P. P., Clerk of this Parish") is entitled to be. This tolerance is limited, however, to cases where there is such a link. If Pope's account of Curll's poisoning had been called *A Complete Guide to Equity and Contract,* we would entertain a claim that the title was false, but it is likely we would prefer to call it misleading. I suspect this extends even to the case where the title is *A Complete Guide to Equity and Contract* and large sections of the subject are left out. Titles, unlike modern publishers' claims on the back cover, are not true or false. They thus conform to Searle's view of proper names in general. As he says, "it may be conventional to name only girls 'Martha,' but if I name my son 'Martha,' I may mislead, but I do not lie" (173). Such unconventional naming may not even mislead; in appropriate circumstances (perhaps I name my daughter Michael or label my plan for eating babies *A Modest Proposal*) it challenges preconceptions and disturbs set responses. If these intuitions are correct, titles belong with ordinary proper names rather than with definite descriptions, no matter how descriptive they may be; they occupy the territory of proper name degeneracy.

Another sense in which a title might be thought to be false is when it is not the author's. We have already seen cases where the modern title of a work departs significantly from the one given by its author. But authors change their minds, and Pope's oeuvre highlights the difficulties for critics and editors who wish to use correct, authorially approved, titles but are reluctant to accept the materiality and changeableness of the text. In his volume of the Twickenham Pope (III, ii) F. W. Bateson spends some considerable space rejecting Warburton's grouping of four poems as "moral essays," insisting on their status as "Epistles to Several Persons" instead. A glance at the history of one poem will show how difficult this question is. In December 1731 appeared "An Epistle to the Right Honourable Richard Earl of Burlington. Occasion'd by his Publishing Palladio's Designs of the Baths, Arches, Theatres, &c of Ancient Rome. By Mr. Pope. London: Printed for L. Gilliver at Homer's Head in Fleet-street, 1731. Price 1s." This is a different combination of generic indicator and name, for this time the name is that of the addressee, but it indicates once more the dependence of literary titling on already existing names. The poem is put forward as an occasional one, and it is an adaptation of an older tradition of patronage. It is addressed to a great man not on his birthday nor on his arrival in London but on his becoming an author, a role that places the experienced author-poet in a position of superiority.

Pope was not finished, however, with this deployment of the title page. He used a half title to indicate a thematic concern over and above the occasion of the poem: "Of Taste, An Epistle to the Right Honourable Richard Earl of Burlington, By Mr Pope." This looks rather like a moral essay. In January he made a change to the opening of the half title in the second edition, "Of False Taste . . . ," and later in the same month he used a third edition to bring the half title into the title: "Of False Taste. An Epistle . . ." (fig. 3). The balance between the former half title and the original title is skillfully maintained. "Of False Taste" is now placed first on the title page, but it is in smaller type, and it is separated by a rule from the former title. Pope includes it, even gives it priority, but he will not allow it to dominate. The revisions Pope was making in this poem at the same time and the different relations deployed have been traced by Julian Ferraro in a series of important papers.[22] The naming of the poem became even more complicated through Pope's plans for an "opus magnum" in which the *Essay on Man* was to be paralleled by a collection of complementary poems and his subsequent abandonment, modification, and revival of this scheme, with consequent groupings and regroupings.[23] The search in cases like this to establish one single, unchangeable title is doomed to failure. The titles belong to the books, and Pope uses different arrangements of his books to

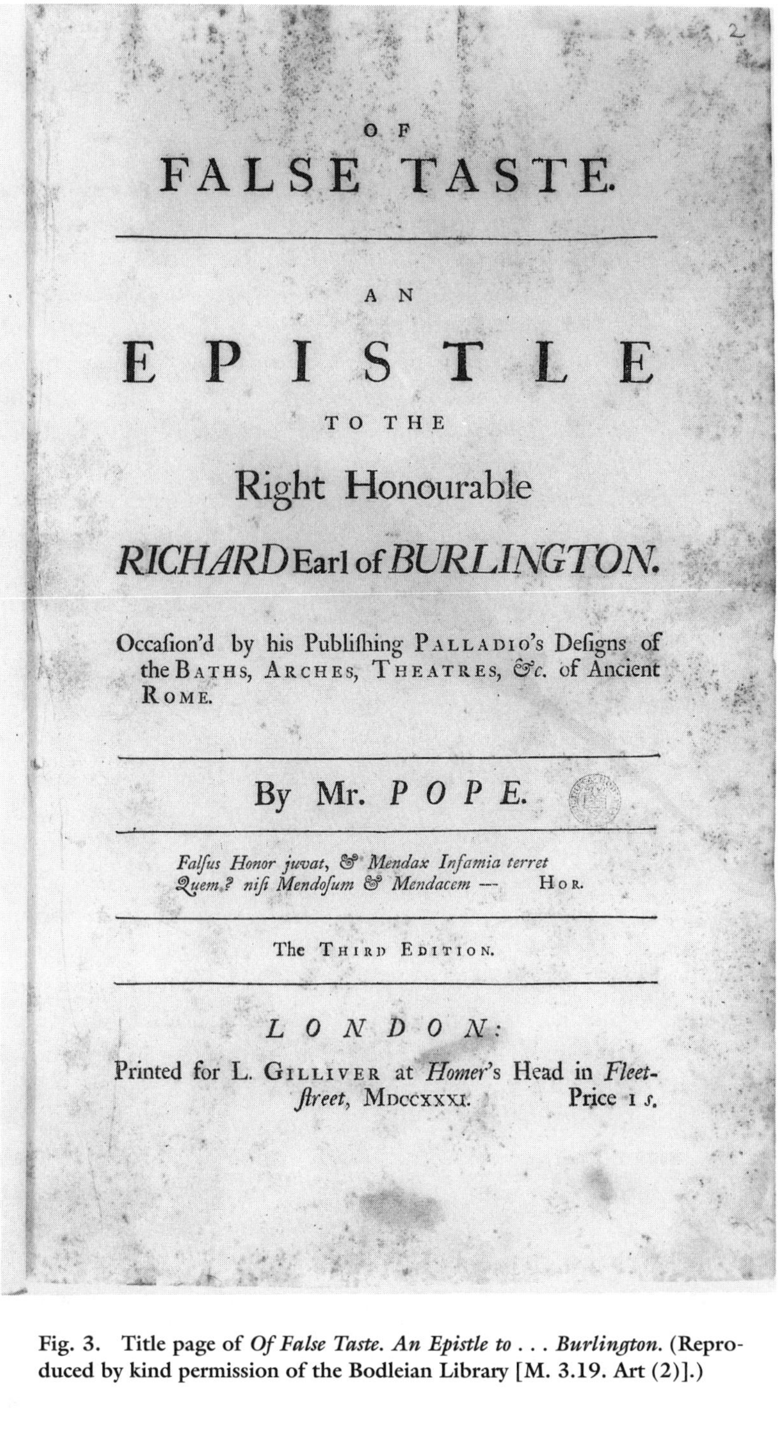

O F

FALSE TASTE.

A N

EPISTLE

TO THE

Right Honourable

RICHARD Earl of *BURLINGTON.*

Occaſion'd by his Publiſhing PALLADIO's Deſigns of
the BATHS, ARCHES, THEATRES, &c. of Ancient
ROME.

By Mr. *POPE.*

Falſus Honor juvat, & Mendax Infamia terret
Quem? niſi Mendoſum & Mendacem — HOR.

The THIRD EDITION.

LONDON:

Printed for L. GILLIVER at *Homer's* Head in *Fleet-*
ſtreet, MDCCXXXI.   Price 1 *s.*

Fig. 3. Title page of *Of False Taste. An Epistle to . . . Burlington.* (Reproduced by kind permission of the Bodleian Library [M. 3.19. Art (2)].)

serve different literary purposes. Accounts of titles not only need attention to the details of title pages; they also need to be diachronic, with attention to the context in which they emerge.

The next section of the title page, which contains the author's name, raises the difficulties about truth and falsehood that have already been addressed. Modern versions of titles have removed some of the original tension and difficulty. Eighteenth-century title pages are rich in anonymity, pseudonymity, and indications of status, which are lost in modern practices of naming. The cases of Defoe's novels are paralleled by other famous works. An original copy of *Gulliver's Travels*, for example, is capable of startling the reader by the thoroughness of its hoaxing style: "TRAVELS I INTO SEVERAL I Remote NATIONS I OF THE I WORLD. I [rule] I IN FOUR PARTS. I [rule] I By *LEMUEL GULLIVER*, I First a SURGEON, and then a CAP- I TAIN of several SHIPS." It is partly the typography that gives the air of authenticity: the largest word is "world" (5 mm), not "travels" (4 mm), giving the emphasis to the scope of the book and its potential for description rather than to the activity of its writer. But the writer too is given his authenticating due, with a frontispiece portrait of Lemuel Gulliver with all conventional attributes, "Captain Lemuel Gulliver of Redriff AEtat. suae 58." The perfectly understandable modern practice of writing of Swift's *Gulliver's Travels* removes the play of fact/fiction, suspension/nonsuspension of illocutionary force, which Swift doubtless enjoyed and framed as an important part of his original meaning.

Anonymity and pseudonymity were both common in the eighteenth century, and, though they are technically distinct, the effort to distinguish them is rarely worthwhile. The most notorious case of unknown authorship, the *Letters of Junius* (1769), was strictly pseudonymous, but it might correctly be said that the author remained anonymous. Anonymity was practiced for a variety of reasons. There was still a vestigial stigma attached to print. Harold Love's study *Scribal Publication in Seventeenth-Century England* shows that many authors, and particularly women, preferred manuscript publication, a form of dissemination over which they could exercise a surprising measure of control.[24] Anonymity was a readily available alternative for the aristocratic, the genteel, the political, the scurrilous, and the obscene. Generic pseudonyms were popular and would play an important role in any study of how status entered the title page in both namings and non-namings of authors. We have seen that Pope eventually moved from being "Mr. Pope" to being "Alexander Pope, Esq;"; Fielding, who published *Joseph Andrews* anonymously, appears on the title page of

The History of Tom Jones, A Foundling as "Henry Fielding, Esq;." When Pope had Bolingbroke's *The Idea of a Patriot King* printed, he said it was "By a Person of Quality." When Lady Mary Wortley Montagu and others published *Verses Address'd to the Imitator of Horace*, it was said to be "By a Lady," and the reply, *Advice to Sappho*, was said to be "By a Gentlewoman." *Tristram Shandy* is properly *The Life and Opinions of Tristram Shandy, Gentleman.*

An alternative to pseudonymity or plain anonymity was cross-reference to other works. Smollett set a pattern that became very common in the nineteenth century with *The Expedition of Humphry Clinker. By the Author of Roderick Random* (1771). The style proved particularly useful to women writers who wanted to remain anonymous but to build on an established reputation. Charlotte Lennox's *Shakespeare Illustrated* (1753), for example, is declared to be "By the author of the Female Quixote," and Jane Austen's novels regularly have cross-references in this way. Pope employs an ingenious and misleading version of this technique in his *Sober Advice*, which is said to be "Imitated in the Manner of Mr. Pope," which indeed it was.

Mottoes appear on the title pages of learned books or works that claim an equivalent dignity. A prime purpose in their use was to display learning as well as to indicate thematic emphasis rather as the subtitle might. Defoe's novels do not have mottoes, but some popular plays did. *The Country Wife* and *Love for Love* have mottoes from Horace that show the learning of the writers and establish their credentials as wits, and even *The Beggar's Opera* has a short motto from Martial. *Tom Jones* is equally modest, using a motto that generally indicates the author's emphasis, "Mores hominum multorum vidit." *Tristram Shandy*, the better to indicate its place in the tradition of learned satire, has its motto in Greek. Mottoes did not have to be in an ancient language, though they commonly were. Locke's *An Essay Concerning Humane Understanding* (1700) has a quotation in English from Ecclesiastes to balance one in Latin from Cicero. As the century progressed, it became more likely that quotations would be translated, even on the title page. Johnson's *Rambler* in 1750 has as its motto an untranslated quotation from Horace, but his *Adventurer* has its motto from Virgil translated into English verse from the second edition of 1754 onwards. The motto seems to have lost importance as the century progressed—Pope did not always use one late in his career—but gained its revenge by invading the novel and its chapter headings as the epigraph during the nineteenth century.

The imprint, like any edition statement, belongs firmly to the printer's and bookseller's side of the book, but even here the boundary is not always clear. The imprint might tell you who printed the book, who owned the copyright, where you could buy it, the year of publication, and the price. Often one or more of these elements was missing. Any listing of members of the book trade, especially if it included their addresses, necessarily had a social significance: Dodsley in Pall-Mall or Brindley in New Bond Street represented a superior branch of the trade to Boreman at the Cock on Ludgate Hill. The names of Dodd, Nutt, or, more certainly, A. Moore suggested something scurrilous afoot. A book from Curll's press was unlikely to be chaste. As David Foxon has explained, other information in the imprint in the early part of the century is coded in ways likely to be misleading to the modern eye. "London, Printed: and Sold by James Roberts" does not mean that Roberts was the printer, merely that he was the distributor, and "London: Printed for James Roberts" does not mean that he was the copyright holder, merely that he was the distributor. In order to interpret the imprint, you needed to know that Roberts's business was as a publisher.[25] Imprints offered other clues that were easier to read. The naming of the printer, "Printed by J. Wright for Lawton Gilliver," suggested that he had a more important role than usual: perhaps he had a share of the copyright, or this was an instance when he was working directly for the author. During the period of Pope's business independence, when he was employing and instructing both John Wright and Lawton Gilliver, their names appeared in his imprints as a kind of identifying badge. When it was important to retain anonymity, as over an *Essay on Man,* Wright and Gilliver were neither used nor mentioned; when Pope wanted to advance the work of his protégé Walter Harte, and add to the confusion over an *Essay on Man* by passing off Harte's *Essay on Reason* as his own work, their names appeared in the familiar way in the imprint, accompanied by the characteristic woodblock that had also appeared on the title page of the *Dunciad Variorum.*

Although imprints merit careful interpretation and sometimes bear different meanings for different readerships, I suspect they differ from other parts of the title page in that, like edition statements, they can be plain false. When Lord Oxford responds to the claim of a copy of *Verses Address'd to the Imitator of Horace* to be the fifth edition by saying that it is a sham of the booksellers (in Bodleian M 3.19 Art), he is probably right. When the 1735 octavo *To Arbuthnot* says it is printed by J. Wright when it is printed by Thomas Ruddiman, it seems to be guilty of falsehood, and the falsehood is associated with unfair dealing, for this is an Edinburgh piracy. Claims that an edition is "revised" or "revised throughout" are common in the eighteenth century, and they are rarely true.

Prices, like imprints, seem to belong safely to the realm of the bookseller, and yet I suspect that in Pope's case even they may signal authorial involvement. In the early part of his career Pope's poems did not appear with a price on the title page: no price appears on an *Essay on Criticism, Windsor Forest, Ode for Musick,* or the *Rape of the Lock.* But, when Pope began the period of alliance with Wright and Gilliver, prices started to appear: *To Burlington, To Bathurst, To Cobham,* an *Essay on Man, To a Lady, Ode to Venus,* most of the Horatian imitations, and the *New Dunciad* all displayed prices on their title pages. Cheap and popular works, many of the pamphlet attacks on Pope, for example, often appeared with prices, and there may be trade developments that account for this change of practice on Pope's title pages, but one possible reason for the printed prices is a form of retail price maintenance to preserve profit margins for the bookseller and author. When Pope persuaded the Earl of Oxford to publish the *Dunciad Variorum* for him, he told him not to sell copies at less than six shillings; at the same time, Gilliver was asking John Stagg not to sell copies to booksellers at less than six shillings; in 1735 Pope asked Samuel Buckley to take some copies of *Works* II but not to sell them to the trade at less than eighteen shillings or to gentlemen at less than a guinea.[26] This concern with maintaining the retail price was surely based on Pope's squeezing of his bookseller, who needed to ensure he made a very good price on the copies he sold in order to meet Pope's demands for copyright payment. It is surprising that someone as aesthetically conscious as Pope allowed prices to appear on his title pages, but the general pattern of his career suggests that if it meant more profit he would probably have insisted on it.

These attempts at interpretation of imprints in relation to the author's intentions are dangerous if they detract from recognition of the repressed truth that these books were commodities. It is not all they were, and some authors may have done their best to resist commodification, but examination of a number of the title pages of this period suggests a worldly wisdom in authors that prevailing romantic ideologies have effaced. There is a lively engagement with the making and marketing of books, an enthusiasm for it as well as a delighted mocking of it, that makes attention to these title pages instructive. The title page anxiety I spoke of at the outset of this essay has lately had a new manifestation in the practice of reprinting original title pages of novels in their modern editions; both Penguin and Oxford have made it a general policy. Unfortunately, at present the practice seems to represent little more than a superstition: the presence of the title page suggests authenticity and editorial seriousness—even if the text is based on a late reprint. But the omen is good. What is now needed is some seepage between the critical introductions that precede these illustrations but ignore them and those bibliographies that faithfully record title pages without quite saying why.

NOTES

1. Geoffrey Tillotson, ed., *The Twickenham Edition of the Poems of Alexander Pope*, vol. 2, 3d ed. (London: Methuen; New Haven: Yale University Press, 1962). The first edition was 1940, the second 1954. The series name has not been taken from the title page but from the advertisement on the verso of the half title. This essay has benefited from stimulating discussions with John Bowen, Jonathan Dancy, David Greetham, and Angus Ross; I regret that it has been possible to follow up only a few of their valuable suggestions here.
2. David Vander Meulen, ed., *Pope's "Dunciad" of 1728* (Charlottesville and London: University Press of Virginia, 1991). I have followed his example in writing "The Dunciad" here, though I have written what came naturally in the rest of the essay. In presenting the title of his book, I have followed the conventions of the *Chicago Manual of Style*, 14th ed. (Chicago: University of Chicago Press, 1993); and the *MHRA Style Book*, 4th ed. (London: MHRA, 1991).
3. *Hart's Rules for Compositors and Readers at the University Press Oxford*, 39th ed. (Oxford: Oxford University Press, 1983), 24. Bradley and Craigie were joint editors of the dictionary in the period after Murray's death, in 1915, until Bradley's own in 1923. The last part of the dictionary did not appear until 1928 (supp. 1933).
4. *MHRA Style Book*, 34; and *MLA Handbook for Writers of Research Papers*, 2d ed. (New York: MLA, 1984), 2.5.1. The *Chicago Manual of Style* favors omission of *The*, especially when it offends syntax (7.135, 15.112).
5. David Foxon, *Thoughts on the History and Future of a Bibliographical Description* (Los Angeles: School of Library Service, 1970).
6. Tanselle, "Issues in Bibliographical Studies since 1942," in *The Book Encompassed*, ed. Peter Davison (Cambridge: Cambridge University Press, 1992), 28. Of course, title page transcriptions are not verbal historical accounts but symbolic representations; their status is very similar to facsimiles, though they are digital, not analogue.
7. Vander Meulen, "A Descriptive Bibliography of Alexander Pope's Dunciad, 1728–1751," MS, University of Wisconsin–Madison, 1981, 44; his is one of the best discussions of this topic. It is cited in Tanselle's "Title-Page Transcription and Signature Collation Reconsidered," *Studies in Bibliography* 38 (1985): 45–81, an essay that raises many important issues. My transcriptions

do not have the same status as those in proper bibliographical descriptions, in that they are based on only one copy.

8. Goodman, *Languages of Art,* 2d ed. (Indianapolis: Hackett, 1985), 60. Music titles raise problems similar to those of paintings. Many are generic (Piano Concerto no. 5) and have titles imposed upon them (*Emperor*); others derive from characters (*Don Juan*); others are thematic (*Tod und Verklärung*). The historical movement seems to be away from generic counting. Musical compositions could have musical titles, and, if it became more common to read musical scores than to perform them, such a practice might develop. Haydn recorded incipits in his "Entwurf-Katalog"; the recent case of six forged sonatas shows the usefulness of incipits as aids to identification and to forgery (*Guardian,* 4 January 1994, 2–3).

9. G. Thomas Tanselle, *A Rationale of Textual Criticism* (Philadelphia: University of Pennsylvania Press, 1989); and in other essays, especially "Textual Criticism and Deconstruction," *Studies in Bibliography* 43 (1990): 1–33, which should be read in relation to D. C. Greetham's response, setting out further possible oppositions involving "text," "[Textual] Criticism and Deconstruction," *Studies in Bibliography* 44 (1991): 1–30; Jerome McGann, *The Beauty of Inflections* (Oxford: Clarendon Press, 1988); and *The Textual Condition* (Princeton: Princeton University Press, 1991); Roland Barthes, "From Work to Text," *Image-Music-Text,* ed. and trans. Stephen Heath (Glasgow: Fontana Press, 1977), 156–57 (title words are actually in capital letters and separated by full rules). Gerard Genette's *Seuils* (Paris: Editions du Seuil, 1987) provides a dazzling taxonomical introduction to the subject of this essay.

10. For an introduction to this history, see Philip Gaskell, *A New Introduction to Bibliography* (Oxford: Clarendon Press, 1974). The best illustrated introduction to the development of the title page from the incipit and beyond is Wytze Gs Hellinga, *Copy and Print in the Netherlands* (Amsterdam: North Holland Publishing, 1962), 111–12 and illustrations. For an account of the layers of the (largely French) book, see Genette, *Seuils.*

11. For an account of legislation affecting the book trade in this period, see John Feather, "The Book Trade in Politics: The Making of the Copyright Act of 1710," *Publishing History* 8 (1980): 19–44; and "The Publishers and the Pirates: British Copyright Law in Theory and Practice, 1710–1775," ibid. 22 (1987): 5–32.

12. Gilliver made his entry on 12 April 1729, see Stationers' Company Records, Liber G (Ann Arbor, Michigan: University Microfilms, 1953), reel 19. For the Licensing Act, see Raymond Astbury, "The Renewal of the Licensing Act in 1693 and Its Lapse in 1695," *Library,* 5th ser., 33 (1978): 296–322.

13. David Foxon, *Pope and the Early Eighteenth-Century Book Trade* (Oxford: Clarendon Press, 1991), 1, quoting Cyprian Blagden, *The Stationers' Company* (London: Allen and Unwin, 1960), 163. For the copyright legislation, see my account in appendix A of that book; and Feather, "Book Trade" and "Publishers and Pirates."

14. See Hellinga, *Copy and Print in the Netherlands,* pl. 147; and Maynard Mack, *The Last and Greatest Art: Some Unpublished Poetical Manuscripts of Alexander*

Pope (Newark: University of Delaware, 1984), for Pope's print hand. I am grateful to Julian Ferraro for prepublication notification of his discovery.

15. Chiswell papers, MS Rawl. D730, fol. 15. The papers are discussed by Michael Brennan ("A Volume of Richard Chiswell's Papers," *Library*, 6th ser., 2 [1980]: 218–19), and some are listed by J. K. Moore, *Primary Materials Relating to Copy and Print*, Oxford Bibliographical Society Occasional Publication no. 24 (Oxford: Oxford Bibliographical Society, 1992).

16. *Mechanick Exercises on the Whole Art of Printing (1683–84) by Joseph Moxon*, ed. Herbert Davis and Harry Carter, 2d ed. (London: Oxford University Press, 1962), 212.

17. "Mr Pope . . . had gott an injunction in chancery against the printers who had pyrated his dunciad; it was dissolv'd again because the printer could not prove any property nor did the Author appear. that is not Mr Gays case for he has own'd his book" (Arbuthnot to Swift, 9 June 1729, *Correspondence of Alexander Pope*, ed. George Sherburn, 5 vols. [Oxford: Clarendon Press, 1956], 3:36–37).

18. Vol. 4 of *The Twickenham Edition of the Poems of Alexander Pope*, ed. John Butt (1939), 111 (lines 215–19). For a more general account, see Marjorie Plant, *The English Book Trade*, 3d ed. (London: Allen and Unwin, 1974).

19. See Foxon, *Pope*, 93–96; and George Sherburn, *The Early Career of Alexander Pope* (Oxford: Clarendon Press, 1934), 248–69.

20. Vol. 5 of *The Twickenham Edition of the Poems of Alexander Pope*, ed. James Sutherland (1943), 64 (line 38).

21. Searle, *Speech Acts* (Cambridge: Cambridge University Press, 1969), 163, referring to Mill, *A System of Logic*. (I would not want to endorse the theory of reference underlying Searle's discussion here, but it has no consequences for my small-scale interest in the topic.) Searle's position has some compatibilities with John McDowell's in "On the Sense and Reference of a Proper Name," in *Meaning and Reference*, ed. A. W. Moore (Oxford: Oxford University Press, 1993), 111–36. The controversy over description theory and causal (dubbing) theory of names also has a relevance to my essay; see Gareth Evans, "The Causal Theory of Names," in the same collection (208–27).

22. Papers were read at the Conference on Literary Theory and the Practice of Editing at Liverpool in July 1993 and at the colloquium preceding Howard Erskine-Hill's Warton Lecture at the British Academy in May 1994.

23. I have outlined some of these changes in "Pope in the Private and Public Spheres: Annotations in the Second Earl of Oxford's Volume of Folio Poems, 1731–1736," *Studies in Bibliography* 48 (1995): 33–59.

24. Harold Love, *Scribal Publication in Seventeenth-Century England* (Oxford: Clarendon Press, 1993). See also J. W. Saunders's seminal essay "The Stigma of Print: A Note on the Social Bases of Tudor Poetry," *Essays in Criticism* 1 (1951): 139–64.

25. Foxon, *Pope*, 2–5.

26. Sherburn, *Correspondence of Alexander Pope*, 3:26–27; Foxon, *Pope*, 129.

The Cosmopolitics of Reading:
Navigating the Margins of John Dee's
General and Rare Memorials

William W. E. Slights

Texts that have been altered at any stage of their production—which is to say nearly all texts—present the textual critic with the challenge of making choices. Which alterations should be credited and reproduced, which suppressed? The kinds of changes, their genesis, and their effect on how the text will be read all need to be assessed as part of the shape of the text and its positioning within a cultural context. The argument I wish to make turns on the nature of textual alterity, by which I mean not only the alterations made before, during, and after production of a printed text but also the "other" voices that speak from the book's physical margins and through a variety of (mis)appropriated, embedded texts. My argument runs entirely counter to the conviction, still deeply held in some quarters, that printed texts must be stable texts.

John Dee's *General and Rare Memorials pertayning to the Perfect Arte of Navigation* (London: John Day, 1577) provides a remarkable case study of the critical problems of assessing marginal supplements and textual alterations.[1] Published anonymously, it contains layer upon layer of printed and manuscript variance, much of it authorially sanctioned, though the notion of authorship itself is deeply perplexed by two prefaces that postulate an originating "Philosopher" who, at the instigation of an "Vnknown Freend," dictated the body of the work to a "Mechanicien," who wrote it down and delivered it in stages to the printer. Questions of textual alterity, particularly in the present case, lead the critic beyond the limits traditionally prescribed by the concept of authorial intention, though a consideration of intention or purpose may provide a useful point of departure.[2] The announced purpose of Dee's book was to persuade members of Queen Elizabeth's Privy Council to underwrite the creation of a "Pety-Nauy-Royall, of Threescore Tall Ships . . . And Twenty other smaller Barks, . . . all, well vittayled, for Six Thowsand, Six hundred, and Sixty Men, . . . maynteyned continually, and that, very Royally, FOR EVER" (18–19). The book defines a discourse of national security and, in Dee's term, "cosmopolitical" maritime imperialism in a series of propositions that undergo systematic revision as Dee hones and adjusts his proposal for its primary intended audience. The material fact of textual alteration may be viewed as analogous to the need Dee saw for changing the basic attitudes of England's rulers toward maritime power. I hope to demonstrate that such "national scriptures" as the *General and Rare Memorials* must be read in their fullest cultural setting as well as in their most minute bibliographical detail and that alternative voices, particularly those occupying the margins of early modern books, must be allowed to speak from their special and powerful places on the printed page.[3]

The heavily marginated *General and Rare Memorials* has attracted some bibliographical attention. It is an extremely rare book, there likely having been at most one hundred and perhaps as few as fifty copies of this handsome folio printed.[4] A brief article by R. J. Roberts in the *Book Collector* includes a helpful checklist of twenty-three "corrections" in eleven copies available in public access libraries in England.[5] Roberts also considers the state of the bindings, probably by Jean de Planche, on several copies and bewails the decision of the custodians of the Royal Institute of Naval Architects to sell its finely bound copy at Christie's in 1974. While Roberts's exercise in analytical bibliography makes a substantial contribution to the collector's knowledge, it leaves questions about the material and cultural resonances of the work unanswered because unasked. The article tends to shut down issues such as the relevance of the work to the contemporary debate over a possible Anglo-Netherlands alliance and the larger issues of authorship, class, gender, and England's imperial power at sea. For example, Roberts remarks, "It is a pity that Dee's tinkering with the make-up of the book obscures in the first three letters of the collation formula a rather quaint piece of self-advertisement" (72). As I hope to show, Dee's investment in revision pays rich dividends to students of early modern naval history and the history of printing in England. Moreover, what Roberts labels "a rather quaint piece of self-advertisement" may more fruitfully be regarded as an imaginative representation of authorship as a complex function of clientage and political persuasion. These "other" considerations, long regarded as beyond the purview of bibliographers, are not marginal but central to the study of Dee's book.

While traditional methods of bibliographical analysis can be usefully supplemented by studies of the sociology of the text, we cannot simply substitute considerations of ideology for the detailed work of the physical bibliographer. The bibliographer's tools are indispensable in unraveling and, sometimes, interrogating the announced aims of an author. In the case of the *General and Rare Memorials* Dee's claims to be concerned with the defense only of the "Precinct of our own Naturall Ilandish walls, and Royallty of our Sea Limits, here, at home, and before our doores" (22) and to be innocent of imperial ambitions are severely damaged by a wealth of conflicting paratextual, marginal, and inset material. The full history of the work must be teased out of its material as well as its ideological matrices.

To accept at face value the account of authorial intentions laid out in the *General and Rare Memorials* would be to overlook the active collaboration of patron, author, printer, scribe, and reader. The transactions among the various parties and the materials with which they work frequently occur at the margins of the text, in which a combination of white space and annotational supplement represents efforts to control access to the "text proper," indeed to control the very genealogy of the text. Such marginal material in early printed books is too often regarded by modern editors as a kind of prop to the text and demoted to the bottom of the page or as a kind of text improper and banished altogether. The point needs to be made that marginal annotation, whether printed or handwritten, can radically alter a reader's perceptions of the centered text, though its force is noticeably diminished by demotion from its original place at the shoulder of the text.[6] In a text such as the *General and Rare Memorials* marginal alterations combine with the literally unlocked and corrected forms and small cancellans slips pasted over sections of text to create the impression of a work very much in process. The volume, replete with cosmopolitical visions and textual revisions, provides an admirable medium to communicate the projector's plan for reshaping his nation's future. Its heavy investment in alterity thematizes change and enhances Dee's ideas for military and economic reform.

Viewing text production and consumption as an ongoing process throws into high relief the concern of many modern editors and textual critics with the instability of texts. Rather than erasing such features as printed side notes, efforts need to be made to retrieve them from the editorial cutting room floor. In our efforts to understand the history of the printed word, we might well wish that more effort had been made by past editors to record the depredations of external censorship as well as the supposed improvements of authorial self-censureship.[7] Indeed, it is extraordinarily dangerous at any given moment in the history of a text for the textual critic or editor to decide that instances of alteration are extraneous and to suppress them. One feels almost grateful that no clear-text version has ever been or ever will likely be produced of such a richly marginated document as the Huntington copy of the *General and Rare Memorials*, even though such a state of affairs ensures that these particular memorials will remain rare indeed.

Considering that well over half the books produced in early modern England contain printed side notes and that other forms of what Gérard Genette calls "paratext" abound in printed works of the period, it is easy to see why textual studies that extend their concerns beyond the "clear," centered text have begun to appear.[8] In a recent article Genette's English-language translator, Marie Maclean, invokes speech-act theory to explain the relational dynamics of text/paratext: "The paratext involves a series of first order illocutionary acts in which the author, the editor, or the prefacer are frequently using direct performatives. They are informing, persuading, advising, or indeed exhorting and commanding the reader."[9] While Maclean's terms describe the performative nature of Dee's prefatory matter, his exceedingly complex "print acts" differ significantly from speech acts.[10] Though dedicated to one particularly powerful courtier and distributed only to the most influential men in the land, the *General and Rare Memorials,* simply by reason of being print matter, addresses an invisible and unpredictable audience. Moreover, the duration of the print act far exceeds that of the spoken word, and its relationship to licensing and validating authorities requires careful definition, particularly since the printed witness entails wide legal accountability. As Evelyn B. Tribble has recently argued, these relationships are often negotiated at the margins of the text:

> The writer seeks to negotiate an uneasy relationship among his literary predecessors, his powerful patrons, his printer/publisher, and his unknown and inchoate audience of readers. Each of these groups can be said to own the book, or at least to have an interest in it, and the writer is embedded in a dense network of potentially competing authorizers. The page, dedicated to displaying and to fictionalizing such relationships, situates the writer in a context at least partially of his own devising.[11]

The delicate choreography of the page in the John Dee / John Day *General and Rare Memorials* marshals print technology to manage the ideological past—from the wars of classical Greece to monuments for Britain's ancient kings to Henry VI's fisheries statutes—with an eye toward altering the political direction of the realm.

The links between the analogous processes of bibliographical alteration and sociopolitical change in the *General and Rare Memorials* are forged in its title, prefatory notes, marginal annotations, embedded texts, typography, stop-press and post-print alterations, and illustrations. I will comment on each of these features of the text in turn to make the case for historicizing the study of bibliography and bibliographizing the study of cultural history.

The first "print act" to present itself to the reader is an act of radical mistitling. The title page offers not the title of the present volume but, rather, the umbrella title of a proposed four-volume work: *General and Rare Memorials pertayning to the Perfect Arte of Navigation: Annexed to the Paradoxal Cumpas, in Playne: now first published: 24. yeres, after the first Inuention thereof.*[12] The twenty-four-year-old work on the paradoxal compass (a maritime navigational instrument, which Dee claims to have invented, only to have the credit claimed by an imposter) is not in fact annexed to the present, first volume, which carries the running title, *The Brytish Monarchie.* As Dee makes clear in a prefatory note, he already knew that the rest of the *General and Rare Memorials* would likely never see print. The second part, called *The Brytish Complement of the Perfect Arte of Navigation,* contained the "Gubernautik," or navigational tables, required to complete or perfect ("complement") the proposals set forth in *The Brytish Monarchie* (sig. ε4). Because it would have been "(in bulk) greater than the English Bible, of the greatest volume" (i.e., the massive Great Bible of 1540), it was simply too expensive for Dee to have printed, and it is now lost.[13] Dee goes on to report that it was the desire of a certain gentleman (likely Edward Dyer, whom Dee subsequently mentions by name in this preface) that the third part of his great work "should be vtterly suppressed, or deliuered to Vulcan his Custody" (sig. ε4ᵛ), perhaps, Peter French speculates, because it was politically dangerous.[14] The last part, entitled *Of Famous and Rich Discoveries,* records expeditions, some legendary, others actual, undertaken in quest of the treasures of the Far East.[15] Considered in its entirety, the work represents an enormous effort, though Dee and his printer knew that they were offering only a small part of it under the title of the whole. The published part was what C. L. Oastler calls a "sounding-line," or a kind of market survey to determine the thinking of the nation's decision makers on the subject of creating a royal navy.[16]

What Dee's labor produced was a carefully crafted piece of special interest lobbying. He urges Hatton in closing:

> I beseche you (Right Worshipfull Sir,) not onely to take these my speedy Trauailes and Collections in good parte, your selfe: But also, to whom so euer, you will deliuer any one of the Copies, (wherof, only one Hundred are to be printed, by the warning of my Instructor:) You would be my Carefull Orator, to this purpose chiefly: That my good will, and exceding zealous Intent herein, dutifully to pleasure this BRYTISH MONARCHIE, might be thankfully accepted: and so, my simple & very faythfull Trauailes, to be rewarded. And finally, that you would very earnestly request them (for the COMMON-WEALTHS CAVSE,) Speedily, Circumspectly, and Paradoxally to vewe this plat. (79–80)

This is Dee's plan, or "*Plat politicall*" (sig. [Δ1]), for what he elsewhere calls "The marveilous Priuiledge of the Brytish Impire" (margin, 8), a concept that would reverberate throughout the history of what was to become Great Britain and her colonies. Whether the Privy councillors read his work "Paradoxally" is anyone's guess.[17] The fact remains that Dee did not become the father of empire in 1577.

Dee's two prefaces, besides laying out the plan for his entire work and deconstructing his title, also cleverly fictionalize the notion of authorship and initiate the elaborate layering of his text. The first of these is headed, with fine, voluminous irony: "A BRIEF NOTE SCHOLASTICAL, FOR THE better vnderstanding of the *Decorum,* obserued, (or, at the *least, regarded*) *in this present Two-fold Treatise, written vnder the Names* of Three diuers Proprieties, States, or Conditions of MAN: Wherby yt may appere, that they are not *Scopae dissolutae:* or, *Du Coq à l'Asne:* but, by the will, and Grace of the Highest, thus Recorded" (sig. [Δ1]). The embedded Latin phrase, deriving from Cicero's critique of certain artless plain stylists (*Orator* 71.235), means an "untied" (hence useless) twig-broom, and the French means a cock-and-bull story—not a highly serious advertisement for what follows.[18] The note mocks the scholastics' penchant for unnecessary annotations and purposely mystifies the identity of the author by likening the three originary forces behind the text (the Philosopher, Mechanicien, and Vnknown Freend) to the three parts of the soul. His complaints about having been "almost oppressed" and "vtterly defaced" refer not only to "slanderous" accusations (sig. Δ3) concerning his familiarity with demons and his subsequent loss of patronage but also to several acts of plagiarism that he details in the second of his prefaces. Ironically, he protests his prior effacement in a work that he chooses to present anonymously, though he finds several occasions to refer to "M. Dee" (always in the third person) in the course of the work.

Why Dee's elaborate authorial ruse, the curious triple layering of identity, combined with an insistent whine about his ill treatment as scholar and author? The answer would seem to be that Dee chooses to figure himself as a societally marginalized thinker, an eccentric whose only refuge is some reinvented, textualized form of the arcana naturae, Dei, and imperii. That is, he chooses to exercise his powers as natural philosopher, divining the will of God and influencing (behind the scenes) the decisions of the prince. The material medium of this grand design becomes the design of his book.

The second preface, called "A necessary Aduertisement," purports to be written by the "vnknown freend" (sig. Δ2) and begins with the phrase, "Lamentable and irkesome, are these our drery dayes." The initial capital *L* is a beautifully engraved figure of the astronomer, holding a large celestial globe in one hand and pointing to the sun with the other, his dog sleeping peacefully at his feet. John Day had used this initial, likely made by John Bettes, in William Cunningham's *Cosmological Glasse* (1559), though it is equally appropriate to one aspect of Dee's self-representation and contributes to the impressive appearance of the *General and Rare Memorials*.[19] The main text will add to the image of Dee as the magus-scientist other layers of identity, including domestic economist, national historian, and political analyst. The "Aduertisement" is a spirited twenty-page defense of the much maligned "Brytish Philosopher," Dr. Dee, and a warning against various "Cosening forgeries" of his works (sig. Δ3ᵛ). The effect on the reader is to authenticate the present work by characterizing its maker as a man of probity and intellectual scope. The preface also places Dee's scholarly accomplishments within a larger "Cosmographicall frame" of divine creation that exists beyond ordinary human sense and further validates the work (sig. ε*1ʳ⁻ᵛ). Finally, it introduces the expressly political theme of extending England's royal power across the seas to remote lands and promises to justify

the lawfull and very honorable Entitling of our most gratious and Soueraigne Lady, QVEENE ELIZABETH, (and so, this BRYTISH SCEPTRE ROYALL) to very large Forrein Dominions: such, as in, and by the same, duly recouered and vsed, the Course of the Diuine prouidence generall, in this present Age, will bring to light and life, matter of great Importance and Consequency, both to the Glory of God, and the benefit of all Christendom, and Heathenes. (sig. ε4ᵛ)

This overt gesture of expansionism, which will later be denied as a motive behind the proposed royal navy, is couched in terms of divine providence and evangelical zeal. The sentiment is distanced from Dee by being placed in the mouth of a secondary author—namely, the prefacer, who also serves as editor and who interpolates documentary "proof" where necessary. One such document is a letter from "the Right honorable Priuy Counsail" to the Bishop of London, commanding him to "cause Iohn Dee, committed to your L. Custody, to be brought before some Master of the Chauncery: . . . And therupon to set him at libertie" (sig. ε2ᵛ). Quoting Dee's name in this legal context momentarily creates the illusion of a reified author, rather than the elaborate literary fiction of the previous pages. The inset letter to the bishop sets Dee at liberty to act as counsel to Elizabeth's Privy Council.

It is fitting that the author figure self-consciously constructed in the preface should exploit the resources of the margins on each page, a space that, as Michael Camille and other medieval scholars have shown, was regularly treated by scribes as the favored habitat of fabulous creatures who ape human behavior on the very fringes of society's institutions.[20] For the magus the margins are the site of radical forms of otherness that present the altered state of England, designated by the Greek letters ΙΕΡΟΓΛΥΦΙΚΟΝ. ΒΡΥΤΑΝΙΚΟΝ (Hieroglyphicon Brytanicon, or the hieroglyph of Britain) printed vertically in the margin (53) beside an ekphrastic recapitulation of Dee's title-page illustration. But this feels like a nostalgic backward glance at the magical world of the Gothic manuscript margins in which, as Camille argues, the usual hermeneutic questions dissolve into a bizarre kind of alterity that could be supported only by a rigidly hegemonic view of divine and human kind at the center of the page, monastery, court, and city. Dee and Day, on the other hand, are publishing in a changed world. The heavily marginated humanist printed texts of the earlier sixteenth century stand between the Middle Ages and the *General and Rare Memorials*. The nation-state is fast overtaking the feudal estate and the city-state in the dominant English political consciousness. Playfully alternative monstricules, jongleurs, and lumpy nudes have migrated from the medieval margins into more confined spaces reserved for the *allos*, or otherness, of Dee's comparatively chaste title-page allegory of Respublica (replete with hermetic signs and political advice) and Day's elaborately engraved capitals.

The medieval marginal drawings of pots, pans, and defecating monkeys give way to the literal commodification of Dee's text in the form of numbers—the numbers of ships, sailors, important dates, enumerated arguments, and page numbers from books by supporting authorities. Still, the margins of *The General and Rare Memorials* continue to be the territory of the other: of supplemental authorities, editorial emendations, and alternate readings. The margins of the early modern book remain a vital location of textual point-counterpoint.

The sixty-four pages of text in the body of Dee's work contain far fewer references to earlier authorities on navigation, geography, and political history than one might expect from the pen of the owner of one of the most comprehensive private libraries in England. There are only a half-dozen references to what might be considered major authorities (Thucydides, Aristotle, Pliny), the same number to lesser lights (Olaus Magnus, Albertus Krantzius, Randulphus Cestreus), and only four biblical citations (one from Proverbs, the other three from Psalms). As is appropriate to a scholar of international renown, all these citations are in Latin, but the side notes are far less intent upon validating the authority of the present author by marshaling past authors than we might anticipate. More numerous—by a factor of ten to one—than citations of prior authorities are the side notes in English (sometimes cryptic single words, sometimes lengthy disquisitions) that do everything from accusing profiteers of smuggling gunpowder for the nation's enemies to summarizing fishing laws. Someone considered these notes important enough to revise, along with the centered text, both in ink and with printed cancellans slips.

When we trace the editorial negotiations carried out with the reader in the margins, we see that some of the notes work centrifugally, pushing the reader out of the present work to consult, for example, works of ancient philosophy or more recent jurisprudence. Other notes work centripetally, pulling the reader deeper into the argument of the centered text by providing a fresh perspective on it. Consider just one example of each kind of note. In discussing the "Necessary Vittayling of the Pety-Nauy-Royall," Dee suggests the possibility of preserving grain in anticipation of poor crop years. The side note contains a tantalizing mention of "The Norimberg Secret . . . of Corne Reseruing well, many yeres" (41) and cites as its source Theophilus Banosius's preface to Petrus Ramus's *Commentariorum de Religione Christiana* (Frankfort, 1576). One must admire the up-to-dateness of Dee's research (Banos's work appearing in the same year that Dee was composing the *General and Rare Memorials*). Upon going to the source, one learns that grain has been kept at Nuremburg for 223 years (*Commentariorum*, sig. e8). What seems more important than this rather stunning piece of information in itself is the context of Banos's praise of a controversial thinker, Peter Ramus, for his keen observations abroad. At a crucial point in his discussion of domestic economic support for his proposed navy, Dee wishes to broaden the vision of Englishmen to include the awareness that, through extraordinary grain-handling techniques practiced elsewhere in Europe, no one need go hungry to keep the proposed British fleet supplied. The pull of this rhetorical ploy in the margins is decidedly centrifugal, broadening the reader's scope of thought beyond the confines of the text.

Precisely the opposite effect is achieved when Dee deplores the yearly waste of "more than Fiue Hundred Cart-loads of good fresh Fish, within this our Ile of ALBION" (43), citing in the margin the Henrician statutes regulating catches.[21] Tracking down the original source offers little in the way of supplementary information. The immediately preceding and succeeding laws deal with quite different matters. Dee's object in citing the legal authority is to send the reader back into the text with a documented legal precedent, a way that Englishmen can deal with the need for a naval infrastructure using only native supplies, if these supplies are properly regulated. A few pages later Dee quotes at length a fisheries statute from the reign of Henry VI to make his point about the adequacy of British resources and the laws affecting them and to keep his readers focused on the immediate argument rather than sending them off to consult other works (46). The centripetal force of such an annotation stresses the intratextual rather than the intertextual reading dynamic. In a text as carefully orchestrated as the *General and Rare Memorials,* then, no part is detachable or expendable, especially not the marginal annotations. The notes are necessary supplements in the sense that signification spills over the edges of the text, creating the effect that Jacques Derrida calls *dé-bordement.*[22]

A representative page of Dee's book reveals the complexity of his marginal strategies, his *dé-bordements.* Page 54 (fig. 1) uses the printer's device of the pointing hand (☞, indicating appropriate places for reader intervention), a keyword (*Cosmopolites*) that identifies the crucial concept of the passage, and the imperialist boast that "The Brytish Monarchy hath byn Capable of the greatest Ciuile Felicity, that euer was . . . If requisite Policy therto, had byn vsed in Due tyme, and Constantly Followed" (margin, 54–55). The centered text being annotated reveals Dee's agenda for colonializing marginal peoples within the British isles:

Ruly, I can not here let pas, an other Little Diſcourſe, (as there are Diuerſe,) of his, much to this Intent : I am not vtterly Ignorant, (Sayd he,) of the Humors, and Inclinations, of the People of this *ALBION*, being ('now') the greater Portion, of the *BRYTISH IMPIRE*. For, although, as well through ſo many Conqueſts; as alſo, great Reſortings hither, of ſundry other Nations, there hath byn made a Maruellous Mixture of People, of Repugnant Conditions : Yet, from Yere to Yere, the Generall Diſpoſition, of the preſent Inhabitants, doth, much alike, Alter to this great Imperfection : That is : Though otherwhiles, they know and Taſte of the Beſt : yet, ſeldome tyme, they do Conſtantly follow, and continue in the ſame : I mean now, in Publik Behauiour, *Et officys Ciuilibus* : For that, their Ciuile Conuerſation, and Induſtry, in many poynts, is nothing ſo anſwerable to the Dignity of Man, As the very Heathens did preſcribe Rules for the Gouernment therof. Let *CICERO*, his Golden Book, *DE OFFICIIS*, be the Euidence againſt them, to the Contrary : And that, in thoſe Poynts, by the Heathen Orator expreſſed, which both greatly are agreable to the moſt Sacred Diuine Oracles, of our *IEOVA* : and alſo, for the Common-Wealths Proſperity, right Excellent.

I haue oftentymes, (Sayd He,) and many wayes, looked into the State of Earthly Kingdoms, Generally, the whole World ouer : (as far, as it may, yet, be known to Chriſten Men, Commonly :) being a Study, of no great Difficulty : But, rather, a purpoſe, ſomewhat anſwerable, to a perfect Coſmographer : to fynde hym ſelf, *Coſmopolites* : A *Coſmopolites* Citizen, and Member, of the whole and only one Myſticall City Vniuerſall : And ſo, conſequently, to meditate of the Coſmopoliticall Gouernment therof; vnder the King Almighty : paſſing on, very ſwiftly, toward the moſt Dreadfull, and moſt Cumfortable Term prefixed :

And I finde (ſayd he) that if this * Brytiſh Monarchy, wold heretofore, haue followed the Aduantages, which they haue had, onward, They mought, very well, ere this, haue ſurpaſſed (By Iuſtice and Godly, ſort) any particular Monarchy, els, that euer was on Earth, ſince Mans Creation. And that, to all ſuch purpoſes, as to God are moſt acceptable : And to all perfect Common-Wealths, moſt Honorable, Profitable, and Comfortable.

But, yet, (ſayd he) there is a Little lock of LADY OCCASION, Flickring in the Ayre, by our hands, to catch hold on : wherby, we may, yet ones more (before, all, be vtterly paſt, and for euer) diſcretely,

The Brytiſh Monarchy hath byn Capable of the greateſt Ciuile Felicity, that euer was any Particular Monarchy, Els, in the whole World : Yea, ſo Incomparably, that it might haue Extended, for the Generall Monarchie,

---

Fig. 1.   John Dee, *General and Rare Memorials* (London: John Day, 1577), 54, showing one of Day's decorative initial letters, several of his typefaces, and part of a lengthy marginal note with manuscript emphasis added. (Reproduced by kind permission of The Huntington Library, San Marino, Calif.)

> I am not vtterly Ignorant . . . of the Humors, and Inclinations, of the
> People of this ALBION, being (now) the greater Portion, of the BRY-
> TISH IMPIRE. For, although, as well through so many Conquests, as
> also, great Resortings hither, of sundry other Nations, there hath byn
> made a Marueilous Mixture of People, of Repugnant Conditions: Yet,
> from Yere to Yere, the Generall Disposition, of the present Inhabi-
> tants, doth, much, alike, Alter to this great Imperfection: That is:
> Though otherwhiles, they know and Taste of the Best: yet, seldome
> tyme, they do Constantly follow, and continue in the same: I mean
> now, in Publik Behauiour, *Et officiis Ciuilibus:* For that, their Ciuile
> Conuersation, and Industry, in many poynts, is nothing so answerable
> to the Dignity of Man, As the very Heathens did prescribe Rules for
> the Gouernment therof. (54)

The chief result of numerous foreign presences in the fledgling British
Empire, according to Dee, is that the people are barely civilized in their
"Publik Behauiour . . . Ciuil Conuersation, and Industry." Something
must be done, and it takes a man of the world, one such as Dee himself or
Christopher Hatton, to stake out the path of national development. This
project is "a purpose, somewhat answerable, to a perfect Cosmographer: to
fynde hym self, *Cosmopolites:* A Citizen, and Member, of the whole and
only one Mysticall City Vniuersall: And so, consequently, to mediate of the
Cosmopoliticall Gouernment therof, vnder the King Almighty." A brief
meditation on the cosmopolitics of the "Mystical City Vniuersall" brings
Dee to the conclusion that Britain's monarch—no King Almighty but a
queen acting rather too timidly—must seize "LADY OCCASION" by the
forelock (54–55). The "General Memorials" referred to on Dee's title page
may, then, partly be reminders to Her Majesty not to go on missing the
brass ring of "Generall Monarchie." Dee takes the occasion to inform his
sovereign that good government begins at home, in the "Brytish Monarchie." Here is Dee the statesman at his most expansive and mystical, using
the margins to consolidate his central message of domestic protection and
imperial conquest.

A certain amount of what might be considered marginal and referential material makes its way into the body of this printed text. A distinctive
characteristic of the volume is the inclusion of various bits of embedded
text—letters, funereal inscriptions, verse, and two entire Latin orations.
The graphic treatment of these materials on the page creates something like

a computerized hypertext window.[23] Consider, for example, the insert letter from the explorer-navigators Martin Frobisher and Christopher Hall, recently embarked from England to discover the Northwest Passage (3, fig. 2). They pause in "Shotland" just long enough to write a letter testifying to the excellence of John Dee's skills and diligence as a navigational instructor. In a window within the ruled window the letter is editorially called "a sufficient witnes," yet another kind of legal testament to the author's credibility. It is the latest news flash (dated 26 June 1576), filling a gap in the reader's knowledge about the cutting-edge nature of Dee's work. The liminal here becomes the interstitial, sifting into the textual cracks, filling lacunae in Dee's overarching narrative of creating a great sea empire for Britain. The ruled margins of the inset represent the printer's effort both to identify different voices within the text and at the same time to forge a continuous story by filling the empty spaces.[24]

The sense of history, both ancient and modern, is vitally important to Dee's project and its presentation on the page. The volume is, in part, a memorial, a reminder of Britain's royal past as well as a promise of its imperial future. Dee dislodges "Triumphant *BRITISH ARTHVR*" from his prime place in the genesis of the nation, preferring instead the "Peaceable, and Prouident Saxon, King Edgar" (56). The monumental record of the deceased king is reproduced within an ornamental border surmounted by the crossed shield of Britain and printed in large capital italics: "*ANGLICI ORBIS BASILEVS, FLOS, ET DECVS AEDGARVS.*" In the carefully reproduced monument Edgar's name is linked with those of Cyrus of Persia, Romulus of Rome, Alexander of Macedonia, Arsaces of Parthia, and Carolus (Magnus, added in ink to the Magdalene College, Cambridge, copy) of France to provide the requisite temporal and spatial sweep to the historian's vision. King Edgar is praised for maintaining not one but four petty navies, each one thousand ships strong. Here if ever was an imitable monarch, a man of peace and preparedness.

In his highly polemical quotation of Edgar's monument we see Dee using the resources of the printed page to create a symbolic language of power that reaches backward in time as well as extending outward in space. His accounts of a glorious national past are designed to stir the royal and royalist imagination, much as his earlier claims of the extent of England's empire were.[25] For Dee the geographic center of British power and policy is Glastonbury, the ancient royal city that he takes as the starting point for the following lament for an expansionist dream deferred:

Where, he found him felf courteoufly and very worfhipfully entetteined.
And at that tyme of his abode there, and after that, at fundry other
tymes, of his Refort, thither, and to their Ships, he proceded fo with
them, according to his Intent: and pleafured them, fo much according
to their defire: That he finding them, quick of apprehenfion, and likely to
remaine * Thankfull, for his pithy in-
ftructing of them: And they, finding
him (aboue their expectation) fkil-
full: And (more then could be wifhed
for) Carefull, for their well doing,
in this their commendable and honorable Attempt: both the one and the
other, became very forry of their fo
late acquaintance and conference,
for thefe their waighty affaires furde-
ring: And greatly mifliked their want
of tyme, fufficient for the *Complemēt*   The Comple-
and principall pointes of the Perfect Art   ment of the per-
of Nauigation learning at his hands.   uigation.
Such pointes, (I meane), as needed
either great knowledge in the *Sciences
Mathematicall*; and *Arts Mechanicall*:

*As (befides many other thinges) this letter,
may feeme to be a fufficient witnes.*

To the worfhipfull and our approoued good
freend M. Dee, giue thefe with fpeed.

This 26. of Iune. 1576. I ariued in Shotland
in the Bay of Saint Tronions in the Latitude of
59 degrees, 46 Minutes.

I wifh M. Hall make our dutifull Commendations to you with as many
thankes as we can wifh, till we be better furnifhed of firmer matters
to fatisfy our duties for your freendly Inftructions: which when we vfe
alfo remember you and hold our felues bound to you as your poore
difciples, not able to be Scholers but in good will for want of lerning,
and that we will furnifh with good will and diligence to the vttermoft
of our powers. The caufe of our ftay here, was, to ftop a leake which I
had in the *Michaell*, and withall filled certayne frefh water and by Gods
grace this night according to my Commiffion I will depart. This prefent
night I haue a fayr winde, God be prayfed. I haue had fharp weather
and Fogs: But all my company continue with a good courage as they began at the firft. Nowes I haue none, but my Barkes fayle very well all-
but the *Gabriell* hath no fellow, fhe paffes halfe her fayles to all men.
Thus I commit you to God. In laft this prefent after noone ready to fet
Saile.

Your louing freend to vfe and
commaund Martin Frobifher.

Yours to commaund
Chriftopher Hall.

or expert Skill, of many *Caufes* and *effects Naturall*. Such points (I fay) to
their affaires, and the *Perfect Art of Nauigation*, incident; he very aptly
could, & right willingly wold haue dealt with them in: Yf that pinch of
tyme, wold haue fo permitted. For, it is very euident, by his defcription
of the Perfect Art of Nauigation (in his forefayd *Mathematicall Præface*, declared) and alfo, common reafon, and dayly experience, will confirme the
fame: that, not onely, fuch fkill and furniture, as both here is rehearfed,
and in that Præface is fpecified: But, other alfo, is moft nedefull for
him to be fraught withall, that fhall be allowed for an exact *Hydrogra-
pher, Pylot-Maior, Arche-Pylot*, or *Grand-Pylot-Generall* of fuch an Incompa-
rable *Ilandifh Monarchy*, as, this BRYTISH IMPIRE hath bene: Yea, as   THE BRYTISH
it, yet, is: or, rather, as it may, & (of right) ought to be: As I haue   MONARCHY.
bene informed by him, who can reafonably declare how:

WHom, also, I haue heard, often and most   A very Com-
hartily Wifh, That all manner of perfons   of a fayhfull
paffing or frequenting any our Seas, appropriate: Subiect.
and many wayes, next enuironing *England*, *Jre-
land*, and *Scotland*, might be, in conuenient & honorable fort (at all tymes,) at the Commaundement
and Order (by Beck or Check) of A PETY-NAVY-ROY-   A PETY-
ALL, of Three fcore Tall Ships, (or more:) but in   NAVY-ROYAL.
no cafe, fewer: and they, to be very well appoyn-

          A.ij.   ted,

Fig. 2. Dee, *General and Rare Memorials*, 3. According to the handwritten
note in the left margin, the insert letter from Martin Frobisher and Christopher Hall was not part of the original manuscript. (Reproduced by kind
permission of The Huntington Library, San Marino, Calif.)

O Glastonbury, Glastonbury: the Threasory of the Carcasses of so famous, and so many rare Persons . . . How Lamentable, is thy case, now? How hath Hypocrisie and Pride, wrought thy Desolation? Though I omit (here) the names of very many other, both excellent holy Men, and Mighty Princes (whose Carcasses are committed to thy Custody,) yet, that Apostlelike Ioseph, That Triumphant BRYTISH ARTHVR, And now, this Peaceable, and Prouident Saxon, King Edgar, do force me, with a certayn sorrowfull Reuerence, here, to Celebrate thy Memory. (56)

By following the example of good, peace-loving King Edgar and seizing the "Little lock of LADY OCCASION," Elizabeth will be able "discretely, and valiantly [to] recouer, and enioy, if not all our Ancient and due Apperte-nances, to this Imperiall Brytish Monarchy, Yet, at the least, some such Notable Portion therof, As, (all Circumstances, duly and Iustly appertayn-ing to Peace and Amity, with Forreyn Princes, being offred and vsed) this, may become the most Peaceable, most Rich, Most Puissant, and most Flourishing Monarchy of all els (this day) in Christendome" (54–55). Any records of "Ancient and due Appertenances, to this Imperiall Brytish Mon-archy" are, of course, lost in the dark recesses of time, but that doesn't stop Dee from making claims on behalf of his queen. The fervor of nascent nationalism is truly upon him, propelling the most remote historical claims out of the margins and into the center of his argument for imperial defense and expansion.[26] Embedding the texts of history in a new and forward-looking work suited Dee's purposes admirably.

Other embedded materials that function as paratext are verses from Psalm 147 (64 and 80); a pair of orations on improving the economy and defense of the Greek islands, written by the Byzantine philosopher Gemistus Pletho to the Emperor Emanuel and his son Theodore in about 1415 (65–79); and a versified closing summary of the genesis and purpose of Dee's book (sig. L). The Latin version of the psalm is accompanied in its first appearance by an English translation.

O Hierusalem, prayse the Lord: Prayse thy God, O Syon. For, he hath Strengthened the Barres of thy Gates, And hath blessed thy Children within thee: He hath made all thy Borders PEACE: And with the good Nutriment of wheat, doth satisfy thee. &c. He hath not done thus, to euery Nation, els: Prayse we all, the Lord therefore. Amen. (64)

The quotation is carefully edited to stress Dee's thematic concerns: strong national defenses, peaceful borders, agricultural plenty, the people's special election by God. The object of the quotation is to figure Britain as the new Jerusalem, divinely chosen for a special destiny. In the immediately following pages Dee also represents Britain as a more northerly version of the islands of the Peloponnisos, a maritime empire taking its proper place in history, though he points out in an extended marginal note that not all the lessons of that ancient seafaring state are applicable to present-day Britain (margin, 73). The final piece of paratext—"annexed," as Dee says, after the fact (sig. [Δ1ᵛ])—is twenty-eight lines of tetrameter verse outlining his request to its dedicatee, Christopher Hatton, to "*imparte . . . this zealous Publik voyce*" to the "*Sacred Senat, or Chief Powr*" of the realm (sig. [L]). This rather presumptuous "Epistle in Meter" offers only the warrant of his "Redy *freend*" (identified in the margin as *E. D. Esq.*, or Edward Dyer) that Hatton would undertake to transmit the proposal for a royal navy to the highest authorities in the land. These rather transparent indirections constitute yet another form of alterity that has Dee always speaking through another's voice, always presenting a thoroughly mediated text.

One of the chief mediators in the process of textual production is the printer, John Day. Day's production job on the *General and Rare Memorials* is lavish, from the elaborate title-page woodcut to the final full-page cut of the Hatton family arms.[27] In between is a meticulously arranged combination of contrasting typefaces, pictorial initials, arabesque fleurons, textual interpolations, dedications, cancellans slips, and a vast array of printed marginalia. C. L. Oastler's study of Day for the Oxford Bibliographical Society devotes several pages to the Dee-Day collaboration but misses the opportunity to link Day's commitment to producing works of militant Protestantism with Dee's subtext that a powerful British fleet might be used to support the Protestant cause in the Netherlands.[28] Dee had previously used and was used by his connections at court to pursue particular matters of public policy, especially an aggressive policy of harassing the Spanish at sea.[29] Ardent adherents to this policy among the queen's Privy councillors were Walsingham, Leicester, and Hatton (who had recently been knighted and was quickly elevated to the position of vice-chamberlain of the household).[30] These men threw their considerable weight behind Martin Frobisher's impossible plan to outflank the Spaniards in the New World by discovering a Northwest Passage to the Orient and Francis Drake's stunningly successful scheme to raid unsuspecting Spanish ships on the west coast of the Americas. The *General and Rare Memorials* appears to have been addressed primarily to the militant Protestant faction at court, those advisors who had previously shown support for British maritime initiatives.³¹ It allies Dee with a cause dear to his printer but not to his queen.

Day went to considerable trouble not only with the original layout of Dee's book but also with canceled and replaced leaves. One of these, sig. A2 (fig. 2), likely had to be reset to accommodate the recently arrived letter from Frobisher and Hall. Others in the "Necessary Aduertisement" (the replaced sig. Δ4 and the immediately preceding leaf) suggest that for Dee this was work-in-progress. He appears to have struggled against the finality of locking it into the forms. The pasted-on cancellans slips in a great many of the surviving copies of the *General and Rare Memorials* further attest to a continuing commitment to altering the text, even after printing and perhaps even gathering and binding were complete. Three of these slips affect side notes in the Huntington copy, suggesting the importance of the margins as a place to record the most recent revisions, in the form of print as well as manuscript additions. In the first instance several lines of type in one of the notes on the "Aduertisement" are canceled with blank paper. The lines conclude a particularly ill-tempered complaint that the author has spent more than three thousand pounds on scientific studies to advance the inhabitants of "his Natiue Cu[n]try aboue all other" and are restored in ink in the Huntington and Folger copies: "how litle so euer they haue (yet) deserued it at his hands" (margin, sig. ε*1). Did Dee think better of his churlishness, only to have it reinscribed by a secretary working from a partially corrected version of his manuscript?

There is a certain irony in Dee's monstrous ego and accompanying tactlessness catching up with him after he had practiced a temporizing erasure. His anger, directed against the ungrateful kingdom, surfaces once again in a printed side note that has been pasted on to page 35 of all the copies I am aware of except the one in the Cambridge University Library. It is a frontal attack on privateers who are "Abusing . . . this Commonwealth, by carying OVR GVN-POWDER out of this Realm." The Huntington copy has the additional manuscript note, "Prouide agt Armor carrying out of Kingdom." Clearly, Dee knows or believes that war matériel is being treasonably smuggled out of Britain into France and certainly not being used to supply the Lowlands Protestants whom he wished to see supported. The need to clarify the matter was evidently felt to be sufficiently pressing to warrant the addition of a carefully printed twenty-five-line side note. The last such alteration occurs in a note attempting to rationalize a discrepancy of eight hundred ships ("besides the other 4 Stationary Pety Nauyes") in the historical records of the size of King Edgar's fleet (margin, 56). Since Edgar is presented as the great precedent for Elizabeth, it would not do to enter these figures erroneously. The margin is the place to get the facts straight, even at the expense of reprinting, cutting, and pasting in the supplemental text.

Further evidence of the continually shifting nature of the text in question and the central importance of altered states of the text is the extensive contemporary pen-and-ink marginalia in the Huntington copy. Some of these are corrections such as might have been intended for a second printed edition of the work, while others are cues for a proper reading response to the text in hand. Michael Lort (1725–90), one of the book's former owners, notes that its "many MS additions & alterations" are "in Dr. Dees own hand writing." But the marginal additions do not match the numerous authenticated samples of Dee's hand that we have. More likely, they were copied by a secretary from Dee's revised manuscript. In any event these notes serve to keep the printed text in flux.

The manuscript marginalist takes the opportunity to reenter material edited out of the original manuscript in printing, to add new material and new emphases, and to correct errors. The first of these possibilities is suggested by three places in which words have been written in the margin then struck out when the writer notices that they are already in the printed text (sigs. ε1, ε*3ᵛ, and A1). An interpolated side note on the first of the Pletho orations observes that the "Peloponisus: peninsula is well known to be rather an Isle then p[ar]t of the main land," thereby reinforcing the parallel with the British isles (margin, 66). Emphasis is added with hastily drawn pointing fingers, the single word *NOW* to stress the urgency of his proposal (10), and extensive underlining. Much of the underlining occurs in the side notes, all sixty lines of annotation being so marked on one page (56). The level of personal vituperation is significantly raised by the handwritten marginalia in the prefatory pages on which Dee defends himself against a variety of accusations (e.g., adding the words *slanderous* and *diabolicall* [sig. Δ3], *damnable,* and *murderous* [sig. Δ4] to his description of his detractors).

Finally, the manuscript additions include the bracketing of several phrases in the text (e.g., at sig. ε3 and pp. 16 and 35). There are a great many parentheses in the text as printed, and the added ones serve to reinforce the sense that Dee worked to distinguish certain kinds of voice and information as being aside from the flow of his text, typographically set apart yet not shifted to the edge of the page. This information, like that included in marginalia, is appositional or supplemental, and it is delivered sotto voce, in a register below the speaker's more usual lecturing, sometimes hectoring, voice. Like the marginal voice, the parenthetical one offers another layer of information, organization, and emphasis as well as a degree of disengagement from the argument of the main text, usually at a lower rather than a higher level of abstraction.

I have postponed until the end one more sense in which Dee's book is deeply and unintentionally implicated in broader cultural notions of marginality, especially in the areas of class and gender. Both in the text and in its illustrations, women and the "Commons" are simultaneously allegorized and disempowered. Queen Elizabeth is made subject to larger divine and cosmographical forces as well as to the distinctly patriarchal advice of her councillors, including her not-so humble subject Dr. Dee. As for the "Commons," Dee's attitude is a potent blend of solicitude and condescension. The subtle play of these representational forces is a further extension of the attempted containment of the text within a dense layer of marginal annotations and the attempted manipulation of royal decision making.

One of the arresting representations of royalty in the book is an ornamental capital letter C (69, fig. 3) in which Elizabeth sits enthroned, bearing the imperial attributes of sword and orb, elevated above the three nobles kneeling at her right. Day had used the cut, possibly based on a design by Levina Teerlinc, in his edition of Foxe's *Actes and Monuments* in 1563 and recycled it in a work by Gabriel Harvey published in 1578, the year after Dee's volume.[32] Other representations of women, one of them Elizabeth, appear on the title page of Dee's book (fig. 4). The naked figure with the prominent forelock is Lady Occasion. The one at the helm of the European ship of state is "our ELIZABETH, (Sitting at the HELM of this Imperiall Monarchy: or, rather, at the Helm of the IMPERIALL SHIP, of the most parte of Christendome: if so, it be her Graces Pleasure)," to quote Dee's later ekphrasis (53). Europa, more fully clad than her engraved counterpart in Dee's original sketch for the title-page woodcut, rides her bull next to Elizabeth.[33] The design is richly symbolic: the title is flanked by Tudor roses and surmounted by Elizabeth's arms; ships sail on stormy seas; the armed archangel Michael hovers over the scene; a narrative sequence involving soldiers making peace unfolds at the bottom of the page; the figure of Respublica kneels in supplication; there are hermetic symbols of sun, moon, ten stars, Tetragrammaton, a hieroglyphic frame, an inverted wheat stalk, and a half-skull. All this seems to be an elaborate representation

Fig. 3. Queen Elizabeth is enthroned within a capital letter *C* appearing on page 69 of Dee's *General and Rare Memorials* and also in Foxe's *Book of Martyrs*. (Reproduced by kind permission of The Huntington Library, San Marino, Calif.)

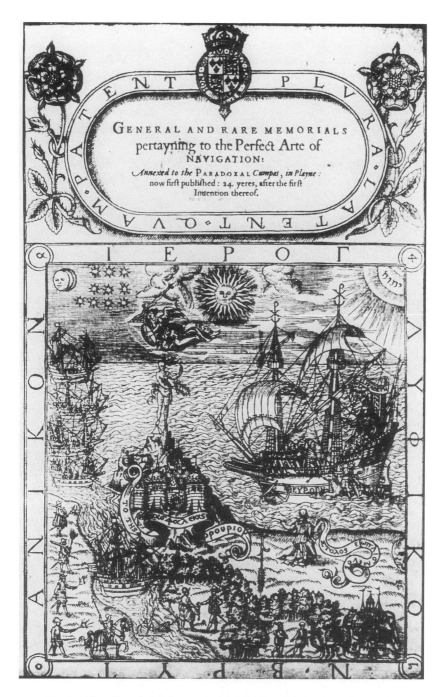

Fig. 4. The allegorical title page designed by Dee for the *General and Rare Memorials*. (Reproduced by kind permission of The Huntington Library, San Marino, Calif.)

of royal power. But what exactly is the relationship between Dee's allegory and the queen? I would argue that the Elizabeth represented here is being rigorously contained by Dee's own expressly male ideology, much as the makers of the book sought to control the reader with marginal annotations, many of which were directed as a form of executive summary to the queen's all-male Privy Council.

Dee's title page includes four female figures—one being carried off to be raped, the second made expressly to be seized and dragged off by the hair, the third (representing the people of Britain) powerless on bended knee with arms outstretched in supplication, and the fourth, Elizabeth, enthroned upon the poop like some latter-day Cleopatra. But is the queen really any more in control than the other unfortunate women? She is represented here doing exactly what Dee wants her to do in the political sphere: she has evidently established the navy Dee wants and is reaching for the power he recommends.

In Dee's account of European power politics Elizabeth's hopes depend on a watchful navy and a tenuous peace. Peter French, identifying a Dutch flag on the ship in the river depicted on Dee's title page, says this "may suggest that Dee advocated an open alliance with the Netherlands."[34] In any event peacemaking certainly seems to be what the cartoon strip series at the bottom of the illustration is all about: the armed figure on horseback poles himself across the river, makes an offering to the gentleman with the sword at his side, is led through the forests, and finally appears with his guide inside the castle at the lower right. But a peculiar idea of peace emerges from Dee's book. On the title page the archangel hovers ominously over all, symbolically wresting the prerogative of violence from the "Commons" and wielding his sword downward through a distinctly patriarchal and hierarchal scheme. Dee quotes (and evidently misquotes, judging from the cancellans slip with the word *keepeth*) "an olde Prouerb. A Sword, keepeth peace: So, this Nauy, by his present readynes, and the Secret of his Circuits, and visitations of sundry forreyn and homish Coasts, obserued: will make the malitious murmurers, and priuy malefactors, of all sortes, to kepe in, and to forbeare their wicked deuises and policies: which, otherwise, against vs, they wold aduenture to execute" (15). Stealth and the constant threat of violent reprisals will be the foundations of his proposed peace. Elizabeth is just along for the cruise.

Dee repeatedly expresses concern for what he calls the "poore Commons" (30, 36, etc.). They are ignorant and childlike, requiring "A Politik. A.B.C." (margin, 8), a simplified version of "Brytish Histories, (by that

Alphabet onely, decyphered, and so brought to their vnderstanding and knowledge)" (9). On the title page they are embodied in the figure of Respublica, begging. She is flanked on either side by sinister, cryptic symbols, the stalk of wheat growing downward and half a grinning skull. Margery Corbett and Ronald Lightbown note Dee's emphasis on hoarding corn supplies in England (*General and Rare Memorials,* 39, 41) and conclude that these are symbols of an artificially induced but nonetheless potentially deadly dearth in the land.[35] The people's lot is not a happy one. And it is not likely to get any happier under the taxation scheme that Dee is proposing for the support of his petty navy. Though it will be a graduated tax and will supersede "other extraordinary TAXES" (13), it will also be perpetual and will extend even to "the wages of all hyred Seruants" (14).

The real benefit Dee proposes for the commonwealth is relief from the exploitation of individual entrepreneurs, particularly those who would trade away the nation's wealth to hostile foreign powers (11, 30, 42). For Dee the real enemy is finally at home, not abroad. He would rather not appear to be advocating a far-flung merchant navy but, rather, a coast guard that will secure the "Precinct of our own Naturall Islandish walls" (22). The resources for the queen's fleet, he argues, are available at home: timber for shipbuilding, fish for "vitualling," saltpeter for making gunpowder.

Dee's vision of a newly secured and largely self-sufficient Britain is carefully circumscribed within a larger "cosmopolitical" frame, much as his title is surrounded by a hermetic aphorism, his title-page illustration by a hieroglyphic pronouncement, his pages by marginalia, and the core of his argument by a pair of narratives. The oval around his title reads, "PLVRA LATENT QVAM PATENT" ("More things are hidden than plain"). The allegory of empire is inscribed within a ruled margin bearing the Greek words HIEROGLYPHICON BRYTANICON. Antique, hermetic, and divine elements add a hint of the unknown to the more sober calculations of natural and human resources available to create and to maintain a strong naval presence. This was a plan to spark the royal imagination as well as to ease anxieties about the royal exchequer. Here, in print form, was a stirring call to national action.

Such an elaborately constructed and meticulously printed and revised volume as the *General and Rare Memorials* leaves no doubt that its makers viewed the printed page as an instrument of direct political influence and the margins as a tool for colonializing its reading audience. In one sense the book failed in its immediate purpose. There were simply too many other demands on Elizabeth's treasury in 1577 to allow for a full-blown royal navy. Dee left England in 1583 to pursue his hermetic and alchemical dreams elsewhere in Europe. Still, in 1588 England managed to muster a sufficient coastal fleet to send the Spanish Armada packing. The great British maritime empire was, after all, well launched by the end of the sixteenth century. And so too was the even more extensive empire of the printed, marginally annotated book.

As several of the essays in this volume forcefully attest, the power of the humble printed side note should never be underestimated. But who, we must ask, wields the power of the margins, and to what ends? Much as an ideologue such as John Dee would like to think that he, as author, controls all the resources of the printed page, the answer to the question involves other players as well. The elaborate set of cues and clues to textual reception that resides at the edges of the text are never issued in an unequivocal voice by a single-minded author. Editors, scribes, printers—even self-revising authors themselves—intervene to alter texts, and they do so without completely erasing traces of their previous signals to readers. The apparent fixity of a printed text is, then, severely compromised by the chorus of self-correcting, de-authorizing, hedging, but vigorously insistent voices from the edge. Even after side notes have been fixed in type, there is a symbiotic relationship between them and the body of the text, the dynamics of which occasionally outstrip or undercut an author's or editor's announced purposes. The pull of the notes may be centripetal, toward the ideological center of the text, or centrifugal, in the direction of alternative constructions of the world. There is no arresting the movement of this process. The interchange between text and margin casts a subtly shifting light on the arguments not only of Dee's alternately expanding and contracting claims for national and imperial power but also on the full range of ideological battles that ranged back and forth across the pages of early printed books. Those debates, their origins, and their consequences become intelligible to today's readers only when we attend to the rich layering and readjusting of text that proceed from the margins.

NOTES

I am grateful to the Social Sciences and Humanities Research Council of Canada for its support as I have prepared this essay and the larger study of printed marginalia in English Renaissance books from which it is drawn.

1. I will take as my primary witness the Lort-Bindley-Britwell copy, which was sold as a duplicate by the British Museum Library in 1787 and is now in the

Huntington Library (RB 82497). I have also inspected the Folger (Harmsworth) copy (STC 6459) and the two now in the British Library, the Sloane (C.21.e.12) and King's Library (48.c.18) copies.

2. In an admirably clear exposition of some of the perplexing editorial problems surrounding the concept of authorial intention, James McLaverty argues that Fredson Bowers's description of an editor's objectives as the "recovery of the initial purity of an author's text" breaks down under the pressure of textual alterity and the demands of emendation. See "The Concept of Authorial Intention in Textual Criticism," *Library,* 6th ser., 4 (1984): 121–38, esp. 126.

3. Jerome J. McGann uses the term *national scriptures* to differentiate the philological questions raised by vernacular works from those provoked by ancient texts. I find the term particularly appropriate to a work that thematizes nationhood as a function of material bibliographical presentation. See McGann's essay "The Monks and the Giants: Textual and Bibliographical Studies and the Interpretation of Literary Works," *Textual Criticism and Literary Interpretation* (Chicago: University of Chicago Press, 1985), 180–99, esp. 185. The essay is one of many in which McGann joins such bibliographical theorists as D. C. Greetham, D. F. McKenzie, and James McLaverty in urging editors and analytical bibliographers to historicize and sociologize their view of textual criticism.

4. A closing address to the work's dedicatee, Sir Christopher Hatton, records that "only one Hundred are to be printed" (79), the handwritten number 50 being supplied in the margin of the Huntington copy. I discuss the nature and provenance of these manuscript notes subsequently. This particular one is called into question by a note Dee wrote in his library catalog next to the entry for this work: "I left 60 of them redy corrected." The fact remains that we are talking here about an extremely rare book.

5. R. J. Roberts, "John Dee's Corrections to his 'Art of Navigation,'" *Book Collector* 23 (1975): 70–75; hereafter cited in the text.

6. Like D. C. Greetham, I am skeptical of G. Thomas Tanselle's argument that the location on the page and in the book of textual apparatus, including side notes accompanying the text as originally published, is an indifferent feature of clear-text editions. Greetham writes, "While it is true that externalization and display do not in themselves guarantee the reader's poststructuralist play in the text, and it is true as well that the converse (concealment of structure does not forbid readerly reconstructions) is also not an automatic response to such texts, the almost universal adoption of concealment over display in eclectic editions cumulatively endorses a disjunct between text and apparatus inimical to the continued intertextual interpenetration of the two." See "Editorial and Critical Theory: From Modernism to Postmodernism," in *Palimpsest: Editorial Theory in the Humanities,* ed. George Bornstein and Ralph C. Williams (Ann Arbor: University of Michigan Press, 1993), 17–18.

7. For a fascinating account of the relationship between censoring and censuring in the English Renaissance, see Richard Burt, *Licensed by Authority: Ben Jonson and the Discourses of Censorship* (Ithaca: Cornell University Press, 1993), esp. 30–31. See also the discussion of these twinned activities in my book *Ben*

Jonson and the Art of Secrecy (Toronto: University of Toronto Press, 1994), 10–11, 170–71.

8. See Genette's *Palimpsestes* (Paris: Seuils, 1981); and *Seuils* (Paris: Seuils, 1987). While medievalists (notable among them Michael Camille, Lilian M. C. Randall, and Lucy Freeman Sandler) have been aware for some time of the riches in the margins of manuscripts, relatively little has been done on the margins of printed texts. Jacques Derrida has labored to theorize the margins, and the work of Lawrence Lipking on margins and modernism, Mary Ann Caws on modernism and postmodernism, Thomas McFarland and Heather Jackson on the Romantics, and Anthony Grafton and Evelyn B. Tribble on Renaissance texts has contributed significantly to our understanding of the history of the printed book. W. Speed Hill has contributed a particularly sensitive account of editing Richard Hooker's marginalia, in the present volume. My own first foray into the arena was an essay entitled "The Edifying Margins of Renaissance English Books," *Renaissance Quarterly* 42 (1989): 682–716.

9. Marie Maclean, "Pretexts and Paratexts: The Art of the Peripheral," *New Literary History* 22 (1991): 274.

10. Peter L. Shillingsburg warns of the limitations of applying speech-act theory to texts in his article "Text as Matter, Concept, and Action," *Studies in Bibliography* 44 (1991): 31–82; and D. F. McKenzie reminds us that in the early modern period speech was thought by some literary, religious, and legal practitioners to be more reliable than impersonal, highly contrived, and variously interpretable written language. See his essay "Speech-Manuscript-Print," in *New Directions in Textual Studies,* ed. Dave Oliphant and Robin Bradford (Austin: Harry Ransom Humanities Research Center, 1990), 87–109.

11. Evelyn B. Tribble, *Margins and Marginality: The Printed Page in Early Modern England* (Charlottesville: University Press of Virginia, 1993), 161. I am grateful to Professor Tribble for suggesting ways to improve the present essay.

12. A lexically tricky title: we may be in for a businessman's memoranda (OED, *memorial,* sb. 4) of an almost universal (general) yet, paradoxically, unusual (rare) sort; or, these may be informal state papers (OED, *memorial,* sb. 6) of a general(ly known) but rare(ly acknowledged) sort. Both these senses (and others, doubtless) fit the text that follows, a detailed account of Britain's foreign and domestic economies that serves as a reminder of the need for naval preparedness. James McLaverty and Thomas L. Berger, in the present collection, give provocative accounts of how titles affect book production and reception.

13. John Dee, *Autobiographical Tracts,* ed. James Crossley (London: Chatham Society, 1851), 61. The term *complement* carried a fine array of scientific meanings appropriate to Dee's geometrical, astronomical, and navigational interests in addition to referring to the number of men required to sail a ship and to the completion or perfecting of his compliment (of which *complement* was a variant spelling) to the queen and her advisors in the preceding volume.

14. Peter J. French, *John Dee: The World of an Elizabethan Magus* (London: Routledge and Kegan Paul, 1972), 183.

15. A manuscript version of this work survives in British Library, Cotton MS

Vitellius C. VII, fols. 25–267. See Nicholas H. Clulee, *John Dee's Natural Philosophy* (London: Routledge, 1988), 290 n. 29.

16. C. L. Oastler, *John Day, the Elizabethan Printer* (Oxford: Bodleian, 1975), 16.

17. In the "Mathematicall Praeface" to *Euclides Elements of Geometry* (d.iv.b) Dee announces that he invented this navigational instrument "for our two Muscovy Master Pilotes" (identified in the margin of the *General and Rare Memorials* as "M. Steuens and M. William Borowgh" [sig. ε3]), to measure a ship's oblique motion in a line that is "neyther circular nor straight, but concurred or winding." See John Davis, *The Seamans Secrets* (London: T. Dawson, 1599), sig. K2ᵛ. Reading paradoxically, then, may mean something like cutting obliquely against the grain of the text to see its larger implications. In 1597 Dee wrote to Edward Dyer (BL Harleian, MS 249, fols. 95–105) with instructions for reading his book to answer a specific question about royal sea rights. See Lisa Jardine and William Sherman, "Pragmatic Readers," in *Religion, Culture and Society in Early Modern Britain,* ed. Anthony Fletcher and Peter Roberts (Cambridge: Cambridge University Press, 1994), 112–13.

18. Erasmus discusses *Scopae dissolutae* as a mocking term in the *Adages.* See *The Collected Works of Erasmus, Adages Ii1 to Iv100,* trans. Margaret Mann Phillips (Toronto: University of Toronto Press, 1982), 466. I am grateful to my colleague Judith Rice Henderson for these references.

19. Oastler, *John Day,* 45.

20. See Michael Camille's learned and delightful book *Image on the Edge: The Margins of Medieval Art* (London: Reaktion Books, 1992).

21. See the 1488 "Act for ye preservacion of the frye of Fyshe," in *The Statutes of the Realm* (London, 1810), 2:543–45. Theodore B. Leinwand has noted that the phrase "Myddle-Sort," which Dee uses to describe fish large enough to bring to market, occurs in a gloss (margin, 43) that combines "ethical, economic, and commonwealth discourses" and may anticipate the use of the term later in the early modern period to characterize a social class. See Leinwand, "Shakespeare and the Middling Sort," *Shakespeare Quarterly* 44 (1993): 290.

22. Jacques Derrida, "Living On: *Border Lines,*" trans. James Hulbert, in *Deconstruction and Criticism,* ed. Harold Bloom et al., 75–176 (New York: Seabury Press, 1976), 81. See also his essay "Some Statements and Truisms," in *The States of "Theory,"* ed. David Carroll, 61–94 (New York: Columbia University Press, 1990); and "This Is Not an Oral Footnote," in *Annotation and Its Texts,* ed. Stephen A. Barney, 192–205 (New York: Oxford University Press, 1991).

23. For more on this highly flexible, emergent form, see George Landow, *Hypertext: The Convergence of Contemporary Critical Theory and Technology* (Baltimore: Johns Hopkins University Press, 1992). The enormous implications of this technology for the practice of textual criticism are just now being realized. For an arresting example of a text expanded—or, rather, exploded—on the printed page into its constituent quotations and allusions, see Samuel Antupit's double-page disassembly of Roy Lichtenstein's "Mural with Blue Brushstroke" in Edward R. Tufte's *Envisioning Information* (Cheshire, Conn.: Graphics Press, 1990), 70–71. Tufte's book traces the various methods (layering, sepa-

ration, use of contour and color) that graphic artists have employed in the print medium to distinguish kinds of information and to make it memorable. His examples range from the earliest printed maps to the most recent computerized cybernetics.

24. In his book *The Writing of History* (trans. Tom Conley [New York: Columbia University Press, 1988]) Michel de Certeau argues that, when *materia* (facts) could no longer be regarded exclusively as signs of revealed truth, they were conflated with *ornamentum* (commentary, especially written commentary, that arranges and interprets "facts") in the form of history. At this point in the recording of the human story, according to Certeau, a new sense of causality emerged. Its abiding concern with *order* and *filiation*—and the historian's consequent abhorrence of a vacuum—was being endlessly reenacted on the pages of the Tudor histories roughly contemporary with the *General and Rare Memorials*.

25. See, for example, *General and Rare Memorials* (sig. ε4); and the statement in Dee's diary that "I declare to the Quene her title to Greenland, Estetiland and Friseland" (*The Private Diary of Dr. John Dee,* ed. James Orchard Halliwell [London: Camden Society, 1842], 4).

26. See William Rockett, "Historical Topography and British History in Camden's *Britannia,*" *Renaissance and Reformation / Renaissance et Réformé,* n.s. 14 (1990): 71–80. Richard Helgerson traces the making of the English nation through its heavily annotated accounts of law, history, geography, and exploration in his thought-provoking study, *Forms of Nationhood: The Elizabethan Writing of England* (Chicago: University of Chicago Press, 1992).

27. Roberts ("John Dee's Corrections") speculates that entries in Dee's diary for June and November 1577, recording loans he had obtained in excess of one hundred pounds, might be related to the extraordinary costs of publication. Dee, a man of large spending and little income, doubtless harbored pecuniary hopes for Hatton's patronage, though we have no record that any such support was forthcoming.

28. Oastler (*John Day*) discusses the Protestant slant in Day's work, especially Latimer's *Sermons* (1549), the *Psalms* (1561, with many editions over the next twenty-three years), Foxe's *Actes and Monuments* (1563 and three other editions), Ælfric's A *Testimonie of Antiquitie* (1566?), and Archbishop Parker's *De antiquitate Britannicae ecclesiae* (1572[-74]). Day wished to support the view that, as D. C. Greetham puts it, "the Protestant revolution in England was in fact merely a return to the original principles of the Anglo-Saxon church." See *Textual Scholarship: An Introduction* (New York: Garland, 1992), 109.

29. Clulee, *John Dee's Natural Philosophy,* 180–89.

30. See Dee, *Private Diaries,* 4; and William H. Sherman, "John Dee's *Brytannicae Reipublicae Synopsis:* A Reader's Guide to the Elizabethan Commonwealth," *Journal of Medieval and Renaissance Studies* 20 (1990): 293–315, esp. 299 n. 17. Sherman's superb book, *John Dee: The Politics of Reading and Writing in the English Renaissance* (Amherst: University of Massachusetts Press, 1995), appeared too late to enrich my thinking about Dee in the present essay.

31. For an older but still reliable account of English maritime enterprise, see Conyers Read, *Mr. Secretary Walsingham and the Policy of Queen Elizabeth* (Oxford: Clarendon, 1925), 3:370–410; and also his history of Dutch-English relations between 1573 and 1578 (1:306–72). I am grateful to Edward Berry of the University of Victoria for encouraging me to pursue this line of inquiry.

32. See Roy Strong, *Gloriana: The Portrait of Queen Elizabeth I* (London: T. Hudson, 1987), 55–56. The capital *C* depicting Elizabeth has been hand-colored in the Bodleian and Trinity College, Cambridge, copies. See Oastler, *John Day*, 49; and Roberts, "John Dee's Corrections," 71.

33. Ashmole Ms. 1789, fol. 50. In the sketch Europa is naked.

34. French, *John Dee*, 184. French's reading is met with skepticism by Clulee (*John Dee's Natural Philosophy*, 290 n. 28) and is flatly contradicted by Margery Corbett and Ronald Lightbown in *The Comely Frontispiece: The Emblematic Title-Page in England, 1550–1660* (London: Routledge and Kegan Paul, 1979), who claim that the flags on the ships in question are English (54).

35. Corbett and Lightbown, *Comely Frontispiece*, 54–55.

"Like a Looking-Glas in the Frame":
From the Marginal Note to the Footnote

Evelyn B. Tribble

Editions are visible yet often unremarked testimonies to the difficulties of managing the past. For what is an apparatus but a sign of the need to transform the text, to assimilate it into a version of the present? The critical role of the structure of the page in shaping reading experience has often been overlooked, in part because of the traditional segregation of social history, bibliography, and literary criticism and theory. Annotations— glosses in the margins and their eighteenth-century successors, footnotes— are consistently undervalued in studies of the history of authorship and publishing. Yet, if rendered visible, the page has much to tell us. Often it is invisible, either because of modern editions that efface so-called extratextual marks or because apparatus becomes so much a part of our mental furniture that it is simply ignored.[1]

Particularly at moments at which paradigms for receiving the past are under stress, the shape of the page can become more than usually visible. In the early modern period, as models of annotation move from marginal glosses to footnotes, the note becomes the battlefield upon which competing notions of the relationship of authority and tradition, past and present, are fought. In this essay, after briefly reviewing the status of the marginal gloss in the sixteenth and early seventeenth centuries, I will examine the shift from marginal glosses to footnotes, which takes place early in the eighteenth century. Lawrence Lipking and others have seen this shift as instituting a newly hierarchical system of knowledge, in which the primary text serenely presides over the bottom matter.[2] While I agree that such a hierarchical system is a goal of this notational practice, what is overlooked here are the strains and stresses inherent in this shift; at its birth the footnote is a heavily contested form: Will it become a vehicle for displaying the critic's taste and breeding or a quasiscientific system for displaying the vicissitudes of textual transmission?³

We can better understand some of the issues at stake in the controversies over footnotes in the eighteenth century through a glance back at glossing practices of the sixteenth and early seventeenth centuries. Such an examination will demonstrate the ways in which the structure of the page becomes associated with a particular mode of organizing and transmitting the past.⁴

As I have discussed elsewhere, for sixteenth-century reformers the *Glossa ordinaria,* the compendium of patristic and scholastic commentary first produced in the thirteenth century, symbolized everything that was wrong with the Catholic Church's reliance on traditions and authorities. Bristling with annotations, abbreviations, obscure references, a jumble of authorities past and present, this page represented all the abuses of scholasticism: its intellectual aridity, its slavishness, its reliance on superannuated traditions at the expense of the simple transmission of God's word to the faithful. Reformers such as Tyndale and Erasmus saw themselves as sweeping away the obfuscations of the past, as presenting, unveiled, the pure and simple truth of the Scriptures. Ironically, of course, the pure and simple truth proved to need supplements and aids of its own, and the glosses of the Geneva Bible crowd the page almost as much as did the notes to the *Glossa ordinaria.*

Classical editions follow a similar trajectory. Throughout the incunabula period and for much of the sixteenth century, the classical past intermingles with the present, as glossed editions reproduce ancient and modern commentators indiscriminately. This is the secular version of scholasticism: a reproduction of the received text along with the full weight of tradition. By the mid-sixteenth century some humanist editors, following the lead of Aldus Manutius, have taken it upon themselves to manage the tradition, to produce editions that look to us more coherent and less jumbled, often produced by a single commentator who sifts through the tradition. In such editions we can see the beginnings of a new conception of the relation between tradition and authority.⁵ Vernacular writers seeking to place themselves within a classical tradition (such as Edmund Spenser and Pierre de Ronsard) used this model. At the same time, as the models of authority and tradition begin to shift from medieval to protomodern, the remaining trappings of scholastic glosses begin to be viewed as pedantry or pretension, a veneer of learning designed to support the writer's claims to have done scholarly work. Thomas Dekker uses this barb against Ben Jonson, who published his masques with so many side notes that (Dekker claims) he seems to have placed his sources on the rack to stretch out as many references as possible.[6]

By the late seventeenth century glosses in the margins begin to decline, associated as they are with residual medieval notions of authorization (in which the author is authorized by others, by his place in a relatively undifferentiated tradition). In the later seventeenth century and the eighteenth century the footnote begins to dominate, a form that promises—but does not necessarily deliver—a hierarchization of knowledge, a firm subordination of text to subtext. By the first quarter of the eighteenth century, the time of Bentley, Pope, and Theobald, annotations have begun either to settle at the bottom of the page, no longer side by side with the so-called main text, or to reside decorously at the end of the volume. The footnote or endnote replaces the marginal gloss in editions of classical poetry and, subsequently, editions of vernacular writers such as Shakespeare and Milton, who were seen as within this classical tradition.

Why does this shift take place at this moment in history? Footnotes are cheaper to print (endnotes cheaper still, as academic authors find). But printers of the period, as far as I can find, do not defend the change in these terms. One eighteenth-century discussion of the footnote instead points toward a revived interest in the aesthetics of printing, a sense that printers and publishers shared with writers and critics of having emerged from a barbaric past, from which they were eager to distance themselves. This separation is accomplished through a series of distinctions and demarcations designed to reorder the world of letters, literally and figuratively, into canons of taste.

John Smith, the author of the midcentury handbook *The Printer's Grammar* (1765), spends much of his energies in distinguishing "modern" printers from their crude seventeenth-century forebears. For Smith the most compelling symbol of the distinction was the move to roman rather than black letter type and the related abandonment of the practice of mixing italic, roman, and black letter on the same page. In his directions to compositors he distinguishes between the "old" way of composing "with Capitals to Substantives, and Italic to Proper names" and "the more modern and neater way," in which "we pay no regard to put any thing in Italic but what is underscored in our Copy: neither do we drown the beauty of Roman Lower-case Sorts by gracing every Substantive with a Capital; but only such as are Proper names, or are words of particular signification and emphasis."[7] The various sections of the book are to be distinguished by changing the point size rather than mixing fonts higgledy-piggledy, as was the practice through the seventeenth century. The dedication, therefore, is to be two points larger than the body, footnotes in smaller type, and so on. Typography is also capable of marking social distinction: Smith discusses the practice of certain printers who set the name of the dedicator "in small letter, and a great distance [which] denotes a profound submission" (219). Thus, the form of the book is to be configured so as to mime contemporary ideals of order, coherence, beauty, and hierarchy.

Footnotes (or bottom notes) rather than marginal notes (or side notes) are also, implicitly, seen as the "modern and neater way." Smith writes:

> Hence we see in the productions of former Printers, that they delighted in seeing the pages lined with Notes and Quotations; which they enlarged on purpose, and contrived to encompass the pages of the text, that they might have the resemblance of a Looking-glas in the frame. By thus crowding the pages with Notes, they could not want so many quotations as we do at present [i.e., in the text?] now we are convinced, that too many Notes are of no advantage to work that is to be called curious: for the Notes being always considerably less than the text, either this will appear too pale, or the other too black; and for this reason those who have a notion of Printing, avoid to write many Side notes. (133)

The curious or elegant work, as opposed, presumably, to the merely learned work, is spoiled aesthetically by the crowded page. Smith thus mocks the aesthetics of an earlier period, which saw beauty in the overelaborate and gaudy framing of the page: implicitly, such a page presented only a show of learning that would reflect a false flattering image of the misguided printer and author. This concern with the aesthetics of the page is borne out by Joseph Trapp's preface to *Praelectiones poeticae:*

> The references for our quotations from the poets are not set out in the margin of the page; since all who are not strangers to their writings will sufficiently recognize the passages; and we thought that the elegance of the page would be diminished by notes added in this way.[8]

The margin can also provide scope for the owner of the book to display his own erudition: Smith writes rather disparagingly of the printers of other countries, who are compelled to make extra wide margins, "since they would disoblige the Literati, were they to deprive them of a large Margin, to write their Notes and Annotations to books of learning" (259–60). Yet another signification of the margin (not mentioned by Smith) must be considered for this period: the eighteenth century is also the era of the large-paper editions, deluxe versions of already expensive books. In addition to listing subscribers by social rank, subscription lists indicate those who have paid out the extra money for large-paper editions, in which the same form is impressed upon larger paper, thus providing an expensive expanse of snowy margin. In this incarnation the margin has become a sign of leisure, in which gentlemen of taste display large margins, marked in the prefatory matter as their own property.

This class marking shows us that footnotes are yet another manifestation of the marked shift in canons of taste that takes place toward the end of the seventeenth century. As I will argue, the role of the note—the shape of the page—becomes of central importance in the struggles to define this emergent notion of taste and the concomitant role of the critic. Central to this critical enterprise are acts of distinction, which are at the heart of the construction of taste. In the remainder of this essay I will examine two such acts: John Dryden's work to distinguish himself from previous translators of the classics, most notably John Ogilby; and Alexander Pope's attempt to distinguish his critical mission from the nascent professionalism of Richard Bentley and Lewis Theobald.

The Ogilby part of the story is told much less often than is the Bentley, for Ogilby, unlike Bentley or Theobald, gets only passing derision in Pope's *Dunciad Variorum*. Forgotten now, Ogilby was the prime translator of Virgil and Homer from the mid-seventeenth century until Dryden's *Virgil*, and, later, Pope's *Homer* came to supplant him. Ogilby was an autodidact, a former dancing master who turned to the serious study of Latin and Greek only after a disabling masquing accident during a performance for the court of Charles I.[9] Despite beginning his study only later in life, during the interregnum Ogilby went on to translate the most famous epics of classical antiquity, including Virgil and Homer. Ogilby published the translations himself, had them printed on fine paper supplemented by copious "sculptures," or engraved illustrations, and sold the books out of his home. (He is also known for several energetically promoted, if less than successful, lotteries to rid himself of old stock and raise money for new projects.)

For Ogilby it was not merely the act of translation that was worthy of note: the material book itself was an epic achievement. In his autobiographical preface to the elaborate travel atlas *Africa*, he describes the success of his first venture into translation:

> And first Rallying my new rais'd Forces, a small and inconsiderable parcel of *Latin*, I undertook no less a Conquest, than the Reducing into our Native Language, the Great Master and Improver of that Tongue, *Virgil*, the Prince of *Roman* Poets; and though I fell much short in this my vain Enterprise, yet such, and so happy prov'd the Version, and so fairly accepted, that of me, till then obscure, *Fame* began to prattle, and soon after I, forsooth, stood forth a new *Author,* so much cheer'd up with fresh Encouragements, that from a *Mean Octavo*, a *Royal Folio* flourish'd, Adorn'd with Sculpture, and Illustrated with Annotations, Triumphing with the affixt Emblazons, Names, and Titles of a hundred *Patrons,* all bold Assertors in Vindication of the Work, which (whate're my Deserts) being Publish'd with that Magnificence and Splendor, appear'd a new, and taking Beauty, the fairest that till then the English Press ever boasted.[10]

Adorned with engravings, "illustrated" with marginal notes, and stamped with the imprimaturs of "a hundred Patrons," the physical book will soar with no middle flight above its peers.

In the case of the annotations or marginal notes, "illustration" seems to have both conceptual and literal implications. In the dedication of his *Virgil* to William, earl of Hertford, Ogilby writes: "Wherein, as I have by the Encouragement of Noble and Generous Personages, mentioned in their several Pieces, us'd the skill and industry of the most famous Artists, in their kinds, for the embellishments of the Work, so there will not, I suppose, be much wanting in the Margents, to any indifferent Reader, for Illustration of the Poem."[11] On the one hand, the poem will be illustrated, or clarified to its readers; on the other, it is literally illustrated by these notes, for they profoundly shape the visual configuration of the page. Ogilby's page does indeed look like Smith's "looking glass within a frame" (see fig. 1): the poems are surrounded on three sides with elaborate annotation. Based in large part on the annotations of de la Cerda, Scaliger, and Caussin, they are typical of their kind in content: identification of references, remarks upon geography and customs of the time, and so on.[12] For example, he identifies "Conan" as "An Excellent Astrologer and Geometrician . . . in the time of *Ptolemy,* and left behind him 7 Books of Astrology" (13). A character described by one of the shepherds as "Him with a *Staff*

VIRGIL'S
' BUCOLICKS:

The First ² Eclog.
Tityrus.

The ³ Argument.

Sad Meliboeus, *banished, declares*
What Miseries attend on Civil Wars :
But happy Tityrus, *the safe Defence*
People enjoy under a setled Prince.

⁴TITYRUS, ⁵MELIBOEUS.

Meliboeus.

 Nder a spreding ᵃ Beech, thou *Ti-*
tyrus ᵇ set,
On slender Reeds do'st Rural
Notes repeat.
We are of Lands, and sweet Fields,
dispossest,
We flie our Country: Thou, in shade at rest,

(1) Pastorals are of several sorts & denominations, according to the diversity of the Subjects and Persons : Those consisting of Shepherds were called *Poimenica,* of Goatherds *Ai̇̇polia,* of Swineherds *Subotia,* of Neatherds *Bucolica :* Which last, *Scaliger* terms the Noblest Species of Pastorals; whose ·Original see in the Scholiast of *Theocritus, Servius, Probus, Sabinus* and *Nannius.*

(2) The word signifies *Selection :* For the first Authors of these kinde of Poems (which commonly were no other than undigested *Rhapsodies*) disrelishing many times the rudeness of their unpolish'd composures, us'd upon second thoughts to select from the gross heap some choice and more studied Peeces, which for that reason they call'd *Eclogs.* *Scalig. l. 1. Poet. c. 4.*

(3) *Among̃st those who took part with the Conspirators and Murtherers of* Cæsar, *was the City of* Cremona, *which* Augustus, *becomming absolute Victor at the Battel of* Philippi, *assigned (with the Lands adjacent) to his Soldiers, at once to reward them, and punish the Inhabitants : But* Cremona *not being wide enough to satisfie the greedy Soldier,* Mantua, *the next Town, was added to enlarge the Assignment. Virgil upon this occasion, amongst other* Mantuans, *ejected out of his Inheritance, went to* Rome *for Redress: where, by* Mecœnas *and others recommended to* Augustus, *he obtein'd so great a share in his favour, that he was not only re-instated in his Lands; but receiv'd so many Gifts and Rewards, as far exceeded them in value. This occasion, to which the World is indebted for all these Poems, is particularly the subject of this.*

(4) A name assum'd by *Virgil* to represent himself under the condition of a Shepherd, either in imitation of *Theocritus,* or in allusion to the Pastoral Pipe call'd *Titvrinus;* or the old *Teretismata,* rustick Satyricall Dances.

(5) In the Original the Word signifies a Neatherd, but covertly in this place the Mantuans, or particularly *Cornelius Gallus,* as *Servius* and *Sabinus* conjecture ; The latter of whom gives this Reason, because *Gallus* was born between *Cremona* and *Mantua.*

(a) La Cerda contends that *Fagus* properly signifies an *Oak,* or *Holm,* but we have chosen the vulgar and more warranted Interpretation. Ingeniously and appositly is our Shepherd seated under a *Mast-Tree,* from which the Antients received not only shelter, but sustentation; to intimate the Tranquillity of his Condition, the Competency of his Fortune.   (b) *Theocritus* (whom our Author imitates)

B   Fair

[who] described the world's great ball" is glossed in this way: "his name purposely omitted to comply with the Rusticity of the Relator; but supposed most probably *Archimedes* that famous Sicilian Mathematician, contemporary and intimate with *Conan*" (13). The notes are reminiscent of those in sixteenth- and early-seventeenth-century translations; to this extent the book looks backward to an earlier set of assumptions about the role of the translator/critic.

John Dryden, who is probably most responsible for the opprobrium in which Ogilby is now held (among those who have heard of him), chose to define himself as translator against his predecessor. Ogilby is given passing mention in "MacFlecknoe" as the MacFlecknoe's "uncle," and thus chief among Dullards. In his dedication to the *Virgil* Dryden refers scornfully to the "botching interpreter" who preceded him. To those he imagines asking, "Why . . . did you attempt [the translation]?" he responds: "No other Answer can be made, than that I have done [Virgil] less Injury than any of his former Libellers."[13]

This judgment is borne out in the prefatory verses to the 1697 *Virgil*, many of which stress Dryden's superiority to those translators who preceded him, particularly "mangling Ogleby's presumptuous Quill."[14] The first anonymous poem casts Dryden as the savior of the spirit of Virgil from the depradations of the immediate past:

> Long the rude fury of an ignorant Age
> With barbarous spight prophan'd his Sacred Page
> The heavy *Dutchmen* with laborious toil,
> Wrested his Sense, and cramp'd his vigorous Style
> No times, no pains the drudging Pedants spare;
> But still his Shoulders must the burthen bear.
> While thro' the Mazes of their Comments led,
> We learn not why he writes, but what they read.[15]

For the author of this poem Virgil's "Sacred Page" is profaned by the burden of pedantic commentary; the "Mazes" of notes surrounding the verse only serve to conceal the poetic genius of the author. Notes are not used to call attention to the particularities of style of the author or to clarify his intentions but, instead, to call attention to the superficial learning of the commentator himself. By the end of the seventeenth century the old tradition of marginal glossing has begun to appear as just that: old and antiquated. Just as Dryden has "endeavour'd to make Virgil speak such *English*, as he wou'd himself have spoken, if he had been born in *England,* and in this present age" (sig. F3v), so too is the appearance of the book to be "modern and neater," to use Smith's terminology, than the magnificent, if ponderous, royal folios of his predecessor.

Though he makes the point more obliquely, Dryden himself seems to concur with this assessment of the marginal freight to editions such as Ogilby's. In his afterword to the *Virgil* he remarks:

> The few Notes which follow, are *par maniere d'acquit,* because I had obliged my self by Articles, to do somewhat of that kind. The scattering Observations are rather guesses at my Author's meaning in some passages, than proofs that he so meant. The Unlearned may have recourse to any Poetical Dictionary in *English,* for the Names of Persons, Places, and Fables, which the Learned need not: But that little which I say, is either new or necessary. (623)

The "unlearned" are instructed to seek their enlightenment elsewhere; the page will not be cluttered up for their benefit. Almost casually, Dryden dismisses one of the most enduring roles of the note: the identification of unfamiliar references. (Another, economic reason seems to be behind the paucity of notes, which Dryden had promised in the prospectus: Jacob Tonson was unwilling to spend the extra money to print all of the notes to which Dryden had committed himself.)[16]

For all the scorn heaped upon him, Ogilby was perhaps not the real threat to emergent constructions of taste, the canon, and the critic. Something of a transitional figure, Ogilby both looks back at the past (in his use of marginal commentary) and ahead to the emergence of the marketplace (in his energetic promotion of his books and his ingenious modified subscription system, by which wealthy patrons sponsored particular engravings that were to bear their coats of arms). The issue that was to divide the educated elite in the eighteenth century was, rather, the technical rigor of scholars such as Richard Bentley and Lewis Theobald. At stake in this debate was the very definition of a critic: Was a critic a gentleman who pointed out the beauties of his poet to an admiring audience or an ink-stained scholar grubbing about with old manuscripts and correcting his betters? In the controversies between Richard Bentley and Charles Boyle, reprised in the quarrels among Pope, Bentley, and Theobald, we see the role of the page and the note in the nascent construction of taste.[17]

If Ogilby was ridiculed for excessively extravagant claims, Theobald and Bentley received censure for the excessive minutiae of their concerns. Bentley achieved early notoriety for exposing the Honorable Charles Boyle's ignorance of classical textual transmission in the latter's edition of the *Epistles of Phalaris*. The resultant furor over scholarship foreshadows the issues at stake in Pope's *Dunciad*. In both cases taste—the definition of true critic—is of prime importance. In response to Bentley's critique, Boyle argues that the minutiae of scholarship are beneath the dignity of a gentleman: "I little imagin'd ever to have been engag'd in a Dispute of this nature. I am not over-fond of Controversie even where the Points debated may be thought of some importance, but in trivial matters, and such as Mankind is not at all concerned in, methinks it is unpardonable."[18] Later he adds: "Begging the Dr.'s pardon, I take *Index-Hunting* after Words and Phrases to be, next *Anagrams* and *Acrostick,* the lowest Diversion a Man can take himself to" (145). Boyle also voices concern lest "worthy Men, who know so well how to employ their hours, should be diverted from the pursuit of Useful Knowledge into such trivial Enquiries as these" (sig. [A4v]). Boyle's scorn of "Index-Hunting" has obvious class implications, as he draws a distinction between worthy, useful knowledge pursued by gentlemen and the "low diversions" (note the sense that all this work is, after all, simply a game) followed by the professional rather than the amateur commentator.

Boyle makes the class sneers explicit at times, as when he ascribes Bentley's attacks to his "Breeding" (sig. A2v). Later in the book he quotes Charles de Saint Euremond in order to clarify his definition of the critic:

The Learned Tribe is my Aversion, who are perpetually busie in restoring corrupted Passages, that when restor'd are at last worth nothing. They set the highest Price on such knowledge, as one who would choose to be without; and know least of those things which most deserve to be known. Having no fine way of thinking and speaking themselves, they can never enter into the Delicacy of another Man's Thoughts or Expression. They would succeed very well in explaining and commenting upon a Grammarian; for His mind is thrown into much the same Mould with Theirs, and his Studies have lain the same way: but when they come to one of the Sensible and Wellbred Writers of Antiquitie, they neither relish nor understand his Sence, and way of thinking, must needs be locked up to 'em; 'tis so very different from their Own. . . . The Genius that animates their admirable Writing is not felt; the Remarkable and Instructive Passages there are not observ'd.[19]

Boyle thus establishes a clear hierarchy between the critic (he spends a considerable amount of time defining the "true" critic) and the scholar/ pedant. The failure of breeding or taste prevents the pedant from apprehending the "Sensible and Wellbred" writers; lacking the ability to understand their Genius, they are thrown back upon such trivial, material details, as finding a "false Accent" (223). Both Ogilby, with his concern only for the beauties of his fair book, and Bentley, with his obsession over trivial marks of punctuation, are blind to the ineffable spirit that animates poetry.

Critiques such as this gained considerable currency in the early to mid-eighteenth century. Bentley became a convenient focal point for attackers in the Battle of the Books. As Peter Cosgrove writes:

> The attack was the culminating point of a social struggle that had been waged since the invention of printing gave new impetus to the revival of learning—a struggle between the hierarchical domination of a relatively easily controlled body of literary and philosophical knowledge, and the erosion of that domination by a combination of the relaxing of ecclesiastical and civil control of the rate of literary diffusion and by increased investigation into the validity of the texts both sacred and secular which upheld the hierarchical social structure.[20]

The stakes are high, then, and Bentley was seen as a threat to far more than a few odd punctuation marks in Terence. These attacks tended to be conducted through parody; Bentley's concern with textual minutiae made his apparatus a convenient target for satire. Most of these efforts—the *Dunciad Variorum* is only the most famous—mimic the form of the scholarly edition.[21] One such is a parody of Bentley's 1712 Horace: *The Odes, Epodes, and Carmen Seculare of Horace, in Latin and English, with a translation of Dr. Ben-ley's Notes. To Which are Added Notes upon Notes in 24 parts complete by several hands.*[22] English and Latin are printed on facing pages, and the "notes upon notes" are designed to "convince him, how ridiculous it is, to presume to correct Horace without Authority, upon the pretended Strength of superior Judgment in Poetry" (sig. A2v).

Another, cruder attempt at parody is *The Session of the Critics: or, The Contention for the Nettle, a Poem. To Which is added, A Dialogue between a player and a poet, with Notes, explanatory and critical, after the manner of the Learned Dr. Bentley.*[23] The slender book is a miscellany of equally slender contemporary critical witticisms. The "Dialogue between a player and a poet" is heavily annotated in a supposedly Bentleian manner:

> A (a)Dialogue *between* W-m P-k-n, *Player*, H-S-, *Poet*
> P (b)How now, (c)Friend S—, why so melancholy?
> You're always used to be alert and jolly.
> S (d)You know my clever (e)Talent at inditing,
> Some verses on my (f)Cousin I've been writing.
> P(g) Some verses, Sir (h)I wish you good night—
> But hold—pray, lend 'em me, I must go sh—te.
>
> (6)

The "explanatory and critical note" on the last line reads: "(h)Reader, take your pen, and blot out the last Letter in the word *shite:* the true reading is *shit.* The word here is in the Present Tense of the Infinite Mood of the Verb *shit,* which is not formed into *shite,* but *shit,* as the most accurate Criticks, Grammarians, and Etymologists agree" (6). This scatological ridicule of the excessive attention to detail demotes Bentley to the lowest regions of the body, an appropriate punishment for a writer whose "pretended strength of superior Judgement in Poetry" has constituted a threat to the canons of taste.

It was Alexander Pope who attempted to find a new critical use for the note, one that would eschew both the prolixity of an Ogilby and the pedanticism of a Bentley. In his Homer, Pope had attempted to define a new province for the note: to train taste by the judicious display of poetical beauty. In his preface to Homer, Pope complains that such concerns were neglected by his predecessors: "there is hardly one whose principal Design is to illustrate the Poetical Beauties of the Author . . . their Remarks are rather Philosophical, Historical, Geographical, Allegorical, or in short rather any thing than Critical & Poetical."[24] Thus, he promises that "the chief Design of the following Notes is to comment upon *Homer* as a poet" (5). Yet this technique fails him for his famous edition of Shakespeare, since the unexpected difficulties of editing the text at all left him with little time for complete annotations. He thus falls back upon the configuration of the page as a substitute for copious notes. Harassed by the difficulties of Shakespeare's text, which he ascribes in part to "the ignorance of the players," he employs a typographical system for apportioning praise and blame:

Some suspected passages which are excessively bad . . . are degraded to the bottom of the page, with an asterisk referring to the places of their insertion. . . . Some of the most shining passages are distinguished by commas in the margin; and where the beauty lay not in particulars but in the whole, a star is prefixed to the scene. This seems to me a shorter and less ostentatious method of performing the better half of criticism (namely the pointing out of an author's excellencies) than to fill a whole paper with citations of fine passages, with general applauses or empty exclamations at the tail of them.[25]

It is worth noting here Pope's exploitation of a newly hierarchical typographical system. "Degrading" excessively bad passages to the bottom of the page visually reinforces the hierarchies of taste and class Pope attempts to impress on the text (one of the reasons the errors imposed by the players are so gross is that "that class of people was then far inferior to what it is in our days. . . . The top of the profession were then mere players, not gentleman of the stage" [172]). The pecking order of good/bad, tasteful/tasteless, is considerably less clear when the suspect passage is placed to the *side*, where the offending passage might be seen to be in direct competition with its betters.

It is appropriate, then, that Pope employs the footnote to degrade his opponents. The *Dunciad Variorum* celebrates Dullness, reigned over by Lewis Theobald, the author of *Shakespeare Restored*, who justifiably took Pope to task for his ignorance of textual editing. Here Pope casts himself as a humanist satirizing the obfuscations of the "herd of commentators," whose notes obscure rather than enlighten:

> There, thy good Scholiasts with unweary'd pains
> Make Horace flat, and humble Maro's strains;
> Here studious I unlucky moderns save
> Nor sleeps one error in its father's grave,
> Old puns restore, lost blunders nicely seek,
> And crucify poor Shakspear once a week.
> For thee I dim these eyes, and stuff this head
> With all such reading as was never read;
> For thee supplying, in the worst of days,
> Notes to dull books, and prologues to dull plays;
> For thee explain a thing till all men doubt it,
> And write about it, Goddess, and about it;

So spins the silkworm small its slender store,
And labours, till it clouds itself all o'er.[26]

To reinforce the point Pope clouds over his own page with notes, some brilliant parodies of Theobald's own notes. In these he mocks the tremendous expenditure of energy that results only in the merest change of a syllable or two: "The Dunciad, sic M.S. It may be well disputed whether this be a right Reading? Ought it not rather to be spelled Dunceiad, as the Etymology evidently demands? *Dunce* with an *e*, therefore *Dunceiad* with an *e*" (59). At the foot of the page he displays and parodies the "low diversions" of his opponents, thus visually embodying the class sneers apparent in the passage from Bentley I quoted earlier.

One of his targets is in fact Ogilby himself. Pope ridicules the naive self-promotion of the quality of his books. On the line "Here swells the shelf with Ogilby the great," he comments: "*John Ogilby* was one, who from a late initiation into literature, made such a progress as might well stile him the *Prodigy* of his time! sending into the world so many *large Volumes!* His translations of *Homer* and *Virgil, done to the life,* and with *such excellent Sculptures!* and (what added great grace to his works) he printed them all on *special good Paper,* and in a *very good Letter*" (78).

The pretensions toward self-canonization—and these on the basis of such material elements as illustrations, type, and paper—are exploded, appropriately enough, at the foot of Pope's page. Both Bentley and Ogilby are cast down, degraded, the one for his obsession with minutiae, the other for his ridiculous boasting of the gaudiness of his productions. Both are bound to the letter—Ogilby to the typographic letter, Bentley to the letter of the manuscript. Both thus miss the higher truths that critics of true taste can discern. The footnote, then, is seized by Pope as a weapon in the constitution of a social and literary hierarchy against those who are seen as its enemies.

NOTES

I am indebted to the members of the panel on "Eighteenth Century Shakespeare" at the Shakespeare Association of America conference (1993) for their helpful comments on an earlier version of this essay. Particularly generous with their time and comments were Bill Slights, Bernice Kliman, Johanna Gondris, and Nick Clary. Thanks are also due to Shannon Miller and Shef Rogers, for reading various versions of this essay.

1. My work is indebted to bibliographical work on the "sociology of the text," which has in turn contributed to a general reconsideration of the role of the material text. See Philip Cohen, ed., *Devils and Angels: Textual Editing and Literary Theory* (Charlottesville: University Press of Virginia, 1991); Jerome McGann, *Textual Criticism and Literary Interpretation* (Chicago: University of Chicago Press, 1985); D. F. McKenzie, "Typography and Meaning: The Case of William Congreve," *Buch und Buchhandel in Europe im achtzehnten Jahrhundert* (Hamburg: Hauswedell, 1981), 81–125; James McLaverty, "The Mode of Existence of Literary Works of Art: The Case of the *Dunciad* Variorum," *Studies in Bibliography* 37 (1984): 82–105; Peter L. Shillingsburg, "An Inquiry into the Social Status of Texts and Modes of Textual Criticism," *Studies in Bibliography* 42 (1989): 44–79. Because my own training is in English Renaissance literature, I have been greatly influenced by the recent work done by Peter Stallybrass, Margreta De Grazia, and others on the materiality of the Renaissance text. See De Grazia, *Shakespeare Verbatim: The 1790 Apparatus and the Reproduction of Authenticity* (New York: Oxford University Press, 1991); Randall McLeod, "Un-Editing Shakespeare," *SubStance* 33–34 (1982): 26–55; Stephen Orgel, "What Is a Text?" in *Staging the Renaissance*, ed. David Kastan and Peter Stallybrass (London: Routledge, 1992), 83–87; and Peter Stallybrass and Margreta De Grazia, "The Materiality of the Shakespearean Text," *Shakespeare Quarterly* 44, no. 3 (Fall 1993): 255–83.
2. Lawrence Lipking, "The Marginal Gloss," *Critical Inquiry* 3 (1977): 609–55. William W. E. Slights has taken issue with many of Lipking's assumptions about the role of the marginal note in the sixteenth and seventeenth centuries. See "The Edifying Margins of Renaissance English Books," *Renaissance Quarterly* 42, no. 4 (Winter 1989): 682–716.
3. Peter Cosgrove has convincingly argued that "the restoration of a history to the device of footnoting may point toward the larger failure of an 'objective' discursive vehicle to escape an inherent instability between its rhetorical and its factual elements." See "Undermining the Text: Edward Gibbon, Alexander Pope, and the Anti-Authenticating Footnote," in *Annotation and Its Texts,* ed. Stephen A. Barney, 130–51 (Oxford: Oxford University Press, 1991), 131. See also Peter Riess, *Towards a Theory of the Footnote* (Berlin and New York: Walter de Gruyter & Co., 1983).
4. The discussion of biblical and early humanist editing practices is derived from the first two chapters of my book *Margins and Marginality: The Printed Page in Early Modern England* (Charlottesville: University Press of Virginia, 1993).
5. See E. J. Kenney, *The Classical Text* (Berkeley: University of California Press, 1974).
6. Thomas Dekker, *The Magnificent Entertainment* (London, 1604), sig. A4v.
7. John Smith, *The Printer's Grammar* (London: for W. Owen, 1765), 201, 202.
8. Quoted in David Foxon, *Pope and the Early Eighteenth-Century Book Trade,* revised and edited by James McLaverty (Oxford: Clarendon Press, 1991), 44.
9. Unless otherwise noted, my discussion of Ogilby is derived from the prime book-length source on his life and times: Katherine S. Van Eerde, *John Ogilby*

and the Taste of His Times (Folkestone, Kent: William Dawson and Sons, 1976).

10. John Ogilby, *Africa: Being an Accurate Description of the Regions of Aegypt, Barbary, Lybia, and Billedulgerid* (London: Printed by Tho. Johnson for the Author, 1670), sig. C1r.

11. John Ogilby, *The Works of Publius Virgilus Maro. Translated, Adorn'd with Sculpture, and Illustrated with Annotations* (London: For the Author, 1654), sig. [A1r].

12. Van Eerde discusses Ogilby's sources in *John Ogilby* (37–39).

13. John Dryden, *Virgil's Aeneis* (London, 1697), sig. [F3v].

14. Henry Grahme, "To Mr. *Dryden* on his Translation of VIRGIL," *Virgils Aeneis,* sig. [††v].

15. Anonymous, "*To Mr. Dryden, on his Excellent Translation of* Virgil," *Virgil's Aeneis,* sig. †r. A possible author for these verses is Edward Howard; see James and Helen Kinsley, *Dryden: The Critical Heritage* (New York: Barnes and Noble, 1971), 217.

16. See John Barnard, "Dryden, Tonson, and Subscriptions for the 1697 *Virgil,*" *BSA* 57 (1963): 129–51.

17. A great deal of valuable material has been published on the role of Bentley in the quarrel between the Ancients and the Moderns. I am particularly indebted to Penelope Wilson, "Classical Poetry and the Eighteenth Century Reader," in *Books and Their Readers in Eighteenth Century England,* ed. Isabel Rivers (New York and Leicester: St. Martin's and Leicester University Press, 1982); Peter Seary, *Lewis Theobald and the Editing of Shakespeare* (Oxford: Clarendon Press, 1990); and Peter W. Cosgrove, "Undermining the Text."

18. Charles Boyle, *Dr. Bentley's Dissertation on the Epistles of Phalaris, and the Fables of Aesop, Examined by the Honourable Charles Boyle, Esq.,* 3d ed. (London: For Thos. Bennet, 1699), sig. A2r.

19. Ibid., 227–28; quotation is from Charles de Saint Euremond, *Ouvres méslees* (Paris, 1668), 28.

20. Cosgrove, "Undermining the Text," 135.

21. As James McLaverty points out, the *Dunciad Variorum* was deliberately configured to resemble Bentley's 1712 edition of Horace. See "The Mode of Existence of the Work of Art."

22. *The Odes of Horace* (London: Bernard Lintot, 1712–13).

23. *The Session of the Critics* (London: For Thos. Cooper, n.d.).

24. Alexander Pope, *Homer* (London: Bernard Lintot, 1715), 3.

25. Alexander Pope, "Preface to Shakespeare," in *Literary Criticism of Alexander Pope,* ed. Bertrand A. Goldgar (Lincoln: University of Nebraska Press, 1965), 174.

26. Alexander Pope, *The Dunciad,* ed. James Sutherland (London: Methuen, 1963), 81–82.

Glossing the Flesh: Scopophilia and the Margins of the Medieval Book

Michael Camille

> *But the handling of books is specially to be forbidden to those shame-less youths, who, as soon as they have learned to form the shapes of letters, straightway, if they have the opportunity, become unhappy commentators, and wherever they find an extra margin about the text, furnish it with monstrous alphabets, or if any other frivolity strikes their fancy, at once their pen begins to write it.*
> *—Richard de Bury,* Philobiblon

Since for medieval readers the pen was often euphemistically described as the penis and the act of writing itself had been allegorized as ploughing more fleshly pages by poets such as Jean de Meung, the shameful youths described in the epigraph were doing more than merely doodling; they were masturbating in the margins. These words expressing horror at the excesses of youth, reminding us of the censorious words of so many con-temporary conservative cultural critics of "youthful excesses" as diverse as graffiti, pop music, and "zines," are from the pen of the fourteenth-century statesman and bishop of Durham, Richard de Bury, and appear in his famous treatise on his "love of books," the *Philobiblon,* which he finished just before his death in 1345.

De Bury devotes much of chapter 17 to this defilement of the objects of his desire by the polluting filth of others. But the "dirt" that he saw filling the margins of books was not merely the result of dusty neglect nor only those products of the idle imagination, the "monstrous" marginal crea-tures, painted and penned by both artists and readers, that we can still see today in so many books from the period. It also consisted of actual products of readers' own bodies. This is clear from his description of how the "lazy

and headstrong youth" snivels and drips his snot on the volumes as he
lounges over his studies, showering them with chewed food and spittle as
he chatters, and who, falling asleep, folds back "the margins of the leaves to
no small injury of the book." He pushes a multitude of straws in the pages,
to mark his place, which "because the book has no stomach to digest them
. . . distend the book from its wonted closing." This desecration is recounted in powerfully eroticized terms in the breathless bishop's rhetori-
cally eloquent Latin as a savage penetration of the pure pages, the boy using
his "wet and perspiring hands to turn over the volumes," thumping the
"white vellum with gloves covered in all kind of dust," his nails, "stuffed
with fetid filth as black as jet, with which he marks any passage that pleases
him."[1] Various bodily juices and fecal matter become new and fantasic
pigments in the production of these gross glossings of the text, making
their margins like those cesspools that surrounded houses and villages,
places for the extrusion of filth, but also like the liminoid edge of the human
body itself, the barrier that protected and yet also registered the impressions of other bodies, what a fourteenth-century medical text called "the
margynes of the skynne." The margins are, in this text, where the book and
the body meet.[2]

The margins were, I shall argue, more generally a site for the confron-
tation and even the intercourse of the flesh and the spirit, which we tend to
separate as dialectical opposites in our teaching and writing about the
Middle Ages. This is partly because since the nineteenth century scholars
have tended to see the book as a static, closed object, as a medieval encyclopedic summa. In this sense the book comes to represent what Derrida
terms "the idea of a totality . . . the encyclopedic protection of theology and
of logocentrism against the disruption of writing" and is used to explain
everything from the Gothic cathedral to the system of medieval aesthetics.[3]
But once it is "used" and "opened" (these metaphors so beloved of idealist
historians and critics), it is totally changed. Susan Stewart's very different
metaphors of the book in action are those of "containment, of exteriority
and interiority, of surface and depth, of covering and exposure, of taking
apart and putting together," and being "between covers" calls to mind "the
titillation of intellectual and sexual reproduction."[4] Richard de Bury's treatise tells us far more about this second nub of interrelated desires—for
books, for bodies, and for progenitors—than previous interpreters have
noted.

The anxiety about defilement and the body's boundedness in relation
to the book are most strongly expressed in chapter 17 on the handling of

books. Here we read that "next to the vestments and vessels dedicated to the Lord's body—unclean hands should not touch them." Restored to their "proper places" and "inviolable custody," "they may rejoice in purity while we have them in our hands." "And surely next to the vestments and vessels dedicated to the Lord's body, holy books deserve to be rightly treated by the clergy, to which great injury is done so often as they are touched by unclean hands." But, rather than these pronouncements, it is the vehement half-disgusted, half-aroused fascination in de Bury's description of the violent mistreatment of volumes that alerts us to the fetishism underlying the bishop's biblophilia.[5] His obsession, repeated throughout the *Philobiblon,* is with policing the margins of his many volumes and keeping them locked away, closed and impenetrable. It can perhaps be seen as an early example of that anal anxiety exhibited by all collectors, but it also discloses an erotic dynamic to the book that is crucial to the medieval conceptualization of knowledge, not only as an inviolate treasure to be guarded but also as a generative, productive process that has to be somatically performed. The bishop complains in one of many extended metaphors associating the creation of books with the fathering (not bearing) of children, that "the pen of every scribe is now at rest, generations of books no longer succeed one another."[6] His repeated concern is with the preservation of texts, the philological dream that is also biological, for their "purity of race" has been contaminated by contact with various others inimical to books who should be allowed no intercourse with them. This group includes women, termed by Bury "that biped beast," "compilers, translators and transformers," who distort texts in copying, and, most significant for us, "painters knowing nought of letters."[7]

This last group of book defilers, decorators and illuminators, is interesting since many of the things that de Bury describes as dirtying the book—the mucky fingers and sweaty bodies of youths, for example—are exactly the bodies that are painted twisting and curling their limbs in the margins or in some cases literally invading the lines of text as animated corporeal line endings. This is the case in a Book of Hours made in England around the year 1300, probably for an Augustinian prior, in which a naked youth lolls across the lines between the words *fornicatio* and *incarnationis* while pointing to his side like a halo-less Christ (fig. 1). Examples like this seem to suffuse the written page with the very dirt that so disturbed the bishop. Even more significant, many of the margins of the most luxurious and expensive illuminated manuscripts of this period are full of the turds of human waste, expelled from the anuses of various creatures. I have written

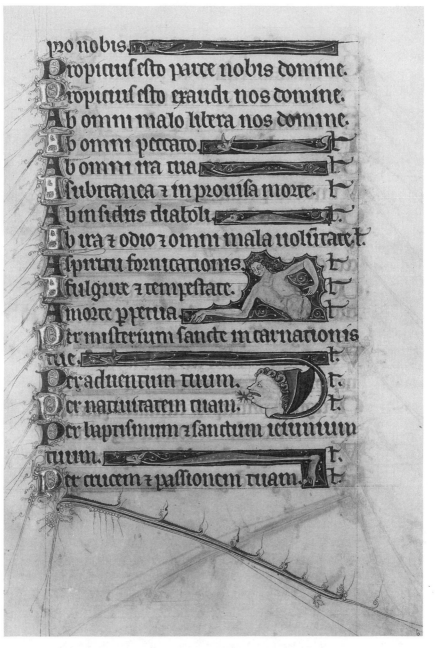

no nobis.

Propicius esto parce nobis domine.

Propicius esto exaudi nos domine.

Ab omni malo libera nos domine.

Ab omni peccato.

Ab omni ira tua.

A subitanea & improuisa morte.

Ab insidiis diaboli.

Ab ira & odio & omni mala uoluntate.

A spiritu fornicationis.

A fulgure & tempestate.

A morte perpetua.

Per misterium sancte incarnationis tue.

Per aduentum tuum.

Per natiuitatem tuam.

Per baptismum & sanctum ieiunium tuum.

Per crucem & passionem tuam.

Fig. 1. Line endings point, eat, and play with the text. (From Walters Art Gallery, Baltimore, MS 102, fol. 30: Psalter and Hours, c. 1300.)

about this scatalogical imagery in the margins elsewhere, relating it to the social construction of a celebratory shitty universe in the courts and cloisters of medieval Europe, which did not classify human excrement as necessarily negative.[8] An aspect that I did not discuss and that I want to take up further in this essay, however, is the way such images might also be activated in the process of reading itself. The bodily signs that fill the margins of medieval manuscripts can be understood in terms not only of social inversions and projections but profoundly psychological ones. The margins, and their fleshly glosses, are a site of a reworking of the imaginary in the thirteenth and fourteenth centuries, related to a new way of reading as well as provid ing a new site for discourse, both visual and verbal.

It is especially in English manuscripts of the late thirteenth and four-teenth centuries that this interest in the gross and productive body as a marginal motif first becomes pronounced. Creatures that seem all body, and yet are not human, eat parts of other bodies, their ravenous mouths seeming to mock the reader's own *ruminatio* of the text. Such bodily inversion played an important and often protective role. In many of the most luxuriant products of the so-called East Anglian school in the 1330s, were manuscripts that Bury himself would have known. There are also numerous anal images, whose "mooning," of course, in folkloristic terms was precisely a way of guarding the text from the evil eye, the anus literally expelling the demonic other by displaying something obscene and fright-ening. Just as such carved gargoyles shit forth their vile liquids from the high gutters of cathedrals and churches, these monsters served to keep the book's pages clean. Illuminators filled the borders and the *bas-de-page* areas of texts with all manner of bodies, not only the usual hybrids and half-human, half-animal creatures but also images that evoke the body's vul-nerability. There are also more narrative images with strong thrusting phal-lic associations, as though the pages were literally being penetrated by nodules of flesh and organs of surprising extension as in the margins of a Parisian manuscript in which little men with erections play out violent fantasies with nuns, animals, and other men (fig. 2). In terms of the gender of these bodies, it is surprisingly most often that of the male that is erot-icized in marginal art. The illuminator of this last example, a Parisian manu-script of a vernacular text, the *Roman de la Rose,* was in fact a woman, Jeanne de Montbaston, and points to the fact that we should not always assume the male heterosexual eye as being the only gaze in the medieval book, either in production or reception.[9]

Two processes that affect books and that are elided with notions of

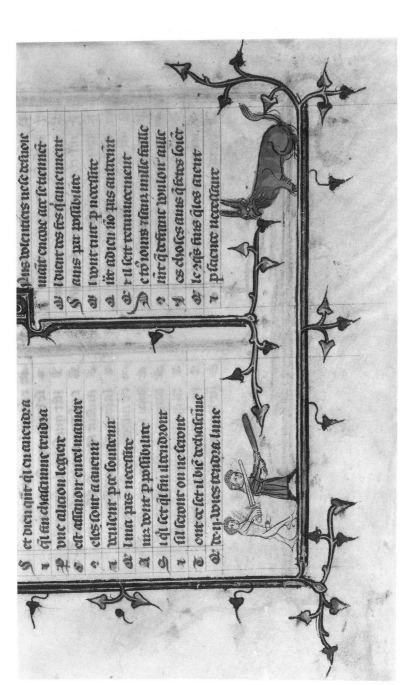

Fig. 2.   Sexual sport in the margins. (From Bibliothèque Nationale, Paris, MS 25526, fol. 130v: *Roman de la Rose*, c. 1340, illuminated by Richart and Jeanne de Montbaston.)

perversion in de Bury's treatise are the translation and the illustration of texts, both indicative of a transference, or crossing of boundaries. Both are excesses that the books themselves complain of in a brilliant display of ventriloquism by which the bishop makes his volumes speak for themselves: "Alas how ye commit us to treacherous copyists to be written, how corruptly ye read us and kill us by medication, while ye supposed ye were correcting us with pious zeal." Art that adorns books is associated directly with perversion: "in us the natural use is changed to that which is against nature '*contra naturam*,' while we who are the light of faithful souls everywhere fall a prey to painters knowing nought of letters, and entrusted to goldsmiths to become, as though we were not sacred vessels of wisdom, repositories of gold leaf *(repositoria bractearum).*"[10] Cosmetics on the faces of male books make them effeminate, just as the new Parisian fashions in philosophy leave books "languishing" and "unmanly." The idea that effeminacy goes with artifice is a traditional trope, but these hints of a sin against nature have, to my knowledge, not been discerned in this text before and are perhaps linked to the preponderance of the naked male body in manuscripts made for monastic celibates. It is significant in terms of the polymorphous perversity exhibited in these images that, although de Bury criticizes the lavish marginal adornment of manuscripts as being "against nature," he freely admits to indulging in it himself elsewhere in the *Philobiblon,* in which he notes that he keeps on his payroll "in our different manors no small multitude of copyists and scribes, of correctors, binders, illuminators, and generally of all who could usefully labour in the service of books."[11]

This should not surprise us, since in the early fourteenth century the taste for marginal book illumination was at its apogee, with many scribes becoming illuminators and cities like Paris specializing in the trade. What is surprising is the range and variety of texts whose margins were being penetrated in this way. It included all genres and audiences. As well as luxurious Bibles and Psalters used by wealthy prelates and monks, there were Books of Hours and Romances in the vernacular read by the rich laity. As well as law books and decretals used by masters and doctors at the universities, even the texts of "scientific" treatises by philosophers such as Aristotle were being illuminated with marginal bodies. Indeed, I would argue that it is from intellectual university centers like Oxford, Bologna, and Paris that the fashion for bodily marginal art had its first exhibition, linked to new attitudes to the page and to reading in the scholastic context. Even those books that lack high-quality illumination, which means most literary and scholarly texts, often include pictorial marginal signs, glosses that can be likened to doodles. In the *bas-de-page* of an English fourteenth-century copy of legal statutes in Princeton, no fewer than three different doodlers added their various bodies (fig. 3). The text itself treats forest law, and the images at the bottom of the page might be seen as responses to it, although what they construct over hundreds of years is a kind of wildman of the woods story with royal overtones. The first glossator depicted the sullen, half-naked king in his underdrawers, saying, "allas, allas, alas." A second, perhaps a half-century later, added a wildman at the left growling, "ware, ware," and again, after an interval of many generations (I would say in the seventeenth century), some less adept doodler made still another monster with a professor's biretta on its head, to create a marvelous accretion, a suggestive narrative incompatible in style but interactive as a trinity of perverse bodies on the page.

The visual world that surrounded texts in the twelfth century had been predominantly a vegetable rather than a corporeal one. In the words of Hugh of St. Victor, "the page is a vineyard and garden," and when he reads he harvests, picking the berries from the lines. The very word *pagina* derives, according to Pliny, from the word for "vines." This metaphor of the trellis of the vine border holding the fruits of the text was perfectly suited to the predominantly oral mode of twelfth-century reading. In the words of Ivan Illich, "as he picks the fruit from the leaves of parchment, the *voces paginarum* drop from his mouth as a subdued murmur."[12] The fruits of the pages were literally mouthed by speakers, and thus the body interpenetrated with the book on a level of the Logos. The great change in the thirteenth and fourteenth centuries in literate modes of production and reception meant that the page was no longer a repository of sounds and voices but, rather, a collection of visually presented texts to be compared again and again, still perhaps read aloud but now structured for the eye/I reading the text. Also new was the systematic use of page layouts we still know today—such as footnoting, indices, and page headings, all of which made the examination of manuscripts for reference and analysis rather than reflection and meditation.[13]

The scholastic book, as used by Richard de Bury was a far more physically tangible presence, partly because of this new emphasis upon the layout of the page and, above all, as the site of and presence of glosses. The written gloss had existed earlier, but the ways in which readers became actively involved in their making texts anew was new. Since books were incredibly expensive luxury objects, students were often the scribes of their own texts

Et tuz les autres q̃ auer point. eient arcs e setes hors de fo
restes e de deinz forestes arcs e piles. Et q̃ veue des armes soit
fete deus foiz par an. Et en chescun Hundred. e fraunchise seient
esluz deus conestables a fere la veue des armes. les conestables
auantditz presenteint deuaunt les Justices assignez q̃nt il vendront
en pais les defautes q̃l aueront trouez de armeure
e de cunes des veilles. e de chemins. Et presenteint auci des genz
qi herbegent genz estraunges en viles de uplaund pur queus
il ne volent respundre. Et les Justices assignez en chescun
parlement repesenteint au Roi. e le Roi sur ceo en fra reme
die. Et bien se gardent desormes viscuntes. baillifs de
fraunchises. e de lors seigniurs. ou maindres qi baillie
ou foresterie vint en fee. ou en autre manere qil ne soit
saciz oue le pais. Et solum ceo q̃l seint. eient chuualx
e armure a ceo fere. Et si nul soit qi nel face. seient les
defautes presentez par les conestables as Justices assignez. e
puis apres par eus au Roi cum auaunt est dit. Et comaunde
le Roi e defend. q̃ feire ne marche desormes ne seient te
nuz en cymiter pur honur de seinte eglise. Done a Wyn
cestre le vnsme iour de Octobre. Le an du regne le Roi
tresime.

Fig. 3. Three doodles. (From Scheide Library, Princeton, MS 30, fol. 90: *Statuta Angliae*.)

anyway, which fostered the idea of writing as transformation. The gloss was a site not only of supplementation; it was also one of contestation, allowing the reader to mark disagreement. The wide margins that frame most texts in the thirteenth and fourteenth centuries are precisely for the purpose of providing this space for emphasis or disagreement, not for focusing attention on the increasingly fixed image of the text, as philologists, always seeking to delimit the boundaries of the text they are editing, would have us believe but, rather, by making the boundaries of the text less solid, more capable of being penetrated by the eye of the reader and even by his body in the act of marking. This phallocentric performance of the pen in writing also represents the beginnings of what the psychoanalyst André Green calls the "voyeurism" of reading:

> Reading and writing, in terms of psychoanalysis, are not primary processes, but complex activities acquired relatively late; they come as a result of training, making use of partial drives tamed by education and the "civilizing process." Reading and writing are sublimations, which means that the underlying partial drives are inhibited from attaining their goals, displaced and desexualized. Once broken down into their constituent parts, those partial drives have to do with scopophilia [voyeurism]. The desire to see is patent in the act of reading. The book cover, the binding function as garments. . . . We are thus talking here about a kind of pleasure experienced by means of the eyes. Of course we can have texts read to us, but this is only a derivative practice, for listening to a text (in the non-psychoanalytical sense) is not reading it.[14]

Richard de Bury had spent ten years at Oxford, and his reading habits were those of his friends, the Oxford scholars and commentators Robert Holcot and Thomas Bradwardine, suffused in Aristotelian epistemology and the "new logic." But he often refers to great authors of the past, ancient and modern, as though they were speaking to him in his library rather than being bound between boards on parchment pages that he had actually to open and to read. When it came to consulting his books, the bishop often had them read aloud to him, especially while he was eating. On the one hand, this might be interpreted as the continuation of earlier medieval modes of reading as oral performance. But it also suggests a direct rejection of the intimacy fostered by the new mode of *lectio,* which, if not silent, was still scopophilic in the sense I have described. For de Bury's reading was still a performance of the whole body and not just the eyes, even if, increasingly, vision was taking a primary role. Is there a link between this increasing corporealization of reading the book with one's own eyes (as the visual object fetishized and feared by de Bury) and the physicality embodied in fourteenth-century marginal art?

The transformation of reading practices from being predominantly oral and aural modes of monastic performance in the earlier Middle Ages to their being held in the hands of individuals and read by them alone—which has remained our idea of reading a book—coincides with the appearance of Gothic marginal art. On one level it is possible to see this in terms of a democratization of reading, something that churchmen like de Bury opposed and which was also articulated as dangerous in manuscripts made for eminent churchmen, such as Stephen of Derby, prior of the Cathedral of Holy Trinity, Dublin, between 1348 and 1362, whose Psalter, now in Oxford, exhibits a similar ambivalence about reading in the margins as that we see in the bishop's treatise (fig. 4). The initial to Psalm 97, "Let us sing to the Lord a new Song," contrasts the public choric reading or singing of the *opus dei* within the letter of the law with the ugly individuality of private reading going on at its edges. The "new song" of the psalm text here is the new horror of lay people gaining access to books. But what are these gawking, squat men holding small open volumes meant to be reading, illicit romances or sexually titillating tales? It is fascinating to consider the fact that pornography as we know it today could only emerge in a culture in which reading was done privately and perhaps silently. Along with exemplifying the kind of dirt that Saint Bernard criticized when he said, "where there are corners there is filth," these two gawking readers are staring avidly at texts that arouse their phallic desire (signaled by their erectile hats). They are having dirty looks in dirty books.

If new modes of literacy help explain why the margins of late medieval manuscripts should be filled with muscular animated bodies rather than the fruits and leaves of literate labor, it is not the only framework for understanding marginal art. The oral traditions of "folk culture," still not totally divorced from Latin literate culture in this period, provide many of the themes we see. We must avoid reading these only from the viewpoint of the priests at the center and remember that the illuminators were, for the most part, laymen and -women who shared in the whole culture, popular, vernacular, and literate. We have to stand on the margins with the monsters and see what vantage point that reveals. The traditional interpretation is that the margins become the site of a satirical and critical attack upon lax

Fig. 4.   Licit and illicit readers. (From Bodleian Library, MS Rawl. G. 185, fol. 81v: Psalter made before 1368 for Prior Stephen of Derby.)

morals, contrasting the fallen flesh at the edge with the spiritual ideals of the text at the center, as in the Psalter of Stephen of Derby. But the monstrous private readers in the margins here who split reading into two books, compared with the one book used by all the choir monks, is the way of the future. Indeed, I would argue that these bodies actually aided in the reading process and were part of the animated materiality of scholastic *lectio*. As a reaction to the optical decorporealization of the pages that scholastic modes of reading introduced, they articulate the return of the repressed flesh and its dangerously ductile sensations. All the open mouths and biting bodies, too, are articulations of a range of tactile and olfactory experiences that were being literally marginalized, as the novel idea of silent reading began.[15] By including little figures pointing, doodled hands functioning like N.B. marks, and tiny men jumping about in between lines to mark especialy important parts of texts, illuminators were returning the text to the body from which it had been repressed. This did not indicate only that the text was a block of visual space; it marked this space as a place in which another reader could come and add his own gloss or disagreement.

Moreover, the page became a site for intertextual intercourse between different texts, a mingling of bodies of discourse as reading became a kind of writing, much as it is celebrated in contemporary critical theory. The difference was that the unfixity of the text was literally embodied in the manufacture and reception of books themselves. This multiple glossing can be seen especially in manuscripts used at the university, where students and masters added notes and their own glosses to the set texts of curriculum in ways students still do today. Rather than the luminous marker, they marked texts with bodies, with squiggles of figures and fingers. These bodies as extensions of their own bodies into the texts mark a point of entry for the reader into the book. This is also the function of the countless heads we see in initials and margins of fourteenth-century books. These staring heads are not merely "decorative." They are representations of internal readers whose eyes scan the pages, whose bodies are literally half-within and half-outside the parchment, cues for the reader's own eyes outside the book. All this suggests that, just as monastic reading was an animated vocalization and performance of texts and not their silent imbibing, reading practices in the later Middle Ages were far more dynamic.

The medieval library, then, was not the stratified space of a disembodied, panoptic display we know today but a much more private, complex, interactive, and, moreover, corporeal space. It was also very small compared to our vast storage houses: the average literate clergyman at

Avignon in the mid-fourteenth century owned an average of nine books.[16] This was what made de Bury's bibliophilia, that one could not visit him in his palaces without stepping on volumes scattered in every room, so astounding to his contemporaries. Yet it was exactly the rarity and the vast expense in having a book written and, especially, illuminated, which charged each volume even more with an aura of power and authority, stimulating an awe and, for an owner, delectation and fervid attention, that we can hardly imagine today, so used to scanning hundreds if not thousands of books and texts in our everyday lives. Medieval readers of all types, whether they be schoolboys being beaten for not repeating their Donatus correctly, laywomen whispering their Books of Hours in the increasingly privatized and isolated domestic spaces, or masters in the schools arguing over their Aristotle, were all performers who were marking their bodies in certain ways with these special instruments—books. According to Michel Foucault, "The imaginary is not formed in opposition to reality as its denial or compensation; it grows among signs, from book to book, in the interstice of repetitions and commentaries; it is born and takes place in the interval between books. It is a phenomenon of the library."[17] The structure and institution of the modern library has been to erase all possibility of fantasy and of bibliophilic fetishism, to exclude the body from the site of reading, to make a silent and desomatized space of the *biblioteca* the simulacrum of purely mental experience, a process that will only accelerate in the future with the increasing incorporeality of the electronic word. Of course, people leave their traces in pages; they doodle in books, deface them, chew them, tear them up, even steal them and sleep with them—but they rarely make them the objects of erotic desire or mark them with genital juices.

The book has today lost much of its corporeal, communicative, and erotic associations with the speaking/sucking mouth, the gesturing/ probing hand, or the opening/closing anus. Reading for the medieval literate was, by contrast, still charged with these associations, which made every turn of the page an act of intense scopophilia and resonant with sensations, from the feel of the flesh and hair side of the parchment on one's fingertips to the lubricious labial mouthing of the written words with one's throat and tongue. Consider the way medieval books were bound with thongs between stamped leather or wooden boards, held shut with metal studs, encased in hide belts and snapped shut with buckle-like clasps, as well as the way they were displayed with their backsides uppermost on desks when taken out of their locked chests and turned for delectation, quite literally on the moving "reading wheel," like the turning wheels that broke not the spines of volumes but, instead, the backs and bones of transgressors of law in the public squares of cities. All this made them into the clunky and physically intimidating objects, attractive to modern S/M and leather fetishists. Likewise, the very act of reading was a libidinal experience, of penetrating the bound volume, that dangerously ductile opening and shutting thing. The result was a promiscuous interpenetration of books, not only with the bodies that read them but also with those that were excluded from them. In *Image on the Edge* I associated the hybridity and monstrosity of bodies in the margins of a book made for a laywoman with the notion of the fecund female body, arguing that these marginal forms were part of an ideology of procreation, urging her to fulfill her maternal destiny in this Book of Hours made for her marriage and dedicated to her name saint, Marguerite, the patron saint of pregnant women (fig. 5).[18] Now I am inclined to see this procreative metaphorics as more widespread in medieval culture, not only aimed at subjugating women's bodies as in the case of Marguerite's book but also used in highly gendered male scholastic discourse, even of the most misogynistic kind, exemplified in Richard de Bury's *Philobiblon*.

Perhaps only today, with the fast-approaching "death of the book," are we able to begin to appreciate and partially recover the cultural history of this submerged corporeality that links textuality to sexuality. For when I open a medieval manuscript this is entirely different from the experience of opening a printed book, for I am conscious not only of the *manuscript* (the manual handling of materials in production, writing, illumination) but also of how in reception the parchment has been penetrated, of grease stains, thumb marks, erasures, drops of sweat, places where images have been kissed away by devout lips, holes of various animal eating places—in short, of how bodies, human, animal and insect, have left their imprints of countless bodies upon it. Every book is a relic of bodily pain, desire, and death.

We should not forget too that books were also produced *from* bodies, first of all in the parchment pages, which were the stretched and treated skins of animals. Inks and colors were often produced with human spittle and urine, according to contemporary recipes. Moreover, the manuscript is a product of the hands and body of human labor that have registered every pressure and point of contact upon the flesh itself. The margins provide a site at which the reader could take part in, and to some extent, interplay with the text already written. In interlinear glosses too the reader could interrupt, interject, and replace. One often finds pasages crossed out in

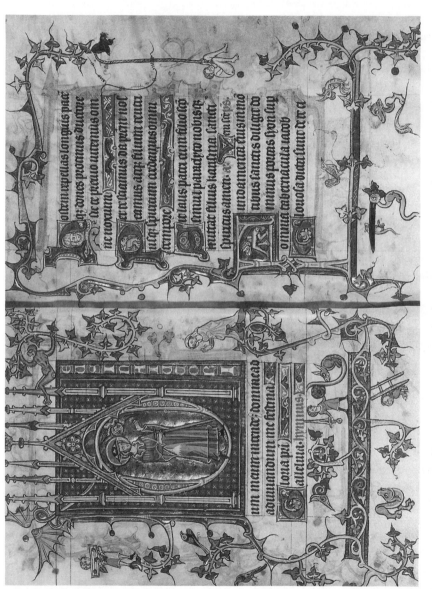

Fig. 5. Marguerite's monsters. (From Pierpont Morgan Library, New York, M. 754: *Hours of the Virgin*, c. 1330.)

medieval texts, far more than in printed books, which have a finality in their uniform means of production that precludes altercation between reader and text. If for no other reason, this association between the margins and the glossing site of resistance gave the illuminator a chance to joke and play upon the text, to experiment with shapes, and to invert stereotypes in ways that seem at first very modern.

But it would be mistaken to see in these irreverent images, the expression of freedom from constraints and limitless "self-expression." This is best explained in terms of a contemporary group of displaced image makers whose work might at first seem to represent the very limits of freedom. Graffiti are, I would argue, like marginal art, products of massive cultural anxiety in response to radical technological and social change. Their perpetrators are often described as merely expressing themselves in manic and antisocial terms not that different from Richard de Bury's attack on the idle, doodling youths of the fourteenth century. Like the medieval artists who often picture themselves adding images in the margins of manuscripts, these modern painter-climbers squeeze their exuberant flourishes at the edges of the monuments of cities, on disused billboards and walls, perching dangerously as I saw them in Berlin, and always on the lookout in case the the police might disturb them (fig. 6). While, of course, the maker of the marginal images in medieval manuscripts was lauded and paid to produce what these young men are doing illegally, there are a number of connections and contrasts between manuscript illumination and contemporary graffiti art that are revealing of both. Apart from the obvious associations of marking boundaries and territory, there is the same interest in the dexterous rapidity of execution in a few telling lines of spray can or quill, in the monstricules created not by the illuminator but the pen flourisher. These can be compared to the quick-fire flow of spray can squirtings. There is the same search for individual *ductus* in the manic repetition of conventional elements aided by the stencil popular among Parisian student graffitists today, just as those on the Left Bank used repeated motifs in their schoolbooks in the Middle Ages, with the model book monsters and tracing and pricking used to repeat elements on the manuscript page. Then there is the erasure of previous words, signs, and images working like later glosses and additions of new owners' arms and heraldry or even as in the erasures one finds in the margins of manuscripts.

The manuscript page, like the wall, is not the site of a single unique and finished "picture" as in an abstract expressionist painting, which fakes the idea of radicality. What is truly radical is that one can come along and

Fig. 6.   Berlin graffitists, 1992. (Photo by Stuart Michaels.)

alter, add, erase, and recreate what is there. There is also the same interest in particular styles and authorial self-inscription, especially with the more elaborate script styles of the spray can graffitists, who identify these vast colorful inscriptions as carefully created as the display script of the Book of Kells by "tags" that allow the same artist to be noticed in his audacious antics throughout the city.[19] Certain marginal illuminators also have tags by which we can identify them, a certain type of bird, a windmill, or, as in the case of the Franco-Flemish artist of Marguerite's manuscript, a certain way of making anuses into a form of epigraphic inscription (see fig. 5). The closeness of writing to drawing are as true for the medieval manuscript as for the New York wall, and also similar is the fact that these exhibitions of supposed self-expression are actually highly conventional, borrowing from the authority of the very advertising codes and slogans that these young image makers are supposedly seeking to subvert. The recent elevation of graffiti art to the status of "works of art" for sale in the Soho galleries has further collapsed notions of center and periphery. What was "dirt" easily becomes "art."

Michel de Certeau argues that today "marginality is becoming universal" and is "no longer limited to minority groups, but is rather massive and pervasive, this cultural activity of the non-producers of culture, an activity that is unsigned, unreadable and unsymbolized."[20] Graffiti are aimed at exactly this loss of visual authority, at the collapse of any coherent visual "truth" in our society, through the display of expressive acts by unknowable artists that are inexplicably overcomplex. Reading Richard de Bury, fulminating against the doodling license of the youth of his day, sounds not unlike many conservative critics of graffiti today, full of the same fear of the bodily violence of an explosive marginal group. If unused urban real estate is marked by the alientated art at its edges in today's cities, books provided a similar locus for the youth of the fourteenth century. If we have become a society of doodlers because of the easy availability of paper and images, we have also developed into a culture in which the book no longer really interacts with the body. Graffitists project their bodies into the spaces of run-down city neighborhoods precisely because they have been excluded from the spaces of script and literate "high" culture, which de-emphasizes the flesh or pretends to—as it has always done. The mass media, having co-opted the body and desire, present everything on such a large scale that resistance has to have its larger space too. Writing can no longer be on the page; it has to be on the wall.

In trying to think once again about the margins of medieval books, I began by comparing medieval manuscripts to bodies (as I argue medieval people often did) and then to the spaces of today's urban graffitists. I want to end briefly by touching upon a less controversial comparison and one already made by a number of recent writers who have juxtaposed the medieval manuscript to the computer. Academics who have written brilliantly about the new electronic systems of text production have often made comparisons with medieval manuscripts. David Bolter describes the hypertextual possibilities of the future as returning us to the interactive world of the glossed, interactive medieval book, and Richard Lanham sees electronic communication reintroducing the complex interplay of word and image that was visible in medieval manuscripts. There will be multiple margins for commentary, rethinking, and rewriting in this future hypertextual space. "Through the infinite resources of digital image recall and manipulation ekphrasis is once again coming into its own, and the pictures and sounds, suppressed into verbal rhetorical figures are now reassuming their native places in the human sensorium."[21]

This dream of a return to a "natural" mode of text reception (as if all textuality were not something totally constructed) and interaction strikes me as wishful thinking, precisely because the computer screen cannot be penetrated like a body, cannot be defiled or dirtied, marked by my own body. It can only be marked and changed within its own system. I send messages that relay messages to another site where my own body cannot be. True, this site/sight is vastly more multiform than any page and can be constantly played around with by me and anyone else who cares to join in. But it is always elsewhere, and, moreover, it can be everywhere. It is not the loss of the reading and writing surface that makes our current communications transformation so profound but, rather, the loss of a space around those text blocks, a space that articulated the closeness of our bodies to our books and allowed us to interpenetrate with that flesh. This word has a different set of associations from *interface,* which suggests a disembodied looking at the icon, the mystic's stare into the face of God. The computer, as we know, can be as much of an object of (especially) macho fetishistic desire as the book used to be for misogynistic medieval churchmen like Richard de Bury. This bishop and bibliophile, who never mentions an individual book, although he fetishisizes countless texts in his collection, and who was only concerned with keeping the vast library he had collected together (guarded by keepers who would allow access to only a select few), would probably have welcomed such a magical thing as a computer, which could keep the thousands of delicate and pure texts from defilement by human hands by storing them as imperceptible impulses on a small disk. This dematerialization is related to a larger issue explored recently by writers such as Judith Butler: the cultural code, as old as Aristotle, that associates ideas and forms with the male and matter and flesh with the female.[22]

Computers, it seems to me, have fallen prey to the same disturbing metaphorics. But, more than that, they have not yet established anything like a scriptable alternative space for the youthful body in today's culture. In their appropriation by business and in their expense they have created a class of experts not unlike the Latin literates of the fourteenth century, together with a rich, graphically sophisticated "Mondo 2000" counterculture on the Internet, with spin-offs in the older technological forms of magazines, films, and videos. But there are still no margins. One can make dates for future intercourse on the Internet, play games on the screen, write obscenities on it, have virtual sex with it, infect it with electronic viruses even, but one cannot leave one's bodily impression upon its surface. The computer ends up being an extension of our wired brains rather than our tired bodies. In the future perhaps we will find new ways of interacting with its surfaceless scripts and even of making margins somewhere in the electronic web for illicit somatic stains, markings of our flesh, and remakings of ourselves that are so crucial for the production of pleasure, knowledge, and desire and which make all medieval manuscripts embodiments of past lives, not just texts about them.

NOTES

1. Richard de Bury, *Philobiblon* (Oxford: Basil Blackwell, 1960), 157–59.
2. See Michael Camille, *Image on the Edge: The Margins of Medieval Art* (Cambridge, Mass.: Harvard University Press, 1992), 16.
3. Jacques Derrida, "The End of the Book and the Beginning of Writing," *Of Grammatology* (Baltimore: Johns Hopkins University Press, 1974), 6–26. And, for an approach antithetical to my own in its acceptance of the book metaphor as a systematic ordering principle, see Jesse M. Gellrich, *The Idea of the Book in the Middle Ages: Language, Theory, Mythology, Fiction* (Ithaca: Cornell University Press, 1984). For the book metaphor in general in addition to the chapter that so influenced Derrida, "The Book as Symbol," by Ernst Robert Curtius (*European Literature and the Latin Middle Ages,* trans. W. R. Trask [New York, 1965], 308–17), see Hans Blumenberg, *Die Lesbarkeit der Welt* (Frankfurt: Suhrkamp, 1981).
4. Susan Stewart, *On Longing: Narratives of the Miniature, the Gigantic, the Souvenir, the Collection* (Baltimore: Johns Hopkins University Press, 1987), 37.

5. This essay forms part of a larger work in progress about the relations between medieval book collectors, reading, and fetishism. For more on de Bury's library, see J. de Ghellinck, "Un bibliophile au XIV siècle: Richard d'Aungerville," *Revue d'Histoire Ecclesiastique* 18 (1922): 271–312, 482–508; 19 (1923): 157–200; and N. Denholm Young, "Richard de Bury (1287–1345)," *Collected Papers on Medieval Subjects* (Oxford: Oxford University Press, 1946), 1–26.

6. De Bury, *Philobiblon*, 107.

7. Ibid., 51.

8. See Michael Camille, "Courtly Crap," *Image on the Edge*, 111–15.

9. For this manuscript, see Camille, *Image on the Edge*, 147–48; and Sylvia Huot, *The* Romance of the Rose *and Its Medieval Readers: Interpretation, Reception, Manuscript Transmission* (Cambridge: Cambridge University Press, 1993), 273–319.

10. De Bury, *Philobiblon*, 51.

11. Ibid., 95.

12. Ivan Illich, *In the Vineyard of the Text: A Commentary to Hugh's* Didascalion (Chicago: University of Chicago Press, 1993), 57. See also Michael Camille, "Seeing and Reading: Some Visual Implications of Medieval Literacy and Illiteracy," *Art History* 8 (1985): 26–49.

13. The best analysis of this crucial change in reading practice is Malcom B. Parkes, "The Influence of the Concepts of *Ordinatio* and *Compilatio* on the Development of the Book," in *Medieval Learning and Literature: Essays Presented to Richard William Hunt,* ed. J. J. G. Alexander and M. T. Gibson (Oxford: Clarendon Press, 1976), 133–35.

14. Andre Green, "The Unbinding Process," *On Private Madness* (London: Hogarth Press, 1986), 342–43.

15. Paul Saenger, "Silent Reading: Its Impact on Late Medieval Script and Society," *Viator* 113 (1982): 367–414.

16. Daniel Williman, *Bibliothèques ecclésiastiques au temps de la papauté d'Avignon* (Paris: CNRS, 1980), 101.

17. M. Foucault, "Fantasia of the Library," *Language, Counter-Memory, Practice: Selected Essays and Interviews* (Oxford: Basil Blackwell, 1977), 91.

18. Michael Camille, "The Pregnant Page," *Image on the Edge*, 48–55. A recent essay on the transmission of texts associated with Saint Margaret describes how words were sometimes literally ingested and how the "eating of the text-apple by the pregnant woman" was part of its transmission (J. Wogan-Browne, "The Apple's Message: Some Post-Conquest Hagiographic Accounts of Textual Transmission," in *Late Medieval Religious Texts and Their Transmission: Essays in Honor of A. I. Doyle,* ed. A. J. Minnis [Bury St. Edmunds: Boydell and Brewer, 1994], 39–55).

19. See C. Castleman, *Getting Up: Subway Graffiti in New York* (Cambridge, Mass.: MIT Press, 1982); and Susan Stewart, "*Ceci tuera Cela*: Graffiti as Crime and Art," *Crimes of Writing: Problems in the Containment of Representation* (Oxford: Oxford University Press, 1991), 206–30.

20. Michel de Certeau, *The Practice of Everyday Life* (Berkeley: University of California Press, 1988), xvii. De Certeau is of course the great theorist of book as body; see especially his essay "Inscriptions of the Law on the Body" (139–42), in which "the skin of the servant is the parchment on which the master's hand writes." For further analysis of the relationship between book and body in medieval visual culture, see Michael Camille, "The Image and the Self: Unwriting Late Medieval Bodies," in *Framing Medieval Bodies,* ed. Sarah Kay and Miri Rubin (Manchester: Manchester University Press, 1994), 62–100.

21. Richard A. Lanham, *The Electronic Word: Democracy, Technology, and the Arts* (Chicago: University of Chicago Press, 1993), especially his essay "The Edge of Chaos" (245). In countering the proposition that visual thinking is inferior to verbal thinking, Lanham asks, "What about all those medieval manuscripts with the demons dancing a marginal commentary on the text?" Jay David Bolter (*Writing Space: The Computer, Hypertext, and the History of Writing* [Hillsdale, N.J.: L. Erlbaum Associates, 1991]) has also made the optimistic association between medieval modes of reading and writing and hypertext; and Rebecca E. Zorach ("New Medieval Aesthetic: Learning from the Nerds of the Middle Ages," *Wired* [January 1994]: 48–49) argues that "on the cusp of a new aesthetic sensibility fueled by a groundswell of decentralized creativity, we might do well to look to the past for clues to our future."

22. Judith Butler, *Bodies That Matter: On the Discursive Limits of Sex* (New York and London: Routledge, 1993), 1–27.

Communication, Semiotic Continuity, and the Margins of the Peircean Text

Mary Keeler and Christian Kloesel

INTRODUCTION

We begin with a brief portrait of Peirce and a description of the quality and scope of his work and the nature and condition of his manuscripts. On this basis we call into question the concept of "text" itself and identify four senses of the term *margins* to consider how his manuscripts challenge current editorial theory and practice. Peirce's ambition was to ground and expand logic on a fundamentally new basis—a general theory of representation he called semiotic—that could account for the continuous nature of thought and communication working together in human experience to generate knowledge. He was convinced, from his work as a physical scientist, that absolute accuracy is unattainable, and his pragmatism is the method that regards truth as a *limit* successively approached by increasingly refined investigations, which depend on communication among collaborating investigators. Peirce's theory has been recognized as a new philosophical perspective responding to (and reconciling the effects of) Cartesian dualism, materialism, and reductionism—the demand for an absolute foundation for knowledge that prevents us from explaining how communication is possible at all. His own corpus exemplifies the futility of attempting to capture the continuity of ideas in a discrete medium of expression and records his awareness of and frustration with this limitation. His work anticipates, in nature and content, the ingenious computer network medium that promises to engender new appreciation for realms and modes of inquiry that our traditional media relegate to the margins of scholarship.

In a discussion of the possibility of building a machine capable of logical inference, Peirce describes a mechanical syllogism-solver invented by Allan Marquand (his former student at the Johns Hopkins University) and asks if this could be a reasoning machine:

> What, then, is the use of designating some formulations of opinion as rational, while others . . . are stigmatized as blind followings of the rule of thumb or of authority, or as mere guesses? When we reason we set out from an assumed representation of the state of things. This we call our *premise;* and working upon this, we produce another representation which professes to refer to the same state of things; and this we call our *conclusion.* . . . The irrationality here consists in our following a fixed method [an algorithm], of the correctness of which the method itself affords no assurance; so that if it does not happen to be right in its application to the case in hand, we go hopelessly astray. In genuine reasoning, we are not wedded to our method. We deliberately approve it, but we stand ever ready and disposed to reexamine it and so improve upon it, and to criticise our criticism of it, without cessation. Thus the utility of the word "reasoning" lies in its helping us to discriminate between self-critical and uncritical formations of representations. If a machine works according to a fixed principle involved in the plan of it, it may be a useful aid in reasoning; but unless it is so contrived that, were there any defect in it, it would improve itself in that respect, then, although it could correctly work out every possible conclusion from premises, the machine itself would afford no assurance that its conclusions would be correct. Such assurance could only come from our critical examination of it. Consequently, it would not be, strictly speaking, a reasoning-machine.
>
> Self-criticism can never be perfectly thorough for the last act of criticism is always itself open to criticism. But as long as we remain disposed to self-criticism and to further inquiry, we have in this disposition an assurance that if the truth of any question can ever be got at, we shall eventually get at it. (MS 831 [1900])[1]

We grasp here the perspective from which the present essay examines the marginal nature of Peirce's work (in text and concept), its challenge for editorial theory, and the promise of a new medium capable of changing the conduct and understanding of creativity, scholarship, and—certainly—critical editing. In the second of his 1903 Pragmatism Lectures, Peirce urges his audience to consider even his own philosophical perspective critically, as he has done:

> I trust that if you can see what my description is meant to convey, you will not find it so hard to see that it is just. And yet I should be really sorry if you were so easily satisfied about a matter of extreme importance. Time is needed to digest these ideas and to form a definitive judgment of their truth,—*much* time. . . . Certainly, in philosophy what a man does not think out for himself he never understands at all. Nothing can be learned out of books or lectures, they have to be treated not as oracles but simply as facts to be studied like any other facts. That, at any rate is the way in which I would have you treat my lectures. Call no man master, or at any rate not me. Only bear in mind that I have been a good many years trying in singleness of heart to find out how these things really are, and always disposed to doubt and criticize my own results. (MS 304)

Peirce captures the essence of "the editorial role" here as, fundamentally, *criticism* (careful examination and interpretation) in thought and expression—which, in its most rudimentary form, is criticism or examination of one's own habits of thought and expression in the conduct of learning.

His life's work can be seen as the struggle to gain the philosophical perspective needed to appreciate how intellectual growth is possible, in terms of our aesthetic, ethical, and logical sense of responsibility based on self-critical control. We can capture this paramount and most human capability in our instruments, which inevitably operate on our instruction, only to the extent that we use them to develop effective relationships that augment our constructive (editorial) ability.

PEIRCE AND HIS TEXT: OBSTACLES FOR SCHOLARSHIP

Charles Sanders Peirce lived from 1839 to 1914. His father, Benjamin, was professor of mathematics and astronomy at Harvard, served as president of the American Academy for the Advancement of Science and as superintendent of the U.S. Coast and Geodetic Survey (the preeminent scientific institution of the period), and was widely regarded as the leading American mathematician of his time. Charles was rigorously trained by his father, and he grew up in a house in which the leading scientific and literary figures of the day frequently gathered.

He took up the study of chemistry at age eight, and of logic at twelve, and he graduated from Harvard at nineteen. From 1861 (when he began his thirty-year employment with the Coast Survey) to 1863 he studied chemistry at Harvard's Lawrence Scientific School and graduated summa cum laude. In 1865, 1866, and 1869–70 he gave extensive lecture series (on the logic of science and on British logicians) at Harvard and the Lowell Institute, and he was elected member of the American Academy of Arts and Sciences in 1867. Following four years (1872–75) as assistant in the Harvard Observatory—where he prepared his only published book, *Photometric Researches* (1878)—he won election to the National Academy of Science in 1877 (and to the London Mathematical Society in 1880). From 1879 to 1884 he worked as part-time lecturer at the Johns Hopkins University, but he never held a permanent academic position. After his retirement from the Coast Survey, he made his living by writing reviews, essays, and dictionary definitions; by giving occasional lectures; and by the generosity of William James and others.

Although his philosophical work was not widely appreciated during his lifetime, Peirce is now regarded as "the most original, versatile, and comprehensive philosophical mind [America] has yet produced."[2] He worked as physicist, chemist, mathematician, astronomer, and geodesist, and was competent in the sciences generally. But he always regarded himself as primarily a logician, though in a far broader sense than we use the term today. He showed how to extend traditional logic to include relations, which made possible the logical analysis of probabilistic reasoning. He developed a system of metaphysics from his logic of relatives, which he hoped could effectively reconcile the dichotomies of modern philosophy (idealism/materialism, rationalism/empiricism). He demonstrated the connections between logic, probability, and inductive reasoning, and he sketched the first known design for an electrical switching circuit that could perform logical and arithmetical operations.

Because of the quality and scope of his work, Peirce has had foundational influence in the American philosophical tradition, which has since been developed by James, Dewey, Royce, Mead, Quine, Morris, Chomsky, Rorty, and Putnam. His ideas continue to grow in relevance to topics now at the leading edge of human intellectual development: machine intelligence, cognitive science, topographical (graphical) logic, abductive logic, probability theory, the theory of representation and communication, the coordination of graphical (iconic) and verbal (symbolic) understanding, and postmodernism in the arts and in critical theory.

As scientist and computer, Peirce worked to advance the physical sciences by experiment and theory development. He was the first to state the length of the meter in terms of wavelengths of light; he designed instruments to measure the force of gravity and to define the shape of the Earth and the Milky Way; and he contributed much to the effort to establish worldwide measurement standards as the basis upon which researchers could rely when comparing the results of their investigations. The scope of his research (scientific and otherwise) includes psychology, statistics and probability, mathematics, astronomy, chemistry, physics, geodesy, comparative biography, criminology, cartography, economics, philology, religion, metaphysics, and (ancient, medieval, and modern) history and philosophy. His semiotic is logic generalized to conceive mentality and cognition as essentially communicational, so that the collaborative communication of inquirers (exemplified in science as learning by collective experience) is the most highly developed form of human behavior, which can be taken as a model for inquiry (research and learning) across the academic spectrum. But his ideas and accomplishments in these and other areas remain essentially obscure and unknown—because his writings are prodigious (and frequently interrelated in topical scope) and because the largest part of his work remains unpublished.

The only large-scale and purportedly comprehensive edition of Peirce's writings is the misnamed *Collected Papers of Charles Sanders Peirce,* published in six volumes sixty years ago (1931–35) and enlarged by two in 1958.[3] Its topical selection omits science and mathematics almost entirely, and it includes few reviews and even fewer historical, psychological, and philological writings. It contains nearly one hundred fifty selections from his unpublished manuscripts, but only one-fifth of those selections consists of complete manuscripts; parts of some manuscripts appear in up to three of the eight volumes, and at least one series of papers is scattered throughout seven.

Several other multivolume editions have appeared more recently. Peirce's *Contributions to "The Nation"* (1975–87, in four pts.) contains the several hundred reviews he wrote for that journal; though chronologically arranged, it is too narrowly specialized for a comprehensive study of Peirce's thought. The four-volumes-in-five of *The New Elements of Mathematics, by Charles S. Peirce* (1976) include a wealth of previously unpublished materials, but their arrangement is topical and many selections are undated and textually unreliable. The same is true of his *Complete Published Works,* the 149-microfiche edition of copies or transcripts of his lifetime publications (1977; enlarged by twelve fiches in 1986), and of the two-volume *Historical Perspectives on Peirce's Logic of Science* (1985). The editorial/textual principle guiding these editions is, on the whole, no more critical or comprehensive than that stated in the first volume of the *Collected Papers:* "Whenever possible Peirce's punctuation and spelling have been retained."

The most reliable (and otherwise satisfactory) edition of his writings now available is the in-progress *Writings of Charles S. Peirce: A Chronological Edition,* projected in thirty volumes. These will not reach his most mature philosophical work, nor be completed, until well into the next century, especially as Peirce's writings become more difficult from a textual point of view and from the perspectives of scholar, typesetter, and printer. Although designed to convey a representative sense of the full range of Peirce's thought and work—in logic and philosophy, in mathematics, history, philology, and psychology, and in the various hard or special sciences to which he made original contributions—it will present less than one-third of his entire work. Moreover, in its paper print format it cannot easily present his progressively more graphical and "colorful" writings: writings permeated with symbols and complicated graphics and enriched by the use of colors, both in words and diagrams.

Besides his one published book and another that he edited (*Studies in Logic by Members of the Johns Hopkins University* [1883]), Peirce saw into print nearly ten thousand pages: several hundred book reviews, several thousand dictionary definitions, many technical and scientific reports (and reports of scholarly meetings and conferences), scores of epistemological, metaphysical, logical, and pragmaticist articles, and several privately printed booklets and brochures. In addition, he left behind at his death enough material to fill over eighty volumes (of five hundred printed pages each), excluding his correspondence. Clearly, not all of these are worthy of publication—in the sense usually applied to multivolume print editions—but, for a serious study of Peirce's polymathic and original work, scholars need access to everything he wrote: whether published article, galley or page proof, printer's copy, fair-copy manuscript, rough outline for a lecture or essay, sketchy notes toward a report or dictionary definition, or proseless calculations, computations, and diagrams.

Peirce's lifetime publications are now available in his *Complete Published Works,*[4] and the majority of his unpublished manuscripts can be inspected in the thirty-eight-reel "Microfilm Edition of the Charles S. Peirce Papers in the Houghton Library of Harvard University" (1964, with supplemental reels issued in 1971). But the microfilm edition is thirty years old, its quality and topical arrangement obstruct efficient use, and much was left out or overlooked in the filming (especially in his correspondence). Moreover, it does not include substantial holdings at the National Archives (in the records of the Coast Survey) and significant smaller collections at Columbia, Princeton, and the Johns Hopkins; the Library of Congress, Smithsonian, and National Ocean Service Library; the Boston and New York Public Libraries; and the library at Southern Illinois University (the repository of materials from the Open Court Publishing Company, in which a number of manuscript printer's copies and proofs of several important articles have recently been discovered). In total, Peirce's unpublished writings (including his correspondence) come to well over one hundred thousand pages, most of which have not been available to scholars since they were first written. The secondary literature demonstrates that only the hardiest of Peirce scholars have made use of his manuscripts, and most of them have done so, by means of photocopies, in their role as contributing editors for the *Writings*.

Joseph Esposito finds that traditional Peirce scholarship is marked by the limited access to his writings and based largely on the *Collected Papers*, which gives a small and misrepresentative sample of the manuscript material in the Harvard collection. He goes on to say:

> From such perspectives Peirce looks like a philosopher who often changed his mind, who was full of brilliant flashes of argument and insight but had no commanding form to his work. This impression has partly been justified by the fact that when Peirce did change his mind he conspicuously announced it to his readers. It is also significant that he never published a systematic book of metaphysical philosophy . . . and that his writings sometime appear to readers of the *Collected Papers* as episodic and fragmentary. . . . In his later years Peirce had ample opportunity to conclude that his lifetime efforts would not be long remembered. Had he known otherwise he might have been inspired to write a short book on his conception of the task of philosophy, a table of contents for future generations to follow. Instead he proposed giant works, works far beyond the scope of a single man to complete even in a lifetime.[5]

Many scholars have found Peirce's philosophy to be self-contradictory, because his practice of revising theories and exploring new ideas cannot be followed in the topically selected manuscript fragments that appear in the *Collected Papers*. The disciplinary specialist who studies Peirce's ideas must be able to follow the skeins of his thought through the entire collection, since his work in logic and experimental science influenced his philosophy (his conceptions of scientific method, language, truth, and reality), and that work in turn suggested new investigations in logic. No one of these had priority in the development of his thought, and material on any one disciplinary subject may be dispersed throughout his writings.

Scholars in diverse fields need complete and chronological access to Peirce's multifaceted and wide-ranging work if they would progress beyond what, having read Lutoslawski's *The Origin and Growth of Plato's Logic* (1897), he himself said regarding the publication of Plato's dialogues:

> Unless we are content to treat the only complete collection of the works of any Greek philosopher that we possess as a mere repertory of gems of thought, as most readers are content to do; but wish to view them as they are so superlatively worthy of being viewed as the record of the entire development of thought of a great thinker, then everything depends upon the chronology of the dialogues. (MS 434 [1902])

Though Peirce is now most widely known as the father of pragmatism, the other two well-known American pragmatists (James and Dewey) enjoy greater reputations, with better and more nearly complete editions of their work. Eighty years after Peirce's death we have (despite great improvements in archival collections throughout the United States) no effective access to the extraordinary breadth and depth of his work and can now only begin to realize that what Peirce said in one of his Pragmatism Lectures of his logical writings refers to his entire corpus:

> But I must tell you that all that you can find in print of my work in logic are simply scattered outcroppings here and there of a rich vein which remains unpublished. Most of it I suppose has been written down; but no human being could ever put together the fragments. I could not myself do so. (MS 302 [1903])

THE MARGINAL NATURE OF PEIRCE'S WORK

Beyond the problem of inadequate access to Peirce's surviving works by traditional scholarly means is the futility of attempting to capture his (philosophical) thought in any discrete medium of expression. His manuscripts even record his awareness of and frustration with the limitations of the linear paper-embodied text in such established media as the printed book or journal article. We can identify four qualities of what Peirce has left as his life's work that indicate why it remains at the margins of scholarship.

1. Peirce's prolific and complex marginalia, both textual and graphical, exemplify the unfinished or in-progress nature of his work and expand the limitations of the written and printed page. Considered without regard to the other marginal aspects of his work, they appear to be like the corrections, annotations, notes, and comments in the writings of other prodigious authors like him, which have always challenged the limitations of paper print media.

2. Because Peirce published an enormous amount of material in many different places and print media, it remains at the margins of scholars' awareness and comprehension. The situation is worse with the much larger part of his work—his unpublished manuscripts—and it will continue to be so despite the several editions that have appeared and are appearing. The most promising of these, the *Writings,* has been an exemplary critical edition in its first five volumes, but, given the growing complexity of Peirce's later and more voluminous writings, those standards will be increasingly tested and, especially because of the publishing demands of the crucial graphical component, may eventually fail to yield the useful resource that authentic scholarship requires—and, with its limitation to thirty volumes, many of Peirce's important writings will remain marginally accessible.

3. Peirce's writings challenge the margins of traditional scholarly publishing by content as well as their condition. Reading and editing Peirce is an extremely difficult task, because he was a polymath—whose work no one person can fully comprehend or critically edit. His writings, no matter what their nominal topic, are perfused with discussions of topics from other disciplines, so that mathematics looms significantly in an epistemological paper, logic in a mathematical one, or geodesy in a metaphysical one. Beyond the limitations of access—his manuscripts are deposited in different places, remain in a deplorable state of order and arrangement, and are nearly unmanageable in size and volume—the task of representing the course he followed in developing his philosophical view within

the confines of the printed page and bound book is all but impossible.

4. Peirce's philosophical view itself fundamentally refuses to define (or delimit) the margins of the known or knowable. In this regard his conceptions of communication and continuity lose their vital essence in the very notion of a (selected) critical or definitive edition. His (semiotic) examination and explanation of how human experience grows through communication calls on us to accept the "editorial role," each in our own way, to extend our own margins of thought—and to progress collectively through self-controlled expression. In a 23 December 1908 letter to Victoria Lady Welby, Peirce wrote:

> Know that from the day when at the age of 12 or 13 I took up, in my elder brother's room, a copy of Whately's *Logic,* and asked him what Logic was, and getting some simple answer, flung myself on the floor and buried myaself in it, it has never been in my power to study anything—mathematics, ethics, metaphysics, gravitation, thermodynamics, optics, chemistry, comparative anatomy, psychology, phonetics, economics, the history of science, whist, men and women, wine, metrology, except as a study of semeiotic. (*SS* 85–86)[6]

And in a postscript written five days later, but not mailed, he said (apologizing for his long letter):

> Well, dear Lady Welby, you deserve this infliction, for having spoken of my having "always been kindly (!!!) interested in the work [on semiotic, which she termed 'significs'] to which my life is devoted," when I have myself been entirely absorbed in the very same subject since 1863, without meeting, before I made your acquaintance, a single mind to whom it did not seem very like bosh. (L 463; *CP* 8.376)[7]

Peirce here expresses his difficulty in finding anyone to appreciate that it is one thing to see mathematics, chemistry, or any other subject through semiotic spectacles and quite another to construct or to inquire into the construction of such a set of spectacles—to extend the margins of philosophical perspective.

PEIRCE'S PHILOSOPHICAL PERSPECTIVE

Christopher Hookway comments on the limited progress of Peircean scholarship, as it appeared when he set himself the task of (studying the manuscripts and) writing the book that he looked for when he began to study Peirce's philosophy:

> Many people share the opinion that . . . Peirce is a philosophical giant, perhaps the most important philosopher to have emerged in the United States. Most philosophers think of him as the founder of "pragmatism" and are aware of doctrines . . . which they describe as "Peircean." But, curiously, few have read more than two or three of his best-known papers, and these somewhat unrepresentative ones. On reading further, one finds a rich and impressive corpus of writings, containing imaginative and original discussions of a wide range of issues in most areas of philosophy: he appears to have anticipated many important philosophical discoveries of the last eighty years. However, the interest of Peirce's work does not consist simply in these detailed examinations of philosophical problems, for he was, above all, a systematic philosopher. Inspired by Kant, he devoted his life to providing foundations for knowledge and, in the course of doing so, he brought together a number of different philosophical doctrines: the new logic of relations and quantifiers invented independently by Frege in Germany and Peirce in the United States; sophisticated insights into the structure of science and the logic of probability; a systematic theory of meaning and interpretation; a developed philosophy of mathematics; a general theory of value; and a metaphysics incorporating an ambitious evolutionary cosmology. It is not wholly surprising that he is not read more widely. . . . He never produced a unified coherent presentation of the system. We have to work from a mass of papers, sets of lecture notes, reviews, and manuscripts, and on that basis—helped by his many programmatic statements—reconstruct the structure and development of his system.[8]

Because of the complexity of its conceptual nature (and the limited access to its holograph expressions), Peirce's philosophy has been interpreted piecemeal—and scholars have been able to construe his ideas as supporting any particular philosophical tradition they want to promote.

Ernest Nagel, for example, concludes that Peirce conceived his semiotic as a theory that would assimilate the findings of both the formal (logical) and the empirical (biologico-social) approaches of inquiry: "He was the first, or among the first to work out an empiricism which could combine recognition of the indispensable function in inquiry of strict logic and other regulative principles, with a recognition of the equally indispensable role of sensory observation." More careful study shows that what Nagel calls "an empiricism" Peirce called "pragmatism": the method he prescribed to avoid the puzzles of traditional philosophy and logical theory, which, as Nagel recognized, "derive almost entirely from isolating knowledge from the procedures leading up to it, so that it becomes logically impossible to attain."[9] Hookway explains that Peirce does not remove philosophical problems by exposing errors in tradition but that his pragmatism makes them "tractable,"[10] and Esposito explicates his work as a comprehensive metaphysics responding to the limitations of modern philosophy.

Peirce himself realized that many of his contemporaries, like his friend William James or his student John Dewey, misunderstood his work. Here is his account of what he saw happening to his conception of pragmatism:

Four different doctrines indeed that would be so describable [as pragmatism] occur to me as possible to be broached by *somebody*. . . . In the first place, then, it is not incredible that somebody should opine that all human thoughts are so indefinite as to render it a pure question of convenience what we should regard as anybody's meaning in any utterance; although to hold that vagueness of thought could, of itself, have such a result would involve a confusion of *vagueness* with *generality in depth*. Yet certainly whosoever should himself have ideas so confused as to think *all* human ideas to be of that more than miraculous vagueness might well be expected to fall into the confusion in question. In the second place, it is conceivable that a person should hold "man to be the measure of things" in so extreme a sense as to make practical convenience his sole criterion of truth; and he might then easily be led to consider this opinion to be what pragmatism consists in. In the third place, a person of positivistic opinions might admit . . . that the meanings of some concepts involve elements other than conceivable practical consequences; while yet, in view of our total ignorance as to what subjects those further elements are true of, and what they are false of, he might think it expedient altogether to ignore those further elements, and might entitle this policy "pragmatism"; and being, like most positivists, a bad logician and a vague thinker, he might be under the delusion that, in doing so, he was basing pragmatism on a "practical preference." In the fourth place, since Professor James's definition of pragmatism . . . says that it is "the doctrine that the whole 'meaning' of a conception *expresses itself* in practical consequences," [The Italics are mine. C.S.S.P] upon which follows a division of the genus "practical consequences" into two species, it is easily imaginable that he holds that some, if not all, concepts are capable of expressing themselves or getting expressed in several ways. (MS 300 [1908])[11]

Peirce's solution to this illegitimate proliferation of meaning was to change the name of his conception from "pragmatism" to "pragmaticism."[12]

Pragmatism, for Peirce, was the method of inquiry implied by his semiotic (theory of experience), as properly understood. It tells us how the conditions of experience, semiotically defined, *effect* learning. Semiotic explains the need for pragmatism (a procedure for learning) and offers a conceptual framework with which to identify and examine what are the necessary conditions for meaning to occur in experience. Pragmatism describes the practice or procedure for creating those conditions: "Nobody will expect of a theory that it should furnish skill or render practice needless" (*CP* 2.201).

Peirce developed semiotic as a means to understand the nature of inquiry (or learning) as the process by which we can examine beliefs, interpretations, and assumptions in the course of our experience, for which he considered traditional logic to be inadequate because it provided no comprehensive account of language and meaning—of communication. He considered science to be the most reliable process of conducting inquiry, and his pragmatism attempts to capture its essential methodological nature in philosophically useful terms: "The single purpose of my whole life has been to do what in me lay toward rendering Philosophy scientific" (MS 296 [1908]). What Peirce means by "scientific" must be appreciated in terms of his theory of experience and the procedure for continuing to develop experience effectively.

[Philosophical theories] have the same sort of basis as scientific results have. That is to say, they rest on experience—on the total everyday experience of many generations. . . . Such experience is worthless for distinctively scientific purposes . . . although all science . . . would have to shut up shop if she should manage to escape accepting them. (MS 291; *CP* 5.522 [1905])

The kind of philosophy which interests me and must, I think, interest everybody is that philosophy, which uses the most rational methods it can devise, for finding out the little that can as yet be found out about the universe of mind and matter from those observations which every person can make in every hour of this waking life. (MS 328; *CP* 1.126)

The primary challenge of any science is to resolve the many different observations (views or experiences of some phenomenon) that are possible, by continuing to formulate and test hypotheses (representations of these views), with some hope that the many views can be brought together in one final explanation. Effective inquiry proceeds only through cooperation of individuals working to represent and express their views (experience), thereby creating a community that can give each member a broader perspective (collective experience) but that can remain vital only through continued individual contributions. Trying to overcome the solipsism or individualism that characterizes both rationalism and empiricism, Peirce (based on his own experience as a working scientist) developed his semiotic and pragmatism to account philosophically for *a community of inquirers* as that which makes knowing possible:

> The real . . . is that which, sooner or later, information and reasoning would finally result in, and which is therefore independent of the vagaries of me and you. Thus, the very origin of the conception of reality shows that this conception essentially involves the notion of a COMMUNITY, without definite limits, and capable of an indefinite increase of knowledge. (*W* 2:239; *CP* 5.311 [1868])

As a practicing scientist and an extraordinarily proficient philosopher, Peirce concluded that, while successful investigation of any sort involves sophisticated instruments and techniques, successful inquiry (the growth of knowledge) relies on effective communicational conditions, operations, and awareness: careful observation and ingenious conceptualization generate knowledge only insofar as they are collaboratively validated and collectively continued.

THE CONTINUITY OF PEIRCE'S TEXT

As he developed his philosophical perspective, Peirce found it increasingly difficult to constrain his thought within the limitations of the formats of expression available to him (which still generally prevail): the book and journal article. Moreover, those aspects of his thought that he regarded as most significant, and are often the subject of the greatest contemporary interest, are typically those that the editors of his own time would not publish because they could not imagine a readership for them. This limitation, taken together with his compositional methods, resulted in a rich corpus of material in respect to which the usual distinction between draft and final version of a paper is all but useless. In fact, there is no useful distinction to be drawn in general between that part of the manuscript material that should be available to any serious scholar and the part that can be neglected either because of redundancy or because it is distinctly inferior in intellectual quality. A description of his method of writing will indicate why.

Typically, if Peirce was aiming at establishing an idea, he would proceed from a certain starting point along a certain line of thought until he realized that, if he pursued the matter further in the way he was headed, he would not get to where he wanted to go, or at least not within the limits set by possible publication. He would then double back a few sentences—or a page or two or ten or fifty pages—until he found a suitable logical forking point and move toward his goal in an alternative way from that point; if the same sort of thing happened again, he would again double back to a forking point and move toward his goal anew. Sometimes a path from a fork would itself have a fork, which is to say that in going back he would go past a fork taken earlier and find one still farther back. Sometimes a fork on a fork would itself have a fork, and so on. Sometimes he would go back to the beginning and blaze another trail from there, still heading toward his original goal but in a quite different way. Sometimes he would abandon that starting point and try another approach. Sometimes he would actually make it to his original goal, but, then, his understanding of it would have changed (grown) in the course of his trying to reach it, forcing him to redefine his objective. What is most valuable to the contemporary reader is Peirce's learning process itself, not witnessing the result (especially what he completed for publication) but joining him along the trails and side trails he pursued.

Peirce referred to himself as a pioneering thinker. Many of his unpublished manuscripts—some are several hundred pages long—are indeed like trails made through a hitherto uncharted conceptual forest, not records of random strolls here and there but, rather, the sort of trails left by a careful explorer. A major reason for the growing contemporary interest in Peirce's work is that the territory he explored is frequently what is only now being investigated by others and staked out for temporary settlement by one discipline or another. But, if his exploratory method of composition makes these writings exciting to read, it also makes them unpublishable in printed and bound form. We could, of course, bind up transcriptions of such intellectual explorations as books, but no publisher would regard material presented in that form to be acceptable as a product of the press, and, in any case, the very binding of the pages would make the printed transcription less useful than the material in its original state. This material must be manipulated, rearranged, set first in one order and then in another, so that even the awkwardness of the unbound paper page is preferable to the diminishment of intellectual value that would result from presenting it in conventional book format.

Certainly, search and retrieval of the material in its present form is a nightmare, made endurable only by the quality of the content with which one is working. Peirce's method of writing, particularly in his later years, was such that almost any topic might be introduced and discussed in almost any given manuscript, regardless of its nominal topic; consequently, we must search through the manuscripts (in photocopy or microfilm) page by page, hoping the right guess has been made about where to search, since the manuscript labels are not usually helpful, and it is impossible to work through the entire hundred thousand pages time and time again. Days can be spent in search of a dimly remembered but crucially important passage, sometimes to no avail. The same can be said of the *Collected Papers*, which, though in the process of being superseded, is still the only overall presentation of his writings available to most readers—but its indices and principles of arrangement are far from adequate for scholarly purposes.

Its topical arrangement, as mentioned earlier, brings about the disruption of actual series of papers, both published and unpublished—so that the six papers published in the *Popular Science Monthly* in 1877–78 as "Illustrations of the Logic of Science" are scattered in three of the eight volumes of the *Collected Papers*, and (some of) his 1903 Lowell Lectures "On Some Topics of Logic" in seven of the eight. Moreover, most of Peirce's manuscripts appear in excerpts only (and we are rarely told what and how much has been left out), and (to reflect the volumes' respective topics) different parts of the same manuscript appear in different volumes. Many of the selections are not dated or are dated inaccurately, and, in a number of instances, parts of different manuscripts are seemingly grafted together (without mention), and some of these grafted manuscripts consist of writings composed more than three decades apart. This state of affairs leaves us with a scholarly tool that is unreliable, obscurantist, and often entirely frustrating.

A brief glance at a bibliography of Peirce's published writings and at various guides to his unpublished writings will indicate the continuity of his work and the fact that he was not finished (writing) when he died.[13] His many productions and numerous observations make clear that he would not have called a single one of his writings "definitive" or "final." Although he intended to get into print considerably more than he did—including several full-length books, which he either did not finish, was unwilling to tailor to publishers' demands, or simply failed to have accepted (primarily because they were too advanced or difficult to become moneymakers), it is fair to say that the largest part of his writings represents "unfinished" work or, better, "work-in-progress." In a 2 December 1904 letter to Lady Welby he clearly marks the difference between publishing material and merely getting it into print:

> Much of my work never will be published. If I can, before I die, get so much made accessible as others may have a difficulty in discovering, I shall feel that I can be excused from more. My aversion to publishing anything has not been due to want of interest in others but to the thought that after all a philosophy can only be passed from mouth to mouth, where there is opportunity to object & cross-question & that printing is not publishing unless the matter be pretty frivolous. (*SS* 44)[14]

The fact that Peirce regarded even his publications as work-in-progress can be seen in comments he made in a number of places, as well as in his habit of marking at least one offprint of his published articles "Working Copy"—and then making corrections, annotations, and comments in it, sometimes many years later. Peirce tells us in one of the Lowell Lectures that he has always been skeptical "with everything I have printed" (MS 465), and, in a lecture on "Multitude and Continuity" given before the mathematics faculty at Harvard, he says that "no sooner is a paper of mine worked up to a finish and printed than I immediately begin to take a critical attitude toward it and go to work to raise all the objections to it big and little that I can"; he concludes, in an alternate version, "And the result has always been that I have found that there were other men who were far better satisfied with them than I myself have been. . . . The truth is that I am far too well acquainted with the depths of my own stupidity to know what it is to be satisfied with any product of my mind" (MS 316a).

It is this very self-criticism that kept Peirce from publishing more than he did and that explains the "unfinished" and "in-progress" nature of his work. He says repeatedly that he struggled for decades with the veracity of his semiotic; for nearly thirty years with the truth of pragmatism; and for over twenty years with his system of graphical logic called Existential Graphs (though he had had it in mind for a dozen years).[15] Peirce saw into print somewhat less than he intended not because he had nothing of interest to say but, rather, because he regarded his work as unfinished and as continually in need of modification and further development. He even described a "method of discussing with [him]self a philosophical question" or his "processes of forming philosophical opinions." These methods and processes exhibit not only the growth and continuity of his thought but also the fact that closure, certainty, and final intentions are (according to his pragmatic maxim) possible only *in the long run.*[16]

SEMIOTIC, PRAGMATISM, AND THE EXISTENTIAL GRAPHS

Peirce clearly felt that he had achieved one objective in his life's work: "Logic, in its general sense, is, as I believe I have shown, only another name for *semiotic*" (MS 798; *CP* 2.227 [1896]). In his recent article on Peirce for the *Johns Hopkins Literary Guide,* Leroy Searle warns: "Perhaps the greatest difficulty for readers of Peirce, aside from the probability that they are born and bred nominalists, is that most will bring to Peirce's writing assumptions about 'logic,' 'metaphysics,' and 'semiotics' or about the idea of the 'sign' that may be fundamentally incompatible with the position Peirce elaborates."[17]

Peirce's semiotic has ancient origins in a theory of "semiosis," an originally Greek conception of how our ability to represent the objects of experience makes it possible for us to generalize (symbolize, categorize, measure): to establish relations that make possible the continuous growth or spreading of ideas. By the end of his life Peirce had developed a comprehensive theory to account for all traditional realms of philosophical investigation. *Ontology* can be viewed as examining one dimension of semiotic; its field of investigation is the structure of the world (elements and relations of existence). *Epistemology* examines a second dimension of semiotic; its field of investigation is the meaning of the world (our relations to the world through representations of its existential relations). *Semiotic* examines the third dimension to incorporate the first two in a field of investigation into the occurrence of meaning in the world (our experiential reliance on representations of the relations in the world, by which we continue to gain knowledge of it). We know what exists to the extent that we are capable of representing our observations effectively (usefully, as a basis for further observation)—and can continue to develop this capability. According to Esposito, Peirce's aim was "to discover a unified theory of logic, psychology, and metaphysics, and to present it in some sort of logical form."[18]

Searle explains why Peirce's philosophy challenges the prevailing attitude and condition of modern philosophy—and its effect on science:

> While philosophical commentators may wish to "ignore the metaphysical side of Peirce's thought" . . . it was crucial for Peirce, whose persistent complaint about metaphysics since René Descartes was that it was unclear, self-contradictory, or confused—not that one could get rid of it or otherwise deconstruct it. His turn to Duns Scotus, the subtlest medieval defender of realism, combined with his study of Kant, led to a version of critical realism in which he rejects the nominalism he finds in virtually all modern philosophers since Descartes. . . .
>
> In general, Peirce took the view that "nominalism" involves a metaphysical reduction of modes of reality to the existence of individual entities . . . thereby hopelessly obscuring the dependence of thought and inquiry on diverse forms of representation and so ensuring in all intellectual pursuits, but especially in experimental science, a chronic state of crisis or confusion over the status of truth claims, as well as the proliferation of destructive and not merely critical forms of skepticism.[19]

Nearly a century ago Peirce developed his semiotic to explain many problems that modern physics has since recognized. Einstein's relativity theories do not account for communication between observers who can compare time intervals, and time is conceived as reversible. We establish experience of the past (in memories and records of all kinds)—even our awareness of the present (to the extent that we turn our attention to it) becomes consciousness of the immediate past—but we cannot have such experience of the future. Peirce's philosophical *observation* of this "asymmetry of experience," based on the irreversibility of time, indicated to him a fundamental "directionality in experience": we are bound in our conscious experience to "go from the past toward the future" (MS 304 [1903]). This metaphysical observation is the foundation for his semiotic as a theory of the continuity of experience (the *growth* of meaning rather than its haphazard expansion). Uncertainty about the future tends to draw us out of the certainty of the past. Notions of probability and chance (tendencies) have no meaning (are of no use to us) without our awareness of time—the rational roots of a sense of *purpose*—which gives us the basis for comparing our experiences through thought and communication.

Medieval scholars further developed Greek theories of semiosis to conceive thought *as* communication (thought is dialogic in form)[20] and investigated the necessary conditions for any form of such *mediation* to occur. A medium of expression does not simply "convey meaning" but becomes a part of our human experience to affect, in some way that cannot be completely predicted, those engaged in its use. In our modern technological conception of communication, we routinely consider the process as no more than the transmission of information, taking no comprehensive account of the conditions that must be part of the occurrence of meaning in anyone's experience. According to Peirce, *ideas* cannot be accounted for in these terms:

> We are accustomed to speak of ideas as reproduced, as passed from mind to mind, as similar or dissimilar to one another, and, in short, as if they were substantial things; nor can any reasonable objection be raised to such expressions. But taking the word "idea" in the sense of an event in an individual consciousness, it is clear that an idea once past is gone forever, and any supposed recurrence of it is another idea. These two ideas are not present in the same state of consciousness, and therefore cannot possibly be compared. (*EP* 1:313; *CP* 6.105 [1892])[21]

Western philosophy, in its symbolic logic tradition and preoccupation with linguistic *structure,* has not fully appreciated what *functional* conditions the Greeks tried to explain and understand. "A sign is a thing which causes us to think of something beyond the impression the thing itself makes upon the senses," as Saint Augustine says.[22] We might say, in modern terms, that, when we use a medium of communication, it can mysteriously become "transparent" for us and so reveal to our thoughts the thing to which it refers.[23]

A chemist by training, Peirce employed the Greeks' conception of sign to examine conditions that we cannot observe by empirical methods (as we can the structure of a medium and the behavior of participants) the way a chemist employs the concept of molecule as the basis for explaining molecular activity underlying the observable behavior of materials in reaction. Mediation is not merely reaction; we cannot discover "the rules" of sign-mediated behavior simply by external observation and statistical summary. Symbolic expressions are the periodic products of semiosis, but their empirically identifiable features (structures) alone do not determine what meaning will be made of them as signs (in semiosis): "In the first place, a sign is not a real thing. It is of such a nature to exist in replicas. Look down a printed page, and every *the* you see is the same word, every *e* the same letter. A real thing does not so exist in replica. The being of a sign is merely *being represented*" (MS 517 [1904]).

An expression has *virtual*, not factual, meaning—meaning that thought and communication continually generate. What makes an expression more than its objective properties is the not-strictly-causal (only vaguely determinable) relation to what *someone's* thought *might* take it to mean. From any (necessarily limited) human point of view the meaning of any expression cannot be simply a matter of *probability* (established conventional response) or *actuality* (conditionally stimulated response) but must include *possibility* (an individual's unique experience in which the interpretation of meaning occurs) that cannot help but generate new meaning—growing experience. The essential continuity of experience, in which meaning is always a possibility in the future, is theoretically fundamental to Peirce's method, or pragmatism—a point ignored by his coeval and modern "pragmatists" alike.

I do not think that the import of any word (except perhaps a pronoun) is limited to what is in the utterer's mind *actualiter*, so that when I mention the Greek language my meaning should be limited to such Greek words as I happen to be thinking of at the moment. It is, on the contrary, according to me, what is in the mind, perhaps not even *habitualiter*, but only *virtualiter* which constitutes the import.*

*This was said in 1868, before declaring for pragmaticism, thus: No present actual thought (which is mere feeling) has any meaning, any intellectual value; for this lies, not in what is actually thought, but in *what* this thought may be connected with in representation by subse-

quent thoughts; so that the meaning of a thought is altogether something virtual. (MS 291 [1905])[24]

Peirce's semiotic conceives experience in a fundamentally *tri-relative*
conceptual structure that captures its generative or continuously growing
nature. He arrived at this conception by beginning with the concepts of
subject and object, because experience cannot be conceived in less than
these two terms. But more than two concepts are needed, because the
theory must account for the *relationship* between the two separate terms
when we speak of a subject *experiencing* an object. The necessary third term
(focusing attention on the *relation of experience* between subject and object
as a phenomenal element in its own right—to define, analyze, and explain)
makes the minimum adequate conceptual structure a tri-relative one.

This "logic of relations" prescribes an essential ordering (time dimension) of conceptual terms, a construct that makes it possible for Peirce to
account for the generative or creative aspect of experience in terms of tri-
relative sign activity. Traditional dichotomous theories (such as Saussure's
of signifier/signified or those of the logical positivists), without this relation of generation, cannot explain the productivity of thought and communication in creating new signs. Because the conditions conceptualized
in these theories are, therefore, timeless (language coded to thought as
accomplished fact), they cannot explain the uniqueness of someone's
meaning in a particular time and place or how it can come to be understood
by others. Without the tri-relation that constitutes experience theoretically
accounted for, communication must be considered irrelevant and even
impossible. On this point Searle remarks:

> While Peirce's "semiotics" may appear intriguingly similar to Saus-
> sure's proposed discipline of "semiology" . . . it should not be over-
> looked that the first of many fundamental differences is that Peirce's
> semiotics is not based on the *word* as "sign" . . . but on the *proposition*
> as that which unifies consciousness and creates intelligibility or com-
> prehension. In this sense, Peirce's semiotics is not a theory of language
> but a theory of the production of meaning.[25]

Beyond accounting for thought and communication as time based and
productively evolving, the generality of Peirce's theory exposed the misconception of basing logic (any explanation of reasoning) on language
alone. In the first place, he said,

Logic, for me, is the study of the essential conditions to which signs must conform in order to function as such. How the constitution of the human mind may compel men to think is not the question; and the appeal to language appears to me no better than an unsatisfactory ascertaining of psychological facts that are of no relevancy to logic. But if such appeal is to be made, (and logicians generally do make it; in particular their doctrine of the copula appears to rest solely upon this,) it would seem that they ought to survey human languages generally and not confine themselves to the small and extremely peculiar group of Aryan speech. (MS 291 [1905])

Peirce also argued that the purely symbolic character of traditional logic fundamentally prevented it from usefully serving us as an observational science, in capturing the essential continuity of experience. He created his Existential Graphs as an instrument for investigating the formal relations of linguistic symbols diagrammatically, "since no reasoning that amounts to much can be conducted with[out] *Icons* and *Indices*" (*SS* 118), to make their logical character *observable*. At the same time, he cautioned against the notion that any mode of reference performs complete representation.

The system of Existential Graphs may be characterized with great truth as presenting before our eyes a moving picture of thought. Provided this characterization be taken not as a flatly literal statement, but as a simile, it will, I venture to predict, surprise you to find what a strain of detailed comparison it will bear without snapping. A picture is visual representation of the relations between the parts of its object; a vivid and highly informative representation, rewarding somewhat close examination. Yet from the nature of things it must fall short of perfection, just as a representation of any kind must. It cannot directly exhibit all the dimensions of its object, be this physical or psychic. It shows this object only under a certain light, and from a single point of view. (MS 291 [1905])

Individual points of view are also accounted for in terms of Peirce's trirelation, which, at the same time, indicates just what constitutes the *potential* advantage of a conventional medium (of symbols), such as language: "It appears to me that the essential function of a sign is to render inefficient relations efficient,—not to set them into action, but to establish a habit or general rule whereby they will act on occasion. . . . a sign is something by knowing which we know something more" (*SS* 31–32).[26]

The last part of this quotation is crucial to understanding what Peirce means by "efficient relations." Just as mediation in a language (when conventionally used by all participants) allows us to treat the medium transparently in order to express ideas, this very transparency can prevent us from examining the generalizing character of that medium's established structure and habituated function. One part of the tri-relation (the relation of idea to sign) may be perfectly automatic, but, if the sign's relation to its object is not well-established (based on the sign user's experience of that object), then the tri-relation as a whole will not be efficient (efficiency entails effectiveness) in its role of referring to *something* for someone. As the units of language (words, sentences, paragraphs, documents, etc.) grow, their combinatorial power increases, while their referential power decreases (symbols can take on a life of their own). We are easily misled by symbolic power, as any rhetorician knows. Our ability to create and use symbolic expressions is certainly our greatest virtue, but, at the same time, it can be our greatest liability in reasoning—if we do not use the pragmatic (experimental) method to investigate their trustworthiness.

The purpose of the pragmatic method is to create truly efficient sign relations by maintaining the unifying function of conventionality while encouraging the diversifying function of representability through any media that can be devised for that purpose. The effective conduct of science provides the best evidence that regularity (procedure) and inexactitude (vagueness of meaning) are not only compatible but also productive, in the long run. From the semiotic perspective the continuity of experience that supports the growth of knowledge depends on our collective capability to examine the validity of related ideas (as concepts) while increasing the reliability of their reference (as representations) to the world. We can know to the extent that we can learn to represent what we observe usefully (to ourselves, at least), in combining many observations over time, by the most efficient media we can create.

SEMIOTIC CONTINUITY

Peirce began his lifelong investigation with the hypothesis that the tendency or urge to generalize across the multitude of distinctions our senses are capable of discriminating is the basis of rational thought. We make sense of what would otherwise be "noise" or sheer confusion by means of our ability to create some apparent order in thought (communication with ourselves) and through communication with others who are capable of creating mutually recognized order. The sensory tendency to detect differences, to particularize experience, must be complemented by the cognitive (communicational) capability to relate the distinguished particulars on some basis, to generalize experience. To be effective (in gaining control in any particular context) this capability must be exercised in some sort of community (by collective cognition), no matter how vague or limited are the conditions for relations among its members.

His semiotic explains how experience can grow, based on the generalizing tendency that works to maintain the relatedness or continuity of ideas. His pragmatism serves as the methodological reminder that generalizing is not an end in itself: the unifying cognitive capability, in turn, must serve the discriminating sensory capability, in a continuing cycle of conceiving and testing ideas against reality. In this continuous effort—to formulate ideas, to test them against sensory experience, to modify them in response, and to test them again—we rely, in semiotic terms, on mediation relations so minute and complex in the subtleties of linguistic expression alone that we could never be aware of or account for them all. While they are all *theoretically* explicable, we need only investigate their unnoticed operation (or transparency) in relational detail when a particular purpose arises. For this purpose Peirce proposed his Existential Graphs.

If most mediation relations did not occur for us automatically, without our conscious thought, none of our remarkable human capabilities would be possible. To the extent that we can establish relations that are trustworthy (concepts), as a result of experience, we can establish habits of thought and behavior (by training and learning)—which operate uncritically unless disturbed by new experience in which they are recognized as dysfunctional. By means of such complex mediation we establish (more or less successful) mediated relations with the world around us. To the extent that these relations are habitual, we tend not to notice them or examine their effectiveness. We learn languages but do not readily examine their "fitness" in representing our experience. We establish habitual relations through tools and technological devices of all kinds that release us from routine, on which we may build to create new pursuits. The human-computer relation may epitomize our capability to establish habitual relations and increasingly build them into the machine itself, once we can define a habit in terms of an algorithm, or routine of interpretation for executing some operation.

The human semiotic capability to generalize—to relate objects (sensed or imagined) through mediation in experience, learn habits of thought, and automate productive behavior—requires human consciousness, or self-awareness, or the ability to "take perspective": to use the objective self to view the subjective self. Peirce clearly enunciated his dialogical concept of cognition in 1905: "A person is not absolutely an individual. His thoughts are what 'he is saying to himself,' that is, is saying to that other self that is just coming into life in the flow of time" (*CP* 5.421). Six years later he expressed the point as follows:

> In reasoning, one is obliged to *think to oneself.* In order to recognize what is needful for doing this it is necessary to recognize, first of all, what "oneself" is. One is not twice in precisely the same mental state. One is *virtually* (i.e. for pertinent purposes, the same as if one were) a somewhat different person, to whom one's present thought has to be communicated. (MS 846; *CP* 7.103)

We can examine our habits and consciously develop new ones, based upon what we can imagine to be possible as the consequence, continually linking the past to the future through ideas. The history of science demonstrates the hazards of mistaking elaborate conceptual generalizations for what they are supposed to refer to, rather than using them as devices to be continually modified as more is learned. In 1905 Peirce made clear that generality is a form of vagueness, that "wherever degree or any other possibility of continuous variation subsists, absolute precision is impossible" (MS 291; *CP* 5.506). In the semiotic explanation of the tri-relative condition, a sign refers to something else for someone: the sign can never *be* the thing referred to (it would have no use in generalizing), and we never know for sure what someone might take it to mean; for, as Peirce said in a 1 December 1903 letter to Lady Welby, "perfect accuracy of thought is unattainable,—*theoretically unattainable.* And undue striving for it is worse than time wasted" (*SS* 11).

Peirce considered what twentieth-century physicists and philosophers call the problem of indeterminacy, in terms of semiotic, to be a circumstance of representational multiplicity, to which his pragmatism responds. Any particular expression or interpretation might well lead to a definite response, which then can be evaluated for its usefulness in that context— but no particular representation can possibly be the end of inquiry or claim to be absolute. Determining meaning, for any particular circumstance, and testing it in further experience is the procedure for maintaining a potential indefinite determinability, in which every proposition (sign) would be part of an endless continuum that never reaches, but approaches the limit of, perfect representation. As Searle explains:

> While this [pragmatist] maxim appears to leave meaning infinitely deferred, it would be more accurate to say that it accepts meaning (as it does thought and reality itself) as a continuous process, which we determine, with arbitrary precision (depending on "different circumstances and desires"), in communities of inquiry. Finally, Peirce's pragmaticism, with its debt to Duns Scotus, reflects Peirce's sense that thinking is normative and in its deepest reaches ethical and aesthetic; it must be these if it is to be scientific. . . . According to the title phrase of one of his most widely read essays, it is by inquiry and experiment that we seek the "fixation of belief" . . . while the ethics of the process is profoundly summarized in the slogan that Peirce would have on "every wall of the city of philosophy: Do not block the way of inquiry" . . . —which is to say, no belief is ever ultimate, and no one ever gets the last word.[27]

Having gained the metaphysical perspective of semiotic continuity, Peirce was particularly concerned about the dominance of deterministic materialism in the science of his time and, in his 1893 "Reply to the Necessitarians," in *The Monist,* he posed four phenomena that cannot be explained by the established mechanistic laws: growth, diversity, generalization, and feeling. His purpose was not to refute the established laws of physics but, rather, to demonstrate that they are not absolute and complete, especially in their ability to account for living matter: "Some of us are evolutionists; that is, we are so impressed with the pervasiveness of growth, whose course seems only here and there to be interrupted, that it seems to us that the universe as a whole, so far as anything can possibly be conceived or logically opined of the whole, should be conceived as growing" (*CP* 6.613).

Peirce says that growth, rather than simply defying the conservation law of physics, must be accounted for in a new law of "an intimate connection between growth and habit" that builds on what the conservative laws describe as an advancement. He concluded that all living organisms require the ordering negentropic (habit-taking) tendency along with the entropic (habit-breaking) tendency in order to conduct themselves successfully in

the mechanistic world of chance (in which regularities have some probability of occurring): "I make use of chance chiefly to make room for a
principle of generalization, or tendency to form habits, which I hold has
produced all regularities" (*EP* 1:310; *CP* 6.63). Esposito explains that
habit breaking requires the concept of chance to give habit-taking activities
the opportunity to become increasingly subject to habit.[28]

Peirce's notion of continuity was conceived to characterize the
negentropic tendency itself. The possibility of systematicity, or regularity,
responds to the conditions of chance, or irregularity: "Supposing matter to
be but mind under the slavery of inveterate habit, the law of mind still
applies to it. According to that law, consciousness subsides as habit becomes established, and is excited again at the breaking up of habit. But the
highest quality of mind involves a great readiness to take habits, and a great
readiness to lose them" (*CP* 6.613).

Peirce worked for five decades developing his philosophy to explain
this quality of mind: how our feelings (intuitions) become effectively related to what (without this mediation capability) would be the brute force
objects in a world of simple reaction, by means of our power to contemplate and converse, which makes it possible for us to "know" (to gain some
control of what happens in our experience). Progressively, he formulated
his semiotic, his pragmatism, and his Existential Graphs into a major metaphysical project toward resolving at least one problem in philosophy that he
had identified in the beginning: "if materialism without idealism is blind,
idealism without materialism is void" (*W* 1:111).[29] Materialism and idealism are merged (as objective idealism) in his semiotically explained metaphysics: the substance of anything we experience is never in question, only
our ability to make it intelligible, by which we understand it in some
measure that continues to grow. Ultimately, knowing is continuing to
represent what we have learned, through observation, in our conduct—
which is the most efficient possible relation to existence.

Semiotic continuity offers a new metaphysical perspective for building
the "spectacles" we need to proceed pragmatically in developing self-
critical control and for appreciating the nature and necessity of communication. Esposito concludes that Peirce's efforts "have left us a legacy of
a truly interdisciplinary metaphysics upon which to build," and Searle
credits him with expanding logic "to cover the whole range of intelligent
inquiry or associative thought for any 'intelligence capable of learning by
experience' . . . without losing the precision that made Peirce one of the
fathers of modern formal logic," so that his metaphysics "does not issue in a

simple ontology, nor does it lead to radical skepticism because the crucial (and subtle) question hinges on the character and function of representability, not being or existence."[30] In 1907 Peirce himself described the results of his efforts:

> I am, as far as I know, a pioneer, or rather a backwoodsman, in the work of clearing and opening up what I call *semiotic*, that is, the doctrine of the essential nature and fundamental varieties of possible semiosis; and I find the field too vast, the labor too great, for a first-comer. (MS 318; *CP* 5.488)

THE DIFFICULTY OF EDITING AND PUBLISHING PEIRCE

As a prodigious author (and publisher and editor), Peirce was aware of all matters concerning writing, editing, and publishing. In 1891 (five years before the appearance of the relevant fascicle in the *Oxford English Dictionary*) he provided a more sophisticated definition of *emendation* than any that had appeared in print; it is "an attempt to restore the true reading of a passage upon historical grounds, external or internal, by means of conjecture or circumstantial evidence" (MS 1167). In 1900 he wrote "The Editor's Manual" (MS 1181), a ninety-two-page manuscript primarily about spelling. And between 1864 and 1908 he published several hundred book reviews, in which he said much about writing, publishing, and editing. In an 1893 review of a new edition of Beckford's *Vathek*, he provided— intimating the novel's actual history—the recipe for an immortal book: "Write it at one sitting in 3 days and 2 nights; devote 3½ years to improving it, and then publish it as near as possible as it originally was." In 1890 he agreed with A. C. Fraser's plea for a new edition of Locke's works and said that "this great man, whose utterances still have their lessons for the world, with wholesome influences for all plastic minds, should be studied in a complete, correct, and critical edition," and in a review of Fraser's 1901 edition of *The Works of Berkeley* he clearly distinguished between what are now called "substantives" and "accidentals": "Whether for an ordinary reader of philosophy, this edition or that in Bohn's 'Philosophical Library' is to be preferred is a delicate question. The text of either is excellent, although neither, we are sorry to say, respects Berkeley's punctuation, which is a part of his style."[31]

An edition of Peirce's own work will be different from many other contemporary editions, especially those that issue previously published book-length works by novelists, psychologists, and philosophers that, even during their lifetimes, went through a number of separate printings and that must, therefore, focus on the collation of all authoritative (and sometimes, unauthoritative) versions of particular documents and on the eradication of editorial and compositorial corruptions. It will be different, because few of his publications (which represent less than one-fifth of his entire work) were printed more than once and because there are few holograph manuscript versions, printer's copies, corrected page or galley proofs, or offprints corrected shortly after publication. It will also be different because, in his unpublished manuscripts, there are few authoritative, and collatable, alternate versions. As indicated earlier, rather than writing a series of (collatable) drafts that are subsumed in a final version, Peirce would generally proceed along a path of thought, return to a crossroads, and then blaze new trails—with the roads not taken becoming at times important stretches of a subsequent exploration. As a consequence, nearly all his manuscripts have their own textual authority, and there are few difficulties (either here or in his publications) in establishing copy-text.

Peirce indicates in his 1902 grant application to the Carnegie Institution (to enable him to write thirty-six memoirs detailing his system of logic) that he has accumulated "a large store of unpublished results" and that "those things I have published have been slight and fragmentary, and have dealt little with the more important of my results" (L 75). (We may also recall that his published works are only "scattered outcroppings of a rich vein" of unpublished fragments that "no human being could ever put together.") Editing and (re)publishing Peirce would be a relatively simple task if his manuscripts were all in one place and properly assembled, dated and complete, textual in the purely linguistic (ASCII character) sense, and fewer in number and smaller in bulk. None, unfortunately, is the case—and that is why editing and publishing them is, at least in the traditional medium of the printed and bound book, enormously difficult. Many of his writings present serious obstacles for traditional publication methods, for they are highly graphical in nature. There is text enclosed in graphical figures, graphics embedded in text, text contoured around graphics, and entire pages of graphics with no text at all. Moreover, Peirce used color in his text and figures to make important distinctions and to key text elements to related graphical elements, and he invented many symbols and the Existential Graphs, which are permeated with colors and tinctures. Who can afford to typeset such material and to print the many lists and tables, and mathematical and scientific formulas, in his writings, not to mention his work in Arabic, cuneiform, and Egyptian hieroglyphics?

The most serious difficulties in editing and publishing Peirce lie in the reassembling and reorganization, and in the dating, of his unpublished manuscripts (at Harvard and in the smaller collections elsewhere). Peirce himself dated only about one-third of his manuscripts, and yet their dates of composition are the sine qua non for our study of the growth and development of his thought; moreover, as he made fundamental discoveries in topology, geodesy, and several theorems and methods of formal logic, some of his manuscripts involve questions of priority. Many of Peirce's manuscripts have, in fact, now been dated, primarily by editors in the Peirce Edition Project in Indianapolis. Using information derived from publications and internal evidence, reports and correspondence, and watermarks and Peirce's handwriting, they have been able to assign definitive dates to several hundred manuscripts (especially those in the years covered in the first six volumes of the *Writings*) and preliminary dates to nearly all. But, given the several thousand fragmentary pages that remain unplaced—and will so remain until each page has been carefully compared and scrutinized in preparation for each of the remaining volumes in that edition—it is fair to assume that the chronological fine-tuning of manuscripts (and discrete manuscript pages) will not be completed until shortly before the completion of the final volume.

The same will be true of the reassembling and reorganization of manuscripts, which have been in a chaotic state of disarray since their arrival at Harvard in 1915.[32] There are literally thousands of loose, incomplete, and fragmentary pages that are collected in so-called fragment folders. Although many of these pages have over the years been moved into their appropriate places in particular manuscripts (in the photocopy collections of the Peirce Edition Project and, to a lesser extent, in the similar collections at the Texas Tech University Institute for Studies in Pragmaticism), many thousand more remain fragmentary for the time being. Moreover, certain gaps will always remain, for pages and papers have been lost or stolen over the years, and, especially during paper shortages (in World War II), some papers were actually given away.

Today the collection is sorted into folders according to a variety of organizational schemes (and pages in one folder are often found to belong to manuscripts in another). Robin's *Catalogue* provides the most valuable and comprehensive view of the disordered manuscripts (and their incomplete representation in the microfilm edition). Unfortunately, it gives a greater sense of order than there actually is, and, even here, the topical arrangement has proven counterproductive. MS 1043, for example, a five-page untitled note on chemical valency, appears in the "Chemistry" section and is said to belong with MSS 1041 and 1042, both entitled "Valency." As it turns out, the note completes a now reassembled excellent twenty-five page version of the 1906 essay on "The Basis of Pragmaticism," consisting of one loose title page from MS 280 (in the "Pragmatism" section), nineteen pages from MS 908 (in the "Metaphysics" section), and the note from MS 1043 (whose first page has Peirce's inscription, in red ink, "Note to be printed in small type at the end of the article"). There are numerous other such instances of disarray (and misappellation), for we find manuscripts in "Mathematics" (or "Pragmatism" or "Metaphysics") that might belong to "Logic," and visa versa, others in "Astronomy" that might belong to "Physics," still others in "Physics" that equally concern "Psychology," and so on. Moreover, many a manuscript (or parts thereof) actually belongs into letters—and parts of letters into manuscripts.

Related to the difficulty of editing and publishing Peirce is the question of access to his letters. Only a small number have been published (like those between Peirce and Lady Welby or the few between Peirce and William Torrey Harris),[33] only a minimal number is included in the *Writings* (and earlier editions), and the microfilm edition lacks hundreds of them. And what is to be done with other such private documents as diaries and personal notebooks? Although these are writings never intended for publication, or the eyes of anyone but Peirce himself, many are highly important in studying the growth and development of his thought.

Foremost among these is the so-called Logic Notebook (MS 339), his journal of logical analyses inscribed in nineteen of the years between 12 November 1865 and 1 November 1909. It can fairly be said that this is the single most fruitful and important of all of Peirce's extant manuscripts, but large parts of it are illegible in the microfilm edition (primarily because of bleed-through in its near–onion-skin paper) and only parts of it have been and will be reproduced in the *Writings*. And yet Peirce himself divined its importance to his work, when he wrote on 23 March 1867: "I cannot explain the deep emotion with which I open this book again. Here I write but never after read what I have written for what I write is done in the process of forming a conception." The remainder of the notebook is devoted to important discussions and representations of formal logic, categoriology, graphical logic, semiotic, mathematics, and metaphysics—

but, due to its private and very graphical nature, it presents profound typesetting and printing difficulties.

There are other profound and seemingly insuperable difficulties in (editing and) publishing Peirce in the traditional medium of the printed and bound book. What, for example, is the editor of a selected critical edition to do with a manuscript that has six (more or less) complete (or incomplete) versions, as in the case of Peirce's Carnegie application? Although the compositional order of the six versions can be established relatively easily and although the seventy-six-page version actually sent to the Executive Committee (and later returned to Peirce, with a "corrected" typescript prepared at the Carnegie Institution) is clearly marked, it is equally clear that only the six versions together (some five hundred pages in all) can come close to representing the full extent of Peirce's intentions for his memoirs. The "final" (actually) sent version is neither the best nor the one that best represents Peirce's final intention; for several of the thirty-six memoirs are here not described at all (beyond their titles) or described and outlined less clearly and fully than they are in other versions. Peirce's "intention," in short, is represented in all six versions.

What is the editor of a selected critical edition to do with the four chapters that make up the 1901–02 "Minute Logic" (MSS 425–34), an incomplete logic book whose completed and continuous text (in the central and "final" versions of the four chapters) amounts to about a thousand pages? But there are as many pages again, representing the sort of trailblazing passages and sections mentioned earlier, which a contributing editor in the Peirce Edition Project worked for over a year to map (in several carefully constructed stemmata) to reveal complex and organic convolutions that are no less important to the development—and understanding—of Peirce's argument than are the continuous central versions of the main trunk. Even if all twenty-three hundred pages of this book were published (in the main body as well as in the editorial and textual apparatus of an edition), the printed page and bound book would keep the reader from seeing, at once (or in real time), the full extent of its many evolutions.

There are several other groups and series of manuscripts like those of the "Minute Logic." Two of Peirce's most important lecture series—both given in 1903, one at Harvard (MSS 301–16a) and the other at the Lowell Institute (MSS 447–78) and both consisting of eight lectures—come, respectively, to about seven hundred and fifteen hundred pages. Although many of these were not read (or covered) in the lectures, they are no less important than those actually presented. And what is the editor to do with MSS 601–79, written between late 1907 and late 1910, which represent various overlapping and interrelated chapters for at least three (interrelated and overlapping) book projects, variously entitled "The Rationale of Reasoning," "Logic Regarded as a Study of Signs," and "Essays on Meaning"? Even if an edition could somehow represent all three book projects, and print all seventeen hundred pages, the usefulness of that representation would be severely limited.

What, finally (though many other examples might be cited), is the editor of a selected critical edition to do with two of the best known and most frequently cited of Peirce's published papers, "The Fixation of Belief" (1877) and "How to Make Our Ideas Clear" (1878)? As foundational expressions of his pragmatism, Peirce intended to use them—each time with extensive revisions, including deletions and additions of sometimes lengthy passages—as chapters in several later book projects. There is no "final" version of either essay, except as tailored for each particular book project, and there is no print edition that, within the limited framework of thirty volumes, can afford to publish the two papers four or five times.

The difficulty of editing and publishing the marginalia in Peirce's work is less serious. These marginalia are like those in any prodigious author's work, in that they correct errors and make other revisions (which sometimes extend into preceding or following versos and are problematical only when Peirce fails either to complete his revision or to insert carets and directional lines); provide references and footnotes and give instructions to typists, typesetters, printers, and editors (the last including Peirce himself, regarding his own writings, whether the present one or others); contain comments upon his own writing or that of others and, in lectures, indicate the number of minutes so far taken; or are mere doodles or pen and ink trials.

One last and somewhat more serious difficulty in editing and publishing Peirce's text (and its marginalia) lies in the fact that several early editors (and catalogers) of his unpublished manuscripts saw fit to use the margins, and the text itself, for a variety of purposes, by writing in corrections, notes, and other annotations; in some cases only the most experienced and astute reader of the manuscripts is able to differentiate, whether in the original manuscripts or in photocopies or microfilm, Peirce's hand from that of others. These marginalia serve the following purposes: (1) to indicate, by numerical notations, the inclusion of certain passages in the *Collected Papers* (as "1.349" or "1.611–15 precedes this"); (2) to identify a given passage or paper ("Lowell Lectures/Lecture I/Vol 2" or "Fragment #104"), to cross-reference it with other papers ("cf Lowell" or "More in Box 18"), or to provide it with a (missing) title or even to modify Peirce's own title; (3) to summarize, by a word or phrase, the contents of a particular passage, paragraph, or section (as "categories" or "thirdness") or even a whole paper (as in one of the Pragmatism Lectures: "Almost nothing on/ Pragmatism"); (4) to "correct" what was deemed incorrect or to add (seemingly) missing words; (5) to give instructions to typists (as "Begin [on fresh page]," "go to p 60," "Type 26½ pp," or "Typist Stop"—and many of these pages have, in addition, beginning and closing brackets as well as passages and whole pages crossed out by the editors) and instructions to typesetters, for a number of Peirce's handwritten manuscripts (and a few of his typescripts) seem to have been used as printer's copy for the *Collected Papers;* it is, moreover, reasonable to assume that some of these manuscripts (and typescripts) have not found their way back into the Peirce Papers collection;[34] and (6), most astoundingly, to evaluate passages, sections, or whole papers by providing them with letter grades (as "A," "B+," or "C"—or following the "Almost nothing on Pragmatism" remark with: "But B–A quality") or adding other comments (as "dup[licate]" or "5 pp too diffuse")—all these intended, it appears, to help the editors in selecting what to include in their edited volumes.

The traditional medium of the printed page and bound book makes the idea of producing an authoritative text that embodies an author's "final intention" seem reasonable. Because of its rigid nature and the cost of producing such texts, the role of an editor is infused with the notion of establishing at least textual intention as an artifact, almost as an end in itself. In this hide-bound mode of existence, representations function to stabilize (pragmatically) the procedure of scholarship but also, at the same time, to abbreviate the critical process that is fundamental to the vitality of the collective scholarly mind. Peirce's semiotic gives us the perspective from which to appreciate the editorial role in the procedure of collective inquiry, in which habit taking is as crucial as habit breaking. But, if we hope to establish Peirce's "intention" in a medium of expression, we must invent a new one for the purpose.

PEIRCE'S "INTENTION" NEVER TO FINISH DEVELOPING
HIS IDEAS

Traditional editing theory would give us the objective, in editing Peirce's manuscripts, of establishing *a text* that represents *his intentions,* which would be dubious from the semiotic perspective. First of all, the notion of a text as the data of our experience from which we interpret Peirce's intentions would be impossible to establish with any credibility (as we have seen). Even if we restrict our objective to determining "what he intended to publish," we know from his own testimony that this would be merely expedient and not serve Peircean scholarship. Selecting a sample to publish, as must be done in producing a critical print edition, implies some basis for judgment—as well as enormous reliance on a manageable number of editors to carry out the work judiciously and accurately. But, even if the whole archive of Peirce's work could at least be arranged in some accurate, chronologically ordered form, the original manuscripts would be the data of experience from which the editors work to infer Peirce's intention at any point of rendering it in textual form. Semiotic tells us that "the data from which inference sets out and upon which all reasoning depends are the *perceptual facts*, which are the intellect's fallible record of the *percepts*, or 'evidence of the senses'" (MS 428; *CP* 2.143 [1902]).[35]

Beyond this most obvious issue of perceptual fallibility lie more subtle difficulties. Which intentions, at which instant in time, could be established? Even if the notion of continuously changing intentions were consistent with current editorial theory, how could this be represented in the print medium, with its already overburdened footnotes and textual apparatus? More difficult yet would be explaining and justifying—and keeping track of—the editorial judgments that result from the editors' interpretation. As Peirce describes semiotic evolution, "every symbol is a living thing . . . [and] its meaning inevitably grows, incorporates new elements and throws off old ones" (*CP* 2.222 [1903]). And even beyond this unimaginable burden (the pragmatic result of the feeble concept of author's intention) would be the complication that symbolic meaning has continued to grow since Peirce's writing: "How much more the word *electricity* means now than it did in the days of Franklin; how much more the term *planet* means now than it did in the time of Hipparchus. These words have acquired information" (*W* 1:496; *CP* 7.587 [1866]). Editors would need to be thoroughly steeped, if that is possible, in what a nineteenth-century mind might "intend" the meaning of the symbols to be in order to "determine" what their meaning *might* have been for Peirce. And what does semiotic tell us about the indeterminacy (multiplicity) of meaning? Worse yet, Peirce's pragmatism claims that meaning is always in the future; the editors would be trying to defy his fundamental principle of communication in their nineteenth-century version. These perils, as shown earlier, have always plagued the editing of Peirce's work.

This very problem of accurate interpretation, considering the complexity of continuously growing meaning, led Peirce to his most challenging work in logic.

> No communication of one person to another can be entirely definite, i.e. non-vague. We may reasonably hope that physiologists will some day find some means of comparing the qualities of one person's feelings with those of another, so that it would not be fair to insist upon their present incomparability as an inevitable source of misunderstanding. Besides, it does not affect the intellectual purport of communications. But whenever degree or any other possibility of continuous variation subsists, absolute precision is impossible. Much else must be vague, because no man's interpretation of words is based on exactly the same experience as any other man's. Even in our most intellectual conceptions, the more we strive to be precise, the more unattainable precision seems. It should never be forgotten that our own thinking is carried on as a dialogue, and though mostly in lesser degree, is subject to almost every imperfection of language. I have worked out the logic of vagueness with something like completeness but need not inflict more of it upon you, at present. (MS 291 [1906])

Peirce's work in semiotic convinced him that objective idealism (what makes it possible for us to suppose that there is a basis for common meaning between individuals and even across cultures), in order to be effective, must be complemented by logical realism (what makes it possible for our ideas to tend toward reliable reference in the world of our experience):

> To satisfy our doubts, . . . it is necessary that a method should be found by which our belief may be determined by nothing human, but by some external permanency—by something upon which our thinking has no effect. . . . It must be something which affects, or might affect, every man. . . . The method must be such that the ultimate conclusion of every man shall be the same. Such is the method of science. (W 3:253–54; CP 5.384 [1877])

Self-controlled collective reasoning was, for Peirce, the scientific method, and science was not a body of certified truths or systematized knowledge; he even suggested that knowledge is not the point of science at all. As Hookway explains: "it is not sufficient because 'knowledge, though it be systematized, may be dead memory; while by science we all habitually mean a living and growing body of truth'; it is not necessary because we can take the activities of, for example, Ptolemy to be genuinely scientific even though most of the propositions he defended were substantially false."[36] The scientific inquirer is a member of a community of those who disinterestedly pursue the truth. Their pursuit advances, essentially, through dialogue and conversation and is sucessful to the extent that it can produce testable representations of reality. "Knowing" is entirely a collective achievement, based on our ability to establish the truth of our representations of it collectively.

From the semiotic perspective Peirce's intention was to *communicate his ideas,* which *necessarily* involves three factors that constitute mediation or semiosis: the medium of expression, the object of the expression, and the idea generated by someone who interprets what might be expressed in the medium about the object. Whether the "someone" was Peirce himself (by means of his own expressions in a manuscript, considering the objects of his own thought) or someone else (scholar, editor, or student attempting to interpret his manuscripts about what he might be trying to express), the very act brings a new experiential point of view into the continuing growth of ideas. For Peirce, communicating with himself in text and drawings generated more conceptual depth and breadth (or helped him "snapshot" his ideas as they progressed to keep track of where they might be headed or where else they might go). For those following Peirce, communicating by means of the manuscript with him generates ideas in their particular experiences of the world, which may establish some continuity of thought with Peirce, as meaning continues to develop.

Peirce's concept of pragmatism serves as example by which to show what happens to concepts in communication—and their author's "intentions." From its early formulation even those who greatly respected Peirce's intellect began to interpret his concept in ways that served their own (more limited) purposes. Today, by dictionary definition and philosophical tradition, the concept is hardly recognizable as what Peirce's manuscripts indicate it meant to him. Because his theory is so comprehensive, pragmatism's commonly accepted meaning is not contrary to Peirce's use of the term, but it falls far short of living up to what it might mean to us if we had fuller understanding of the continuity in his development of its meaning. On the other hand, its current meaning may well have served some essential evolutionary purpose and can always be reexamined for its usefulness, once we appreciate the continuous nature of Peirce's "intention."

The essential nature and purpose—and virtue—of communication is *not* simply to transmit messages accurately (what information theory was conceived to do) but also to modify or add to them in the process (to generate new ideas about the objects of our thoughts, no matter how abstract or general they may be). In communication we keep ideas growing and responding to our collective experience of the conditions that confront us—whether they are presented by natural phenomena or by our creative expressions, which together constitute our experience, and whether or not they refer to anything of pragmatic value. That always remains to be discovered in the future.

THE NEW MEDIUM

If not absolutely necessary, it is entirely fitting that Peirce's work has had to wait for publication until the advent of a medium capable of capturing its nature and purpose. The virtues as well as limitations of the book have defined the conduct and character of inquiry for over five hundred years, and we have no idea just how much this "medium is the message." The new computer network medium, soon fully capable of bringing together all previous media, promises a new semiotic era for collective inquiry. Countless methods and procedures that have been established over the centuries to support the current publisher-library-academy circumstances are already changing through technological innovation.

Until now the limitations of the paper print medium have determined what intellectual resources we could create. With digital media—integrated modes of representation under user control (interactive multimedia of sound, text, and image)—we gain new freedom of expression; digital storage allows us to keep track of expressions and their authors, and digital networks give us access to, and the capability to select, what serves specific communication purposes as they arise. Now that each of us has the potential to be a publisher or broadcaster, we will all need to understand better the purpose of the "editorial role," pragmatically, to support semiotic continuity (avoid intellectual chaos and yet not "block the road to inquiry" with rigid structures of control).

Our traditionally established structures of organization and control have supported the misconception that knowledge can be located somewhere. The prospect of a worldwide, high-speed, high-capacity, computer-linking network transmission medium, by which we can learn and research as a "collective mind," forces us (even without Peirce's philosophical perspective) to question our belief in knowledge as an established, immutable structure. Along with the development of such a pervasive capability will come the need to create unprecedented new facilities for communication, collaboration, and critical control.

Great amounts of money continue to be spent on the production of artistically, historically, and philosophically significant work in the form of large print editions. The required critical editorial work, using traditional methods and tools, is painfully slow. Not only does this work need the efficiency to be gained from the new medium, but scholarly work has begun to *require* the electronic enhancement of the products, in the form of computer-based resources and tools. At a minimum these tools will automate (make more efficient to use) such features as tables of contents, indices, and bibliographies that are essential to an edition's effective critical purpose. Such means of finding and keeping track of content will be even more crucial to research conducted in computer network media, and the work of those who develop these means (editors and their staffs) will continue to become more valuable—though their methods (habits and procedures) will need to change in response to the new potential. Unfortunately, just as printers tried to automate the process of manuscript production in the transition from handwritten pages to printed books, we are now trying to automate the book and have not yet begun to understand how the electronic form makes both technological and behavioral change necessary (and in concert).

According to Brian Gaines, we have entered a new era of digital technology innovation and development that will focus "as much on the content and intentions of computer-based activities as on the underlying technologies of hardware, software, communications and human-computer interfaces."[37] The innovation must not only involve new technologies, such as those for knowledge representation and acquisition (hypermedia and intelligent agents), but also our judicious application of them, as they become our primary means of academic discourse on a worldwide communication network. We must become more closely engaged in determining what we want automation technology to do for us.

Computer network technology has the potential to increase dramatically our powers of observation, exploration, application, and interpretation, by giving us common access to far more material than we can "track through" or "track down" by any other means. In addition, it gives us the means to establish virtual communities built on the components of reliable archives, efficient access, and effective communication. With sufficient design and coordination among network systems managers, publishers, librarians, researchers, and students, network communities could develop and maintain intellectual resources virtually, analogous to the way geographically based communities develop and maintain their physical resources. Network community activities would include:

> libraries and publishers collaborating to archive works of established scholars and provide useful (tailored application) access for students in particular fields of investigation to explore that body of work;
>
> researchers collaborating to conduct joint investigation into the origins and implications of recorded events; and
>
> editors, teachers, students, and researchers collaborating to prepare a selected portion of material from a database collection, tailored according to some pedagogical need or research requirement.

Resource materials would be more efficiently available to more individuals, and individuals' contributions to building resources would be more efficiently available for consideration in the virtual community of inquiry. In semiotic terms what are now inefficient relations (in the realms of archiving, publishing, teaching, and research) could be made much more efficient.

In the transition, as we lose the printed page (and with it the book, the bookshelf, and the floors of indexed storage), we will need what Patricia Battin calls a "new set of lifelines."[38] The operations of searching, sorting, selecting, and keeping track of where related ideas seem to be going and where they came from will be essential in the on-line environment of communication and collaboration. These functions are already essential in the scholarship of an individual investigator; they will take on dramatically new "overhead dimensions" in the on-line community, in which communication will be nearly as convenient as thinking.

THE PROMISE OF THE NEW MEDIUM FOR ELECTRONIC EDITIONS

Many of the technological requirements for so-called electronic (or hyper-) editions already exist, but further critical functions need to be specified and responded to in digital systems development, if we are to use these resources effectively in scholarship and continue their development in virtual communities of inquiry. Without addressing the matter of editing, George Landow summarizes the coming impact of the new medium: "Electronic text processing marks the next major shift in information technology after the development of the printed book. It promises (or threatens) to produce effects on our culture, particularly on our literature, education, criticism, and scholarship, just as radical as those produced by Gutenberg's movable type."[39] Our conscious behavioral changes will be at least as significant and necessary as those provided by technological advancements.

Several other scholars, each involved with editing projects, have examined the influences of the new technology on editing to identify advantages and problematic effects. Charles Faulhaber discusses the TLG (Thesaurus Linguae Graecae), ARTFL (American and French Research on the Treasury of the French Language), and ADMYTE (Archivo Digital de Manuscritos y Textos Españoles) and concludes that "the decisive change between the current practice of textual criticism and that of the 21st century will be the use of the computer to produce machine-readable critical editions."[40] Reese Jenkins, editor of the Edison Papers, sees advances beyond machine-readable text into the realm of hypermedia and says: "As we are nearing the end of the century during which images, objects and sound have increasingly come to dominate our culture, we as historians and documentary editors need to broaden our verbal conception of a document, learn the diverse languages expressed in forms rather than words, and find ways of incorporating and integrating into our monographs and editions, words, images, artifacts and sound."[41] Jerome McGann, originator of the Rossetti Hypermedia Archive, assures us (in his allusive essay "The Rationale of HyperText") that network hypermedia "is no more a sign of the Last Days than was moveable type five centuries ago."[42] And Peter Robinson, a participant in the Voltaire and Canterbury Tales electronic edition projects at Oxford (and the author of two important reports on the digitization and the transcription of primary textual sources), concludes that "there are no longer any technical obstacles in the way of creating electronic editions and distributing these at reasonable cost. The obstacles are political, financial, and ideological."[43]

Although none of these scholars details the possibilities and advantages of on-line editorial and scholarly communities on the World Wide Web (which may, however, be implied in McGann's reminder that "the word 'text' derives from a word that means 'weaving'" and which is exemplified at least in the network collaborative transcription process of the Canterbury Tales Project), clearly they are aware of it. The most forward-looking conception of on-line electronic editions was presented several years ago at an editing conference in Toronto:

One of the most interesting possibilities that the electronic edition opens up . . . is that of maintaining a fluid, on-line copy, to which corrections and additions by the editors, or suggested to them by other . . . scholars, could continually be appended, with their source and date indicated. The application would seem to entail a partially new conception of the function of critical editions. . . . An on-line version . . . holds out the prospect of an edition that will form a centre of a much more useful kind: a central copy, available to all scholars, that is continually updated. The on-line copy could thus become a continuing focus and clearing-house for scholarship.[44]

Electronic editions continue to lag behind the new technology, primarily because they seem unable to free themselves, as Robinson says, from "the tyranny of the printed page and the bound volume." McGann points out that "the book or codex form has been one of our most powerful tools for developing, storing, and disseminating information" and that "critical and other scholarly editions of our cultural inheritance are among the most distinguished achievements of our profession," but he adds that, "in an age of print publication, manuscripts of writers tend to stand in *medias res,* for they anticipate a final translation into that 'better world' conceived as the printed word," and that "history has slowly revealed the formal limits of all hardcopy's informational and critical powers." Faulhaber identifies the goal of most current electronic editions as "still the printed text itself, the material object to be placed in the hands of the linguist and the literary critic" and notes that "to date most computerized textual criticism has conceived of the computer primarily as a tool to facilitate the production of printed texts."[45]

The bulk of the secondary literature on the use of computer technology in editorial projects is on word processing and entering, filing, and storing text; the creation of databases and the preparation of catalogs, chronologies, bibliographies, indexes, concordances, and lists of words and variants (and the means of sorting and searching them); stylistic, stylometric, and statistical analysis; formatting, page making, and typesetting (and proper encoding thereof); collating and proofreading; and scanning and optical character readers (and their inefficiency with handwritten materials). But what good is an electronic edition, Peter Shillingsburg asks, if it "simply does what a book does, even if it does it better?"[46] According to Robinson, computer technology will enable editors "to present all the instances of a text in as many different forms as they wish, together with all the additional material they can find or imagine."

An electronic edition that takes full advantage of the new technology will "provide all of the information currently provided in print editions—but in a form both easier to use and more powerful,"[47] and it will include bibliographic information and tools, retrieval and analysis programs, and digitized images of all transcribed texts, whether handwritten or printed. As a consequence, individual volumes will become cheaper and more quickly disseminated and, with more efficient relatability among their "texts," immensely more useful (by allowing paradigmatic in addition to syntagmatic study). They will be more widely useful if, instead of being available in proprietary systems like that used by the TLG, they are made accessible across platforms by being encoded in SGML (the Standard Generalized Markup Language that specifies how languages describing texts might be constructed) and its dialect for describing scholarly texts developed by the Text Encoding Initiative.

The three basic aspects of electronic editions or hyper-editions are, according to Faulhaber, content, creation, and use. In content "the top layer is the critical text itself, but underlying that . . . are the paleographical transcriptions of all witnesses, in turn underlain by the digitized facsimiles of the MSS themselves"; if the edition moves toward a hypermedia system that allows for "the incorporation of graphics, video, sound, and animation," we transcend "the traditional conception of a critical text."[48] In fact, McGann argues that what is needed is a "critical archive" rather than a "critical edition"—or, according to Robinson, "a resource bank" that is "an accumulation of materials without the privileging of any one text at all"—that stores "data in the most complete forms possible (both as logically marked-up etext and as high-resolution digitized images)" and that "must be able to accommodate the collation of pictures and the parts of pictures with each other as well as with all kinds of purely textual materials." He goes on to say that hyper-editions "need not organize their texts in relation to a central document, or some ideal reconstruction generated from different documents. An edition is 'hyper' exactly because its structure is such that it seeks to preserve the authority of all the units that comprise its documentary arrays . . . [and it] resembles that fabulous circle whose center is everywhere and whose circumference is nowhere"—or, we might say, whose circumference has no permanent margins.

In the creation of the hyperedition "the goal . . . is *not* to produce a critical text through mechanistic means but rather to present the editor with as much usable evidence as possible, allowing human judgment to operate as efficiently as possible." Regarding its use, finally, the hyperedition "must provide facilities to allow users to annotate the text by attaching commentaries to it, commentaries which might form the basis for an article or a class discussion, or merely contain a query concerning a puzzling feature of the text. In turn it must be possible to filter out these commentaries on the basis of the author, their date of composition, or their subject matter."[49]

Both Faulhaber and McGann conclude with important comparisons between print and electronic editions. According to McGann, "The exigencies of the book form forced editorial scholars to develop fixed points of relation—the 'definitive text,' 'copy text,' 'ideal text,' 'Ur text,' 'standard text,' and so forth—in order to conduct a book-bound navigation (by coded forms) through large bodies of documentary materials. Such fixed points no longer have to govern the ordering of the documents. As with the nodes on the Internet, every documentary moment in the hypertext is absolute with respect to the archive as a whole, or with respect to any subarchive that may have been (arbitrarily) defined within the archive." And Faulhaber stresses that hyper-editions "must rely more than ever on cooperation with their peers and with specialists from other disciplines, particularly computing and information science," and that "far more than in the traditional print environment, advances in electronic scholarship will depend on enlightened collaboration among specialists in widely separated fields."[50]

THE PROMISE EXEMPLIFIED IN AN ON-LINE PEIRCEAN
COMMUNITY OF INQUIRY

There have been no serious attempts yet to create an on-line research community in the humanities—a network computer–enabled collaborating group comparable to those of the Nematode Worm Community, the Human Genome, or the Sequoia 2000 Global Change projects in science. Unlike science researchers, humanities scholars have little experience in collaborative work beyond joint authorship and do not yet appreciate the potential of a communication medium to support continuous inquiry among members of communities of common interest. Breaking this habit of solitary operation, the TLG demonstrates that (even with rudimentary network support for digital access and dissemination) a humanities discipline can be transformed in scope and quality of research, with students contributing what could not be dreamed of by scholars not long ago.

There may be no better subject than the work of Peirce on which to build, demonstrate, and develop a model for the new digital communication medium. His life's work brought the many domains of inquiry together in a philosophy of human experience, in which communication occurs continuously in the growth and spread of ideas; pragmatism directs intellectual pursuit in semiotically responsible growth, and his existential graphs can lead us beyond the transparency of what has become established as text, toward more effective implementation of multimedia. This system of graphical logic has become the basis for a worldwide group of computer science researchers (collaborating by network communication) to develop effective methods of knowledge representation, called Conceptual Graphs, for use in building automated systems in many fields of application.[51] Such "intelligent" digital systems (with multimedia-based data manipulation, pattern recognition search and retrieval, intelligent database and network management, and user-defined interface access) will be needed to coordinate the work of academic communities in efficiently developing and maintaining their collective intellectual resources in digital form.

Many academics have already experienced the rudimentary improvement of semiotic efficiency in access to resource materials and communication with colleagues; better semiotic examination would guide further development to serve the needs of collaborative inquiry. In these advancements we might even hope to reverse the trend of technology-driven digital systems development and begin to create a medium to serve the new editorial role that computer network technology not only makes possible but also demands if we are to make effective use of it.

Building an on-line community based on Peirce's work as a digital resource would begin with what we could consider the primary data: his manuscripts. Each manuscript page would be digitized (as raster image, character-based transcript, and index record) and could be retrieved and viewed or linked to any other page, for the purpose of searching and sorting the collection into compositional order and for selecting manuscript pages to order in other ways (such as reading or topical order) for specific purposes, as they arise. Network access and communication would then make it possible to increase the contributions of scholars to the editorial process that, in semiotic terms, will require a regularizing procedure to bring their many views together on some (tentative) basis. An authoritative version would be established (tentatively) by essentially the same process we now rely on to prepare works for publication, although new automated instruments will be required to keep its progress collectively intelligible.

In any work prepared for publication an author explains to colleagues how to reach a certain conclusion about the subject in question, calling on others to test it by replicating the procedure to see if they reach the same results. This form of communication can be logically treated as an argument, with premises (assumptions about the evidence), conclusions (results of interpreting the assumed evidence), and an account of the interpretational procedure by which the result is reached from the evidence. The procedure may include complex measurements and experiments, but it may simply be based on symbolic operations. In any case the argument form of the communication represents the author's experience of something (in this case pages of manuscript) and prepares it for validation in a particular field of study. If validation occurs (which constitutes tentative acceptance), the conclusion can function as a premise in the continuing inquiry of those who are participating. The effectiveness of any collaboration depends on such a validation process through communication, even when the contributors are not consciously in collaboration. Semiotically, any particular observation becomes significant only as it becomes accepted in the general context of a realm of investigation. Ideas in a particular field or group will continue to develop in this pragmatic fashion, depending on how well the communication procedure for validating individual interpretive contributions works.

Here Peirce's pragmatism cautions: in any realm of inquiry, in which the validation of individual interpretations occurs by explicit procedure, judgment should proceed heuristically—not algorithmically (maintained by permanent authority or habit of mind). The basis for judgment established by any group of inquirers may, at any time, be mistaken. With inquiry conceived as an ongoing, sophisticated communicational challenge, we know that individual interpretations will be expressed more or less effectively for consideration by the group in a validation process that works more or less effectively to establish the validity of the individual contributions. The collective editorial role in this procedure is to stabilize collective inquiry by tracking the possible directions it might be taking—to construct a metarepresentation (a sort of map of collective self-reflection) of all individual contributions—without determining its results: semiotically, we might say, to keep the *matter* of inquiry (texts or mediational products) from becoming the hide-bound substitute for the continuity (growth) of mind. (Modern complexity theorists might say that the editorial role is to maintain the complexity between order and chaos, stagnation and confusion.) To the extent that we can explicate, examine, and improve this procedure, we can identify how digital technology might truly augment the process, without expecting ever to build an algorithm for its execution.

The flexibility of digital text, with hypertext interlinkability as originally conceived by Ted Nelson,[52] makes possible a virtual community of inquiry that can maintain diversity in its unity: establish habitual tendencies of conceptual development based on collective critical assessment of individual contributions in a continuous mode of development that efficiently tests these assumptions against new contributions (views of the evidence). Hypertext can preserve and efficiently display the course and context of an argument as it develops. Members of such a community can more easily take other members' perspectives on any evidence in question, working to comprehend rather than exclude what appears to be marginal, with the hope of bringing their many views together and learning more.

Technological progress during this century has given us the opportunity to create a new medium of communication for effective research and learning, across the academic spectrum. Now, at the end of the century, we can begin to see that science without effective humanist perspective is aimless and foolhardy and that humanism without effective scientific procedure is blind and canon bound. If we are to realize the evolving power of the new medium—in forms that support the efficient expression, exchange, and growth of ideas—we must be able to examine traditional *editorial* processes and products, better specify their purposes, experiment with enhancements and alternatives, and transform the entire enterprise of inquiry. In the next century the new (editorial) medium and a new (evolutionary) metaphysical perspective may give us the chance to establish semiotic continuity among intellectual disciplines while we pragmatically extend their margins.

NOTES

1. Quotations from Peirce's manuscripts at Harvard are referenced (in parentheses in the text) according to the numbering system in Richard S. Robin, *Annotated Catalogue of the Papers of Charles S. Peirce* (Amherst: University of Massachusetts Press, 1967); quotations from his letters are identified by L followed by the (Robin) correspondence folder number. (Dates of composition are either Peirce's or ours.In quotations from his text, we have changed neither spelling nor punctuation.)
2. Ernest Nagel, "Charles Sanders Peirce, a Prodigious but Little-Known American Philosopher," *Scientific American* 200 (1959): 185. But even in his life-

time Peirce was known as the greatest living logician. Ernst Schröder, the leading European logician at the turn of the century, sent the following encouragement to Peirce in 1896: "However ungrateful your countrymen and contemporaneans might prove, your fame [will] shine like that of Leibniz or Aristoteles into all the thousands of years to come" (L 392).

3. The editions listed here and in the next two paragraphs are *Collected Papers of Charles Sanders Peirce,* 8 vols., ed. Charles Hartshorne, Paul Weiss, and Arthur Burks (Cambridge: Harvard University Press, 1931–58); *Charles Sanders Peirce: Contributions to "The Nation,"* 4 pts., comp. Kenneth Laine Ketner and James Edward Cook (Lubbock: Texas Tech Press, 1975–87); *The New Elements of Mathematics, by Charles S. Peirce,* 4 vols., ed. Carolyn Eisele (The Hague: Mouton, 1976); for *Complete Published Works,* see *A Comprehensive Bibliography of the Published Works of Charles Sanders Peirce,* 2d ed. rev. by Kenneth Laine Ketner (Bowling Green, Ohio: Philosophy Documentation Center, 1986); *Historical Perspectives on Peirce's Logic of Science: A History of Science,* 2 vols., ed. Carolyn Eisele (Berlin: Mouton, 1985); *Writings of Charles S. Peirce: A Chronological Edition,* 5 vols. (of 30 projected), ed. Max H. Fisch et al. (Bloomington: Indiana University Press, 1982–).

4. It is quite likely that additional unsigned reviews will be identified as Peirce's, especially in the *Nation* and *New York Evening Post.*

5. Joseph L. Esposito, *Evolutionary Metaphysics: The Development of Peirce's Theory of Categories* (Athens: Ohio University Press, 1980), 1.

6. Quotations from Peirce's letters to Lady Welby (referenced in parentheses in the text as *SS,* followed by page number) are taken from *Semiotic and Significs: The Correspondence between Charles S. Peirce and Victoria Lady Welby,* ed. Charles S. Hardwick (Bloomington and London: Indiana University Press, 1977).

7. Quotations from the *Collected Papers* are referenced (in parentheses in the text) as *CP,* followed by volume and paragraph numbers; from the *Writings* as *W,* followed by volume and page numbers.

8. Christopher Hookway, *Peirce* (1985; reprint, London and New York: Routledge and Kegan Paul, 1992), ix.

9. Ernest Nagel, foreword, in *Charles Peirce's Empiricism,* by Justus Buchler (1939; reprint, New York: Octagon Books, 1980), xvi.

10. Hookway, *Peirce,* 3.

11. James's definition is in J. M. Baldwin's *Dictionary of Psychology and Philosophy* (1902), 2:321b.

12. In *CP* 5.414 Peirce gives this explanation for the change: "It has probably never happened that any philosopher has attempted to give a general name to his own doctrine without that name's soon acquiring in common philosophical usage, a signification much broader than was originally intended. . . . my word 'pragmatism' . . . begins to be met with occasionally in the literary journals, where it gets abused in the merciless way that words have to expect when they fall into literary clutches. . . . So, then, the writer, finds his bantling 'pragmatism' so promoted, feels that it is time to kiss his child good-by and relinquish it to its higher destiny; while to serve the precise purpose of expressing the

original definition, he begs to announce the birth of the word 'pragmaticism,'
which is ugly enough to be safe from kidnappers."

13. See especially the *Comprehensive Bibliography* and Robin's *Catalogue*. Peirce's
published writings began in 1857 and ended in 1909; his unpublished writings
began (by his own account) when he was eleven, at which time he wrote a
"History of Chemistry," and ended (by his second wife's account) when he was
lying on his deathbed in April 1914.

14. In his 1902 application to the Carnegie Institution, Peirce said: "What has
chiefly prevented my publishing much has been, first, that my desire to teach
has not been so strong as my desire to learn, and secondly, that so far from there
being any demand for papers by me, I have found considerable difficulty in
getting them printed as a favor to myself" (L 75).

15. Having realized that his graphical logic could provide a proof of pragmatism,
Peirce said in one of his Pragmatism Lectures: "When I first got the general
algebra of logic into smooth running order [in 1884], by a method that has lain
nearly twenty years in manuscript and which I have lately concluded is so
impossible to get it printed that it had better be burned,—when I first found
myself in possession of this machinery I promised myself that I should see the
whole working of the mathematical reason unveiled directly" (MS 303).

16. The method and processes are most clearly detailed in MS 311, which contains
this lengthy but highly significant paragraph:

> In the first place, I endeavor, as far as possible, to avoid attacking questions
> which seem possibly to depend upon questions which I have not already
> thoroughly considered at least once. I then set down my question in writing as
> accurately as I can, which is in itself, sometimes, a matter of difficulty and
> doubt. That done I write down in the briefest, but most complete and exact
> terms, every argument I have read heard or can imagine to be maintained, first
> on one side and then on the other of the question. Some of these arguments
> admit of brief and decisive refutations which I also set down. I then reflect
> upon the matter and, without entering into the merits of the case, state what
> the general nature of the considerations appears to me to be upon which the
> decision should be made to turn, with the reasons. I add the indication, or
> sometimes a full statement of other ways of considering the question which I
> know to have been employed or which might naturally be employed, and
> show as clearly as I can what degree of weight ought to be attributed to each
> and why. There usually appears to me to be but one way in which the question
> can be decisively discussed, and I proceed to set down the points of that
> discussion, together with all the doubts that may arise. If I find the question
> depends upon some other which I have not fully considered, I put the whole
> thing aside, until that other question shall have been considered. Frequently
> the original question will take a new and broader form, so that I amend what I
> have written or begin over again. Or it may be that while a broader question is
> suggested and noted, the discussion is completed on the original lines. Some-
> times I come upon indications that there is some other way of considering the
> matter without my being able to formulate that other way. In that case, I shall

have a mass of tentative notes which may prove useful when I shall come [to] understand the subject better. I ultimately amend again and again reviewing every part of the argument as critically as I can. It then very often happens that besides this preferred mode of treatment some others merit some attention, especially if it turns out that they tend to modify the conclusion. I set down whatever seems worth noting respecting each. I now go back to my two lists of arguments first set down, which will by this time probably have been augmented and briefly note, in regard to each one, what seems to dispose of it in the way of acceptance or rejection. Arrived at this point, I put away my notes and pass to something else. But in process of time I shall recur to the original question, probably in a somewhat different form, and from a different point of view; and I am always disposed to be sceptical about the value of my former discussion. Indeed, what brings me back to the question will commonly be some new light in which I see, or suspect, that there is some consideration whose importance I had not appreciated, and I find myself disposed and encourage the disposition to regard my former discussion as wooden and unintelligent. I now do the whole thing over again without consulting my former notes of which I do not retain any precise recollection. Having completed this second examination, I get out my former notes, and critically compare them. Even where they agree there will sometimes be a slight difference which upon careful consideration suggests some doubt. Now it is precisely doubts that I am at this stage endeavoring to develope. Combining the two discussions, I do the best justice I can to the problem and again lay it aside. After a time, usually a long time, the matter comes up for a third time, and I now invariably find that my ideas have, as it were, become shaken down into a more compacted, connected, and generalized mass. I go over my notes once more, work out to the end any doubts that I am able to resolve, and get a thorough grasp of my own opinions. What is not now indelibly impressed upon my mind I would rather it were disencumbered from. For now is to begin a long course of cultivation of the conceptions I have thus far gained. This process I continue to perform, for the most part, pen in hand. I draw up my statement afresh, omitting what seems to be of too little worth for preservation. I criticize it in every philosophical aspect which seems to me just. I endeavor to enlarge it and especially to make it join homogeneously with other results. In that way statements which I may print and which to readers who take them for momentary inspirations may seem decidely brilliant are to me who remember what dozens of times they have gone through my mill, are well-known for the monuments of my stupidity that they really are.

If we take seriously Peirce's description of his thinking and writing methods, as well as his remarks about representing "the entire development of thought of a great thinker," we must conclude that every publication and every manuscript page—with deletions, additions, and other revisions; with references and allusions to all other published and unpublished materials; with citations of letters and private notebooks; and with directions toward memos, notes, and scraps—is required to represent the continuity and full development of his thought.

17. Leroy F. Searle, "Peirce, Charles Sanders," in *The Johns Hopkins Guide to Literary Theory and Criticism,* ed. Michael Groden and Martin Kreiswirth (Baltimore and London: Johns Hopkins University Press, 1994), 559.

18. Esposito, *Evolutionary Metaphysics,* 147.

19. Searle, "Peirce," 559. For the commentators who "ignore . . . thought," see Doede Nauta, "Peirce's Three Categories Regained: Toward an Interdisciplinary Reconstruction of Peircean Frameworks," in *Proceedings of the C. S. Peirce Bicentennial International Congress,* ed. Kenneth L. Ketner et al. (Lubbock: Texas Tech Press, 1981), 121.

20. The belief that thought is dialogic recurs frequently in Peirce; see, for examples, MSS 634 and 637 (1909).

21. For the two *EP* references in this essay, see volume 1 of *The Essential Peirce: Selected Philosophical Witings,* ed. Nathan Houser and Christian Kloesel (Bloomington and Indianapolis: Indiana University Press, 1992).

22. *Saint Augustine's "On Christian Doctrine,"* trans. D. W. Robertson (Indianapolis: Bobbs-Merrill, 1958), 2.1.1 (34).

23. See Mary A. Keeler, "Investigating Transparency in the Conditions of Mediation from a Semeiotic View," *Semiotica* 82, no. 1–2 (1990): 15–41.

24. Peirce's footnote is taped to the bottom of the manuscript page.

25. Searle, "Peirce," 560. Peirce called his theory of sign and representation *semeiotic* (his preferred spelling) or *semeiotic; semeiotics* occurs once in his manuscripts, *semiotics* never.

26. The date of this letter from Peirce to Lady Welby is 12 October 1904; the one quoted in the preceding paragraph is dated 14 March 1909.

27. Searle, "Peirce," 562. For "every wall . . . inquiry," see *CP* 1.135.

28. See Esposito, *Evolutionary Metaphysics,* 169–70.

29. From Peirce's 12 November 1863 oration at a reunion of the Cambridge High School Association; first published in the 21 November 1863 *Cambridge Chronicle.*

30. Esposito, *Evolutionary Metaphysics,* 231; Searle, "Peirce," 559–60. For "intelligence . . . experience," see *CP* 2.227.

31. For the three reviews, see Peirce's *Contributions to "The Nation,"* 1:198, 1:96, and 3:38.

32. What follows, in this and the next paragraph, focuses on the papers at Harvard, for the smaller collections elsewhere are considerably less problematical. Although the several thousand pages of Peircean scientific materials that have been discovered in Record Group 23 in the National Archives are scattered through hundreds of linear feet of the records of the Coast Survey, they have been photocopied and are now available, and chronologically assembled, in the collections of the Peirce Edition Project.

33. See Wallace Nethery, "C. S. Peirce to W. T. Harris," *Personalist* 43 (1962): 35–45. Harris was the founding editor of the *Journal of Speculative Philosophy,* the first philosophical journal in the United States (published in St. Louis beginning in 1867).

34. This is probably the case with the two-paragraph opening section of the 1887–88 "A Guess at the Riddle," which is included in the *Collected Papers* (1.1–2)

but can no longer be found in the manuscripts; see *EP* 1:245–47 (including n. 8 for item 19).

35. Our underline.
36. Hookway, *Peirce,* 67–68.
37. Brian R. Gaines, "Representation, Discourse, Logic and Truth: Situating Knowledge Technology," in *Conceptual Graphs for Knowledge Representation: First International Conference on Conceptual Structures, ICC '93, Quebec City, Canada, August 1993—Proceedings,* ed. Guy W. Mineau et al. (Berlin: Springer-Verlag, 1993), 39.
38. Patricia Battin, "The Library: Center of the Restructured University," *College and Research Libraries* 45 (1984): 172.
39. George P. Landow, *Hypertext: The Convergence of Contemporary Critical Theory and Technology* (Baltimore: Johns Hopkins University Press, 1992), 19.
40. Charles B. Faulhaber, "Textual Criticism in the 21st Century," *Romance Philology* 45 (1991): 123.
41. Reese Jenkins, "Words, Images, Artifacts and Sound: Documents for the History of Technology," *British Journal for the History of Science* 20, no. 1 (1987): 56. (Jenkins has recently retired from the Edison Project.)
42. Jerome McGann, "The Rationale of HyperText," a World Wide Web document whose URL is http://jefferson.village.virginia.edu/public/jjm2f/rationale.html; quotations from this document are not otherwise referenced here. (See also his more recent essay "The Rossetti Archive and Image-Based Electronic Editing," by substituting *imagebase* for *rationale* in the URL.)
43. Peter Robinson, "The Electronic Editions of Voltaire and the Canterbury Tales" (paper delivered at the joint meeting of the Association for Computers and the Humanities and the Association for Literary and Linguistic Computing, April 1994, Paris); quotations from this paper are not otherwise referenced here. For the two reports, Oxford University's Office for Humanities Communication Publications Nos. 4 and 6, see *The Digitization of Primary Textual Sources* (1993) and *The Transcription of Primary Textual Sources Using SGML* (1994).
44. George M. Logan, David T. Barnard, and Robert G. Crawford, "Computer-Based Publication of Critical Editions: Some General Considerations and a Prototype," in *Computers and the Humanities: Today's Research, Tomorrow's Teaching* (Toronto: University of Toronto, 1986), 325. (See also John Price-Wilkin, "Using the World Wide Web to Deliver Complex Electronic Documents: Implications for Libraries," *Public-Access Computer Systems Review* 5:3 [1994], 5–21 [Web URL—http://www.lib.virginia.edu/staffpubs/jpw/yale.html].)
45. Faulhaber, "Textual Criticism," 123.
46. In a private communication between Shillingsburg and Richard J. Finneran.
47. Faulhaber, "Textual Criticism," 128.
48. Ibid., 135, 136.
49. Ibid., 139, 143.
50. Ibid., 145.
51. The so-called CG community began forming after John Sowa's *Conceptual*

Structures had appeared in 1984, with the aim of building "intelligent computer systems" for knowledge representation. Its theoretical and applied work is based on conceptual graphs (and thus combines the expressive power of natural languages with the precision of logic), which are in turn based on Peirce's existential graphs. The so-called PEIRCE Workbench provides the virtual context and tools for constructing and testing models (much as designers build and test models of physical objects), relying on graphs to model functional and dynamic systems and to show thought processes (and contradictions). Conceptual Graphs represent a unified diagrammatic tool that can integrate entity-relationship and dataflow diagrams, Petri Nets, and Finite State Machines.

52. See Theodor Holm Nelson, *Literary Machines* (1980; reprint, Sausalito, Calif.: Mindful Press, 1992) (revised and published at least eight times).

Commentary upon Commentary upon Commentary: Three Historicisms Annotating Richard Hooker

W. Speed Hill

It is a truth universally acknowledged, that a work in possession of a scrupulously edited text, must be in want of a commentary. If you ask a colleague how he or she will use a scholarly edition, the answer will be: "for the commentary"—meaning the discursive, annotational commentary, not the strictly textual apparatus. However laborious, the establishment of the text is taken for granted by the layperson and its apparatus criticus largely ignored.[1] What will *really* be used is what the editor has to say about that text. Yet in the early 1970s (i.e., when the editorial committee of the *Folger Library Edition* of Richard Hooker met to design its commentary) there was little guidance in print as to how to do so,[2] although there was an embarrassing surplus of advice about how to construct a text. Writing in 1969, George Watson had remarked on "how little formal attention has been paid in any language to the writing of a commentary. There is no philosophy of the footnote, though any editor with experience in establishing a text and writing a commentary upon it will know that the second function is usually more demanding than the first."[3] Nonetheless, we proceeded as if there existed a scholarly consensus, silent, untheorized, but substantially intact, as to just what a commentary was and what it should set out to do, and it was this consensus that our "Statement of Editorial Policy" set out to uncover, articulate, and apply to the annotation of Hooker's texts.[4]

The text of *The Lawes of Ecclesiasticall Politie* was published in 1977–81, the associated commentary in 1993.[5] Why the delay? There were two reasons: (1) textual editors competent to edit the text did not have the equivalent expertise in church history, patristic Latin and Greek, liturgics, historical theology, and/or early modern political theory; and (2) textual editors, in our experience, produce texts more expeditiously than commentators produce commentaries. Those of us editing texts could not afford professionally to wait for our commentary colleagues to complete their work before ours appeared in print. To American editors within the Greg-Bowers-Tanselle tradition of copy-text editing, this division of labor seemed quite normal at the time (Watson's remark acknowledges as much). The texts of Fredson Bowers's landmark edition of Dekker had appeared 1953–61; the commentary, subcontracted to Cyrus Hoy, did not appear until 1980–81. The Kane-Donaldson text of *Piers Plowman* is only now being supplied its associated commentary.[6] The Oxford Burton has likewise issued the text volumes of *The Anatomy of Melancholy* in advance of its associated commentary,[7] which is being prepared by a different set of editors in a different country. And Hans Walter Gabler's edition of James Joyce's *Ulysses* has been annotated by Don Gifford, in a separate volume published by a different publisher, as a wholly independent enterprise.[8]

The split is ratified in the *Introductory Statement* of the MLA's Committee on Scholarly Editions (CSE) (successor to the Center for Editions of American Authors [CEAA]), whose principal author was G. Thomas Tanselle. After itemizing the "four categories of data" deemed "crucial" to a scholarly edition (record of emendations; list of variants; discussion of difficult readings; line-end hyphen list), the 1977 *Statement* added:

> Obviously, other information—such as a historical introduction or explanatory annotation—may also be helpful. . . . Whether or not this material is included in the edition may depend on the nature of the work, on the nature of the audience envisaged for the edition, or on various practical considerations. By not insisting on annotation that goes beyond the discussion of textual cruxes [category 3 of textual data], the CSE is reflecting its sense of priorities: the first responsibility of an editor is to establish a text. It is not suggesting, however, that these other materials cannot provide valuable adjuncts to a text. . . . But the CSE's primary concern is with the texts themselves.[9]

Tanselle's statement in his later 1981 survey of "Textual Scholarship," is more balanced: "The editor's focus cannot be narrower than the full meaning of the text,"[10] but the earlier *Introductory Statement* was highly influential and fairly represents the state of the question in the 1970s.

The privileging of text over commentary, however, is a comparatively recent phenomenon. Reviewing J. Churton Collins's 1905 edition of Robert Greene, W. W. Greg remarked: "no competent critic will probably deny, that the business of an editor is primarily with his author's text, that it is in that department that he can do the most valuable and lasting work, and that biographical, critical, and exegetical matter are at once more easily superseded and instrinsically less important."[11] Greg's assumptions remain current in American copy-text editing. The CSE now condenses Tanselle's earlier paragraph as follows: "Many, indeed most, scholarly editions include a general introduction—either historical or interpretive—as well as explanatory annotations to various words, passages, events, and historical figures. Although neither is essential to the editor's primary responsibility of establishing a text, both can add to the value, that is the usefulness, of the edition."[12] And T. H. Howard-Hill writes: "it hardly appears that the transmission of meaning has been or could be the task of a critical editor," and "there is no room in editions for editors to exhaust the meanings of their texts and no obligation on them to do so."[13]

But why should the person who knows the text so intimately be inhibited from commenting upon what he or she takes that text to mean? To be sure, there is the economic argument: adding a lengthy discursive commentary to an already elaborate textual apparatus is expensive. But the economics of scholarly publication describes a situation without explaining it. A more likely cause, as Jerome McGann has suggested, is the schism in the profession between textual criticism and hermeneutics.[14] In the 1970s that schism was itself orthodox. "Critical and interpretive material likely to date ought to be confined to introductions," I wrote ex cathedra in our "Statement of Editorial Policy," whereas "exegesis, which should be as valid fifty years from now as it is now, belongs in annotation" (27). At the first scholarly conference I attended, "Editing Sixteenth Century Texts," in Toronto in 1965, participants routinely objected to editors' obtruding personal interpretations into scholarly editions.[15] Believing, with Greg (and others), that in establishing texts lay the permanence of scholarly fame and that texts, once established, were stable, scholarly editors were advised to eschew criticism that might date their editions, and end users—then as now—resented idiosyncratic interpretations' assuming authoritative status because they flanked established texts in standard editions.

Such assumptions now seem very naive. The very concept of a scholarly edition is itself under attack. McGann is less concerned with editing as such than with assembling a multimedia archive,[16] and discriminating between commentary that will or will not date over the next fifty years has a how-many-bagels-on-the-head-of-a-pin unreality about it. Still, the subjective/objective, critical/scholarly, and indeterminate/determinate binarisms re-

main residually operative within both the guild of scholarly editors—
including its principal funding agency, the NEH—and the profession at
large. As editors, we may dismiss our colleagues' critical practice as in need
of a freshness date, "better if consumed by——," in order to claim that we
alone create monuments of unaging intellect. Yet in the 1960s, when the
CEAA editions were first being conceived and poststructuralism was a
cloud on the horizon no bigger than a man's hand, editorial focus on
establishing the authoritative text complemented the autonomous decon-
textualized text so esteemed by New Criticism.[17] Such commentary as was
deemed admissable—the glossing of obsolete words, the identification of
historical allusions and immediate source texts, the supplying of cross-
references to parallel passages in the same author's works—represented
long-standing traditions of historical and philological scholarship at their
most empirical, objective, and reliable. "Annotation," I wrote, in 1973,
"ought to be factual, objective, verifiable, noncontroversial," by which I
meant doctrinally neutral (28). And yet, while as editors we seek a longer
shelf life for the products of our textual scholarship than the scholarly
monograph typically enjoys, it would be a sad victory if textual immortality
were to be purchased at the price of interpretive silence or self-censorship,
whether economically or hermeneutically driven.

Framing the problem of scale is the audience a given level of annotation assumes, and that level is a function of the intended audience's prior
information. In 1973 I assumed it "would be that of a states-side graduate
student in the relevant fields of English literature, church history, theology,
or political science; an advanced undergraduate in England, in the same
fields; or a specialist in these or related fields who may wish to pursue his
interest in Hooker outside the traditional texts with which he may already
be familiar" (26). We judged that readers from a variety of present scholarly
disciplines, and not just English literature, might consult our commentary.
In 1996, that audience is substantially smaller, less well informed, more
heterogeneous, more fragmented.

More concretely, we may ask: Which other books can we assume our
readers have ready access to? Classroom editions typically do not gloss
words found in a college-level dictionary—even when the meaning is obsolete and the word continues in current use—though few of us would
claim a personal lexicon coextensive with the *American Heritage Diction-*
ary. To conserve space we do not quote biblical passages cited in the text
unless the editor makes a particular point of Hooker's use of them. Yet
Holy Scripture is Hooker's principal source, and it is misleading not to find

it itemized. Instead, we list the citations in a separate schedule, which is more economical of space, and we assume that any serious reader of Hooker will have a Bible within reach and will look them up. We do quote passages from Hooker's sources, "if Hooker had the passage before him when he was writing and does not himself quote it"; we note discrepancies between texts he quotes and a standard critical text when "there is a substantive or interpretive point at issue"; but we "summarize or paraphrase . . . omitted material" from Hooker's own quotes, "unless their quotation will materially help our reader to understand Hooker's use of the material"; and we translate "all texts in foreign languages, modern as well as classical, . . . whether quoted by us or by Hooker, unless Hooker's Latin or Greek in his footnotes is there to supply the original which he translates or paraphrases in his own text" (29). We do not assume that our reader has to hand Migne's *Patrologiae Latina et Graeca,* University Microfilms of STC books, or any of the standard series of ecclesiastical texts we cite.

There are three reasons why our procedures were, and would still be described as, conservative. First, Hooker himself annotated *The Lawes;* our annotations build on his. Second, Hooker himself—as well as most of his readers today—was prepoststructuralist;[18] though he rejected Plato's notion of innate Ideas (*FLE,* 1:74.17–28), he had no quarrel as such with Western metaphysics since Plato. Deferential to the powerful, he was successively the protégé of a bishop (John Jewel) and an archbishop (John Whitgift), and the *Lawes* defended an institution with which Hooker had personally come to identify himself.[19] Third, full-dress scholarly/critical editions, being retrospective, are inherently conservative, poised ideologically between the residual and the dominant.[20]

The first reason is the one germane to the concerns of the present volume. The *Lawes* is a learned work, and its scholarly documentation is part of its original public dress.[21] Insisting on that public layer were Hooker's earliest readers, Edwin (later Sir Edwin) Sandys, who personally underwrote the publication of Hooker's treatise,[22] and George Cranmer, grand-nephew of the martyred archbishop of Canterbury.[23] Their notes on a manuscript of Book VI, which itself has not survived, were first printed by John Keble in 1836 and are reedited in our edition (*FLE,* 3:107–40). While the English text of the *Lawes* is perfectly accessible to readers with small Latin and less Greek, the marginal notes—which supply the authorities for texts cited, quoted, or discussed in cryptically abbreviated form as well as many of the originals of texts in Latin or Greek that Hooker translates or paraphrases—are not. Cranmer and Sandys are keenly sensitive to this dual audience. Cranmer suggests (and Sandys concurs)[24] "that as little as might be were in the margent but rather, if it be of moment, in the text."[25] There are frequent adjurations to "Cite your author," "quote the booke,"[26] and "Translate yt"[27] keyed to particular references, as well as more general reminders: "Looke to the quotations in the margine that they be right and rightly placed. And that care is to be had through the whole booke" (3:115.14–15). The relation between the marginal note and the text is occasionally queried (3:115.16–18, 134.25–26) or a call issued that "Some auctority must be alleaged for this point" (3:116.9–10; cf. 127.6–8) or that he "Cite [his] authorities, both for this and other like antiquities. A bare narration, unquoted, uncredited" (3:136.24–25). Sandys counsels, "I would never have Greeke authors cited in Latin" (3:136.15).

Most of what Cranmer and Sandys urge is familiar enough to anyone who has ever read a manuscript for a university press. What is distinctive about their notes is their freedom in advising a person who was, after all, their own former tutor (at Corpus Christi College, Oxford) and their frankly political aim. While the protocols of scholarly debate are to be observed, the goal remains disputational conquest. The point not very delicately put:

> because this quæstion of Layelders and the next of Bishops are the most essentiall pointes of all this controversy, I could wishe that although in the other bookes you have rather beaten backe their arguments then brought any proof for our assertions, yet in theis two quæstions if you did deale with them ἀνασκευαστικῶς καὶ κατασκευαστικῶς ["through dismantling and contriving against them"], I thinke it were not amisse. . . . What proofes therefore you can alleage out of scripture or antiquity or reason to breake the necke of their presbytery, I thinke it were not labour lost to alleage them. (3:126.1–9; cf. 3:140.6–9)

Cranmer summarizes his advice:

> *To conclude.* I could wishe that through all the bookes you should be carefull of the quotations both of their sentences [opinions, views] and of other auctorityes alleaged . . . 2 that in the margine you sett as little as may be: 3. that thinges only probable be indefinitely affirmed. 4. That in awnswearing their arguments you do not onely satisfy your self

and those which are learned, but as farre as may be, even the simplest; which must be done by persecuting them when you have them at a lift [disadvantage], not by hard wordes but by layeng open the inconsequence of their argumentes as plainely as may be. (*FLE*, 3:129.4–13)

While Sandys concedes that "trueth must be only aymed at" (3:135.22), five lines later he warns, "Remember your adversaries," who will (in this instance) seize upon the fact that Hooker is not always consistent in his translations (3:135.25–27). The polemical aim is to be kept foremost: "I would wish you allwaies where you graunt anie thing to them ἐκ περιουσίας ["so as to bring it to advantage"], verie playnly to signifie that you graunt it not for truehts sake, but admitt it by way of disputation to shew their utter weakenes" (3:140.6–9). Growing exasperated ("I will here put you in mynd once for all . . ."), Sandys insists:

that you must needes set down Mr Cartwrights and W. T. [Walter Travers] woords at large in the margent of this booke wheresoever they are impugned. Els will your discourse want much credit of sinceritie: which in your former [books] it hath especially by that meanes. (3:137.20–24; cf. 139.4–6, 22–26)

(Thomas Cartwright was Hooker's principal opponent in the *Lawes* and Walter Travers his antagonist in a notable public controversy at the Temple [*FLE*, 5:264–69, 641–48]).

Implicit in Sandys's polemical counsel is a quite distinct motive for Hooker's scrupulous documentation of his attack on Cartwright or Travers: the reader is to have before him—in the margins—the very text Hooker is controverting. This in fact is the convention that obtained in the two principal Elizabethan controversies that had preceded Hooker's *Lawes*, Whitgift's with Cartwright and, earlier, Jewel's with the Roman Catholic Thomas Harding. In the Admonition Controversy, to which Hooker's contribution is the only text now remembered, the initial salvo had been an anonymous pamphlet called *An Admonition to the Parliament* (1572),[28] a 56-page octavo in black letter (STC 10847; see fig. 1). Whitgift answered it immediately (STC 25427), in a quarto that reprinted the *Admonition* section by section, with his "answers" interspersed, the alternating discourses being distinguished by size of type, still in black letter (fig. 2). Cartwright's *A Replye to An Answere made of M. doctor Whitgifte*, another quarto (STC 4712), answered Whitgift's *Answere*, and Whitgift in

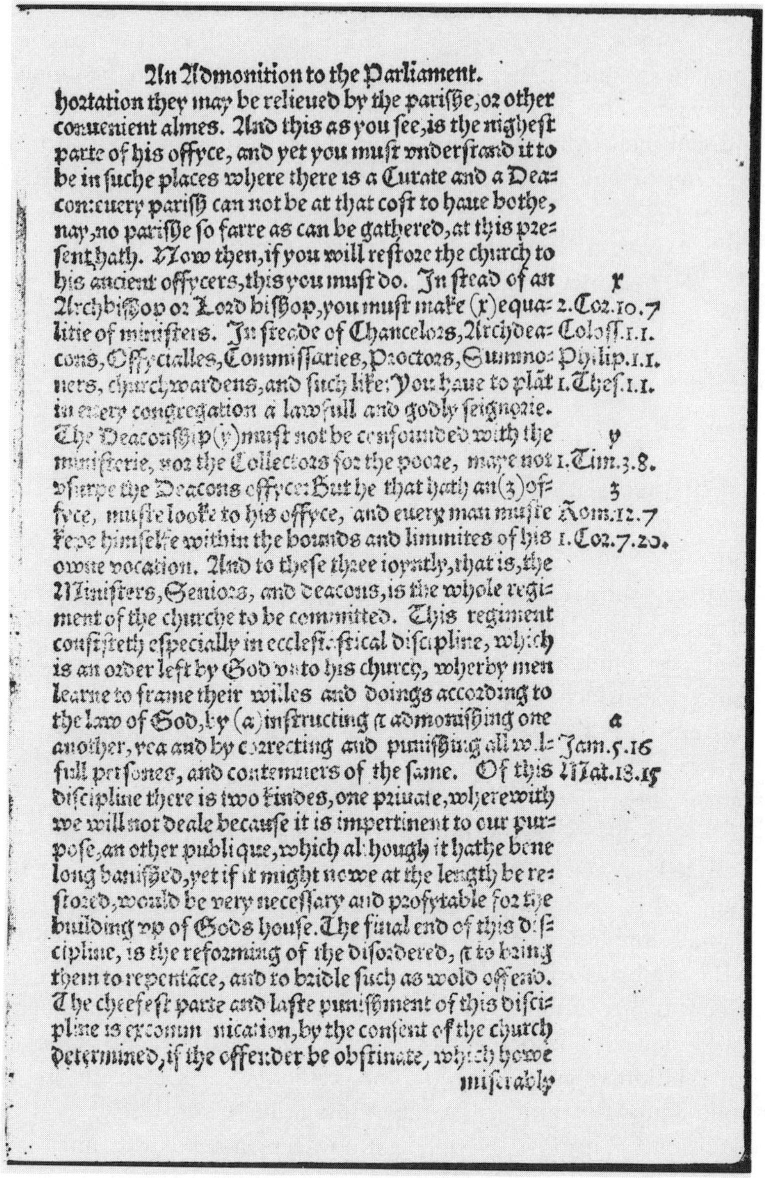

hortation they may be relieued by the parishe, or other
conuenient almes. And this as you see, is the nighest
parte of his office, and yet you must vnderstand it to
be in suche places where there is a Curate and a Dea=
con:euery parish can not be at that cost to haue bothe,
nay,no parishe so farre as can be gathered,at this pre=
sent hath. Now then,if you will restore the church to
his ancient officers,this you must do. In stead of an
Archbishop or Lord bishop,you must make (x)equa=   **x**
litie of ministers. In steede of Chancelors,Archdea=   2.Cor.10.7
cons,Officialles,Commissaries,Proctors,Summo=   Coloss.1.1.
ners,churchwardens,and such like:You haue to plât   Philip.1.1.
in euery congregation a lawfull and godly seigniorie.   1.Thes.1.1.
The Deaconship(y)must not be confounded with the
ministerie,nor the Collectors for the poore, maye not   **y**
vsurpe the Deacons office:But he that hath an(z)of=   1.Tim.3.8.
fice, muste looke to his office, and euery man muste   **z**
kepe himselfe within the bounds and limmites of his   Rom.12.7
owne vocation. And to these three ioyntly,that is,the   1.Cor.7.20.
Ministers,Seniors, and deacons,is the whole regi=
ment of the churche to be committed. This regiment
consisteth especially in ecclesiastical discipline, which
is an order left by God vnto his church, wherby men
learne to frame their willes and doings according to
the law of God,by (a)instructing admonishing one   **a**
another,yea and by correcting and punishing all w.=   Jam.5.16
full prisoners, and contemners of the same. Of this   Mat.18.15
discipline there is two kindes,one priuate,wherewith
we will not deale because it is impertinent to our pur=
pose,an other publique,which although it hathe bene
long banished,yet if it might nowe at the length be re=
stored,would be very necessary and profytable for the
building vp of Gods house.The final end of this dis=
cipline, is the reforming of the disordered, (t is bring
them to repentâce,and to bridle such as wold offend.
The cheefest parte and laste punishment of this disci=
pline is excommunication,by the consent of the church
determined,if the offender be obstinate, which howe
                          miserably

Fig. 1. Signature A6ʳ of *An Admonition to the Parliament* (1572; STC 10848), the originary document of the Admonition Controversy (see *FLE*, 6:384–92). (By permission of the Folger Shakespeare Library.)

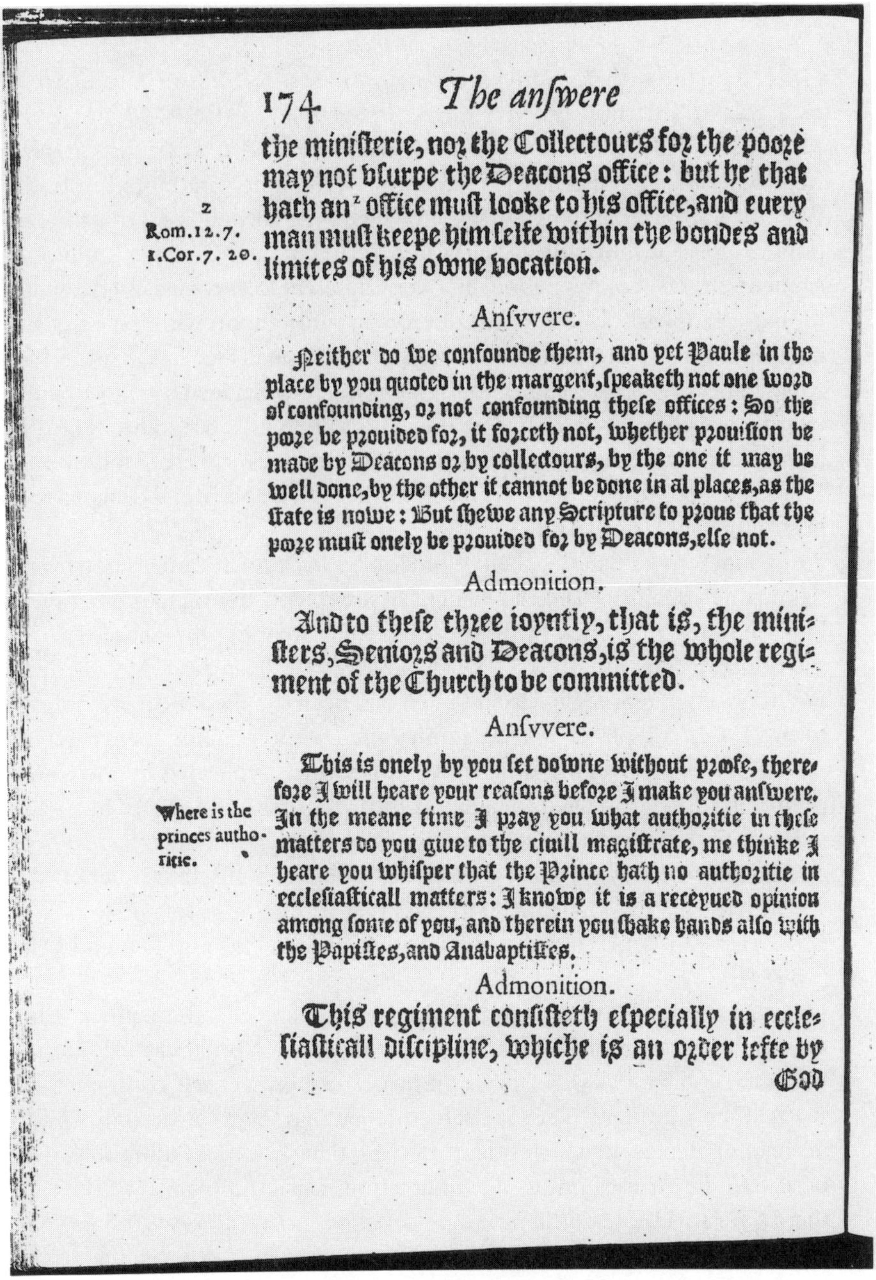

the miniſterie, no2 the Collectours fo2 the poo2e
may not bſurpe the Deacons office: but he that
hath an office muſt looke to his office, and euery
man muſt keepe himſelfe within the bondes and
limites of his owne bocation.

z
Rom.12.7.
1.Cor.7. 20.

Anſvvere.

Neither do we confounde them, and yet Paule in the
place by you quoted in the margent, ſpeaketh not one wo2d
of confounding, o2 not confounding theſe offices : So the
poo2e be p2ouided fo2, it fo2ceth not, whether p2ouiſion be
made by Deacons o2 by collectours, by the one it may be
well done, by the other it cannot be done in al places, as the
ſtate is nowe : But ſhewe any Scripture to p2oue that the
poo2e muſt onely be p2ouided fo2 by Deacons, elſe not.

Admonition.

And to theſe th2ee ioyntly, that is, the mini-
ſters, Senio2s and Deacons, is the whole regiment of the Church to be committed.

Anſvvere.

This is onely by you ſet downe without p2oofe, there-
fo2e I will heare your reaſons befo2e I make you anſwere.
In the meane time I p2ay you what autho2itie in theſe
matters do you giue to the ciuill magiſtrate, me thinke I
heare you whiſper that the P2ince hath no autho2itie in
eccleſiaſticall matters: I knowe it is a receyued opinion
among ſome of you, and therein you ſhake hands alſo with
the Papiſtes, and Anabaptiſtes.

Where is the
princes autho-
ritie.

Admonition.

This regiment conſiſteth eſpecially in eccleſiaſticall diſcipline, whiche is an o2der lefte by
God

Fig. 2. Page 174 of John Whitgift's *An Answere to a certen libel intituled,
An Admonition* (1573; STC 25429). The *Admonition*'s assertions are re-
printed (in larger type) and answered by Whitgift. (By permission of the
Folger Shakespeare Library.)

turn responded with *The Defense of the Aunswere to the Admonition, against the Replie of T.C.*, now grown to an 823-page folio (STC 25430; fig. 3; cf. *FLE*, 6:385–90).[29] While both the *Admonition* and Cartwright's *Replye* were officially suppressed, their *texts* were scrupulously reprinted in both Whitgift's *Answere* and his *Defense*, in which their allegedly seditious assertions reappear authoritatively "answered." Sandys's and Cranmer's admonishments, then, connect Hooker's very different controversial style and format—Hooker's folio text is set in roman throughout, with italic signaling quotation, in continuous unparagraphed chapters (see figs. 8 and 9)—to his patron Whitgift's earlier stratigraphic manner. Indeed, the documentational revisions asked for by Cranmer and Sandys were a significant factor in the *Lawes'* interrupted publication: only Books I–V were published in Hooker's lifetime (1593, 1597; he died in 1600); Books VI–VIII appeared posthumously (1648; 1662).[30]

Cranmer and Sandys, then, pull Hooker back to an earlier controversial manner, against Hooker's evident desire to construct an argument on his own terms, unframed by his predecessors' format.[31] One can see this in the printer's copy for Book V, which survives (Bodleian Add. MS C.165). When his amanuensis, Benjamin Pullen, has been supplied the relevant text from "T. C.," it is placed in the margin if there is room; if not, it encroaches on the text column. This same contest for space is replicated by the compositor in John Windet's print shop; compare figures 4 (fol. 22[r]) and 5 (sig. D3[r] [1597]). When the relevant text came to hand *after* Pullen had copied out his transcript, as in fol. 24[r–v], Hooker is obliged himself to squeeze "T. C." into the margin available; so too was Windet's compositor; see figures 6 and 7 (fols. 24[r] and 24[v]) and compare figures 8 and 9 (sigs. D4[r] and D4[v] [1597]).[32]

It takes no Derrida to detect the fissure between "Remember your adversaries" and "trueth must be only aymed at." Nonetheless, Hooker, Cranmer, and Sandys were at one on this issue, however self-contradictory (to us) their argument. They speak truth, their opponents error; only willful misreading denies on which side truth rests; that such misreading shall not occur requires conscientious documentation. In fact, the only response to the *Lawes* in Hooker's lifetime, *A Christian Letter of Certaine English Protestants* (1599; STC 4707), studiously ignores Hooker's documention. Hooker had framed his argument on explicitly disciplinary (not doctrinal) grounds, for fear of provoking a destructive and intransigent sectarianism. His disciplinary arguments are, in effect, conceded by *A Christian Letter*, and he is attacked for denigrating Calvin (chap. 19), for relying upon

The Prin-
ces right in
Ecclesiasti-
cal matters
694   The defenfe of the anfwere   Tract.20

But if the inftitution of widowes be fo neceffary, why fhould they not be in euery congregation as wel as Deacons: for the Apoftle fpeaketh as direcly of them in his epiftle to Timothie, as he doth of Deacons. Againe if this be a fufficient excufe why the church hath no widowes, to fay that they cannot be gotten, or there is none mate, why will not the excufe ferue the church for lacke of your Seniors alfo. &c.

Of the Authoritie of the ciuill Magiftrate
in Ecclefiafticall matters. *Tract.20.*

The .1. Diuifion.

Admonition.

ANd to thefe three ioyntly, that is, the Minifters, Seniors, and Deacons, is the whole regiment of the Church to be committed.

Anfvvere to the Admonition.Pag.126.Sect.vlt.

*(margin: eathere is the princes autho-
ritie.)*

This is only by you fet downe wythout proofe, therefore I wyll heare your reafons before I make you anfwere. In the meane tyme I praye you what authoritie in thefe matters doe you giue to the ciuill magiftrate, me thinke I heare you whifper that the Prince hath no authoritie in ecclefiafticall matters: I knowe it is a receiued opi-
nion among fome of you, and therein you fhake handes alfo with the Papiftes and Anabaptiftes.

T.C.Pag.153.Lin.vlt.&c.

*(margin: (b) Note thefe
fpeaches.)*

*(margin: (b) What i no
more but to. fee
them executed i
how differe.h
this from Papi
ftes h
(c) The prince
fpoyled of an-
thority to make
Ecclefiafticall
orders.)*

Unto all the reft vntill the end of the firft parte of the Admonition, I haue anfwered already, yet there is a poynt or two whiche I w ifte touche, whereof the firft is in the .126.pag, where hee would beare men in hand that the authours of the Admonition & fome other of their minde, would fhut out the ciuill magiftrate and the prince from all authoritie in Ecclefiafticall matters. Whiche furmife although I fee it is not fo much, bicaufe either he knoweth or fufpecteth any fuch thing, as bicaufe he meaneth hereby to lay a bayte to entrappe withal, thinking that where (a) he maketh no confcience to giue he careth not what authoritie to princes, wee will be loth to giue more than the fworde of God will permit, wherby he hopeth to drawe vs into difpleafure with the prince: yet for bicaufe he fhall vnderftand, we nourifhe no opinions fecretly, which we are afhamed to declare o-
pely, & for that we doubt not of the equitie of the prince, in this part, which knoweth that although hir authoritie be the greateft in the earth, yet it is not infinite, but it is limited by the word of God, & of whom we are perfuaded, that as her maieftie knoweth, fo fhe will not vnwillingly heare y truth in this behalf, thefe things I fay beyng confidered, I anfwere in the name of the authors of the Admonition and thofe fome other which you fpeake of, that the prince and ciuill magiftrate (b) hath to fee, that the lawes of God touching his worfhip, and touching all matters and orders of the church be executed and duly obferued, & to fee that euery ecclefiafticall perfone do that office whereunto he is appointed, & to punifh thofe which faile in their office accordingly. (c) So for y making of y orders and ceremonies of the church, they do (where there is a conftituted and ordered churche) perteyne vnto the minifters of y church, & to the ecclefiaftical gouernours, & that as they medle not with the making of ciuill lawes, & lawes for the common wealth: fo the ciuill magiftrate hath not to ordeyne ceremonies perteining to the church: But if thofe to whome that both apperteyne make any orders not meete, the magiftrate may and ought to hinder them, & driue them to better, for fo much as the ciuill magiftrate hath this charge to fee that nothing be done againft y glory of God in his dominió.

Io.Whitgifte.

*(margin: The Admoni
tors & T.C.
ioyne with
the Papiftes
againft the
Queenes fu-
premacie in
matters eccle
fiafticall.)*

The words of the Admonition pag.126. be thefe : and to thefe three ioyntly, that is, the Minifters, Seniors, and Deacons, is the whole regiment of the church to be committed. Wher-
fore they fpoile the ciuill magiftrate of all gouernment in Ecclefiafticall matters: for if the whole gouernmét of the church is to be committed to Minifters, Seniors, & Deacons, what authoritie remaineth to the ciuil magiftrate in y gouernment of it? Agreable to this difobedient fpirit & erroneous & Papifticall doctrine, is that in the fecond Admenitió Fol.8.&.9. where the authors of that booke take from the ciuill magiftrate al fupremacie in
Eccle-

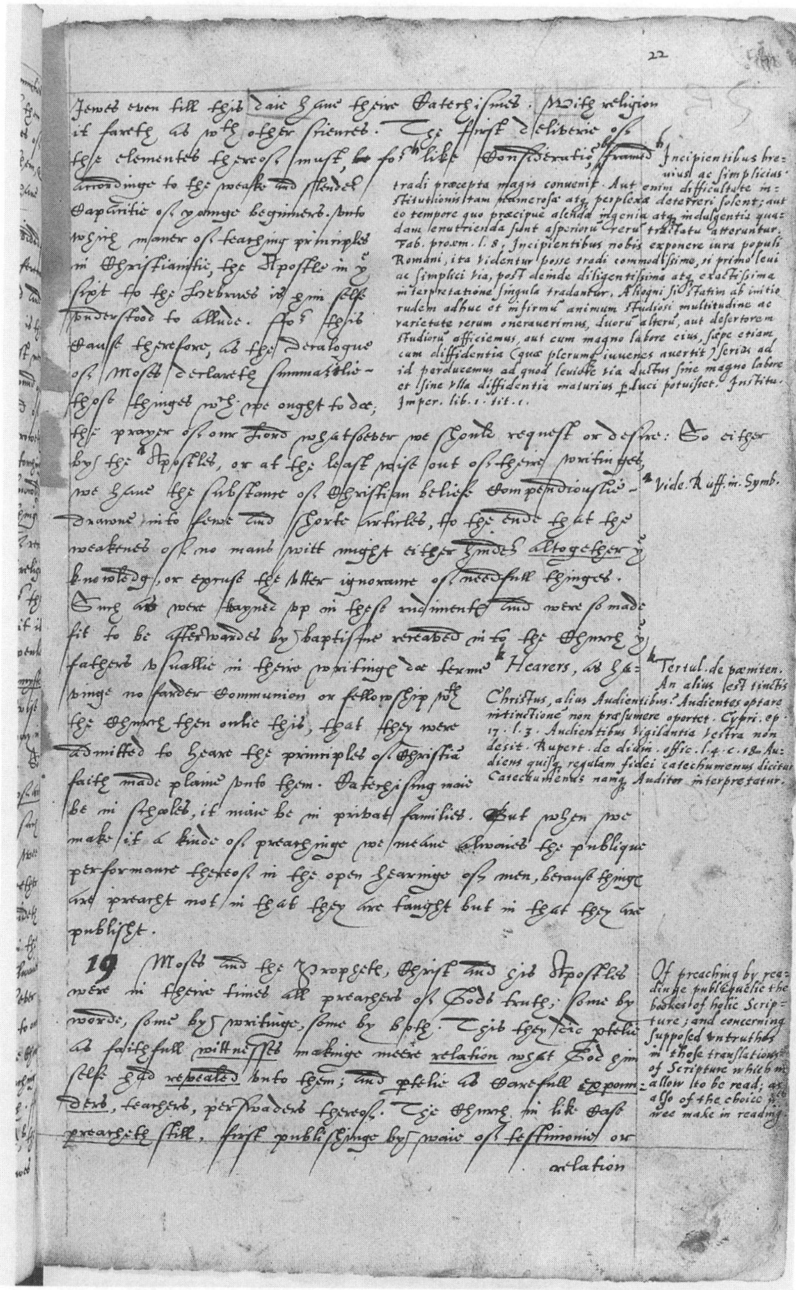

Fig. 4. Benjamin Pullen's fair copy of Hooker's Book V, the printer's copy for the 1597 edition (Bodleian Library, MS Add. C. 165, fol. 22ʳ). Pullen cuts into the body of the text (in secretary) in order to transcribe the quotations (in italic) from Quintilian's *Oratoriarum Institutionum*, Justinian's *Institutiones* (n. *h*), and Tertulian's *De poenitentia* (n. *k*). (By permission of the Bodleian Library, Oxford.)

day haue their Catechifmes. With religion it fareth as with other Sciences. The firſt deliuerie of the elements thereof muſt, for ᵃ like conſideration, be fra-med according to the weake and ſlender capacitie of young beginners: vnto which manner of teaching principles in Chriſtianitie, the Apoſtle in the ſixt to the Hebrues is himſelfe vnderſtood to allude. For this caufe therefore, as the Decalogue of Moſes declareth ſummarily thoſe things which we ought to do; the prayer of our Lord what-ſoeuer we ſhould requeſt or defire: ſo either by the ᵇ Apoſtles, or at the leaſtwife out of their writings, we haue the ſubſtance of Chri-ſtian beliefe compendiouſly drawne into few and ſhort articles, to the end that the weake-nes of no mans wit might either hinder altoge-ther the knowledge, or excuſe the vtter igno-rance of needefull things. Such as were trayned vp in theſe rudiments, and were ſo made fit to be afterwards by Baptiſme receiued into the Church, the Fathers vſually in their writings do tearme ᶜ *Hearers*, as hauing no farther com-munion or fellowſhip with the Church then only this, that they were ad-mitted to heare the principles of Chriſtian faith made plaine vnto them. Catechiſing may be in ſchooles, it may be in priuate families. But when we make it a kinde of preaching we meane alwayes the publique performance thereof in the open hearing of men, becauſe things are preacht not in that they are taught, but in that they are publiſht.

19 Moſes and the Prophets, Chriſt and his Apoſtles were in their times all preachers of Gods truth; ſome by word, ſome by writing, ſome by both. This they did partly as faithfull *witneſſes*, making meere *relation* what God himſelfe had *reuealed* vnto them; and partly as carefull *expounders*, teachers, perſwaders thereof. The Church in like caſe *preacheth* ſtill, firſt publiſhing by way of *teſtimonie* or relation the truth which from them ſhe hath receyued euen in ſuch ſort as it was receiued *written in the ſacred volumes of ſcripture*; ſe-condly by way of *explication*, diſcouering the myſteries which lye hid therein. The Church as a witneſſe preacheth his meere reuealed truth by *reading* pub-liquely the ſacred ſcripture. So that a ſecond kind of preaching is the reading of holy writ. For thus we may the bouldlier ſpeake, being ſtrengthneḍ ᵈ with the example of ſo reuerend a Prelate as ſaith, that *Moſes* from the time of auncient generations and ages long ſince paſt had amongſt the Cities of the very Gen-tiles them that preached him, *in that* he was read euery Sabboth day. For ſo of neceſſitie it muſt be meant, in as much as we know that the Iewes haue alwaies had their weekely readings of the *law of Moſes*; but that they alwayes had in like maner their weekely *ſermons vpon ſome part of the law of Moſes* we no where finde. Howbeit ſtill we muſt heere remember, that the Church by her publique reading of the booke of God preacheth only *as a witneſſe*. Now the principall thing required in a witneſſe is fidelitie. Wherefore as we cannot excuſe that Church, which either through corrupt tranſlations of Scripture deliuereth in ſtead of diuine ſpeeches any thing repugnant vn-

Marginal notes:

ᵃ *Incipientibus breuius ac ſim-plicius tradi præcepta magis conuenit. Aut enim difficultate inſtitutionis tam numeroſæ atque perplexa deterreri ſolent; aut eo tempore quo præcipue alenda inge-nia atque indulgentia quadam enutrienda ſunt aſperiorum rerum tractatu atteruntur. Fab. proœm. lib. 8. Incipientibus nobis exponere iura, populi Romani, ita videntur poſſe tradi commodiſſime, ſi primo leui ac ſimplici via, poſt deinde di-ligentiſſima atque exactiſſima interpretatione ſingula tra-dantur. Alioqui ſi ſtatim ab initio rudem adhuc & infir-mum animum ſtudioſi multitudine ac varietate rerum one-rauerimus, duorum alterum, aut deſertorem ſtudiorum aſ-ficiemus, aut cum magno labore eius, ſæpe etiam cum diffi-dentia (qua plerumque iuuenes auertti) ſerius ad id perdu-cemus ad quod leuiore via ductus ſine magno labore & ſine ulla diffidentia maturius perduci potuiſſet. Inſtitu. Imper. lib. 1. tit. 1.* ᵇ *Vide Ruff. in Symb.*

ᶜ *Tertul. de pœ-niten. An aliud eſt tinctu Chri-ſtus, alius Au-dientibus? Au-dientibus optare intinctionem non præſumere oportet. Cypr. epiſt. 17. lib. 3. Audientibus vigilantia veſtra non deſit. Rupert. de diuin. offic. lib. 4. ca. 18. Audiens quiſque regu-lam fidei Catechumenus dicitur. Catechumenus namque Auditor interpretatur.*

of preaching by reading publiquely the bookes of ho-lie Scripture; and concer-ning ſuppoſed vntruthes in thoſe tranſla-tions of Scrip-ture which we allow to be read; as alſo of the choice which wee make in rea-ding. ᵈ *Act. 15. 21.*

D 3   to that

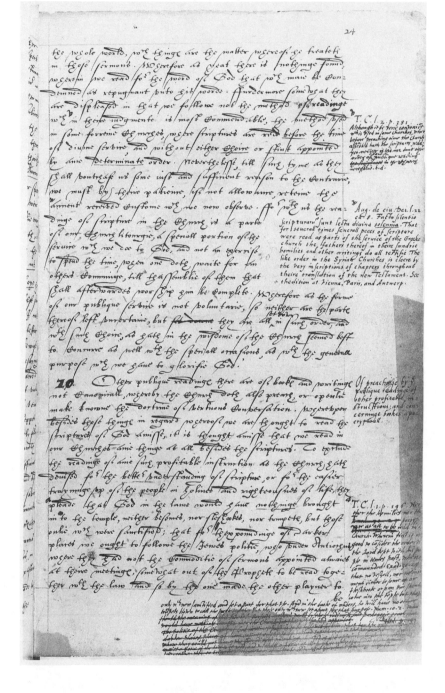

Fig. 6.   On this folio (Bodleian Library, MS Add. C. 165, fol. 24ʳ) Hooker
has added a quotation from Thomas Cartwright's *Second Replie* (1575) in
the margin of folio 24ʳ (n. *v*) and added a quotation to a citation of Cartwright's first *Replye* (1573). Because Pullen had already copied the folio,
Hooker's addition spills over into the bottom margin. (By permission of the
Bodleian Library, Oxford.)

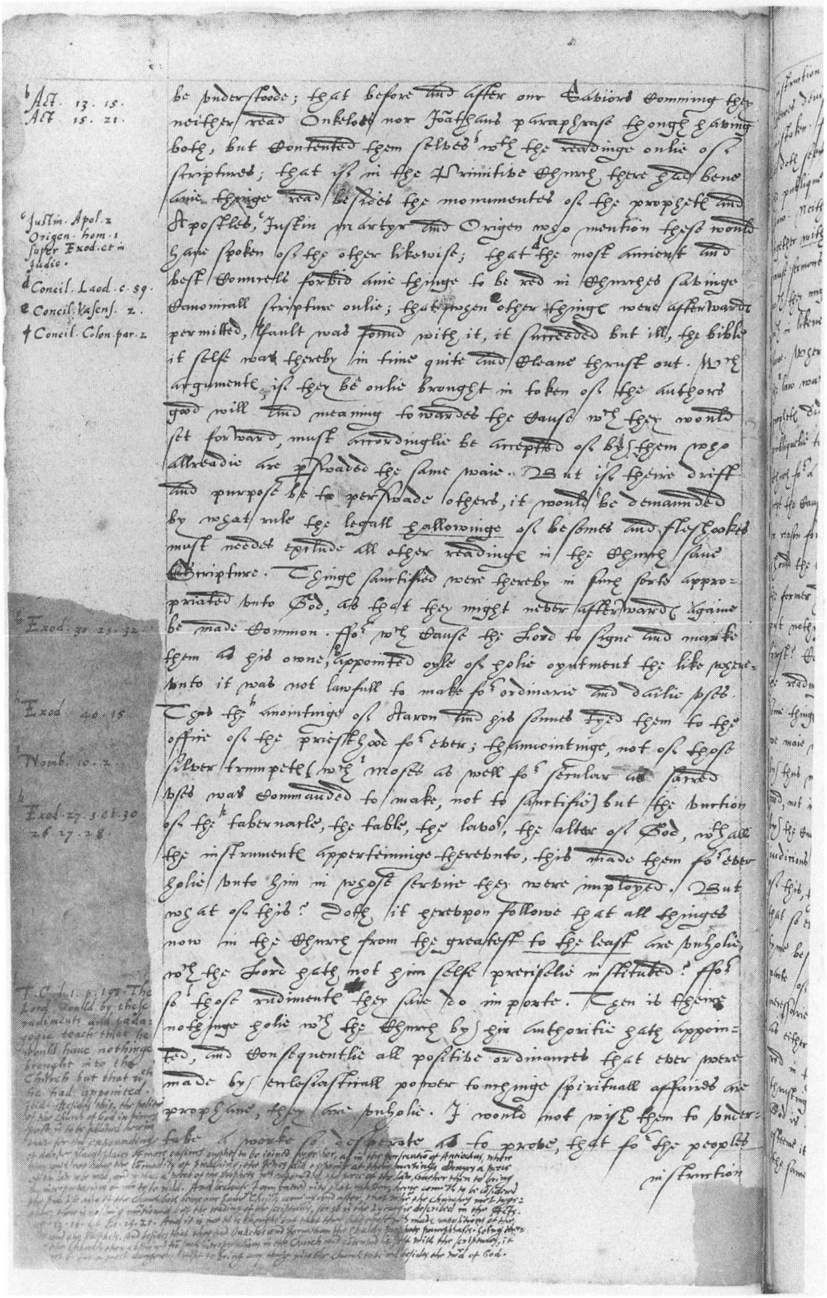

Fig. 7. On this folio (Bodleian Library, MS Add. C. 165, fol. 24ᵛ) Hooker has added to the brief quotation from Cartwright's *Replye* (n. *l*), which again spills over into the bottom margin. (By permission of the Bodleian Library, Oxford.)

the matter it selfe will easily enough likewise suffer) if the Ægiptians being meant by both, it be said that *they*, in regard of ª their offer to let go the people, a *Exod.10.14.* when they saw the fearefull darkenes, *disobeyed not* the word of the Lord ; and yet that they *did not obey* his word, in as much as the sheepe and Cattle at the selfe same time they withheld. Of both translations the better I willingly acknowledge that which commeth neerer to the very letter of the originall veritie: yet so that the other may likewise safely enough be read, without any perill at all of gainesaying as much as the least iot or syllable of Gods most sacred and precious truth. Which truth as in this we do not violate, so neither is the same gainesayed or crost, no not in those very preambles placed before certaine readings, wherein the steps of the latine seruice booke haue bene somewhat too neerely followed. As when we say Christ spake b *to his disciples* that b The Gospell which the Gospell declareth he spake c *vnto the Pharisees.* For doth the Gospell on the second Sunday after affirme he spake to the Pharisees *only ?* doth it meane that they and besides Easter, and on them no man els was at that time spoken vnto by our Sauiour Christ ? If not, the 20. after then is there in this diuersitie no contrarietie. I suppose it somewhat probable, c *Iohn.10.11,* that S.Iohn and S.Mathew which haue recorded those Sermons heard them, *Math.22.1.* and being hearers did thinke them selues as well respected as the Pharisees, in d T.C.lib.2. that which their Lord and Maister taught, concerning the pastorall care he had pag. 381. Although it be ouer his owne flocke, and his offer of grace made to the whole world, which very conuenithings are the matter whereof he treateth in those sermons. Wherefore as yet ent which is there is nothing found, wherein we read for the word of God that which may Churches, be condemned as repugnant vnto his word, Furthermore somewhat they are where before displeased in that we follow not the method of reading which d in their iudge- preaching time ment is most commendable, the method vsed in some forreine Churches, assembled hath where scriptures are read *before* the time of diuine seruice, and without either the scriptures *choice* or *stint appointed* by any *determinate* order. Neuerthelesse, till such time as read; yet neither is this nor they shall vouchsafe vs some iust and sufficient reason to the contrary, we must any other orby their patience, if not allowance, reteine the e auncient receiued custome der of bare which we now obserue. For with vs the reading of Scripture in the Church is ding in the a part of our Church Litourgie, a speciall portion of the seruice which we do Church neto God, and not an exercise to spend the time, when one doth waite for an o- e *Aug. de ciuit.* thers comming, till the assemblie of them that *Dei.lib.22.ca.8. Facto silentio scripturarum sunt lecta diui-* shall afterwards worship him be complete. *na solennia.* That for seuerall times seuerall peeces of Scripture were read as parts of the seruice of the Greeke Wherefore as the forme of our publique ser- Church, the Fathers thereof in their sundry Homilies and uice is not voluntarie, so neither are the parts other writings do all testifie. The like order in the Syrian thereof left vncertaine, but they are all set throughout their translation of the new Testament. downe in such order, & with such choice, as See the edition at Vienna, Paris, and Antwerp. hath in the wisedome of the Church seemed best to concurre as well with the speciall occasions, as with the generall purpose which we haue to glorifie God.

20 Other publique readings there are of bookes and writings not Canoni- Of preaching call, whereby the Church doth also preach, or openly make knowne the doc- by the publique reading trine of vertuous conuersation : whereupon besides those things in regard of other profiwhereof we are thought to reade the scriptures of God amisse, it is thought a- table instructimisse that we reade in our Churches any thing at all besides the scriptures. To ons; and conexclude the reading of any such profitable instruction as the Church hath de- Apocryphall. uised for the better vnderstanding of scripture, or for the easier trayning vp of the

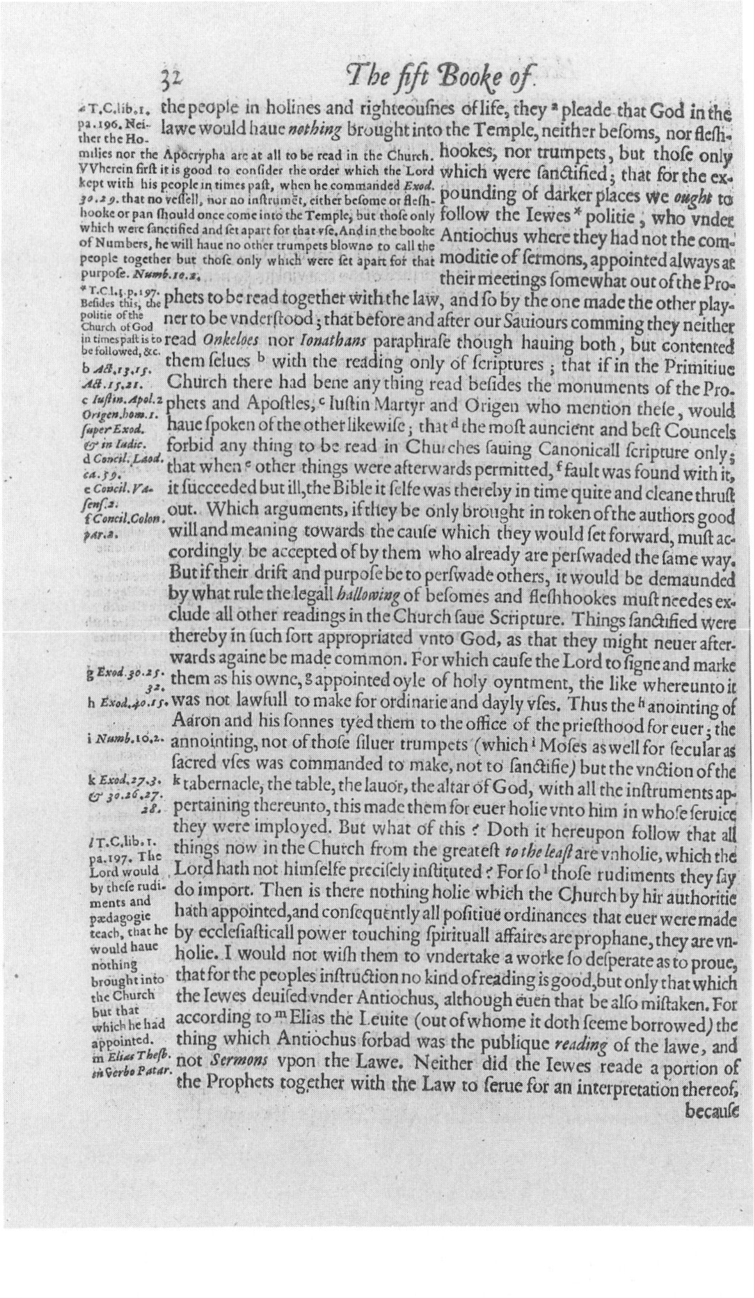

T.C.lib.1. pa.196. Neither the Homilies nor the Apocrypha are at all to be read in the Church. VVherein firſt it is good to conſider the order which the Lord kept with his people in times paſt, when he commanded Exod. 30.29. that no veſſell, nor no inſtrumēt, either beſome or fleſh-hooke or pan ſhould once come into the Temple, but thoſe only which were ſanctified and ſet apart for that vſe. And in the booke of Numbers, he will haue no other trumpets blowne to call the people together but thoſe only which were ſet apart for purpoſe. Numb.10.2.

the people in holines and righteouſnes of life, they *pleade that God in the lawe would haue *nothing* brought into the Temple, neither beſoms, nor fleſhhookes, nor trumpets, but thoſe only which were ſanctified; that for the expounding of darker places we *ought* to follow the Iewes * politie, who vnder Antiochus where they had not the commoditie of ſermons, appointed alwayes at their meetings ſomewhat out of the Pro-

T.C.l.5.p.197. Beſides this, the politie of the Church of God in times paſt is to be followed, &c.

b Act.13.15. Act.15.21.
c Iuſtin.Apol.2 Origen.hom.1. ſuper Exod. & in Ladic. d Concil. Laod. ca.59. e Concil. Valenſ.2. f Concil.Colon. par.a.

phets to be read together with the law, and ſo by the one made the other plainner to be vnderſtood; that before and after our Sauiours comming they neither read *Onkeloes* nor *Ionathans* paraphraſe though hauing both, but contented them ſelues *b with the reading only of ſcriptures; that if in the Primitiue Church there had bene any thing read beſides the monuments of the Prophets and Apoſtles, *c Iuſtin Martyr and Origen who mention theſe, would haue ſpoken of the other likewiſe; that *d the moſt auncient and beſt Councels forbid any thing to be read in Churches ſauing Canonicall ſcripture only; that when *e other things were afterwards permitted, *f fault was found with it, it ſucceeded but ill, the Bible it ſelfe was thereby in time quite and cleane thruſt out. Which arguments, if they be only brought in token of the authors good will and meaning towards the cauſe which they would ſet forward, muſt accordingly be accepted of by them who already are perſwaded the ſame way. But if their drift and purpoſe be to perſwade others, it would be demaunded by what rule the legall *hallowing* of beſomes and fleſhhookes muſt needes exclude all other readings in the Church ſaue Scripture. Things ſanctified were thereby in ſuch ſort appropriated vnto God, as that they might neuer afterwards againe be made common. For which cauſe the Lord to ſigne and marke

g Exod.30.25. 32.
h Exod.40.15.
i Numb.10.2.

them as his owne, *g appointed oyle of holy oyntment, the like whereunto it *h was not lawfull to make for ordinarie and dayly vſes. Thus the *h anointing of Aaron and his ſonnes tyed them to the office of the prieſthood for euer; the annointing, not of thoſe ſiluer trumpets (which *i Moſes as well for ſecular as ſacred vſes was commanded to make, not to ſanctifie) but the vnction of the

k Exod.27.3. & 30.26.27. 28.

*k tabernacle, the table, the lauor, the altar of God, with all the inſtruments appertaining thereunto, this made them for euer holie vnto him in whoſe ſeruice they were imployed. But what of this? Doth it hereupon follow that all

l T.C.lib.1. pa.197. The Lord would by theſe rudiments and pædagogie teach, that he would haue nothing brought into the Church but that which he had appointed. m Eliæ Theſb. in Verbo Patar.

things now in the Church from the greateſt *to the leaſt* are vnholie, which the Lord hath not himſelfe preciſely inſtituted? For ſo *l thoſe rudiments they ſay do import. Then is there nothing holie which the Church by hir authoritie hath appointed, and conſequently all poſitiue ordinances that euer were made by eccleſiaſticall power touching ſpirituall affaires are prophane, they are vnholie. I would not wiſh them to vndertake a worke ſo deſperate as to proue, that for the peoples inſtruction no kind of reading is good, but only that which the Iewes deuiſed vnder Antiochus, although euen that be alſo miſtaken. For according to *m Elias the Leuite (out of whome it doth ſeeme borrowed) the thing which Antiochus forbad was the publique *reading* of the lawe, and not *Sermons* vpon the Lawe. Neither did the Iewes reade a portion of the Prophets together with the Law to ſerue for an interpretation thereof,

becauſe

Fig. 9.   Signature D4ᵛ of Hooker's *Lawes of Eccleſiaſticall Politie*, Book V, corresponding to folio 24ᵛ of Benjamin Pullen's fair copy. Hooker's addition to note *l* could not be included by the compositor, because signature D5ʳ was already in type, and the body could not be cut into it to make room for the quotation; an abbreviated reference was therefore added in the margin above, keyed by an asterisk and in smaller type, followed by "&c." to signal the ellipsis (see *FLE*, 2:74, 504). (By permission of the Folger Shakespeare Library.)

"Schoolemen, Philosophie, and Poperie" (chap. 20), for his intricate prose style (chap. 44), and for misconstruing seventeen of the Thirty-Nine Articles,[33] issues unaddressed by the documentation to the earlier Admonition Controversy.

Such documentation has few analogues in modern scholarly discourse. Indeed, modern copyright law explicitly protects the copyright holder from unauthorized reproduction "except by reviewers for the public press," and a publisher would not normally permit such a wholesale reprint if its aim was refutation or ridicule (a self-conscious exception would be Derrida's *Ltd. Inc.*). When Hooker is not quoting Cartwright by the yard, his documentation follows a more familiar pattern. The base text is to be intelligible to "even the simplest"; controverted texts appear there in English, the original Latin or Greek in notes, to satisfy "those which are learned." Thus, the argument proceeds simultaneously on two levels: in the vernacular for the lay reader; in the language of scholarly citation for the linguistically adept, university-trained reader. Cranmer and Sandys repeatedly remind Hooker of the dual decorums of the treatise's two audiences. Many of us deploy just such a strategy in our own scholarly writing, preferring it to the parenthetical citational style dictated by the MLA, because it allows a simultaneously offensive and defensive rhetoric, the main text conducting the argument, the documentation authorizing it, defending it against possible attack, sustaining it logistically with citations of allies, supplying evidence in greater detail than is deemed appropriate for the main text, even conceding opponents' points in the decent obscurity of its smaller type, marginal placement, or displacement to the end of the chapter or volume.

In this respect the bulk of Hooker's non–T. C. citations are familiar enough. But there are differences. Because Hooker's annotations normally appear in the margins adjacent to their in-text references (normally referenced by superscripted italic letters), both in the scribal transcript and in the published folio, they are often puzzlingly abbreviated. Placing all of them at the foot of the page, which Keble's editions, beginning in 1836, were the first to do,[34] where abbreviation occasioned by the narrow measure of the margin is no longer physically necessary, makes them doubly difficult to read. First, the eye must now glance down to pick up the reference and then go back to the text; second, unless one is already familiar with the work being cited, the citation itself is cryptic without a list of short titles appended as a key.

Most readers recognize biblical citations, then as now, but these too were coded by Hooker for the learned, as when Vulgate forms were preferred (e.g., "I. Reg." for 1 Kings). But the relative uniformity of citational form for biblical references conceals a wide variety of occasions for their deployment.[35] They supply historical analogues (true and false), or they had come to have doctrinal force, or they were traditional proof texts. Similarly, Hooker was obliged to interpret, or reinterpret, the multiple patristic texts that themselves had long histories in the earlier controversy, in addition to citing texts that were his distinctive contribution to the debate. In the first case the citation is defensive, to ensure that he and his opponents are, literally, on the same page; in the second, to point to recognized authorities whose support—alleged by Hooker but novel in the context of the controversy itself—is adduced to buttress Hooker's own arguments.

Any editor commenting on Hooker, then, is obliged first to master a precursor commentary. Again, surviving manuscripts help us. Corpus Christi College, Oxford, MS 215b is Hooker's own copy of *A Christian Letter,* densely annotated with Hooker's responses to their attack (the title page speaks in the plural of *"certaine English Protestants"* as its authors). Cranmer and Sandys had commented on a finished draft; MS 215b supplies the initial stages of composition.[36] Apart from spontaneous eruptions of contempt ("Ignorant asse" [*FLE*, 4:22.10]; "O Witte" [4:53.18]; "A terme as fit as is a saddle for a cowes back" [4:65.23]), Hooker jots down texts to be used in his reply ("vide Hilarium pag. 31. Vide et Philon. p. 33 <et p. 81> Dionys. p. 338" [4:17.21–22]), admonishes himself ("Remember heer S. Jeromes Epistle in his own defense. Forget not Picus Mirandulaes judgment of the Schoolemen. Bezaes judgment of Aristotle. Ad also Calvins judgment of philosophie. Epist. 94. ad Bucerum" [4:65.9–12]), and drafts key propositions and assertions. Actual page references are attached to quoted authorities, whereas in the *Lawes* citation is commonly by book and chapter or epistle number. Again, the basic pattern of Hooker's notes to himself is perfectly familiar: academic argumentation has not fundamentally changed since the late sixteenth century—or at least so it seemed to us in 1970.

Because the later annotator necessarily builds on Hooker, that commentary constitutes a Derridean "supplement," a commentary upon a commentary. Thus, in his first (1836) edition, Keble expanded, clarified, and corrected Hooker's notes. Though all are now at the bottom of the page, the careful reader will observe brackets separating "Keble" from "Hooker." Still intended for the learned, Latin and Greek excerpts remain untranslated. Ronald Bayne's edition of Book V (1902) followed Keble's, though by now the supplements and clarifications swamp Hooker's originals, and translations are supplied. The commentary in the *Folger Library Edition*, however, follows Hooker's text. The brackets that before divided editorial from authorial commentary have become distinct sections either within the same volume (as in vols. 4 and 5) or in a separate volume (as in vol. 6). Only textual notes—and only the briefer ones of those, the longer discursive ones being collected in the textual commentary at the end of the text volumes—appear at the foot of our text pages.[37] In this respect our model was the Yale Saint Thomas More Edition, supplemented by the Bowers-Tanselle dictum that the text and only the text should appear on the text page, not the Yale edition of Milton's prose, which places annotation at the foot of the text page. Our reader is presented with a text page that mimics its original state when it was published four hundred years ago, but as a bare text it is unintelligible to any reader not already familiar with its originating polemic.[38]

The difference is subtle but important. Because our commentary is self-standing, not visually an extension of or supplement to Hooker's, our editors were freer to examine critically Hooker's own documentation, to assess the extent to which he is quoting fairly or accurately. In fact, he usually is: in the overwhelming number of instances we endorse Hooker's use of his authorities, and miscitation or misuse of a cited authority is rare. But, whereas Bayne conducts his dialogue with Hooker within the confines of the editorial bracket, in close proximity to the text he is commenting upon, we reconstruct Hooker's notes anew and place that reconstruction in the back of the volume or in a separate one.[39]

The formal divide between sixteenth-, seventeenth-, and early-eighteenth-century editions of Hooker and later-eighteenth- and nineteenth-century ones, then, is the two-step migration of marginal notes to the foot of the page; that between nineteenth-century editions and ours, the physical separation of our annotation from Hooker's. The first implies that Hooker is no longer fully intelligible without editorial supplementation but that he remains an author whose works are relevant to the issues of the day; the second concedes that the author's importance is largely historical, that it is *his* work that is the object of attention, not the "laws of ecclesiastical polity" that Hooker himself deemed to be his subject. Keble's editions (eight in fifty-five years) found an audience for which the ecclesiastical, social, and political issues Hooker debated were still very much alive; ours finds its users among coteries of professional academics. The disestablishment of bishoprics was an issue in nineteenth-century England on which an informed reading of Hooker might supply a useful perspective. A comparable issue today, the ordination of women within the Church of England, is one upon which Hooker, read literally, is not notably helpful.[40] This does not mean that, in their discursive introductions, our editors do not function as advocates for the author to whom they have devoted a substantial amount of their professional time, effort, and research skills. They do. But it is not expected that they will fight anew the political and liturgical wars of the sixteenth and seventeenth centuries either in their introductions or their annotations. Indeed, it is explicitly stated in the editorial guidelines that they not do so.

Such older historicist assumptions would occasion no comment were there not now so wide a gap between them and more current poststructuralist or New Historicist ones.[41] Just as there is a schism between those for whom Hooker remains authoritative as a theologian or Anglican apologist and those for whom he is a figure of major historical but diminishing current relevance, so is there a schism between the older historicism that underwrites our commentary and newer paradigms. As time runs in only one direction, it was manifestly impossible that such an edition as ours, designed in the 1970s, should proleptically meet the later expectations of the 1990s, its designers being then innocent of the contemporaneous Big Bang of Theory that now describes the Standard Model of our Professional Universe,[42] textualists not excepted. Author-centered editions, devoted (as ours is) to the recovery of authorial intention, no longer enjoy the authoritative status they had a generation ago,[43] a change none of us anticipated. And a scholarly edition erected on deconstructionist foundations is a contradiction in terms.[44] Barbara Mowat suggests that Barthes's concept of a "text" as a "network of meanings," not an authorially centered or authorially dependent "work," usefully opens up the editing of Shakespeare.[45] But, insofar as Hooker's *Lawes* is a work, it was already and explicitly, in the sixteenth century, a network of meanings, and the distinction (which is more Mowat's than Barthes's) is without a difference. Were one to wish to decenter Hooker within the *Lawes*, remove Hooker's authorial imprint and challenge his authorial control, one would have to begin by deconstructing the carefully articulated, preexisting substructure of annotation and documentation that is integral to the *Lawes* as a work of religious controversy.

Historically, the authors of *A Christian Letter* declined to do so, but it would not now be so difficult. The excess of buttressing authorities betrays the work's own internal strains, independent of the conflict between

Cranmer's regard for "trueth" and the cervical fracture he sought for "their presbytery," for such contradictions are necessarily embedded in any discourse of power. A cultural materialist would see Hooker's appeal to natural law as equally suspect, for it "naturalizes" what are, after all, social and political constructs whose aim, obviously enough, was to keep political power in the hands of those who already had it. A Derridean reader of Hooker would seize upon that documentation precisely because it exemplifies the endless deferral of meaning said to be inherent in all literary texts. But to sustain an argument for the retention of the liturgy of the Prayer Book uniform throughout the realm and to defend a church administered by an episcopate whose power devolved from the sovereign as its "supreme governor," as Hooker set out to do, by challenging his opponents' reading of Scripture (as well as of Jerome and Cyprian and Augustine et al.) is to refer the politically problematic to the textually even more problematic. Scripture, after all, was the ultimate term of reference—the transcendental signifier—for both sides. Yet to which text? Masoretic? Septuagint? in which translation? Vulgate? Bishops' Bible? Geneva? Douai? interpreted with the aid of whose commentary? Medieval? Reformed? Catholic? Humanist? on what hermeneutical authority? In Hooker's favor is his distinctively humanistic biblical hermeneutics,[46] his own—for the time, novel—historical contextualization of proof texts offered by the presbyterians. His hermeneutical assumptions are, by and large, ones we remain comfortable with, whereas the homologies alleged by Cartwright between the apostolic church and the Church of England as normative for the latter are ones that we too would be skeptical of.[47]

Hooker was himself under no illusions that Scripture was either univocal or hermeneutically transparent. First of all, it was not uniform; parts were divinely inspired, other parts not. Neither a single work nor a pair of typologically matched "Testaments," Scripture was a collection of individual books, "having had each some severall occasion and particular purpose which caused them to be written, the contents thereof are according to the exigence of that speciall ende whereunto they are intended." Different kinds of truth are found there: "naturall, historicall, forreine [i.e., non-Judaeo-Christian], and supernaturall" (*FLE*, 1:127.22–26). Inspired interpretation is to be distinguished from that which is not: when Peter and Paul "recited out of the Psalmes to prove the resurrection of Jesus christ," their "exposition" is sustained by "*intuitive revelation, wherein there was no possibilitie of error*" (1:31.12–13), for the texts themselves imply that David was referring to himself, not foretelling Christ (1:233.11–12, nn. *h*, *i*).

When you or I expound Scripture, we dare not so presume, for "the operations of the spirit . . . are as we know, things secret and undiscernable even to the very soule where they are, because their nature is of another and an higher kind" (1:232.33–233.2). Indeed, this hermeneutical distinction is itself historical: Scripture represents a period of God's direct participation in human affairs now ceased, and that cessation is a "manifest token that the way of salvation is now sufficiently opened, and that wee neede no other meanes for our full instruction" (1:128.1–3). Anabaptists supply the standard cautionary example of the dangers of untrammeled hermeneutical subjectivity: "*When they and their Bibles were alone together, what strange phantasticall opinion soever at any time entred into their heads, their use was to thinke the Spirit taught it them*" (1:44.24–26).

David Noel Freedman succinctly describes the aims of modern biblical commentary as "explanation, explication, and expansion, so that the modern reader will command the same supporting data that informed the ancient hearers and readers regarding the original."[48] He points out that, in addition to the many gaps in our knowledge of ancient texts, there are complementary instances in which we now know more, not less, than the original readers did (246). *Mutatis mutandis,* that has been the aim of the *Folger Library Edition*'s commentary. The difference between ours and that of Hooker's (on which we build) is that the twentieth-century commentator has simultaneously to imagine him- or herself within a sixteenth-century ecclesiastical controversy and to evaluate, judge, and weigh the cited texts of his original, which themselves have since been subject to further scholarly analysis; the first requires sympathetic identification with a distant past and its often alien historical assumptions; the second, mastery of the tools of contemporary historical scholarship, with its rather different assumptions. An editor-commentator in 1996, who knows both less and more than Hooker (or Keble or Bayne) did, must continually negotiate the gap between Hooker's historicism and his or her own, which itself is continually shifting.[49] As in Cranmer's and Sandys's advice to Hooker, the modern commentator too has a dual audience: Hooker himself, an authorial presence imaginatively recreated from writings four hundred years old, and a heterogeneous audience of twentieth- (and twenty-first-) century users of the edition. As the ambient culture accelerates away from Hooker's own— the Church in England is, institutionally and politically, a shadow of its nineteenth-century self, much less its sixteenth-century one—that duality becomes increasingly strained, and its underlying conflicts increasingly hard to suppress or deny.

One response is simply to withdraw from the field, to give over "critical editing" as inherently fallacious, authoritarian rather than authoritative. The most provocative proponent of the nonediting school of editing is Randall McLeod, though he restricts his critique of editors to their treatment of texts, not commentary.[50] A more constructive response is to acknowledge the obvious: that all textual interpretation is inherently contextual, that contexts cannot be legislated, and that the author of a commentary cannot control, finally, the context a reader will choose to place the text in.[51] Hooker (and Cranmer and Sandys) understood this perfectly well, for the function of documentation as they understood it was precisely to delimit, define, and control context so as to control interpretation, especially the interpretation of Holy Scripture. The subjectivities of the Anabaptists were merely exemplary; laws generally (of which the laws governing the polity of the English church were a subcategory), however humanly devised, were objective, eternal, divinely ordained, and, in Hooker's view, both reasonable and accessible to human understanding. That understanding had both a diachronic and a synchronic component. Historically, Aristotle, Thomas Aquinas, and Henry Bracton (*inter multa alia*) are all cited as supplying relevant contexts for an understanding of the laws governing "politic societies" in sixteenth-century England.[52] "The Censure of the grave and reverend prelates within this land" and "the judgment of learned men"[53] sustained and enforced for Hooker a consensus within the boundaries of which truth was held to reside.[54] The twentieth-century editor is charged with reconstituting that consensus, a task made more difficult now that the author has dissolved into "the author-function" and boundaries now exist only to be redrawn.[55] Unavoidably, the contemporary commentator reinforces boundaries drawn long before his or her arrival on the scene, affirming authorial affiliation by fulfilling authorial intention.

NOTES

1. Jo Ann Boydston ("In Praise of Apparatus," *TEXT* 5 [1991]: 1–13) was unable to cite a single published use of the elaborate apparatus of her *Collected Works of John Dewey*. See also Fredson Bowers, "Why Apparatus?" *TEXT* 6 (1994): 11–19, his last published article.
2. There still is not, but the situation is improving. Two earlier essays are frequently cited: Arthur Friedman, "Principles of Historical Annotation in Critical Editions of Modern Texts," *English Institute Annual* (1941): 115–28; and Martin Battestin, "A Rationale of Literary Annotation: The Examples of Field-

ing's Novels," in *Literary and Historical Editing,* ed. George L. Vogt and John Bush Jones (Lawrence: University of Kansas Libraries, 1981); reprinted in *Studies in Bibliography* 34 (1981): 1–21. More recent discussions include Anne Middleton, "Life in the Margins, or, What's an Annotator to Do?" in "New Directions in Textual Studies," *Library Chronicle of the University of Texas at Austin,* ed. Dave Oliphant and Robin Bradford, intro. Larry Carver, 20, nos. 1–2 (1990): 167–83; Stephen A. Barney, ed., *Annotation and Its Texts* (New York and Oxford: Oxford University Press, 1991); Ralph Hanna III, "Annotating *Piers Plowman,*" *TEXT* 6 (1994): 153–63; Richard Knowles, "Variorum Commentary," *TEXT* 6 (1994): 35–47; Betty Bennett, "The Editor of Letters as Critic: A Denial of Blameless Neutrality," *TEXT* 6 (1994): 213–23; Ronald Schuchard, "Yeat's Letters, Eliot's Lectures: Toward a New Form of Annotation," *TEXT* 6 (1994): 287–306; Lawrence Rainey, "The Letters and the Spirit: The Correspondence of Ezra Pound," *TEXT* 7 (1995): 365–96, esp. 381–83; Ian Small, "The Editor as Annotator as Ideal Reader," in *The Theory and Practice of Text-Editing,* ed. Ian Small and Marcus Walsh (Cambridge: Cambridge University Press, 1991), 186–209.

For older studies, see Alice Walker, "Principles of Annotation: Some Suggestions for Editors of Shakespeare," *Studies in Bibliography* 9 (1957): 95–105; W. J. B. Owen, "Annotating Wordsworth," in *Editing Texts of the Romantic Period,* ed. John D. Baird (Toronto: University of Toronto Press, 1972), 47–71; John Carroll, "On Annotating *Clarissa,*" in *Editing Eighteenth-Century Novels,* ed. G. E. Bentley Jr. (Toronto: A. M. Hakkert, 1975), 49–66; Philip Edwards, "The Function of Commentary," in *Play-Texts in Old Spelling: Papers from the Glendon Conference,* ed. G. B. Shand, with Raymond C. Shady (New York: AMS Press, 1984), 97–104; S. P. Zitner, "Excessive Annotation: Piling Pelion on Parnassus," in Shand, *Play-Texts in Old Spelling,* 131–39; Marvin Spevack, "Shakespeare Synchronic and Diachronic: Annotating Elizabethan Texts," in *Festschrift für Karl Schneider,* ed. Kurt R. Jankowsky and Ernst S. Dick (Amsterdam and Philadelphia: John Benjamins, 1982), 441–53; A. C. Hamilton, "The Philosophy of the Footnote," in *Editing Poetry from Spenser to Dryden,* ed. A. H. De Quehen (New York and London: Garland, 1981), 127–63; Mary-Jo Kline, *A Guide to Documentary Editing* (Baltimore and London: Johns Hopkins University Press, 1987), 183–99 (currently in revision). See also items listed under "annotation," in Beth Luey, comp., *Editing Documents and Texts: An Annotated Bibliography* (Madison, Wisc.: Madison House, 1990), 279.

3. *The Study of Literature* (London: Allan Lane, 1969), 132–33; quoted in Hamilton, "Philosophy of the Footnote."
4. The first version is dated 1 June 1970, and its third and final revision was issued 15 January 1979. Its specifications for "Preparing Annotation and Commentary" date from 1 December 1973.
5. W. Speed Hill, gen. ed., *The Folger Library Edition of the Works of Richard Hooker,* vols. 1–5 (Cambridge and London: Belknap Press of Harvard University Press, 1977–90); vol. 6 (Binghamton: Medieval & Renaissance Texts & Studies, 1993), cited as *FLE.* For an account of its origins, personal, intellec-

tual, and institutional, see W. Speed Hill, "Editing Richard Hooker: A Retrospective," *Sewanee Theological Review* 36, no. 2 (Easter 1993): 187–99.

6. See Hanna, "Annotating *Piers Plowman*"; and Middleton, "Life in the Margins."

7. Three volumes to date (Oxford: Clarendon Press, 1989–94).

8. Don Gifford, with Robert J. Seidman, Ulysses *Annotated: Notes for James Joyce's* Ulysses, 2d ed. (Berkeley: University of California Press, 1988).

9. *The Center for Scholarly Editions: An Introductory Statement* (New York: MLA, 1977), 3.

10. *Introduction to Scholarship in the Modern Languages and Literatures,* ed. Joseph Gibaldi (New York: MLA, 1981), 49. More fully: "Nothing has been said about historical or explanatory annotation—notes or discussions that identify allusions, define unusual terms, and the like. Many scholarly editions do not include this kind of information, on the grounds that the essential function of a scholarly edition is to establish a text and that the textual apparatus must therefore take precedence. To the extent that textual and historical annotation can be separated, this position is defensible, although one would scarcely wish to see the latter excluded if it is feasible to present both. Actually, the provision of historical, linguistic, and other clarifying information is not easily separable from editing. In order to establish a text, the editor must investigate and understand the allusions and linguistic subtleties it contains and is then in the best position to elucidate them; discussing these points is a legitimate, often essential, part of an editor's explanation for retaining, or altering, a reading. The editor's focus cannot be narrower than the full meaning of the text."

11. *Modern Language Review* 1 (1905): 238. C.f. R. C. Bald, writing in 1950: "By common consent the constitution of an author's text is the highest aim that a scholar can set before himself" ("Editorial Problems—A Preliminary Survey," *Studies in Bibliography* 3 [1950]; 17; cited by R. J. Schoeck, intro., *Editing Sixteenth Century Texts,* ed. R. J. Schoeck [Toronto: University of Toronto Press, 1966], 10).

12. Committee on Scholarly Editions, "Guidelines for Scholarly Editions" (New York: MLA, 1992), 1.

13. "Theory and Praxis in the Social Approach to Editing," *TEXT* 5 (1991): 37–38.

14. See *A Critique of Modern Textual Criticism* (Chicago and London: University of Chicago Press, 1983; reprinted, Charlottesville: The University Press of Virginia, 1992) and "The Monks and the Giants," in *Textual Criticism and Literary Interpretation,* ed. Jerome J. McGann (Chicago and London: University of Chicago Press, 1985), 180–99.

15. C.f. S. Schoenbaum, writing of Irving Ribner's edition of Marlowe (New York: Odyssey Press, 1963) and referring to "a highly controversial interpretation of *Faustus*" that Ribner had offered in his critical introduction: "The *raison d'être,* as I see it, of such an edition is to provide a sound text and such aids to the understanding as glosses for difficult, obscure, or archaic words and phrases. When the editor proceeds beyond these limited objectives to indulge in fancy

criticism, is he not in effect having a free ride at the expense of a captive audience that has paid its money for the plays?" (*Editing Sixteenth Century Texts,* 20).

16. *TEXT 7* (1994): 95–105.

17. D. C. Greetham, "Textual and Literary Theory: Redrawing the Matrix," *Studies in Bibliography* 42 (1989): 1 and nn. 3–4.

18. See W. Speed Hill, "Scripture as Text, Text as Scripture: The Example of Richard Hooker," *TEXT 9* (1996): 93–110.

19. In *Puritans and Anglicans? Presbyterianism and English Conformist Thought from Whitgift to Hooker* (London: Unwin Hyman, 1990) Peter Lake argues that Hooker's agenda was not wholly defensive but that, under the cover of his conformist apologetic for the status quo, he was in fact creating what has subsequently come to be known as "Anglicanism" (see chap. 4, esp. 225–30).

20. See W. Speed Hill, "The Politics of Funding," *TEXT 6* (1994): 93–99.

21. Although some of Hooker's *Tractates and Sermons* are quite as learned as the *Lawes,* they were not published in his lifetime, and they lack this element of self-presentation. To annotate them the editor is obliged to start ab ovo. No reference supplied by Hooker in the text of *Of Pride,* for example, hints that Aristotle's *Nicomachean Ethics* was an important source (*FLE,* 5:800–831), whereas in the *Lawes* both Aristotle's *Politics* and the *Ethics* are regularly cited.

22. See C. J. Sisson, *The Judicious Marriage of Richard Hooker and the Birth of the "Laws of Ecclesiastical Polity"* (Cambridge: Cambridge University Press, 1940). The younger Sandys was the son of the archbishop of York, of the same name.

23. On the relation of these early readers to the character of the *Lawes'* self-presentation, see William P. Haugaard's introduction to The Preface (*FLE,* 6:51–62).

24. Sandys had Cranmer's notes before him as he prepared his; "those wherein I thoroughly agree . . . I will note with this mark. + If I happen clearly to dissent, I will note them with this mark. O. The rest I will leave unmarked" (*FLE,* 3:130.14–17).

25. *FLE,* 3:108.21–22. Cf. 111.16–17; 112.4–6, –2–1; 116.–8–7; 118.1–2.

26. *FLE,* 3:108.–2; 110.2. Cf. 115.10, 15, –4; 116.3, 20–22; 121.–3; 132.19–20; 134.–1; 136.20; 137.11, 14, 15, 16.

27. *FLE,* 117.–3; 123.17, 22; 127.18–19; 132.4.

28. It is now thought to be by John Field and Thomas Wilcox. Apart from volume 6 of the *FLE,* see Peter Milward, *Religious Controversies of the Elizabethan Age: A Survey of Printed Sources* (Lincoln and London: University of Nebraska Press, 1977), 29–33.

29. Cartwright's two responses to Whitgift's *Defense, The Second Replie . . . Agaynst Master Doctor Whitgiftes Second Answer* (1575) and *The Rest of the Second Replie . . . Agaynst Master Doctor Whitgifts Second Answer* (1577), added, respectively, 710 and 285 pages. They were never formally answered, although Hooker cites from both.

30. See W. Speed Hill, "The Evolution of Hooker's *Laws of Ecclesiastical Polity,*" in *Studies in Richard Hooker: Essays Preliminary to an Edition of his Works* (Cleveland and London: Press of Case Western Reserve University, 1972), 117–58;

FLE, 6:51–62, 187–93. Book VII, published by John Gauden early in the Restoration, may well reflect the state of Hooker's unrevised text (i.e., the state analogous to the draft version of Book VI that Cranmer and Sandys comment on), whereas Book V inserts long excerpts from Cartwright, frequently keyed only to Hooker's own chapter headings—evidence, I would argue, of its having been substantially revised prior to its publication late in 1597.

31. Richard Helgerson remarks of Milton's *Defense of the English People:* it is "a book so dependent for its emphases and structure on the work of its opponent that it can scarcely claim an independent existence" (see *Self-Crowned Laureates: Spenser, Jonson, Milton, and the Literary System* [Berkeley: University of California Press, 1983], 274–75).

32. In reviewing Pullen's fair copy for the press, Hooker inserted some thirty-eight additional notes—some evidently while the work was being set in type (*FLE*, 2:504).

33. See *FLE*, 4:9–53. As Patrick Collinson pointed out at the recent Hooker conference (Washington, D.C., 24–26 September 1993), the authors of *A Christian Letter* were right: Hooker was indeed attempting a redefinition of the Church of England (cf. Lake, *Puritans and Anglicans?*) and so had substantive grounds for distancing himself from the format of the earlier Whitgift-Cartwright controversy.

34. Evelyn B. Tribble's essay in this volume dates the shift from "early in the eighteenth century." I place it, as regards Hooker's *Works*, in the late eighteenth century, specifically 1793, the date of the first three-volume octavo edition. Format seems determinative here. The last folio reprint (1723) retains side notes, cutting into the text when the quotation is extensive. These migrate to the foot of the text page in the 1793 Oxford University Press edition and its subsequent reprints (1807, 1820); the practice is followed in the 1821 octavo printed for John Bumpus and others and by Benjamin Hanbury in his edition of 1825, in which Hanbury placed his own additions within brackets.

35. For a census of Hooker's scriptural citations, see the two indices of scriptural references in *FLE* (5:851–909 and 6:1101–56).

36. The *FLE* reprints both the tract and Hooker's marginalia in volume 4. In addition, newly discovered manuscripts at Trinity College, Dublin, supply further notes on Hooker's contemplated riposte to *A Christian Letter* as well as extensive notes on Book VIII of the *Lawes* (see *FLE*, 3:462–554; 4:83–97; 6:233–47, 1055–99).

37. As prescribed by G. Thomas Tanselle in "Some Principles for Editorial Apparatus," *Studies in Bibliography* 25 (1972): 41–88; reprinted in *Selected Studies in Bibliography* (Charlottesville: University Press of Virginia for the Bibliographical Society of the University of Virginia, 1979).

38. Were I doing it again, I would place *all* textual commentary on the text page, not divided between footnotes on the text page and a textual commentary relegated to an appendix, but, given the pragmatically necessary division of labor between textual and commentary editors, I would still opt for a commentary that follows the text, whether in the same volumes (as in our vols. 4–5) or in a separate one (as in our vol. 6).

39. As to the utility of having the commentary and text in the same volumes (as in the Yale *More*) or in volumes devoted wholly to commentary (as in the Oxford *Ben Jonson*), one could argue either way. Practically, it was necessary that we get out our text volumes as they were completed in order to secure ongoing NEH and CUNY funding, itself dependent on editorial productivity as well as the professional survival for the general editor. Additionally, in our experience the textual editor could produce a text far more expeditiously than a commentator could properly annotate it, though the commentary editor could have materially assisted the textual editor in establishing the correct reading, especially for the controverted, posthumously published Books VI-VIII, had the work of the two editors been better synchronized.

40. He allows baptism by women (i.e., midwives) in an emergency, but he is opposed to women as teachers or priests: "To make wemen teachers in the howse of God were a grosse absurditie," he avers, citing 1 Timothy 2:12 (*FLE*, 2:269.1–3 and n. z). Stephen Sykes argues differently (see "Richard Hooker and the Ordination of Women to the Priesthood," *Sewanee Theological Review* 36, no. 2 [Easter 1993]: 200–214).

41. For an acute analyses of the shifting sands of historicism, see J. C. C. Mays, "Editing Coleridge in the Historicized Present," *TEXT* 8 (1995): 217–38; and Small, "Editor as Annotator as Ideal Reader."

42. Brian Vickers (*Appropriating Shakespeare: Contemporary Critical Quarrels* [New Haven: Yale University Press, 1993]) dates the origin of what has come to be called "poststructuralism" from the student uprisings in Paris in the spring of 1968. For the dates of the Hooker edition's "Statement of Editorial Policy," see n. 4.

43. See my review of papers from "New Directions in Textual Studies" (Harry Ransom conference, University of Texas, 30 March–1 April 1989) *Library Chronicle of the University of Texas at Austin* 20, nos. 1–2 (1990), in *TEXT* 6:370–82; and "The Jutting Ledge: Editorial Theory Today," reviewing *Palimpsest: Editorial Theory in the Humanities,* ed George Bornstein and Ralph G. Williams (Ann Arbor: University of Michigan Press, 1993), for *Yeats: An Annual of Critical and Textual Studies,* forthcoming.

44. Cf. Small, "Editor as Annotator as Ideal Reader," 191.

45. "The Problem of Shakespeare's Text(s)," MS (distributed to members of the Folger Institute's 1993 seminar on "Editing after Poststructuralism").

46. See William P. Haugaard, "Introduction, Books II, III, & IV," *FLE*, 6:153–68.

47. See Haugaard, n. 41; and Hill, "Scripture as Text, Text as Scripture." On Hooker's biblical hermeutics, see Egil Grislis, "The Hermeneutical Problem in Richard Hooker," *Studies in Richard Hooker* (1972): 159–206.

48. "Editing the Editors: Translation and Elucidation of the Text of the Bible," in *Palimpsest,* ed. Bornstein and Williams, 245. Freedman is the general editor of the Anchor Bible Commentary Series and the Anchor Bible Reference Library.

49. Ralph Hanna III speaks to the issue of the problematic, anachronistic, and excessive "plenitude" of information that contemporary annotators bring to earlier texts in "Annotating *Piers Plowman*," 158. Small analogously speaks of the annotator as the "ideal, perfectly knowledgeable, and perfectly competent

reader" but notes that "the problem is not simply that no such reader exists. Rather, it is that no such reader *can* exist" ("The Editor as Annotator as Ideal Reader," 189).

50. See, inter alia, "*from* Tranceformations in the Text of 'Orlando Furioso,'" in "New Directions in Textual Studies," 61–85; and my review, *TEXT* 6 (1994): 370–82. Other scholars (e.g., Michael Warren and Steven Urkowitz) have expressed a preference for unedited texts, especially of Shakespeare's plays.

51. See Gerald Graff, "Determinacy/Indeterminacy," in *Critical Terms for Literary Study*, ed. Frank Lentricchia and Thomas McLaughlin, chapter 12 (Chicago and London: University of Chicago Press, 1990).

52. See W. D. J. Cargill Thompson, "The Philosopher of the 'Politic Society': Richard Hooker as Political Thinker," *Studies in Richard Hooker* (1972): 3–76; reprinted in *Studies in the Reformation: Luther to Hooker*, ed. C. W. Dugmore (London: Athlone Press, 1980).

53. As Hooker noted on the title page of the 1599 quarto of *A Christian Letter*: "All thinges written in this book I humblie and meekly submitt to the Censure of the grave and reverend prelates within this land, to the judgment of learned men, and the sober consideration of all others. Wherein I maie happilie erre as others before me have done, but an heretike by the help of almighty God I will never be" (*FLE*, 4:5). Keble used this as the epigraph to his edition (1:iv).

54. On the importance of consensus in Hooker, see Egil Grislis, "The Role of *Consensus* in Richard Hooker's Method of Theological Inquiry," in *The Heritage of Christian Thought: Essays in Honor of Robert Lawry Calhoun*, ed. Robert E. Cushman and Egil Grislis (New York: Harper and Row, 1965), 64–88.

55. See *Redrawing the Boundaries: The Transformation of English and American Studies*, ed. Stephen Greenblatt and Giles Gunn (New York: MLA, 1992).

Contributors

William L. Andrews is E. Maynard Adams Professor of English at the University of North Carolina at Chapel Hill. He is a coeditor of the *Norton Anthology of African American Literature* (1996) and the *Oxford Companion to African American Literature* (1997) and the general editor of Wisconsin Studies in American Autobiography.

Jonathan Bate is King Alfred Professor of English Literature at the University of Liverpool. Among his recent books are the Arden edition of *Titus Andronicus* (1995) and *Shakespeare: An Illustrated Stage History* (1996).

Thomas L. Berger is Piskor Professor of English, St. Lawrence University. He is coeditor of *New Variorum HENRY V* and author of a recent article on "Looking for Shakespeare in Caroline England." He is also a former editor of the New Cambridge *Troilus and Cressida*.

Michael Camille is Professor of Art at the University of Chicago. He is author of *The Gothic Idol: Ideology and Image-Making in the Medieval Art* and *Image on the Edge: The Margins of Medieval Art*. His current research interests include medieval art theory and relationship between science and art in the Gothic period.

Jonathan Goldberg is Sir William Osler Professor of English Literature at The Johns Hopkins University and also holds appointment as Professor of English at Duke University. He recently completed the manuscript of a book, *Desiring Women Writers in the English Renaissance*. The essay in this volume is part of work in progress on the relationships between colonialism and the history of sexuality.

David Greetham is Distinguished Professor of English and Medieval Studies at CUNY Graduate School. He has edited Trevisa and Hoccleve, and his books include *Textual Scholarship: An Introduction* and *Theories of the Text*. He is also editor of MLA's *Scholarly Editing: A Guide to Research* and coeditor of *TEXT: An Interdisciplinary Annual of Textual Studies*. He is at work on a hypermedia research archive of citation and digital morphing.

W. Speed Hill is General Editor of *The Folger Library Edition of the Works of Richard Hooker*. He teaches English at Lehman College and The Graduate Center, CUNY, and is coeditor of *TEXT: An Interdisciplinary Annual of Textual Studies*.

Mary Keeler is Senior Research Scholar in the Center for the Humanities at the University of Washington and Research Associate at Indiana University, where she serves as consultant to the Peirce On-Line Resource Testbed Project in the effort to create a computer-mediated, collaborative editing environment, as a first step toward building a network-distributed database of the entire work of the philosopher-scientist Charles S. Peirce. Her teaching, research, and professional experience is in the field of electronic media and the study of Peirce's logic (semiotic).

Christian Kloesel is Professor of English at Indiana University and Director of the Peirce On-Line Resource Testbed Project. He worked in the Peirce Edition Project for seventeen years, the last ten as director, and served as editor for volumes 3 through 5 of the *Writings of Charles S. Peirce: A Chronological Edition*. He has long been concerned with the problem of determining how automation technology might be applied in the preparation of a scholarly edition of Peirce's work and how to begin producing such an edition in electronic form as a means to improve the editing process.

Gerald MacLean is Professor of English at Wayne State University, Detroit. He has edited the 1677 English translation of Poullain de la Barre's *The Woman as Good as the Man* (1988), and *Culture and Society in the Stuart Restoration: Literature, Drama, History* (1995), and he coedited *The Spivak Reader* (1996). He is coauthor of *Materialist Feminisms* (1993) and author of *Time's Witness: Historical Representation in English Poetry, 1603–1660* (1990), in addition to numerous articles on seventeenth-century literary history, feminist theory, and textual criticism. He is currently at work on an edition of the English poems celebrating the Stuart Restoration of 1660.

Sonia Massai studied at the universities of Siena and Liverpool. She is a research associate of the University of Wolverhampton, undertaking bibliographic work for the Oxford edition of the complete writings of Sir Francis Bacon. She has completed a study of the interrelations of Shakespearean source, text, and adaptation.

James McLaverty is a lecturer in English at the University of Keele. He is the editor of David Foxon's Lyell Lectures, *Pope and the Early Eighteenth-Century Book Trade,* and is currently preparing the late David Fleeman's bibliography of Samuel Johnson for publication.

Brenda R. Silver is Professor of English at Dartmouth College. Her works include *Virginia Woolf's Reading Notebooks, Rape and Representation,* and an edition of Woolf's unfinished history book, *"Anon" and "The Reader."* She is currently completing a study of Virginia Woolf's construction as cultural icon, tentatively entitled *Mrs. Woolfe Goes to Hollywood,* and editing Woolf's *Between the Acts.*

William W. E. Slights is the author of *Ben Johnson and the Art of Secrecy.* In addition to his work on Shakespeare, Marston, Middleton, Pascal, Conrad, and Frost, he has published essays on the taxonomy and function of printed marginalia and on the theological politics of annotating English bibles in the period 1525–1611. He is working on a book about the production and reception of annotated books in early modern England and another on the image and icon of the heart in the English and continental Renaissance. He teaches English at the University of Saskatchewan in Saskatoon, Canada.

Ann Thompson is Professor of English and Head of the English Department at Roehampton Institute, London. She edited *The Taming of the Shrew* for the New Cambridge Shakespeare series (1984) and is currently one of the General Editors of the Arden Shakespeare (third series), for which she is also co-editing *Hamlet* with Neil Taylor. She is General Editor of a series of books on feminist criticism of Shakespeare forthcoming from Routledge and co-editor with Sasha Roberts of *Women Reading Shakespeare, 1660–1900* (forthcoming from Manchester University Press).

Evelyn B. Tribble is Associate Professor of English at Temple University. She is the author of *Margins and Marginality: The Printed Page in Early Modern England* (1993). She is currently working on a book entitled *Transubstantiation the Renaissance: Early Modern England and the Problem of Religion.*

Index

Hirshhorn Museum, 165
Hirst, Robert (ed.), Mark Twain Edition, 54n. 12
Hoffman, Nicholas, 78n. 14
Holcot, Robert, 254
Holden, Stephen, "Film from New Directors Taking Literary Licence," 81n. 40
Holderness, Graham, and Brian Loughrey (eds.), *The Taming of a Shrew*, 98, 99
Holland (manuscript layout in), 178
Holy Trinity, Cathedral of (Dublin), 255
Homer, 23n. 43, 233
Honigmann, E. A. J., 89, "Shakespeare's Revised Plays: *King Lear* and *Othello*," 101n. 18
Hooker, Richard, 224n. 8, 323–52 passim; *An Admonition to the Parliament*, 329, 330; *Lawes of Ecclesiasticall Politie*, 323–52 passim; *Of Pride*, 349n. 21; *Tractates and Sermons*, 349n. 21
Hookway, Christopher, 279, 280, 305; *Peirce*, 317nn. 8, 10, 321n. 36
Horace, 193, 241, 244nn. 21, 22
Hostetler, Norman, and Robert Bergstrom (eds.), The Major Works of Harold Frederic, 55n. 18
Hotson, Leslie, 163; *The First Night of "Twelfth Night,"* 171n. 32
Houghton Library, 235
Hours of the Virgin, 260
Houser, Nathan, and Christian Kloesel (eds.), *The Essential Peirce: Selected Philosophical Writings*, 320n. 21. *See also* Peirce, Charles Sanders
Howard, Edward, 244n. 14
Howard-Hill, T. H., 325; "Theory and Praxis in the Social Approach to Editing," 348n. 13
Howland, A. C. (ed.), *Materials toward a History of Witchcraft* (Henry Charles Lea), 127n. 14
Hoy, Cyrus, 324
Huet, Marie-Helene, *Monstrous Imagination*, 128n. 23
Huggett, Richard, *Curse of Macbeth, and Other Theatrical Susperstitions: an Investigation*, 171n. 38
Hugh of St. Victor, 252
Hughes, Langston, 50; *Collected Poems of Langston Hughes* (ed. Arnold Rampersad), 55n. 19

Hulbert, James (trans.), Jacques Derrida, "Living On: *Border Lines*, 225n. 22
Hulme, Peter, *Colonial Encounters: Europe and the Native Caribbean, 1492–1997*, 41n. 5, 110, 125n. 3, 128n. 26
Human Genome Project, 313
Humphreys, A. R. (ed), Shakespeare, *Henry V*, 102n. 40
Hungerford, William Lord, 114
Huntington Library, 209, 215, 218, 219, 223n. 1, 223n. 4
Huot, Sylvia, *The Romance of the Rose and Its Medieval Readers: Interpretation, Reception, Manuscript Transmission*, 266n. 9
Huppert, Isabelle, 79n. 29
Hurston, Zora Neale, 49, 51, 52; *Folklore, Memories, and Other Writings*, 55n. 16; *Novels and Stories*, 55n. 16
Hutchinson, Anne, 115, 128n. 23
Hutchinson, Lucy, 39, 40
Hutchinson, Colonel, *Memoirs of the Life of Colonel Hutchinson* (ed. C. H. Firth), 43n. 26
Huxley, Aldous (ed. Lawrence letters??), 12

Iachimo (Shakespeare, *Cymbeline*), 92
Iannone, Carol, 69
Illich, Ivan, 252; *In the Vineyard of the Text: A Commentary to Hugh's Didascalion*, 266n. 12
Imogen (Shakespeare, *Cymbeline*), 91, 92
Indiana, Gary, "Spirits Either Sex Assume," 80n. 39, 81n. 40
Inquisition, 113
Internet, 313
Irving, Henry, 92
Isabella (Shakespeare, *Measure for Measure*), 91

J'Accuse: Virginia Woolf (television series), 79n. 24
Jackson, Heather, 224n. 8
Jacobs, Harriet, *Incidents in the Life of a Slave Girl* (ed. Jean Fagan Yellin), 47, 49, 54n. 7
Jacques (Shakespeare, *As You Like It*), 94
James I, King, *Basilikon Doron*, 109, 126n. 7
James, William, 272, 276, 280, 317n. 11